# Teaching Students with Emotional and Behavioral Disabilities

# Teaching Students with Emotional and Behavioral Disabilities

**Brittany L. Hott, PhD**
**Kathleen M. Randolph, EdD, BCBA-D**
**Lesli Raymond, MS**

5521 Ruffin Road
San Diego, CA 92123

e-mail: information@pluralpublishing.com
Website: https://www.pluralpublishing.com

Typeset in 11/13 Palatino by Flanagan's Publishing Services, Inc.
Printed in the United States of America by McNaughton & Gunn, Inc.

Library of Congress Cataloging-in-Publication Data

Names: Hott, Brittany L., author. | Randolph, Kathleen M., author. |
  Raymond, Lesli, author.
Title: Teaching students with emotional and behavioral disabilities /
  Brittany L. Hott, PhD, Kathleen M. Randolph, EdD, BCBA-D, Lesli Raymond,
  MS.
Description: San Diego, CA : Plural Publishing, Inc., 2022. | Includes
  bibliographical references and index.
Identifiers: LCCN 2020027008 | ISBN 9781635502251 (paperback) | ISBN
  9781635502497 (ebook)
Subjects: LCSH: Mentally ill children—Education. | Problem
  children—Education. | Behavior modification.
Classification: LCC LC4165 .H68 2022 | DDC 371.93—dc23
LC record available at https://lccn.loc.gov/2020027008

# CONTENTS

# 3 Service Delivery 59

# 4 Mathematics Strategies and Interventions 85

# PREFACE

Students with emotional and behavioral disabilities (EBD) deserve a quality, evidence-based education. Capitalizing on the expertise of three authors who have served as general education teachers, special education teachers, interventionists, Board Certified Behavior Analysts, school-based and district administrators, and university faculty with over 60 years of combined experience, along with contributors who are currently practitioners working directly with students who have EBD and children with challenging behavior, our text provides an excellent resource for those dedicated to improving outcomes for children with behavioral challenges. We have supported students, teachers, administrators, paraprofessionals, and families of children from birth to age 21 and beyond. This text provides a comprehensive resource for advanced undergraduate to graduate preservice teachers, and in-service teachers supporting students with EBD and their families. The idea for this book grew out of our own experiences in special education—both the successes and the challenges—within the education system.

This book provides readers with an inclusive approach to teaching and supporting students with EBD. We present service delivery models and also highlight evidence-based reading, writing, math, and study skills strategies. These are important when educating any student, but are especially helpful when supporting students with EBD in academic settings. We provide behavioral interventions on multiple levels, including those that can be initiated and directed by teachers, students, and peers. We also include specific chapters to support the development of quality Individualized Education Programs, Functional Behavior Assessments, and Behavior Intervention Plans, along with a chapter on progress monitoring, which is critical to continued student success.

On the PluralPlus companion site, we are excited to offer instructors and students additional resources to accompany each chapter. Instructor resources include PowerPoint lecture slides, lecture outlines, chapter quizzes, and 2 to 3 in-class activities per chapter. Student resources include links to videos, online learning modules, printable forms, and case studies.

We are thrilled to provide educators with a resource that spans the teacher continuum (i.e., preservice to in-service)—a textbook that can be referred to beyond the college classroom and one that provides resources for meeting the needs of students. Thank you for supporting students with EBD—our students deserve amazing teachers, advocates, and cheerleaders.

# ACKNOWLEDGMENTS

This book would not have been possible without an amazing team who supported us each step of the way. The insight and valuable feedback from faculty who reviewed our proposal and who provided suggestions for improvement as we developed our book was nothing short of amazing. We received stellar support from the project editors at Plural Publishing, Christina Gunning and Nicole Hodges, who gave generously of their time and went above and beyond to ensure that we met deadlines and had all of the resources needed. We also appreciate Hope Partin, University of Oklahoma Master of Special Education student, who served as the project assistant. Ms. Partin kept us organized, provided editorial assistance, and formatted chapters. Finally, we are most thankful for the educators who choose to teach students with emotional and behavioral disabilities. Your work makes a difference and we are hopeful that our text serves as a useful resource.

# CONTRIBUTORS

**Lauren Berlingo, MA**
DESE Doctoral Student
Florida Atlantic University
Boca Raton, Florida
*Chapter 9*

**Nicolette M. Grasley-Boy, PhD, MEd, BCBA**
Doctoral Candidate
Department of Special Education, School Psychology, and
    Early Childhood Studies
University of Florida
Gainesville, Florida
*Chapter 13*

**Sarah Heiniger, MEd, EdS, NCSP, BCBA**
Founder and CEO
Nexus Solutions for Autism
Geneva, Illinois and Oklahoma City, Oklahoma
*Chapters 11 and 12*

**Brianna Joseph, EdD**
Visiting Instructor
Department of Exceptional Student Education
Florida Atlantic University
Boca Raton, Florida
*Chapter 8*

**Nelly Kaakaty, PhD**
Learning Specialist
Alcuin School
Dallas, Texas
*Chapter 5*

**Kelly B. Kearney, EdD, BCBA-D**
Department of Exceptional Student Education
Florida Atlantic University
Boca Raton, Florida
*Chapter 10*

**Jennifer Sears, PhD**
Assistant Professor
Department of Teacher Education
Elementary and Special Education
University of North Georgia
Dahlonega, Georgia
*Chapter 2*

**Wilhelmina Van Dijk, PhD**
Postdoctoral Scholar
Department of Psychology and Florida Center for Reading
    Research
Florida State University
Tallahassee, Florida
*Chapter 13*

# REVIEWERS

Plural Publishing, Inc. and the authors would like to thank the following reviewers for taking the time to provide their valuable feedback during the development process:

**Rocio Delgado, PhD**
Multicultural Special Education
Associate Professor of Education
Trinity University
San Antonio, Texas

**Alandra Devall, PhD**
Educational Psychologist
Professor at Benedictine University
Lisle, Illinois

**Suzanne Gikas, PhD**
Assistant Professor
Special Education
Augsburg University
Minneapolis, Minnesota

**Margaret King-Sears, PhD**
George Mason University
Fairfax, Virginia

**Christen Knowles, PhD**
Department of Special Education and Clinical Sciences
The Center on Human Development
University of Oregon
Eugene, Oregon

**Michael F. Shaughnessy, PhD**
Professor
Eastern New Mexico University
Portales, New Mexico

**L. Kathleen Sheriff, EdD**
Stephen F. Austin State University
Nacogdoches, Texas

**Amanda Walkup, BS, MA, EdS**
Lander University Lecturer in Special Education and
    Coordinator of Field Experiences
Greenwood, South Carolina

**Awilda E. Ramos Zagarrigo, PhD**
Associate Professor
SUNY Buffalo State College—Exceptional Education
    Department
Buffalo, New York

*We dedicate this book to Asher, Ava, Henry, Kameran, Kassidy, Kaylee, Luke, and Noah.*

# 1

# Teaching Students with Emotional and Behavioral Disabilities

## INTRODUCTION

Welcome to teaching students with emotional and behavioral disabilities! The purpose of this book is to provide a well-rounded approach to working with students identified as having an **emotional and behavioral disability** (EBD). Formally identified in the Individuals with Disabilities Education Act (2004) as "Emotional Disturbance," this book will use the term emotional and behavioral *disability*, which is aligned with people-first language and provides a less stigmatized identification in special education than the previous and commonly used terms, emotional and behavior disorder or emotional and behavior disturbance. **Person-first** (or people-first) **language** places the emphasis on the person's identity before their disability (McLeskey et al., 2017). Figure 1–1 provides examples of person-first language.

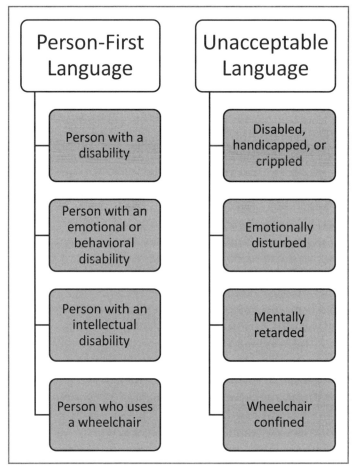

*Figure 1–1. Person-first language*, *or people-first language, emphasizes a person before their disability.*

Based on Public Law 94-142, the Individuals with Disabilities Education Act (IDEA) was enacted in 1990 to ensure that all children with disabilities continued to have access to a free and appropriate public education (FAPE). IDEA was reauthorized in 1997 and again in 2004 as the Individuals with Disabilities Improvement Education Act (2004). IDEA defined an **Emotional and Behavioral Disability (Emotional Disturbance)** as "a condition exhibiting one or more of the following characteristics over a long period of time and to a marked degree that adversely affects a child's educational performance" (IDEA, 2004, §300.8(c)(4)).

Under IDEA (2004), there are five specific subsets of eligibility criteria that would deem a student eligible for special education services as a student with EBD, including:

1. *An inability to learn that cannot be explained by intellectual, sensory, or health factors* (IDEA, 2004, §300.8(c)(4)(i)(a)). This means that students have not made behavioral or academic progress despite any instructional frameworks, strategies, or targeted support provided, and the student does not have an identified learning disability, intellectual disability, neurological impairment, brain injury, or other medical condition impeding learning.

2. *An inability to build or maintain satisfactory interpersonal relationships with peers and teachers* (IDEA, 2004, §300.8(c)(4)(i)(b)). This means that the student is unable to create or retain relationships with students and adults alike. Students who meet this criterion struggle to demonstrate interpersonal skills, including making friends, demonstrating sympathy or empathy, and working and playing both with others and independently.

3. *Inappropriate types of behavior or feelings under normal circumstances* (IDEA, 2004, §300.8(c)(4)(i)(c)). This means that students demonstrate age-inappropriate behavior or feelings that vary significantly from what a typical peer of a similar age, gender, and culture would convey in a similar circumstance.

4. *A general pervasive mood of unhappiness or depression* (IDEA, 2004, §300.8(c)(4)(i)(d)). This means that the student is experiencing unhappiness or depression across most or all of the situations they encounter in life over a consistent period of several months. This cannot be attributed to substance abuse, medication, or medical factors or to typical life scenarios, such as grief due to the death of a loved one.

5. *A tendency to develop physical symptoms or fears associated with personal or school problems* (IDEA, 2004, §300.8(c)(4)(i)(e)). This means that the student's physical symptoms cannot be attributed to medical conditions, there is a specific connection to psychological factors, the person isn't aware of the conflict the symptoms are causing, and the symptoms are not related to a cultural response pattern.

Further, as defined by IDEA, EBD includes schizophrenia but does not include children who are identified as socially maladjusted, unless it is determined that a child has EBD (IDEA, 2004, §300.8(c)(4)(ii)). As with any other special education identification process, the decision to identify a child with a disability of any kind requires a team decision after a comprehensive evaluation has been completed with input from all team members (e.g., teachers, parents, student, administration), and the team decides the most appropriate way to support the student. An EBD identification, along with an Individualized Education Program team decision for educational placement and goals, ensures that students receive the appropriate accommodations and support within the setting appropriate to their needs. Special education settings, service delivery, and supports will be discussed in Chapter 3.

## Social Maladjustment

As mentioned above, students who are socially maladjusted are typically not eligible for special education as a student with an emotional and behavioral disability. This is problematic for several reasons, including that it provides an incomplete EBD definition for eligibility, that the definition is not comprehensive enough to determine true EBD, there is a lack of reliable and valid instruments to determine both EBD and social maladjustment (Olympia et al., 2004), and the current definition is limited (Smith et al., 2015). All of these reasons could lead to underidentification of students with EBD because of the exclusionary criteria (Smith et al., 2015). The debate has been ongoing (Sullivan & Sadeh, 2014) as to how social maladjustment and EBD can be distinguished from one another. All but four states, Indiana, Iowa, Minnesota, and Wisconsin, exclude social maladjustment from EBD eligibility. This inconsistency can lead to inequitable implementation of IDEA for students with EBD across the country (Olympia et al., 2004).

## Comorbidity/Comorbid Disabilities

Comorbidity is defined in the medical community as one or more conditions occurring at the same time within the same person (Valderas et al., 2009). Comorbidity in disabilities is similar in that disabilities can occur both individually and simultaneously within the same person. This means that students may meet the criteria for more than one disability category identification, and given individualized supports, these students have unique needs. Emotional and behavior disabilities are often comorbid with a range of other disabilities, including learning disabilities, autism spectrum disorder, attention-deficit/hyperactivity disorder, intellectual disability, and communication disorders, along with mental health disorders.

## Learning Disability

Learning disability is defined as "a disorder in one or more of the basic psychological processes involved in understanding or in using language, spoken or written, that may manifest itself in the imperfect ability to listen, think, speak, read, write, spell, or to do mathematical calculations, including conditions such as perceptual disabilities, brain injury, minimal brain dysfunction, dyslexia, and developmental aphasia" (IDEA, 2004, §300.8(c)(10)).

## Autism Spectrum Disorder

Autism spectrum disorder (ASD) is defined as "a developmental disability significantly affecting verbal and nonverbal communication and social interaction, generally evident before age three, that adversely affects a child's educational performance" (IDEA, 2004, §300.8(c)(1)). Students with behaviors as the result of emotional behavioral disability identification are not typically identified as having ASD.

## Attention-Deficit/Hyperactivity Disorder

Attention-deficit/hyperactivity disorder (ADHD) is defined as a brain disorder characterized by a continuous pattern of one or a combination of the following: inattention, hyperactivity, and impulsivity. ADHD eligibility criteria in schools has a pattern of behavior that interferes with academics (National Institute of Mental Health, 2016) and falls under the Other Health Impairment eligibility category.

## Intellectual Disability

Intellectual disability is defined as "significantly subaverage general intellectual functioning, existing concurrently with deficits in adaptive behavior and manifested during the developmental period, that adversely affects a child's educational performance" (IDEA, 2004, §300.8(c)(6)).

## Communication Disorders

Communication disorders are defined as "a communication disorder, such as stuttering, impaired articulation, a language impairment, or a voice impairment, that adversely affects a child's educational performance" (IDEA, 2004, §300.8(c)(10)).

## RATIONALE FOR INCLUSIVE EDUCATION

Throughout the text, we will continue to exert that placement in general education, or inclusive education, is the preferred and appropriate placement for most students with disabilities, including students with EBD. According to McLeskey et al. (2017), inclusive education with students with disabilities is preferred, with the formal definition of inclusion as follows:

> Students with disabilities are included as valued members of the school community. This suggests that they belong to the school community and are accepted by others; that they actively participate in the academic and social community of the school; and that they receive supports that offer them the opportunity to succeed. (p. 441)

Typically referred to as the least restrictive environment (LRE) in special education law (IDEA, 2004), the LRE stipulation in IDEA requires each local education agency (i.e., schools and school districts) to educate children with disabilities with their peers who do not have disabilities to the maximum extent possible (IDEA, 2004, §114.a.2.i). The LRE for most students receiving special education is an inclusive environment. According to the U.S. Department of Education's National Center for Education Statistics (NCES, 2018), approximately 13% of school-aged students (ages 3 to 21) have received special education services, and of those students. Additionally, the NCES (2017) reported that approximately 95% of students with disabilities ages 6 to 21 were provided services in neighborhood schools.

## EVIDENCE-BASED PRACTICES

We will continue to reference the EBD definition throughout this book, and we will cover important aspects of working with students with EBD in this book in all settings. As the reader, you will find many strategies and different **evidence-based practices** (EBPs) that work with students with EBD, with all students with disabilities, as well as their general education counterparts. Evidence-based practices are those that are proven effective by a depth of research (Cook et al., 2008; Odom et al., 2005). The use of EBPs is important because, if they are implemented correctly, they improve student performance, academically and behaviorally. The issue teachers find with EBPs is in implementation within the classroom, which ones work with their students, and where they can find EBPs that are appropriate. The Council for Exceptional Children (CEC) has provided guidelines for determining if a practice is an EBP (CEC, 2014). A list of quality indicators and specific criteria were created to evaluate different programs with a depth of research. Evidence-based practices reviewed in this book will span all chapters.

## DISPROPORTIONALITY

"Special education was borne out of, and owes debt to, the civil rights movement" (Skiba et al., 2008, p. 264). Prior the civil rights movement, parents of color battled for their children to have an inclusive and equal educational opportunity. Throughout the years, struggles of special education students and the fight for appropriate services based on individualized needs have been at the forefront of special education. Theoretically, the passage of Public Law 94-142 in 1975 should have been the beginning of equal education for all students with disabilities, regardless of ability level, race, or ethnicity.

Concerns around disproportionate representation of students of color in special education have been documented since the 1960s, when Dunn (1968) mentioned disproportionality as a concern (Skiba et al., 2008). Reports of **disproportionality** have remained steady since the 1980s. Though overrepresentation of students of color in special education is discussed constantly as a concern, actual numbers of overrepresented students of color and ways to reduce and improve the rates of overidentification are not consistently and accurately reported by school districts.

Disproportionality in special education has two implications. The first, and more widely publicized, is that of overrepresentation of Black students in the Learning Disability (LD), Emotional/Behavioral Disability (EBD), and Intellectual Disability (ID) categories of special education placement (Skiba et al., 2008). Traditionally, the LD, EBD, and ID categories are more subjective and can be swayed by a teacher's influence or judgment and the context in which students are being evaluated (Hibel, Farkas, & Morgan, 2010). Black males from low socioeconomic backgrounds have the most consistently reported rate of disproportionality within special education.

The second, less publicized, aspect of disproportionality is the lack of students of color receiving gifted education services (Ford, 2012). A disproportionately low number of students of color are enrolled in gifted programs across the country. Not as much emphasis has been placed on gifted education because of the variance in requirements across states (i.e., mandates and funding), but it has contributed to the discussion of segregated special education settings for students of color (Vincent et al., 2011).

Themes of disproportionality fall into several categories of concern. Overall, disproportionality itself is the problem. However, the special education referral process is fraught with inadequacies, inaccuracies, and inconsistencies. Several factors affecting the referral process cited in the literature include misperception of behavior, misunderstanding of cultural backgrounds by the referring teacher, and perception of home life (Hart et al., 2009; Vincent et al., 2011; Shealey et al., 2011). Though Response to Intervention (RtI) is supposed to be used as a behavioral intervention as well as an academic one, it is a slow process that requires consistent intervention, documentation, and data to support its success or failure. Rates of disproportionality are inconsistent, since actual calculation of disproportionality varies by state and locality as well as nationally. Inconsistent reporting patterns and requirements may be to blame for the lack of agreement in disproportionality data between those entities (Skiba et al., 2013).

## DISPROPORTIONALITY VERSUS OVERREPRESENTATION

Disproportionality and overrepresentation are often used interchangeably. According to Ford (2012), they are similar but have different emphases. Disproportionality is a broader term than overrepresentation and considered to have more of a pattern, with the possibility for miscalculation causing a false positive. Disproportionality in special education refers to representation of students of color compared to the student population overall in special education and in special education versus gifted education.

Disproportionality varies between schools, school districts, states, and nationally. Issues regarding disproportionality for students of color, specifically those with disabilities, led to the major antidiscrimination laws, including the Rehabilitation Act of 1973, the Education for All Handicapped Children Act in 1975 (PL 94-142), and eventually the Individuals with Disabilities Education Act of 1997 (IDEA), reauthorized as the Individuals with Disabilities Education Improvement Act in 2004 (Skiba et al., 2013). The biggest and most significant disproportionality concern is centered on Black males who are labeled as EBD and placed in the most restrictive settings.

### Determining Disproportionality

Factors used to determine disproportionality include risk ratio and composition index. Risk ratio is the extent to which a group is found eligible for service at a rate differing from other groups. In order to calculate risk ratio, the total number of students identified in a given disability category is divided by the total number of enrolled students in that group. In order to calculate the risk ratio for EBD disproportionality, the number of Black males identified as EBD is divided by the total number of students identified as EBD. Composition index is the extent to which a group is over- or underrepresented in proportion to the general population. To calculate the composition index for disproportionality overall, Black males in special education are compared to the overall special education population (Skiba et al., 2008).

### Theories Behind Disproportionality

Many theories have been posited for possible causes to disproportionality in the identification of Black males with EBD. The effects of both interpersonal and intrapersonal factors and their likelihood to be used in order to determine eligibility and identification within a specific special education category have a profound effect on placement decisions for those students (Bal et al., 2013). Other theories include the possibility of a cultural mismatch between White teachers and students of color, the use of incorrect or inappropriate interventions, inconsistent referral patterns and processes, misunderstanding of behaviors considered to be culturally normed, lack of appropriate instruction, testing, teacher or psychologist bias, poor classroom management, pressures to identify students, level of state conservatism, discipline practices at the school level, and school climate and culture (Bal et al., 2013; Ford, 2012; McKenna, 2013; Raines et al., 2012). One theory that has been a concern for many years is that the psychologists conducting special education evaluations often have the ability to manipulate special education identification and placement for a student based on perception, judgment, and pressure from the school environment (Bean, 2013; Skiba et al., 2013; Sullivan & Bal, 2013; Wiley et al., 2013).

## Risk Factors

Race and socioeconomic status are cited as the biggest risk factors throughout the literature surrounding disproportionality. Specifically, for Black males from low socioeconomic backgrounds, referral and identification rates in the high-incidence disability areas of SLD, ID, Other Health Impairment (OHI), Speech/Language Impairment (SLI), and the EBD categories of special education are consistently disproportionate, as compared with the majority of special education identification and placement for their White peers within the same disability categories (Sullivan & Bal, 2013). Additional risk factors for Black male students are possible biological trauma, environmental toxin exposure, neighborhood, and issues related to parental demographics, incarceration, or mental health status (Hibel et al., 2010). The most influential factors that lead to the EBD label are teacher skill, assessment bias, and administrative policies of the school. EBD is perceived by many school personnel to be an intrinsic condition that is stereotypical of Black families who live in poverty, largely based on the condition of their home life and effect of the family structure and environment (Hart et al., 2009).

The deficit model in LD identification and placement mirrors that of the EBD process with the assumption of deficit within social behaviors and skills as compared to academic skills. Instead of using a strengths-based approach, school-based teams use the presumed social deficits for placement within an EBD setting, which researchers identify as schools stereotyping Black male students (Artiles et al., 2010). Additionally, factors that influence the placement of Black males in a more restrictive setting include the definition of EBD operationalized inconsistently, inconsistent language across states, and preconceived notions that Black males don't have the skills to succeed, all of which impact inappropriate placement (McKenna, 2013).

## FEDERAL LAWS

In the Individuals with Disabilities Education Act (IDEA), reducing dispro-portionality in special education was a top priority. Requiring states to monitor and address educational needs of the children in their special education programs, IDEA noted the disproportionality of students of color identified as EBD in restrictive placements (Hart et al., 2009). However, the passage of IDEA found disproportionality increasing with students of color in predominantly White schools, creating a higher percentage of the population of students of color receiving special education services when compared to that of their White peers (Artiles et al., 2010).

IDEA included six major mandates to reduce the problem of dispropor-tionality in special education overall: a zero reject model, nondiscriminatory evaluation, Free and Appropriate Public Education (FAPE) based on an Indi-vidualized Education Program (IEP) that is monitored and updated at regular intervals, education in the least restrictive environment (LRE), due process procedures for both parents and schools, and the requirement of parental and student (when appropriate) participation during the entire process (Artiles et al., 2010). According to Skiba et al. (2013):

> Three of the most notable changes were that the 2004 Act (a) made special education disproportionality one of three priority areas for monitoring and enforcement, (b)shifted from an emphasis fixing noncompliance with special education law to prevention in the general education setting, and (c) made interventions mandatory, including the use of 15% of the district's IDEA funds spent on early intervening services when racial dispropor-tionality was deemed significant in identification, placement or discipline, thus focusing change efforts on the general education setting. (p. 110)

Significant disproportionality and disproportionate representation are listed in separate sections of IDEA (2004, §618, §6162). This has contributed to confusion with states and local reporting agencies due to inconsistent language used to identify the separately mentioned, but incredibly similar and often overlapping, mandates in the law. The Office of Special Education Programs operationalized the definition as follows: Significant disproportion-ality includes only issues of overrepresentation of racial and ethnic groups in educational environments, and disproportionate representation is interpreted as including both issues of overrepresentation and underrepresentation, excluding disproportionality but including school discipline (Skiba et al., 2013). Even with the definitions clarified, confusion and ambiguity continue to plague special education disproportionality in appropriate referral, iden-tification, and placement procedures for Black males with an EBD label. Researchers presume that the problems will continue unless the definitions are combined and clarified, and the government provides stricter reporting guidelines and addresses the problem of disproportionality as one issue.

## Educational Placement

Though research supports placing students in the least restrictive environment, this is often not the case. Students with disabilities who spend the majority of their time in general education classrooms have better attendance, are academically closer to their grade levels, and perform higher on standardized testing than their peers who spend the majority of their time outside of the general education classroom (Artiles et al., 2010). Black males labeled as EBD are often placed in the most restrictive settings rather than a minimally restrictive general education setting with accommodations to support their behavioral needs, which contributes to the disproportionality problem (Skiba et al., 2013). Placement in the more restrictive setting is commonly attributed to school disciplinary policies, projective testing used during the identification process, and the school's perception of the student's home life. Placement may also depend on the school's resources, the philosophy of the psychologist, and the teacher's tolerance levels (Hart et al., 2009).

Black male students from low socioeconomic backgrounds who are identified as EBD, while already coming into the educational setting with a perceived disadvantage, are placed within the most restrictive environment and are then at a further risk for negative outcomes. The dropout rate for students identified with EBD is 50% to 59% and is higher for Black males with EBD. Comparatively, the dropout rate for students with LD is 33%. Rates of involvement in correctional facilities (30% to 70%) and those students with disabilities who seek postsecondary education (30%) are concerning for special education as a whole, but in particular to students of color who are identified as EBD (Artiles et al., 2010). Overall, special education placement leads to social isolation, low self-esteem, higher dropout and unemployment rates, and lower academic expectations (Raines et al., 2012). Black male students identified as EBD and placed in more restrictive settings are at the highest risk for the most negative outcomes.

## Impact of EBD

Though being placed into special education with an EBD label is only the beginning of the struggle for Black male students placed into special education, the EBD label will continue to have a profound impact on them throughout their educational journey. While perception and stereotypes influence the placement process, they also continue to affect students throughout their years until they complete school. An EBD label leads to more judgment and perception regarding the student, his or her family, and disability (Artiles et al., 2010; Hart et al., 2009).

Stereotyping students based on one of more factors, whether they are actually the truth or just perception, is detrimental to students' success within both the general and special education environments. "Culture-specific behaviors can be and are misunderstood, leading to unnecessary special education referrals" for those students (Ford, 2012). Black male students referred for behavioral issues have a high probability of being labeled EBD using a perpetuated stereotype of Black families in poverty and the belief in EBD as an intrinsic condition due to the home environment (Hart et al., 2009).

Special education has many ways to qualify. It does not, however, have the same number of ways to exit, if any exist at all. Once a student is placed into special education, that student is labeled as exceptional, and the experience depends on the quality of education offered and the teachers assigned to the individual student. "Teachers who are more concerned with being nice, rather than demanding brilliance from their learners, often lower expectations for ethnically diverse learners and consequently do more harm than good" (Vincent et al., 2011). Effective teachers are at the forefront of positive outcomes for students.

Outcomes of Black male students identified as EBD are disheartening. Placement of a child into special education in general has been linked to stigma, negative educational outcomes, and possible incarceration. This reflects back to the laws that are supposed to be protecting students, which may actually be more harmful than helpful, and unfortunately, "policy makers and practitioners did not consider cultural-historical factors that might result in unintended outcomes" (Artiles et al., 2010).

## RECOMMENDATIONS TO ADDRESS DISPROPORTIONALITY

Throughout the literature, the problem of disproportionality is highlighted and continuously mentioned. Its basis in the civil rights movement and the laws that are designed to prevent disproportionality often place more of an emphasis on concerns of overidentification and may result in lower rates of identification in more conservative states (Wiley et al., 2013). Culturally responsive teaching, responsible implementation of Response to Intervention (RtI), universal screening, and the consideration of classroom and school context in the referral and placement process are the keys to reducing the number of inappropriate referrals and placement practices for Black males within the EBD category of special education.

### Culturally Responsive Teaching

McKenna (2013) described culturally responsive teaching as making a connection between a student's personal and educational experiences to maximize student learning and engagement. The first step in becoming a culturally responsive teacher is to acknowledge personal cultural background and identity. Next, teachers must develop the awareness that all human behavior is shaped by race, culture, language, and gender. Teachers must engage in reflective teaching and acknowledge the role of personal experience within their practice. Finally, teachers must have high standards and expectations for culturally and linguistically diverse learners (Vincent et al., 2011). Though it may not currently inherently exist in a current teacher, it is possible to develop into a culturally responsive teacher.

Culturally responsive teaching begins in teacher preparation programs at the postsecondary level. Future teachers need to be prepared and learn teaching strategies and culturally responsive pedagogy. Culturally responsive teaching makes connections to students' culture, prior experiences and learning, and performance to provide instruction that gives students empowerment with the goal of transforming their lives and impacting families (Vincent et al., 2011). Teacher preparation programs must be prepared to arm their students with the tools necessary to be effective culturally responsive teachers.

As previously mentioned, the first step in becoming a culturally responsive educator is to acknowledge your own culture. It is highly likely that while this is going on, professionals may feel uncomfortable with the idea of acculturation and education mixed, but it is the most effective way of eliminating a possible cultural mismatch. Teachers should try to understand their students' cultures, because it will help them become more culturally responsive and they will be able to meet the needs of their students more effectively (Ford, 2012). This will help teachers to appropriately teach those students and guide them to their successful adult lives.

Shealey et al. (2011) proposed culturally responsive behavior management and provided several suggestions for a successful schoolwide program, similar to those included in culturally responsive teaching. Similar to those for culturally responsive teaching, the following factors need to be included in a culturally responsive behavior support program: increasing staff members' cultural self-awareness, validating others' cultures, increasing cultural relevance, establishing cultural validity, and emphasizing cultural equity. The implementation of a Schoolwide Positive Behavior Support (SWPBS) program is recommended in order to have a culturally relevant and appropriate way to reduce inappropriate discipline referrals based on misunderstood cultural norms and expectations.

## Implementation of RtI Practices

The main purpose of RtI is to support student behavioral and academic performance from an environmental perspective rather than as an internal attribute (McKenna, 2013). An appropriately implemented RtI program is instrumental in addressing problem behaviors before they warrant a referral for special education services. General education teachers identify struggling students, and the teachers are given specific interventions to implement for a predetermined amount of time before declaring a success or failure. Students' progress through the levels of RtI, with Level 1 consisting of universal interventions and Level 3 being the most intense individual level of intervention, if needed. If they are successful, interventions that work are documented, data are collected, and interventions continue to be implemented. If they don't make progress, students are given more specific and intense intervention in order to address their increasing behavioral demands. The burden is placed on the referring general education teacher and requires rigorous intervention and documentation. RtI has been successful with many students and has the potential to lessen the inappropriate referrals to special education (Vincent et al., 2011).

## Universal Screening

Raines and colleagues (2012) recommend the use of universal screening to reduce disproportionate placement of minority students in special education. Universal screening includes self-reports completed by students of all ages, with professionals reading the reports to students who are unable to read these reports themselves due to their reading ability or are too young to do so. With the potential to provide early risk identifiers, the goal is to eliminate prolonged exposure to risk for students displaying any factors that could possibly warrant future placement in special education. Universal screening also limits the potential for stigma in subgroups and reduces labeling mistakes, and it can predict student achievement, difficulty, and academic or behavioral issues (Raines et al., 2012).

Based on the results of screening self-reports, interventions can be provided for students considered to be at risk in order to lessen risk factors and foster their growth and eventual success. The traditional referral process involves teacher interpretation, which is removed with universal screening. Students are also not looked at in a deficit lens, but rather in a proactive, early intervening model where school-based teams are able to determine individual student need, use culturally sensitive and appropriate intervention, and consider the effect of culture on learning and behavior. Data-driven decision making is reinforced in the universal screening process. Several advantages to the self-report model of universal screening are mentioned, including accurately reporting information related to self-perception of behaviors, emotions, and internalizing symptoms. Self-report screening is reported as a low-cost intervention and can be easily conducted with large populations of students in a short time. Most self-reports are electronically scored, which is considered the most efficient and accurate way for a large-scale universal screening to be conducted (Raines et al., 2012).

## Classroom Contexts

Included in suggestions for more accurate placement of Black males in EBD settings is consideration of the classroom context during the referral process. Poor instruction, impact of the classroom context or school policies on student behavior, and subjective referrals contribute to disproportionate EBD identification and placement for students of color (Hart et al., 2009). Things that should be considered within the classroom context include poor or ineffective teachers, lack of classroom management, peer group interactions, bullying, social inequity, and behavior as a response to something that happened in the classroom. Lack of reference to the classroom context in special education referrals should be a concern for school-based teams (Artiles et al., 2010).

Disproportionate identification of Black males with EBD will continue unless mandates are reinforced at all systemic levels. From local school districts to the federal level, guidelines must be both clearly understood and enforced in order to ensure that students are receiving appropriate interventions prior to being referred for a special education evaluation. Collaboration and cooperation from multiple levels of stakeholders in special education policy and practice are required for disproportionality to be address at the local, state, and national levels.

Disproportionality as a whole must be addressed, a solution must be proposed, and stakeholders must be engaged in the process. Creating culturally responsive teaching and behavior support programs is integral to effectively reducing and eventually eliminating the stereotypes often associated with students of color from low socioeconomic backgrounds. Responsible and effective implementation of RtI in order to support student behavior within the general education classroom setting is necessary. Universal screening to identify risk factors for students at an early age is a proactive way to provide early intervening. The consideration of classroom context in the referral and placement process is necessary for schools. In combination, the previously mentioned strategies will help to reduce the number of inappropriate referrals and placement for Black males within the EBD category of special education.

## CHAPTER SUMMARY

In Chapter 2, multitiered systems of support (MTSS) will be explained in detail. Multi-tiered systems of support involve a systemic, continuous-improvement framework in which data-based problem solving and decision making are practiced across all levels of the educational system for supporting students. MTSS grew out of the RtI framework.

Service delivery for students with EBD is an important aspect of supporting those students. In Chapter 3, we will review different options for service delivery for students with EBD. Inclusion with typical peers in the general education curriculum is the ideal place for students with EBD to receive the bulk of their instruction. While inclusion may not be appropriate for all students with EBD, we will define, describe, and review service delivery options available.

We will provide strategies and interventions in all academic content areas (reading, writing, math, and study skills) in Chapters 4, 5, and 6. Effective study skills will be reviewed in Chapter 7. Chapters 8, 9, and 10 discuss different types of interventions in schools that can be teacher, student, or peer directed.

Additional aspects of teaching students with emotional and behavioral disabilities, such as the administrative and paperwork aspects of special education, are included. Chapters 11 to 13 will provide guidance for writing quality programs and plans for students with EBD. Chapter 11 will support teacher development of meaningful Individualized Education Programs. Chapter 12 will provide guidance for Functional Behavior Assessments, and Chapter 13 will provide the structure to develop quality Behavior Intervention plans.

 **DISCUSSION QUESTIONS**

1. What is the definition of an emotional or behavioral disability?

2. What are the five subsets of eligibility criteria to determine if a child has an emotional or behavior disability?

3. Why is it important to use person-first language?

4. What can school personnel do to prevent disproportionate referrals to special education for students of color?

5. How can an inappropriate label impact a child?

## RESOURCES

### Evidence-Based Practices

https://www.cec.sped.org/Standards/Evidence-Based-Practice-Resources-Original

https://iris.peabody.vanderbilt.edu/resources/ebp_summaries/

https://ies.ed.gov/ncee/wwc/

### Person-First Language

https://www.thearc.org/who-we-are/media-center/people-first-language

https://www.cdc.gov/ncbddd/disabilityandhealth/pdf/disability poster_photos.pdf

### Calculating Disproportionality

https://ideadata.org/resources/resource/1484/spreadsheet-application-for-calculating-disproportionality-measures-and

### Determining Social Maladjustment

https://www.cde.state.co.us/cdesped/topicbrief_sed_socialmal adjustment

## REFERENCES

Algozzine, B., Schmid, R., & Conners, B. (2017). Republication of "toward an acceptable definition of emotional disturbance." *Behavioral Disorders*, 42(3), 132–135. doi:10.1177/0198742917702116

Artiles, A. J., Kozleski, E. B., Trent, S. C., Osher, D., & Ortiz, A. (2010). Justifying and explaining disproportionality, 1968–2008: A critique of underlying views of culture. *Exceptional Children*, 76(3), 279–299. doi:10.1177/001440291007600303

Bal, A., Sullivan, A. L., & Harper, J. (2013). A situated analysis of special education disproportionality for systemic transformation in an urban school district. *Remedial and Special Education*, 35(1), 1–12. doi:10.1177/0741932513507754

Bean, K. F. (2013). Disproportionality and acting-out behaviors among African American children in special education. *Child and Adolescent Social Work Journal, 30*(6), 487–504. doi:10.1007/s10560-013-0304-6

Centers for Disease Control and Prevention (CDC). (n.d.). *Communicating with and about people with disabilities.* Retrieved from https://www.cdc.gov/ncbddd/disability andhealth/pdf/disabilityposter_photos.pdf

Cook, B. G., Tankersley, M., Cook, L., & Landrum, T. J. (2008). Evidence-based practices in special education: Some practical considerations. *Intervention in School and Clinic, 44*(2), 69–75. doi:10.1177/1053451208321452

Council for Exceptional Children. (2014). Standards for evidence-based practices in special education. *Exceptional Children, 80*(4), 504–511. doi:10.1177/0014402914531388

Dunn, L. M. (1968). Special education for the mildly retarded—is much of it justifiable? *Exceptional Children, 23,* 5–21.

Ford, D. Y. (2012). Culturally different students in special education: Looking backward to move forward. *Exceptional Children, 78*(4), 391–405. doi:10.1177/0014 40291207800401

Hart, J. E., Cramer, E. D., Harry, B., Klingner, J. K., & Sturges, K. M. (2009). The continuum of "troubling" to "troubled" behavior: Exploratory case studies of African American students in programs for emotional disturbance. *Remedial and Special Education, 79*(4), 475–494. doi:10.1177/0741932508327468

Hibel, J., Farkas, G., & Morgan, P. L. (2010). Who is placed into special education? *Sociology of Education, 83*(4), 312–332. doi:10.1177/0038040710383518

Individuals with Disabilities Education Act. (2004).

McKenna, J. (2013). The disproportionate representation of African Americans in programs for students with emotional and behavioral disorders. *Preventing School Failure: Alternative Education for Children and Youth, 57*(4), 206–211. doi:10.1080/10 45988X.2012.687792

McKenna, J. W., Solis, M., Brigham, F., & Adamson, R. (2018). The responsible inclusion of students receiving special education services for emotional disturbance: Unraveling the practice to research gap. *Behavior Modification, 43*(4), 587–611. doi:10.1177/0145445518762398

McLeskey, J. L., Rosenberg, M. S., & Westling, D. L. (2017). *Inclusion: Effective practices for all students.* Pearson.

National Institute of Mental Health. (2016). *Attention-deficit/hyperactivity disorder.* Retrieved from https://www.nimh.nih.gov/health/topics/attention-deficit-hyper activity-disorder-adhd/index.shtml

Olympia, D., Farley, M., Christiansen, E., Pettersson, H., Jenson, W., & Clark, E. (2004). Social maladjustment and students with behavioral and emotional disorders: Revisiting basic assumptions and assessment issues. *Psychology in the Schools, 41*(8), 835–847. doi:10.1002/pits.20040

Odom, S. L., Brantlinger, E., Gersten, R., Horner, R. H., Thompson, B., & Harris, K. R. (2005). Research in special education: Scientific methods and evidence-based practices. *Exceptional Children, 71*(2), 137–148. doi:10.1177/001440290507100201

Raines, T. C., Dever, B. V., Kamphaus, R. W., & Roach, A. T. (2012). Universal screening for behavioral and emotional risk: A promising method for reducing disproportionate placement in special education. *The Journal of Negro Education, 81*(3), 283–296. doi:10.7709/jnegroeducation.81.3.0283

Shealey, M. W., McHatton, P. A., & Wilson, V. (2011). Moving beyond disproportionality: The role of culturally responsive teaching in special education. *Teaching Education, 22*(4), 377–396. doi:10.1080/10476210.2011.591376

Skiba, R., Albrecht, S., & Losen, D. (2013). CCBD'S position summary on federal policy on disproportionality in special education. *Behavioral Disorders, 38*(2), 108–120. doi:10.1177/019874291303800202

Skiba, R. J., Simmons, A. B., Ritter, S., Gibb, A. C., Rausch, M. K., Cuadradro, J., & Chung, C. G. (2008). Achieving equity in special education: History, status, and current challenges. *Exceptional Children, 74*(3), 264–288. doi:10.1177/001440290807400301

Sullivan, A. L., & Bal, A. (2013). Disproportionality in special education: Effects of individual and school variables on disability risk. *Exceptional Children, 79*(4), 475–494. doi:10.1177/001440291307900406

Sullivan, A. L., & Sadeh, S. S. (2014). Differentiating social maladjustment from emotional disturbance: An analysis of case law. *School Psychology Review, 43*(4), 450–471. doi:10.17105/SPR-13-0038.1

U.S. Department of Education, National Center on Education Statistics. (2018). Retrieved from https://nces.ed.gov/programs/coe/indicator_cgg.asp

U.S. Department of Education, National Center for Education Statistics. (2017). *Digest of Education Statistics, 2016* (NCES 2017-094). Retrieved from https://nces.ed.gov/fastfacts/display.asp?id=59

Valderas, J. M., Starfield, B., Sibbald, B., Salisbury, C., & Roland, M. (2009). Defining comorbidity: Implications for understanding health and health services. *Annals of Family Medicine, 7*(4), 357–363. doi:10.1370/afm.983

Vincent, C. G., Randall, C., Cartledge, G., Tobin, T. J., & Swain-Bradway, J. (2011). Toward a conceptual integration of cultural responsiveness and schoolwide positive behavior support. *Journal of Positive Behavior Interventions, 13*(4), 219–229. doi:10.1177/1098300711399765

Walker, H. M., & Gresham, F. M. (Eds.). (2014). *Handbook of evidence-based practices for emotional and behavioral disorders: Applications in schools.* Guilford.

Walker, H. M., Severson, H. H., & Feil, E. G. (2014). *Systematic screening for behavior disorders administrators guide: Universal screening for K–9.* Retrieved from https://www.ancorapublishing.com/wp-content/uploads/2018/08/SSBD_Portfolio.pdf

Wiley, A. L., Brigham, F. J., Kauffman, J. M., & Bogan, J. E. (2013). Disproportionate poverty, conservatism, and the disproportionate identification of minority students with emotional and behavioral disorders. *Education and Treatment of Children, 36*(4), 29–50. doi:10.1353/etc.2013.0033

# 2

# Educating Students with EBD within Schoolwide Systems of Support

*With Contributions from Jennifer Sears*

## KEY VOCABULARY

Differentiated Instruction

Positive Behavioral Interventions and Supports

Response to Intervention

Universal Design for Learning

## LEARNING OBJECTIVES

By the end of this chapter, you should be able to . . .

- Develop an understanding of differentiated instruction and Universal Design for Learning.
- Determine ways to assist in the planning of instruction for students with EBD in the general education classroom.
- Discuss schoolwide PBIS and serve students with EBD within the model.
- Define the differences between differentiated instruction and Universal Design for Learning as it relates to students, teachers, and planning for instruction.

# INTRODUCTION

As students with EBD are included into general education classrooms with increasing frequency, it is essential that teachers are provided with effective strategies (Snyder et al., 2016). Regardless of placement, students need access to quality education. Therefore, it is important to understand frameworks and strategies that include the use of differentiated instruction in the classroom, use of **Universal Design for Learning** framework, a prereferral process that is clear and easy to follow, and a clear continuum of support within the school. In this chapter, we explore these frameworks and provide strategies and consumables for teachers to use.

# DIFFERENTIATED INSTRUCTION

The IRIS Center defines **differentiated instruction** as "an approach whereby teachers adjust their curriculum instruction to maximize the learning of all students (e.g., typical learners, English language learners, struggling students, students with learning disabilities, gifted and talented students); not a single strategy but rather a framework that teachers can use to implement a variety of evidence-based strategies" (The IRIS Center, 2010, p. 1). Landrum and McDuffie (2010) further explain differentiation in terms of four areas, namely, (1) students differ in readiness, experiences, and life circumstances; (2) the differences impact what and how students learn, the pace that they learn, and support needed; (3) students learn best when they can make connections to real-life experiences; and (4) teachers need to maximize learning. In each classroom, differentiated instruction can take on multiple forms. Teachers can, and should, be incorporating this throughout their instruction, and this should begin in the planning phase.

For teachers to truly differentiate instruction, they must begin with the students in mind. This requires the teacher to know their students in terms of multiple ways. They must understand the students' readiness, interest, and learning profile (Tomlinson, 1999, 2000, 2014; The IRIS Center, 2010).

Readiness relates directly to a student's current knowledge and level of skill. This can be evaluated by assessments that are given in class, both formal and informal, and often varies across different content areas, especially for students with EBD. A student may excel in the area of reading, but when it comes to math fluency, they are unable to understand their multiplication tables. It may further be influenced by background factors and knowledge and experiences.

Interest is simply stated as what piques a student's curiosity. A teacher can tap into knowledge that a student has by finding out what their activities are outside of school. This can be explored through interest inventories, journal entries, or conversations with students. Teachers can then differentiate their instruction for groups of students by bringing their interests into the conversation in the classroom.

Differentiation of instruction happens across three areas in instruction, namely, content, process, and product (Tomlinson, 2014). Each of these areas can be differentiated in relation to the needs of the students. After the teacher does the initial assessment of her class, it is then that differentiation begins.

The first area to consider is content. When differentiating for content, the same concept or skill is taught but different curriculum is used for different groups of students. Some examples of this can include using different-level texts, scaffolding instruction, or the use of supplemental materials. For instance, a teacher could be teaching about the concept of point of view. Some students may be reading independently a grade-level text to understand point of view while other students may be using an audio recording of the same text, and a third group of students may be reading aloud a text that is below grade level. However, all students are working on the same skill, point of view.

The next area is the process by which a student accesses the curriculum that is presented by the teacher. Once again, the same content is taught, but in this case, the process that the students access the curriculum is differentiated. Some examples of this are the use of manipulatives in mathematics, graphic organizers, or interactive journals. Further, the teacher can differentiate the process by giving students extended time to complete the activity. As with differentiating for content, the students are all working on the same grade-level standards.

The final way that teachers can differentiate for instruction is by the product that the students are producing. The teacher is always assessing the same standard, but the way in which students show their knowledge may look different. This can be done as easily as shortening the length of an assignment to having a completely different assignment for the final product. Further, teachers can use a menu of choices for the students to choose from when they are putting together their final product.

## IMPLEMENTING DIFFERENTIATED INSTRUCTION

As teachers begin to look at their instruction, it is often found they already have a start in differentiating instruction. When a teacher begins instruction, they often give students choices on what they can do to reach a specific goal. This is an example of differentiation. Another common feature found in classrooms is the use of small groups where students are working on different activities; again, this is differentiation. What teachers do not always realize is what they are differentiating. In Table 2–1, an example of what teachers "say" is given followed by an explanation of what the teacher is differentiating and finally the goal of the activity.

**Table 2–1.** Differentiation in Practice

| What the teacher says ... | What makes this an example of differentiation ... | The goal of this activity ... |
|---|---|---|
| Today we will be learning about point of view in a short story. You may choose to listen to a short story to identify the point of view, read a short story to identify the point of view, or write a short story that points out the point of view. | This example can be described as differentiating the students' access to the content, or differentiating the process by which the student engages in the content. It also can be related to the learning style preferences (visual, auditory, kinesthetic). | The goal of this activity is to determine if a student understands the concept of point of view. |

The next step for teachers is to examine their class and purposefully differentiate their instruction. An example of this strategy is provided in Table 2–2. The teacher has divided the class into three groups based on their ability level. Group 1 includes students who are performing at grade level; they understand the math concepts based on a teacher's preassessment. This group understands and is able to compute numbers with regrouping up to two-digit regrouping. Group 2 is performing slightly below grade level. They understand regrouping but can only regroup with one digit. They need a small amount of remediation. Group 3 is the lowest group. This group of students does not understand regrouping even with one digit and struggles without a visual cue. Based on this information, the teacher develops a table to plan out the differentiation for each group in relation to content, process, and product.

## UNIVERSAL DESIGN FOR LEARNING

Universal Design for Learning (UDL) is described by the Center for Applied Special Technology (CAST) as "a framework to improve and optimize teaching learning for all people based on scientific insights into how humans learn" (CAST, 2018). UDL consists of three main principles to guide instruction, namely, providing multiple means of engagement, representation, and action and expression (CAST, 2018). Often, UDL includes some type of technology (King-Sears, 2014). UDL relates in many ways to differentiated instruction as it takes into account the students' needs, but UDL is a proactive approach that is incorporated at the beginning planning stages of instruction as opposed to

**Table 2–2.** Differentiated Instruction Planning

| Standard | Content | Process | Product |
|---|---|---|---|
| Use place value understanding and properties of operations to perform multidigit arithmetic | 1. Students use three-digit numbers to show their knowledge. | 1. Students use the standard algorithm and do not require differentiation. | 1. Students show their knowledge by completing a worksheet that contains two- and three-digit numbers with regrouping. |
| | 2. Students use two-digit numbers to show their knowledge. | 2. Students use graph paper to line up their numbers so that they are able to show the place values. They may use base 10 blocks if needed. | 2. Students show their knowledge by completing five math problems that have two-digit regrouping and one math problem that has three-digit regrouping to see if they can extend their knowledge. |
| | 3. Students use two-digit numbers to show their knowledge but only one digit requires regrouping. | 3. Students start with base 10 blocks to add numbers. They work in a small group with a teacher or a paraprofessional. They then move to using graph paper and have their work monitored after each problem. | 3. Students show their knowledge by completing three math problems with two-digit regrouping with a teacher or paraprofessional guiding their progress. They use manipulatives to answer the questions as needed and gradually move to a removal of the manipulatives. |

an accommodation or adaptation to instruction. Within each of the guidelines of engagement, representation, and expression, UDL further breaks down into the areas of access, building, and internalizing with an ultimate end goal in mind. The three main areas are described below.

## Engagement

The first principle of UDL instruction is engagement. Because not all students are engaged in the same way, there must be multiple options for engagement (CAST, 2018). The three guidelines that fall under engagement are (a) recruiting interest, (b) sustaining effort and persistence, and (c) self-regulation. To reach the self-regulation stage, the teacher must incorporate the first two areas. For many, the engagement is the "hook" or the way that the student is initially introduced to material.

Student curiosity is piqued when recruiting interest, and a teacher might utilize information from student interest inventories. For students with EBD, this could include allowing students to choose how they access the curriculum, where they sit in the classroom, or whether to work in a small group or individually.

In sustaining effort and persistence, goals and objectives are created with the students in mind. The teacher may include the students in the creation of rubrics or demands, there is a sense of collaboration among students and teachers, and demands are varied. For a student with EBD, this might include the teacher evaluating the process as opposed to the product, positive behavior support systems, and a large amount of feedback from the teacher that is specific.

Self-regulation is the third guideline in engagement. When implemented after recruiting interest and sustaining effort, students then move into self-regulation where motivation moves from extrinsic to intrinsic. This area, for all students but especially students with EBD, must be explicitly taught. Self-regulation, as described by CAST, is the ability to "modulate one's emotional reactions or states in order to be more effective at coping and engaging with the environment" (CAST, 2018). Within self-regulation, teachers promote expectations and beliefs, facilitate personal coping skills, and develop self-assessment (CAST, 2018). For students with EBD, this could include the use of self-monitoring charts, a menu of coping skills and strategies to use, and the understanding that the student is in control of their emotions. An example of a self-monitoring chart is available in Appendix 2–1. In this behavior chart, both the student and the teacher monitor the behavior and conference at the end of the class or section of the school day. The student has a "goal of the day," which often would last for longer than 1 day.

While engagement is not the same for all learners, it is essential that teachers understand the needs of their students and provide multiple means for engagement so that students are able to access the curriculum. By following the guidelines of engagement, the ultimate goal of having learners who are purposeful and motivated should be achievable.

## Representation

The second guideline of UDL is providing multiple means of representation. Whereas the engagement guideline addresses the "why" of learning, representation addresses the "what" of learning. Each student approaches content differently within the curriculum based on ability, disability, language, or cultural differences. Options must be included for students to use in order to access the curriculum. The three main guidelines for representation are perception, language and symbols, and comprehension, with the main goal of representation being having expert learners who are resourceful and knowledgeable (Cook et al., 2017; Rapp, 2014).

The first guideline under representation is perception. Once again, this guideline provides the learner with multiple access points to the curriculum. These access points are based on the way that the specific student learns and accesses information through visual or auditory means. This can include enlarged text, changed fonts, the speed in which auditory information is provided, or providing physical objects. The teacher may use descriptions of text that is spoken or visually represented and objects that relate to the curriculum.

The next guideline is providing options for language and symbols. Through this guideline, teachers clarify vocabulary and syntax, support decoding, promote understanding, and illustrate through multiple media (Rapp, 2014). This guideline requires the teacher to make symbols and vocabulary explicit in its demonstration. An example of this could be in mathematics when teaching students about integers and how to add and subtract. The teacher would teach this concept in multiple ways such as using a number line, chips with positive and negative signs, or the standard algorithm. The students see this concept presented in the differing ways but then choose on their own how to solve the problems. By using this technique, all students are able to access the curriculum through their own means.

The final guideline in representation is providing options for comprehension. Through using schema to activate prior knowledge, providing explicit cues, teaching strategies to process and visualize information, and generalizing information, teachers are able to provide these options for comprehension (CAST, 2018). Teachers must explicitly teach these strategies to students prior to them being able to generalize and utilize the information. For instance, before a student can use a graphic organizer for writing such as the POW+TREE model, they must be explicitly taught the strategy. A research-based strategy that has been shown to be effective for students with EBD is Self-Regulated Strategy Development (SRSD). This model of developing background knowledge, discussing it, modeling it, memorizing it, supporting it, and establishing independent practice allows students with disabilities, specifically EBD, to internalize and generalize the use of mnemonic devices, graphic organizers, and other information to promote success in the class-room when used effectively (Ennis, 2016; Lane et al., 2008; The IRIS Center, 2008). Chapter 5 will provide a more detailed overview of effective writing interventions to support students with EBD.

The ultimate goal of developing learners who are resourceful and knowl-edgeable can be achieved by following the three guidelines of representation. Students with and at risk for EBD will be able to develop strategies that they are able to internalize and use throughout their academic career when these strategies are explicitly taught to students and teachers provide multiple means of access to the curriculum.

## Action and Expression

The final area in the UDL framework is providing multiple means of action and expression. This area addresses the "how" of learning and explores how students express their knowledge to teachers (King-Sears, 2014). The three guidelines under action and expression are physical action, expression and communication, and executive functions, with each leading to allowing students with options for action and expression.

Physical action explores how students may interact with materials and tools. In this area, teachers begin using more assistive technology and vary how students may respond to a question. A student might write an answer on a whiteboard and hold up their answer, or teachers may choose to use technology such as Quizlet or Plickers or create an online scavenger hunt for students to respond to a prompt (Chng & Gurvitch, 2018; Lowe et al., 2019). Students with limited speech might use a choice board to answer questions so that they are actively engaged.

The next is expression and communication that explores the concept that there is no medium that works for all learners (King-Sears, 2014). By providing multiple means of expression, teachers are able to level the playing field for students. Under this guideline, teachers should provide multiple media for communication, use multiple tools for construction, and build upon fluency by providing levels of scaffolding and support for practice and performance. The use of manipulatives in mathematics, allowing students to use different graphic organizers of varying degrees for writing, and using the gradual release model for supporting learning all are ways that teachers might address this guideline. For example, some teachers use a graphic organizer to support students' writing, sometimes referred to as the "hamburger" method. For some students, they will need a picture of the hamburger with explanations in each of the areas. For still other students, they will need a picture of the hamburger but without explanations of the different areas. A different group of students might need just the prompts of the graphic organizer to write. By using this method, all students may express the answer to the writing prompt that the teacher has given.

At the highest level of action and expression are executive functions. Executive functions are described as a set of skills that includes working memory, flexible thinking, and self-control (Meltzer, 2018). Many students with EBD have difficulties with executive functioning skills as they lack the self-control and flexible thinking needed. In the UDL framework, executive functions guidelines include guiding appropriate goal setting, supporting planning and strategy development, facilitate managing information and resources, and enhancing capacity for monitoring progress (CAST, 2018). Students cannot be expected to independently set appropriate goals without instruction and support; therefore, teachers must help in this area by providing prompts, models, and scaffolding information. They should post the information so that students are able to follow the goals. Further, teachers must assist students in managing their information by providing graphic organizers and prompts to access their information. Gradually, students will be able to monitor their own progress, but this takes explicit instruction from the teacher. For students with EBD, the behavior chart shown previously is used as a scaffold to assist students with self-regulation and monitoring of behavior.

The ultimate goal of action and expression is to develop learners who are strategic and goal directed. This is the highest level of the UDL framework and takes time and strategic, explicit instruction to attain. However, when students with and without disabilities are provided with the UDL framework, the classroom is accessible to all students.

## IMPLEMENTING UDL

As teachers prepare to incorporate UDL strategies into their classroom, they must begin with the end in mind and start with goal setting, unit planning, and lesson planning. Appendix 2–2 is a UDL planner that includes the UDL guidelines so that teachers can begin to assess their current level of UDL preparation. To use this, the teacher first notes the subject that is being taught. Next, the teacher identifies each student in the class and the preferred learning style for that specific subject. This is done explicitly because dependent upon the subject matter, a student may have a different learning style. Next, the teacher indicates the technology available and appropriate for the subject being taught. Finally, the teacher indicates the parts of the UDL frameworks to be included in the specific lesson plan. This UDL planner is meant for teachers to have an overarching plan of UDL prior to their individual lesson planning.

The next step in the process of planning for UDL is to create a lesson plan. Appendix 2–3 is a template that can be used for lesson planning. Within the lesson plan are common elements such as goals, assessment planning, and key vocabulary. The UDL lesson plan takes planning one step further by including areas within the lesson plan to indicate the UDL frameworks of multiple means of expression, representation, and engagement. This lesson plan utilizes the information from the UDL planner to a more specific level by creating individual day-by-day strategies.

## DIFFERENTIATED INSTRUCTION AND UNIVERSAL DESIGN FOR LEARNING

Differentiated instruction and UDL have many similarities and some notable differences. Each has the common goal of meeting the needs of students and allows for all students to access the content and curriculum. The two, when used in conjunction, will meet the needs of almost all learners in a general education setting. However, there are several differences between the two. Table 2–3 gives more information about the similarities and differences.

**Table 2–3.** Differentiated Instruction and Universal Design for Learning

| Differentiated Instruction | Similarities | UDL |
|---|---|---|
| Student focused | Meet needs of all students | Lesson (curriculum) focused |
| Response to learner needs | Give all students access | Anticipation of learner needs |
| Process to teaching | Engaging activities | Theoretical framework |
| Meet each student where they are | Emphasize critical thinking | |
| | Assess student progress before, during, and after instruction | |

## RESPONSE TO INTERVENTION

**Response to Intervention** (RtI) is a framework that relies heavily on the use of tiered instructional practices, assessment, and monitoring for the early identification of students with learning and behavioral needs (Fuchs & Fuchs, 2006). There are five essential components to the RtI process: (a) high-quality, scientifically based classroom instruction; (b) ongoing student assessment; (c) tiered instruction; (d) parent involvement; and (e) a team of teachers, administrators, and support staff who review the process (child study team). Without these components, implementation of the RtI model is not complete.

The next component is the three tiers of support. This tiered model of support can vary from school to school or district to district. Some other terms that are used are multilevel, trilevel, three-tiered, and four-tiered (Polloway et al., 2018). Despite differences in term use, each level of support includes specific core requirements. The three tiers include (1) high-quality core instruction, (b) targeted supplemental intervention, and (c) high-quality intensive intervention. Figure 2–1 shows how the tiers move from affecting the most students (Tier 1) to the fewest students (Tier 3).

## Tier 1—Core Instruction

Through core instruction, teachers are providing instruction to students at a high level using systematic, research-based, and challenging curriculum all in a general education classroom (Fuchs & Deshler, 2007). This is the stage where differentiation occurs as well as core curriculum instruction. Teachers should be using these techniques and assessing student progress through multiple means during this step of the process. Further, universal screening of all students should be taking place either during the Tier 1 phase or before it.

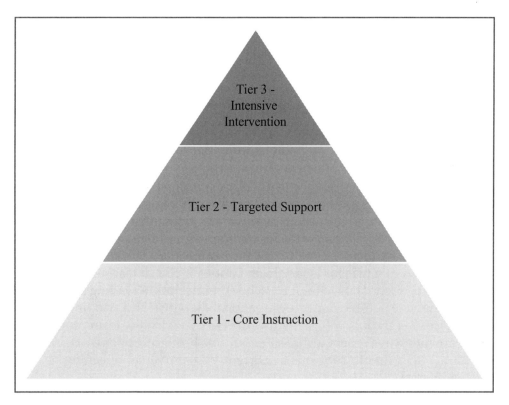

**Figure 2–1.** *RtI tiered process.*

## Tier 2—Targeted Support

If students do not respond adequately to the Tier 1 interventions, then targeted support is put into place for students. During this phase, students are receiving further differentiation, targeted instruction, instructional adaptations, and possibly technology to meet their needs (Polloway et al., 2018). Further, documentation must be gathered during Tier 2 of interventions that have been used and their success or lack thereof. These interventions may occur either in the classroom or in small group settings outside of the classroom by an interventionist. A plan should be in place to set specific goals, interventions applied, and data collection of the results.

## Tier 3—Intensive Intervention

When students, after a determined amount of time, do not respond to Tier 2 interventions, then the most intensive interventions are put into place. Depending on the school or district you work in, Tier 3 interventions may occur before or after a referral to special education takes place. Regardless of referral, during Tier 3 interventions, students will receive high-quality, research-based interventions. Some of these interventions may include programs such as Wilson Reading, Orton-Gillingham, Math Recovery, or specialized behavior interventions. There are cases when a student is able to move from Tier 3 back to Tier 1, but this is only with extensive intervention.

## CHILD STUDY

One integral part of the RtI process is the use of a child study (CST) or student support team. This team often consists of the classroom teacher and support staff (special educators, reading specialists, administration, etc.). The team and name of the team and members vary by school and/or district. In one school in a small district in the Northeast, the team met on a weekly basis where teachers brought data on student progress to the team to be reviewed. A flowchart describing the team process can be found in Figure 2–2. This team consisted of a teacher leader from Grades K to 2, a teacher leader from Grades 3 to 6, a school psychologist, school counselors, a reading specialist, a speech-language pathologist, an occupational therapist, and an administrator. Appendices 2–4 through 2–6 show the process by which the team progressed. There are two ways where a student would be brought up for discussion by the team, either due to previous or current year universal screening or by a teacher referral.

If a student is brought to the team by a teacher, then the teacher must start with the Step 1 form and answer each question. From there, the teacher would

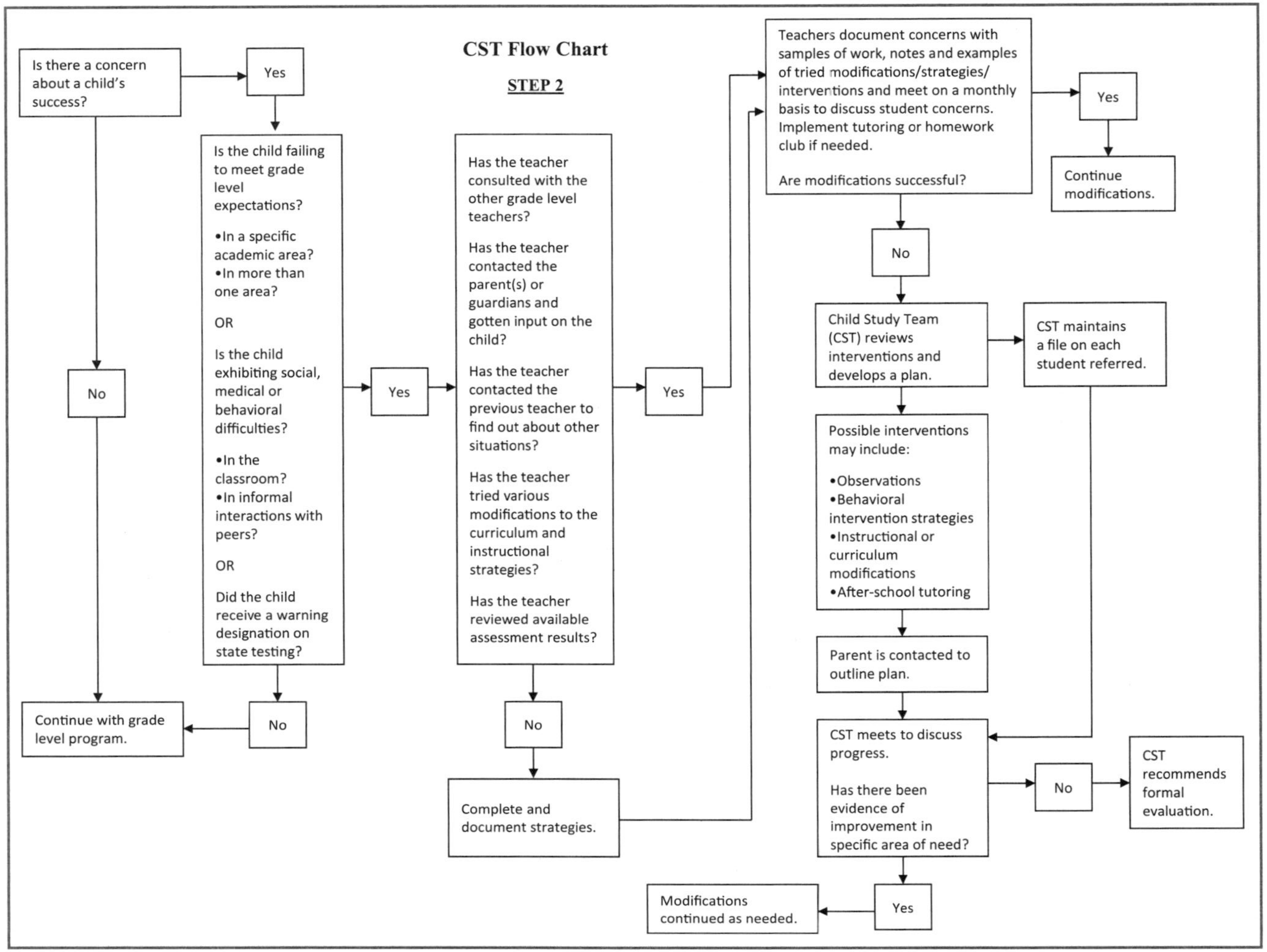

**CST Flow Chart**

**STEP 2**

Is there a concern about a child's success?

Yes

No

Continue with grade level program.

Is the child failing to meet grade level expectations?

- In a specific academic area?
- In more than one area?

OR

Is the child exhibiting social, medical or behavioral difficulties?

- In the classroom?
- In informal interactions with peers?

OR

Did the child receive a warning designation on state testing?

Yes

No

Has the teacher consulted with the other grade level teachers?

Has the teacher contacted the parent(s) or guardians and gotten input on the child?

Has the teacher contacted the previous teacher to find out about other situations?

Has the teacher tried various modifications to the curriculum and instructional strategies?

Has the teacher reviewed available assessment results?

Yes

No

Complete and document strategies.

Teachers document concerns with samples of work, notes and examples of tried modifications/strategies/interventions and meet on a monthly basis to discuss student concerns. Implement tutoring or homework club if needed.

Are modifications successful?

Yes

Continue modifications.

No

Child Study Team (CST) reviews interventions and develops a plan.

CST maintains a file on each student referred.

Possible interventions may include:
- Observations
- Behavioral intervention strategies
- Instructional or curriculum modifications
- After-school tutoring

Parent is contacted to outline plan.

CST meets to discuss progress.

Has there been evidence of improvement in specific area of need?

Yes

Modifications continued as needed.

No

CST recommends formal evaluation.

*Figure 2–2. Child study team flowchart.*

33

complete the referral form. The referral forms (Appendices 2–7 and 2–8) are used to determine if the teacher is using differentiated instruction, following student data, considering home situations, and identifying strengths and weaknesses. The teacher is then assigned a date to meet with the CST.

The CST meets on a weekly basis for 1 hour, and each student is given full consideration, with the teacher leaders taking the lead in the meeting. The classroom teacher attends the meeting to discuss the students. The team then develops an intervention plan (Appendix 2–9) and sets a date to meet again. Both before and after the meeting, the teacher is responsible for contacting the parents to discuss the concerns and outcome of the meeting. The team sets a time to meet to follow up on the student progress at a time determined by the team (generally 4 to 6 weeks).

During the intervention period, data are collected on the strategy and intervention page (Appendix 2–10). The person charged with implementing the intervention (classroom teacher, special educator, reading interventionist, etc.) collects data on a weekly basis or more often if determined by the CST. During the follow-up meeting, the team once again evaluates the students' progress. If they continue to make progress using the Tier 2 interventions, then these interventions continue. If the student is not making progress, then the team can decide to continue with the process, or they can move on to the Tier 3 interventions. Again, a follow-up meeting is planned, goals are defined, and parent communication and interventions continue.

This process continues until a student either moves out of the RtI process due to progress or a referral to special education is made. The length of time is determined by student growth or lack thereof. This process can be used for any types of needs, academic or behavioral. If it is determined that a child needs further support, the school team (in this case) moves forward with a full special educational evaluation to determine if there is a disability.

This example is only one of many that can be found; however, it is a common process that occurs in all schools and districts. It is essential as a teacher that you find out exactly how the process works in your school/district.

## POSITIVE BEHAVIORAL INTERVENTIONS AND SUPPORTS

**Positive Behavioral Interventions and Supports** (PBIS) is an evidence-based framework that has been adopted by many schools and districts across the country. According to the Center on Positive Behavioral Interventions and Supports, over 25,000 schools currently implement PBIS in their schools (Center on Positive Behavioral Interventions and Supports, 2018). Much like the RtI framework, schoolwide PBIS is a three-tiered system directly related to the behavior and academic outcomes of students. The three tiers for PBIS are primary prevention, secondary prevention, and tertiary prevention (Center on Positive Behavioral Interventions and Supports, 2018; Horner & Sugai, 2015; Kittelman et al., 2019). Within each tier, there are foundational systems and practices that relate directly to student levels of support. Figure 2–3 is a model of the three tiers of support, and it shows that each tier supports a different subsection of students.

## Tier I

Tier 1 of the PBIS model includes universal prevention for all students. Tier 1 supports all students and staff and impacts everyone across all settings in a school (Center on Positive Behavioral Interventions and Supports, 2018). The foundational systems within Tier 1 include an established leadership team, meetings on a regular basis, a statement of support for promoting positive schoolwide culture, data-based decision making, professional development, and a personal evaluation plan (Center on Positive Behavioral Interventions and Supports, 2018). The Tier 1 practices include having schoolwide expectations and behaviors that are taught, classroom expectations, encouragement

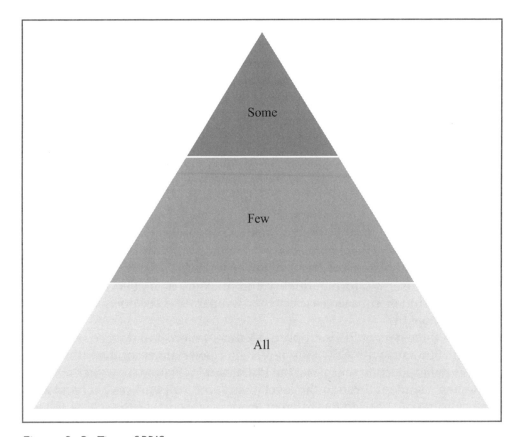

**Figure 2–3.** *Tiers of PBIS support.*

of expected behavior, and strong family/school partnerships. In some schools, the Tier 1 supports of the PBIS model may include a curriculum such as Responsive Classroom or Leader in Me. It is essential that professional development is included for all stakeholders in the school as well as for students so that the expectations are understood across the school. Professional development for parents is also essential so that parents understand the expectations. Schools should look internally at their current systems in place to determine the needs of the school.

## Tier 2

Tier 2 of the PBIS model is targeted prevention where some students are included into this area who are not successful with the Tier 1 interventions. The focus is on students who may develop more significant behavior problems and generally includes groups of students. It is a more targeted intervention than Tier 1 but not as intense as Tier 3. The foundational systems within Tier 2 include an intervention team, data collection, fidelity of implementation, screening process, and access to training. Some practices may include increased supervision, opportunities for positive reinforcement, precorrections, focus on the function of the behavior, and increased academic supports. Teams of specifically trained faculty (e.g., behavior specialists, counselor, and special educator) collect data and set specific goals for students who have moved into the Tier 2 interventions.

## Tier 3

Tier 3 is the most intensive prevention and is individualized to the students; a small subset of students, about 1% to 5% (Center on Positive Behavioral Interventions and Supports, 2018), is included in this tier. The intensive interventions are intended for students who have not been successful at Tier 1 or 2. These strategies are often used for students with disabilities such as autism or EBD or students who have not yet been identified but show signs of disability. The foundational systems of Tier 3 include a multidisciplinary team, behavior support expertise, and formal fidelity and outcome data collected. The practices include function-based assessments, wraparound supports, and cultural and contextual fit.

In all three tiers of PBIS support, documentation, and data collection are essential. Students with EBD may receive supports at any of the PBIS levels, and this data collection will assist the PBIS team in relation to further referrals or moving a student through the level of support. Appendices 2–11 and 2–12 are forms that can be used for different levels of support. As the school collects these forms, they compile data on the student to determine if it is necessary to move a student into Tier 2 or 3 of the PBIS tertiary model.

## CASE STUDY

*Correine is a second grader who has received Tier 1 and 2 supports to address walking out of the classroom, destroying school property, and cursing. Ms. Josephson, the school guidance counselor, and Ms. Randolph, her teacher, are considering a referral to the Child Study team. Describe the steps needed to complete the Child Study process.*

## CHAPTER SUMMARY

The Individuals with Disabilities Education Act (IDEA) provides every student eligible for special education services the right to a free and appropriate public education (FAPE) in the least restrictive environment. For many students, the least restrictive environment is the general education classroom or, at the very least, a public school. Students with disabilities therefore need access to the curriculum and to the behavior supports provided within the school. Differentiated instruction, universal design for learning, response to intervention, and positive behavior intervention supports help schools and teachers to be better equipped to provide the instruction necessary to include all students and provide a more inclusive environment for all.

## DISCUSSION QUESTIONS

1. Compare and contrast differentiated instruction and Universal Design for Learning.

2. What should be considered when planning for differentiated instruction?

3. When planning for UDL, what are three essential areas to consider?

4. Describe the PBIS tiered model of intervention.

## RESOURCES

http://www.cast.org/

https://www.pbis.org/

http://www.rtinetwork.org/

# REFERENCES

Center for Applied Special Technology (CAST). (2018). *Universal Design for Learning Guidelines Version 2.2.* Retrieved from http://udlguidelines.cast.org

Center on Positive Behavioral Interventions and Supports. (2018). *Schools that are implementing SWPBIS.* Retrieved from www.pbis.org

Chng, L., & Gurvitch, R. (2018). Using Plickers as an assessment tool in health and physical education settings. *Journal of Physical Education, Recreation & Dance, 89*(2), 19–25. doi:10.1080/07303084.2017.1404510

Cook, S. C., Rao, K. R., & Collins, L. (2017). Self-monitoring interventions for students with EBD: Applying UDL to a research-based practice. *Beyond Behavior, 26*(1), 19–27. doi:10.1177/1074295617694407

Ennis, R. P. (2016). Using self-regulated strategy development to help high school students with EBD summarize informational text in social studies. *Education and Treatment of Children, 39*(4), 545–568. doi:10.1353/etc.2016.0024

Fuchs, D., & Deshler, D. D. (2007). What we need to know about responsiveness to intervention (and shouldn't be afraid to ask). *Learning Disabilities Research & Practice, 22*(2), 129–136. doi:10.1111/j.1540-5826.2007.00237.x

Fuchs, D., & Fuchs, L. S. (2006). Introduction to response to intervention: What, why, and how valid is it? *Reading Research Quarterly, 41*(1), 93–99. doi:10.1598/RRQ.41.1.4

Horner, R. H., & Sugai, G. (2015). School-wide PBIS: An example of applied behavior analysis implemented at a scale of social importance. *Behavior Analysis in Practice, 8*(1), 80–85. doi:10.1007/s40617-015-0045-4

King-Sears, P. (2014). Introduction to learning disabilities quarterly special issue on Universal Design for Learning: Part one of two. *Learning Disabilities Quarterly, 37*(2), 68–70. doi:10.1177/0731948714528337

Kittelman, A., McIntosh, K., & Hoselton, R. (2019). Adoption of PBIS within school districts. *Journal of School Psychology, 76*, 159–167. doi:10.1016/j.jsp.2019.03.007

Landrum, T. J., & McDuffie, K. A. (2010). Learning style in the age of differentiated instruction. *Exceptionality, 18*(1), 6–17. doi:10.1080/09362830903462441

Lane, K. L., Harris, K. R., Graham, S., Weisenebach, J., Brindle, M., & Morphy, P. (2008). The effects of self-regulated strategy development on the writing performance of second-grade students with behavioral and writing difficulties. *The Journal of Special Education, 41*(4), 234–253. doi:10.1177/0022466907310370

Lowe, M. S., Macy, K. V. & Stone, S. M. (2019). Contingent teaching through low-tech audience response systems: Using Plickers to support student learning and assessment. *Journal of Information Literacy, 13*(2), 235–252. doi.org/10.11645/13.2.2633

Meltzer, L. (Ed.). (2018). *Executive function in education: From theory to practice.* Guilford.

Polloway, E. A., Patton, J. R., Serna, L., & Bailey-Joseph, J. W. (2018). *Strategies for teaching learners with special needs.* Pearson.

Rapp, W. (2014). *Universal design for learning in action [electronic resource]: 100 ways to teach all learners.* Brookes Publishing.

Snyder, T. D., de Brey, C., & Dillow, S. A. (2016). *Digest of Education Statistics 2015* (NCES 2016-014). Washington, DC: National Center for Education Statistics, Institute of Education Sciences, U.S. Department of Education.

The IRIS Center. (2008). *SRSD: Using learning strategies to enhance student learning.* Retrieved from https://iris.peabody.vanderbilt.edu/module/srs/

The IRIS Center. (2010). *Differentiated instruction: Maximizing the learning of all students* [Training module]. Peabody College, Vanderbilt University. Retrieved from http://iris.peabody.vanderbilt.edu/module/di

Tomlinson, C. (1999). *The differentiated classroom: Responding to the needs of all learners.* Association for Supervision and Curriculum Development.

Tomlinson, C. (2000). Reconcilable differences? Standards-based teaching and differentiation. *Educational Leadership, 58*(1), 6–11.

Tomlinson, C. A. (2014). *The differentiated classroom: Responding to the needs of all learners.* ASCD.

## APPENDIX 2–1
## Self-Monitoring Chart

Student Name _____

Behavior 1 _____

Behavior 2 _____

Behavior 3 _____

| Behavior 1 | 1 | 2 | 3 | | Behavior 1 | 1 | 2 | 3 |
| Behavior 2 | 1 | 2 | 3 | | Behavior 2 | 1 | 2 | 3 |
| Behavior 2 | 1 | 2 | 3 | | Behavior 2 | 1 | 2 | 3 |
| Student Total ___ | | | | | Student Total ___ | | | |
| Teacher Total ___ | | | | | Teacher Total ___ | | | |
| Behavior 1 | 1 | 2 | 3 | | Behavior 1 | 1 | 2 | 3 |
| Behavior 2 | 1 | 2 | 3 | | Behavior 2 | 1 | 2 | 3 |
| Behavior 2 | 1 | 2 | 3 | | Behavior 2 | 1 | 2 | 3 |
| Student Total ___ | | | | | Student Total ___ | | | |
| Teacher Total ___ | | | | | Teacher Total ___ | | | |

My goal for the day: _____

## APPENDIX 2–2
# UDL Planning

Subject: _____Unit: _____

Goals/Outcomes: _____

_____

## Student Learning Styles:

| Student Name | Visual | Auditory | Kinesthetic | Other Information |

## Technology (check all that apply)

| | | |
|---|---|---|
| SMART Board | S. Laptop | Printer |
| Chromebook | iPad/Tablets | 3D Printer |
| Projector | Mp3 Player | Microscope |
| Scanner | Camera | Other |
| Speakers | Webcam | Other |
| Calculator | FM System | Other |

| **Multiple Means of Representation** | **Multiple Means of Action/Expression** | **Multiple Means of Engagement** |
|---|---|---|
| __1—Provide options for perception | __4—Provide options for physical action | __7—Provide options for recruiting interest |
| __1.1—Offer ways of customizing the display of information | __4.1—Vary the methods for response and navigation | __7.1—Optimize individual choice and autonomy |
| __1.2—Offer alternatives for auditory information | __4.2—Optimize access to tools and assistive technologies | __7.2—Optimize relevance, value, and authenticity |
| __1.3—Offer alternatives for visual information | __5—Provide options for expression and communication | __7.3—Minimize threats and distractions |
| __2—Provide options for language, mathematical expressions, and symbols | __5.1—Use multiple media for communication | __8—Provide options for sustaining effort and persistence |
| __2.1—Clarify vocabulary and symbols | __5.2—Use multiple tools for construction and composition | __8.1—Heighten salience of goals/objectives |
| __2.2—Clarify syntax and structure | __5.3—Build fluencies with graduated levels of support for practice and performance | __8.2—Vary demands and resources to optimize challenges |
| __2.3—Support decoding of text, mathematical notation, and symbols | | __8.3—Foster collaboration and community |

*continues*

**APPENDIX 2–2.** *continued*

| **Multiple Means of Representation** | **Multiple Means of Action/Expression** | **Multiple Means of Engagement** |
|---|---|---|

**Multiple Means of Representation**

__2.4—Promote under-standing across languages

__2.5—Illustrate through multiple media

__3—Provide options for comprehension

__3.1—Activate or supply background knowledge

__3.2—Highlight patterns, critical features, big ideas, and relationships

__3.3—Guide information processing, visualization, and manipulation

__3.4—Maximize transfer and generalization

**Multiple Means of Action/Expression**

___6—Provide options for executive functions

__6.1—Guide appropriate goal setting

__6.2—Support planning and strategy development

__6.3—Facilitate managing information and resources

__6.4—Enhance capacity for monitoring progress

**Multiple Means of Engagement**

__8.4—Increase mastery-oriented feedback

__9—Provide options for self-regulation

__9.1—Promote expectations and beliefs that optimize motivation

__9.2—Facilitate personal coping skills and strategies

__9.3—Develop self-assess-ment and reflection

Notes:

## APPENDIX 2–3

# UDL Lesson Plan

| Lesson: | Teacher: | Course: | Date: |
|---------|----------|---------|-------|

**TOPIC of This Lesson or Essential Question**

**Common Core State Standards and/or Subject Specific State Standards**

**Mastery Objectives (Skills)**

**Materials/Technology/Resources Needed for the Lesson**

| Academic Language Vocabulary | Academic Language Function |
|------------------------------|----------------------------|

| Formative Assessments | Summative Assessment |
|-----------------------|----------------------|

| Instructional Strategies | Multiple Means of Representation |
|--------------------------|---------------------------------|

| Multiple Means of Engagement | Multiple Means of Expression |
|------------------------------|------------------------------|

**Opening/Activity (Do Now)**

**Agenda**

**Closure (check for understanding)**

## APPENDIX 2–4

# Child Study Team Process:  Step 1

### Step 1:  What Is Your Concern?

Is the child failing to meet grade-level expectations?   Yes_____   No_____

When did you first observe the child's struggles to meet grade-level expectations? _____

What is the specific area(s) of concern?

_____

_____

_____

_____

### OR

Is the child exhibiting social, emotional, medical, or behavioral difficulties?
Yes_____   No_____

When did you first observe the child's struggles? _____

Is the child struggling in any of these areas *within the classroom*?
Yes_____   No_____

Is the child struggling in any of these areas in *informal interactions with peers*?
Yes_____   No_____

Describe your specific concerns:

_____

_____

_____

_____

### OR

Did the child receive a warning designation on State Assessments?
Yes_____   No_____

In what specific academic area was the warning?

_____

**If the answer is YES to ANY of these questions, move on to Step 2.**

## APPENDIX 2–5

# Child Study Team Process: Step 2

### Step 2: What Have You Done So Far?

Have you consulted with other grade-level teachers regarding this child?
Yes_____ No_____

Date of consultation: _____

Who did you consult with: _____

Recommendations:

_____

_____

_____

_____

Did you contact the parent(s) or guardian of the child?   Yes_____ No_____

Date of contact: _____

Who did you contact: _____

Information discussed:

_____

_____

_____

_____

Did you contact the lead teacher to find out other situations regarding this
child?   Yes_____ No_____

Date of contact: _____

Name of crew teacher: _____

Information discussed:

_____

_____

_____

_____

Have you tried modifications to the curriculum and instructional strategies?
Yes_____ No_____

Date strategies and modifications were utilized: _____

Modifications implemented:

_____

_____

_____

_____

Have you reviewed available assessments?    Yes_____ No_____

Date reviewed: _____

Name of assessments: _____

Thoughts regarding assessments:

_____

_____

_____

_____

## APPENDIX 2–6

# Child Study Team Process:  Step 3

### Prior to Step 3

- Teachers should document concerns with samples of work, notes, and examples of tried modifications/strategies/interventions and meet on a monthly basis to discuss student concerns. Tutoring or the homework club can be implemented if needed. If these implementations are unsuccessful, a Child Study Team (CST) Referral will be submitted to the
CST Liaison.

### Step 3:  Child Study Team Referral

- CST meeting is scheduled and the team gathers together to review interventions and develop a plan to address the needs of the child.

- Possible interventions may include:
  - Observations
  - Behavioral intervention strategies
  - Instructional or curriculum modifications
  - After-school tutoring

- Parent is contacted to outline the plan.

- CST meets to discuss the child's progress in a scheduled follow-up meeting.

- If there has been evidence of improvement in the specific area of need, modifications will continue as needed.

- If there is no evidence of improvement, the team may recommend a formal evaluation through the Special Education Department.

## APPENDIX 2–7

# Child Study Team Process:
# Middle School Referral Form

**Student Name:** _____

**DOB:** _____

**ELL Level:** _____

**Teacher/HR/Grade:** _____

**Past/Present Teachers/Staff Involved with the Student:** _____

_____

_____

_____

**Referring Person:** _____

**Date of Referral:** _____

1. **Why are you referring the student?** _____

   _____

   _____

   _____

   _____

2. **In what areas does the student succeed in school?** _____

   _____

   _____

   _____

   _____

3. **In what areas does the student struggle in school?**

   ☐ Math                      ☐ Sensory

   ☐ Reading                   ☐ Motor

   ☐ Written expression        ☐ Other

   ☐ Social/emotional/behavioral

**4. Is the student able to perform at grade level?**

| | Above | At | Below |
|---|:---:|:---:|:---:|
| Count | ☐ | ☐ | ☐ |
| Add | ☐ | ☐ | ☐ |
| Subtract | ☐ | ☐ | ☐ |
| Multiply | ☐ | ☐ | ☐ |
| Fractions (concept) | ☐ | ☐ | ☐ |
| Fractions (compute) | ☐ | ☐ | ☐ |
| Read CVC words | ☐ | ☐ | ☐ |
| Decode at grade level | ☐ | ☐ | ☐ |
| Write a paragraph | ☐ | ☐ | ☐ |
| Write complete sentences | ☐ | ☐ | ☐ |
| Complete assignments in a timely manner | ☐ | ☐ | ☐ |
| Read numbers | ☐ | ☐ | ☐ |
| Add multiple digits | ☐ | ☐ | ☐ |
| Subtract multiple digits | ☐ | ☐ | ☐ |
| Divide | ☐ | ☐ | ☐ |
| Decimals (concept) | ☐ | ☐ | ☐ |
| Decimals (compute) | ☐ | ☐ | ☐ |
| Comprehend at GL | ☐ | ☐ | ☐ |
| Tell time | ☐ | ☐ | ☐ |
| Recall passage | ☐ | ☐ | ☐ |
| Write legibly | ☐ | ☐ | ☐ |

**5. What types of inappropriate behavior does the student display in your class?**

| | |
|---|---|
| ☐ Talking back | ☐ Incomplete assignments |
| ☐ Speaking out of turn | ☐ Gum chewing |
| ☐ Disrupting class | ☐ Not following directions |
| ☐ Leaving room w/o permission | ☐ In hallway without pass |
| ☐ Late to class | ☐ Disrespectful to peers |
| ☐ Fighting | ☐ Argumentative |
| ☐ Lying | ☐ Other (please specify) |

*continues*

**APPENDIX 2–7.** *continued*

### 6. Is the child failing to meet grade-level expectations due to:

☐ Poor effort                    ☐ Completion of work

☐ Ability to follow directions          ☐ Other (please specify)

### 7. What types of accommodations/modifications are you currently providing for the student?

| Accommodations Tried in Class | Not Helpful | | Neutral | Very Helpful | | NA |
|---|---|---|---|---|---|---|
| | 1 | 2 | 3 | 4 | 5 | |
| Extra time on assignments | | | | | | |
| Redirection of attention | | | | | | |
| Preferential seating | | | | | | |
| Multiple modality instruction | | | | | | |
| Structured class routines | | | | | | |
| Highlight important information | | | | | | |
| Behavioral contracts | | | | | | |
| Modified tests (shorter) | | | | | | |
| Graphic organizers | | | | | | |
| Repeated instructions | | | | | | |
| Comprehension clues | | | | | | |
| Use of dictionary/spell check | | | | | | |
| Outlines | | | | | | |
| Other (please specify) | | | | | | |
| | | | | | | |
| | | | | | | |
| | | | | | | |

## APPENDIX 2–8

# Child Study Team Process:
# Primary School Referral Form

**Student Name:** _____

**DOB:** _____

**ELL Level:** _____

**Teacher/HR/Grade:** _____

**Past/Present Teachers/Staff Involved with the Student:**_____

_____

_____

_____

**Referring Person:** _____

**Date of Referral:** _____

1. **Why are you referring the student?** _____

   _____

   _____

   _____

   _____

2. **In what areas does the student succeed in school?** _____

   _____

   _____

   _____

   _____

3. **In what areas does the student struggle in school?**

   ☐ Math                      ☐ Sensory

   ☐ Reading                   ☐ Motor

   ☐ Written expression        ☐ Other

   ☐ Social/emotional/behavioral

*continues*

**APPENDIX 2–8.** *continued*

## 4. Is the student able to perform at grade level?

| | Above | At | Below |
|---|:---:|:---:|:---:|
| Count | ☐ | ☐ | ☐ |
| Add | ☐ | ☐ | ☐ |
| Subtract | ☐ | ☐ | ☐ |
| Multiply | ☐ | ☐ | ☐ |
| Recognize alphabet | ☐ | ☐ | ☐ |
| Write alphabet | ☐ | ☐ | ☐ |
| Read CVC words | ☐ | ☐ | ☐ |
| Spell 3/4 letter words | ☐ | ☐ | ☐ |
| Write sentences | ☐ | ☐ | ☐ |
| Knows colors | ☐ | ☐ | ☐ |
| Read numbers | ☐ | ☐ | ☐ |
| Add multiple digits | ☐ | ☐ | ☐ |
| Subtract multiple digits | ☐ | ☐ | ☐ |
| Tell time | ☐ | ☐ | ☐ |
| Read nonsense words | ☐ | ☐ | ☐ |
| Read at grade level | ☐ | ☐ | ☐ |
| Write name | ☐ | ☐ | ☐ |
| Write at grade level | ☐ | ☐ | ☐ |
| Write paragraph | ☐ | ☐ | ☐ |

## 5. What types of inappropriate behavior does the student display in your class?

☐ Talking back   ☐ Incomplete assignments
☐ Speaking out of turn   ☐ Gum chewing
☐ Disrupting class   ☐ Not following directions
☐ Leaving room w/o permission   ☐ In hallway without pass
☐ Late to class   ☐ Disrespectful to peers
☐ Fighting   ☐ Argumentative
☐ Lying   ☐ Other (please specify)

**6. Is the child failing to meet grade-level expectations due to:**

☐ Poor effort ☐ Completion of work

☐ Ability to follow directions ☐ Other (please specify)

**7. What types of accommodations/modifications are you currently providing for the student?**

| Accommodations Tried in Class | Not Helpful | | Neutral | Very Helpful | | NA |
|---|---|---|---|---|---|---|
| | 1 | 2 | 3 | 4 | 5 | |
| Extra time on assignments | | | | | | |
| Redirection of attention | | | | | | |
| Preferential seating | | | | | | |
| Multiple modality instruction | | | | | | |
| Structured class routines | | | | | | |
| Highlight important information | | | | | | |
| Behavioral contracts | | | | | | |
| Modified tests (shorter) | | | | | | |
| Graphic organizers | | | | | | |
| Repeated instructions | | | | | | |
| Comprehension clues | | | | | | |
| Use of dictionary/spell check | | | | | | |
| Outlines | | | | | | |
| Other (please specify) | | | | | | |
| | | | | | | |
| | | | | | | |
| | | | | | | |

## APPENDIX 2–9

# Child Study Team Process:
# Intervention Plan and Documentation

| | |
|---|---|
| **Student Name:** | **DOB:** |
| **Starting Date:** | **Follow-Up Meeting Date:** |
| **Academic/Behavioral Goal 1:** | |
| **Responsible Person:** | |
| Intervention: | |
| **Academic/Behavioral Goal 2:** | |
| **Responsible Person:** | |
| Intervention: | |
| **Academic/Behavioral Goal 3:** | |
| **Responsible Person:** | |
| Intervention: | |
| **Academic/Behavioral Goal 4:** | |
| **Responsible Person:** | |
| Intervention: | |

Please sign below if you are in agreement with the intervention plan that is in place for this child.

# APPENDIX 2–10
# Intervention Plan Tracking

## STRATEGY PAGE/INTERVENTION RECORD

**Student** _____     **Date** _____

**School** _____     **Grade/Tier** _____

**Completed by** _____     **Title** _____

**Identify Objective (What do you want the student to be able to accomplish?)**

_____

_____

**Instructions:** Enter the date and results for each monitoring session.

| | Date | Score (%) | Goal (%) | Description of intervention, progress monitoring, and score definition with goals. |
|---|---|---|---|---|
| **BL** | | | | |
| 1 | | | | *Intervention: |
| 2 | | | | _____ |
| 3 | | | | _____ |
| 4 | | | | *Progress Monitoring: |
| 5 | | | | _____ |
| 6 | | | | _____ |
| 7 | | | | *Score Definition: |
| 8 | | | | _____ |
| 9 | | | | _____ |
| 10 | | | | *Goal: |
| 11 | | | | _____ |
| 12 | | | | _____ |

*continues*

**APPENDIX 2–10.** *continued*

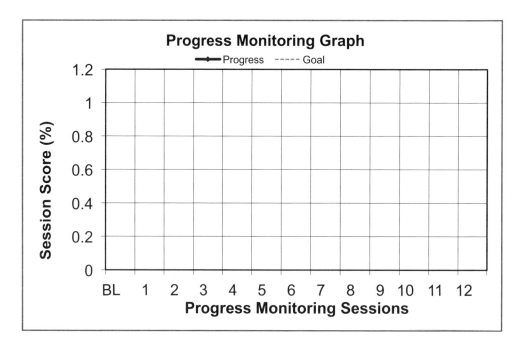

**APPENDIX 2–11**

# PBIS Office Discipline Referral (Minor Offense)

Student Name: _____     Grade: _____

Referred by: _____     Homeroom: _____

Location (circle one):

| |
|---|
| Classroom          Hallway          Cafeteria          Playground<br>Field Trip      Bus      Special Class: _____      Other _____ |

| Student was not **SAFE** | Student was not **RESPECTFUL** |
|---|---|
| __ Physical contact<br>__ Property misuse<br>__ Other _____ | __ Not following directions/<br>    defiance<br>__ Disruptive to the learning<br>    environment<br>__ Use of inappropriate language<br>__ Other _____ |

| Student was not **RESPONSIBLE** | Student was not **CARING** |
|---|---|
| __ Missing materials<br>__ Missing assignments<br>__ Other _____ | __ Name calling/unkind words<br>__ Other _____ |

| Staff Response | Others involved |
|---|---|
| __ Reteach behavior<br>__ Contact parent<br>__ Loss of privilege<br>__ Other _____ | __ None<br>__ Peer<br>__ Staff<br>__ Teacher |

| Comments | Possible Motivation |
|---|---|
| | __ Avoidance<br>__ Attention<br>__ Obtain item |

## APPENDIX 2–12

# PBIS Office Discipline Referral (Major Offense)

Student Name: _____    Grade: _____

Referred by: _____    Homeroom: _____

Location (circle one):

| | | | |
|---|---|---|---|
| Classroom | Hallway | Cafeteria | Playground |
| Field Trip    Bus    Special Class: _____ | | Other _____ | |

---

**Student was not SAFE**
__ Fighting (aggressive behavior)
__ Play fighting
__ Physical harassment
__ Weapon
__ Throwing objects
__ Other _____

**Student was not RESPECTFUL**
__ Gross disrespect
__ Stealing/forgery
__ Cheating/lying
__ Vandalism
__ Defiance of authority
__ Other _____

---

**Student was not RESPONSIBLE**
__ Persistent tardiness
__ Persistent missing of assignments
__ Other _____

**Student was not CARING**
__ Verbal harassment
__ Bullying
__ Other _____

---

**Administrative Response**
__ Conference
__ Time in office
__ Contact home
__ Loss of privilege
__ In-school suspension
__ Out-of-school suspension

**Others involved**
__ None
__ Peer
__ Staff
__ Teacher

---

**Comments**

**Possible Motivation**
__ Avoidance
__ Attention
__ Obtain item

# 3

# Service Delivery

## INTRODUCTION

Public Law 94-142, or the Education for All Handicapped Children Act (1975), changed the face of public education and made a **free appropriate public education (FAPE)** a legal right for students with disabilities. Schools were no longer able to say that they could not provide students with education because they did not have resources or facilities. However, what the law and its subsequent reauthorizations and amendments—Public Law 99-457, the Handicapped Children's Protection Act, PL 101-476, and the Individuals with Disabilities Education Act (2004)—did not do was provide specific guidance on how students should be served within educational settings. This chapter will provide background information on laws and protections for students with emotional and behavioral disabilities (EBD) and provide suggestions and options for providing support for students with EBD and other students with similar needs in the appropriate educational settings, along with suggestions for classroom management strategies to support students with EBD in the classroom setting.

## WHAT DRIVES SERVICES FOR STUDENTS WITH EBD?

All students with disabilities are entitled to a free and appropriate public education and should be educated with their peers in the least restrictive environment. This decision is made by the IEP team, which includes parents, the child, special education teachers, general education teachers, related service providers, and administrators. All the services provided within the local public school are done at no cost to families (IDEA, 2004, §300.39(a)(1)). Schools are supposed to adapt to the needs of students with disabilities and provide what students need, when they need it, in the environment where they will have the most success.

## FREE AND APPROPRIATE PUBLIC EDUCATION

**Free and appropriate public education** (FAPE) is not a new concept. FAPE was first introduced in the Education for All Handicapped Children Act (i.e., PL 94-142) in 1974 and later reauthorized as the Individuals with Disabilities Education Act (IDEA) in 1990. The FAPE mandate was enacted to ensure students with disabilities received an individualized education appropriate to their level of need and linked to federal funding specific to those students. Provided through the IEP process, the FAPE provision is an important legal right for students with disabilities. FAPE ensures students with disabilities are placed in the least restrictive environment, receive specially designed instruction, have access to appropriate related services, and have an appropriate IEP to meet their individual needs.

## LEAST RESTRICTIVE ENVIRONMENT

**Least restrictive environment** is defined by the Individuals with Disabilities Education Act as the school's responsibility to ensure that:

> (i) To the maximum extent appropriate, children with disabilities, including children in public or private institutions or other care facilities, are educated with children who are nondisabled; and (ii) Special classes, separate schooling, or other removal of children with disabilities from the regular educational environment occurs only if the nature or severity of the disability is such that education in regular classes with the use of supplementary aids and services cannot be achieved satisfactorily. (IDEA, 2004, §300.114.a.1-2

Simply stated, the **least restrictive environment** (LRE) should be the first place that students with disabilities receive services, and schools should have the appropriate supports in place for students to be successful. The school district and school IEP team are supposed to interpret this for each student and should evaluate the student's strengths and needs, as well as consider these when a placement decision is made. The least restrictive environment is loosely defined as the one where students without disabilities would receive services, which is typically the general education classroom. All resources should be applied to ensure the student is successful in the least restrictive setting, and the student should make academic and behavioral progress in this setting. If, after a certain amount of time passes with appropriate data to support it, and all resources have been exhausted in the LRE, schools can look at applying additional layers of support to provide the student with the resources needed to be successful. If this requires making a change to the environment where the student receives additional supports and spends additional time outside of the general education classroom, this must also be an IEP team decision.

Placement is determined annually, at the IEP team meeting; it is based on the child's strengths and needs, and it should be offered as close as possible to the child's home (IDEA, 2004, §300.116.b), commonly referred to as the neighborhood school. Placement decisions should be made based on the student rather than what the school has available. All efforts should be made to provide services to students eligible for the general education setting with minimal supports before referring students out.

Federal law (i.e., IDEA, 2004) does not provide specific requirements for educating students in the least restrictive environment, but it does provide indicators for services under Part B, Indicator 5, Sections A to C regarding the amount of time that students with disabilities should be involved in the class-room. The indicators are listed below in further detail related to the amount of time students with disabilities spend in the general education classroom:

- Indicator 5.A—80% or more of the school day
- Indicator 5.B—less than 40% of the school day
- Indicator 5.C—separate school (i.e., center-based school), residential treatment

## SERVICE DELIVERY OPTIONS

Service delivery is an important IEP team decision, with the considerations for how long students spend in the general education classroom being individual and determined by the student's strengths and needs. The amount of time spent in general education is considered to be on a continuum of environments and can vary from 100% of the time to none of the time. In the IEP, the anticipated frequency, location, and duration of services, along with necessary accommodations and modifications, are listed and specifically developed to benefit the student academically and behaviorally. Figure 3–1 illustrates the continuum of special education supports for students with EBD. Specific details about service delivery in the IEP include the amount of time per day and week the child receives services, where the services are provided (i.e., general education or special education classroom), how long those services are provided for, who provides those services, and when the services will begin and end (IDEA, 2004).

Service delivery models are guided by state education laws and may look different state to state. Students are typically classified by the percentage of time spent outside of the general education classroom and may be classified as itinerant (i.e., consultation), supplemental (resource), or full-time (often a center-based school). Consult your state special of education website for caseload and classification information. For example, in Pennsylvania, student participation in special education outside the general education curriculum is broken down into percentages as follows: itinerant (0% to 19.9%), supplemental (20% to 79.9%), and full-time (more than 80%). For many students, this is the general education setting with support provided to the general education teachers by the special education teacher.

## INCLUSION

This is also called an inclusive classroom because of the **inclusion** of students with disabilities and those without. Some may refer to inclusion as "main-streaming," but this term is outdated, and we prefer the term inclusion,

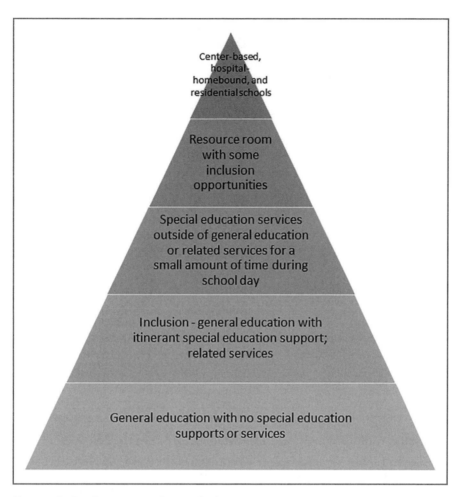

**Figure 3–1.** *Continuum of special education services.*

because it describes the environment in which all students are included. Inclusion is often interpreted in many different ways. The first way that people may interpret inclusion is one where a student remains in the general education classroom with peers for the entire school day, and the supports are provided to the student in the classroom. For example, a student who receives consultation services for occupational therapy will receive those services from the occupational therapist in the classroom, where they work on skills that are appropriate to the student's needs in that specific setting.

A student with EBD who spends all their time in the general education classroom requires minimal support behaviorally and academically. Any student with disabilities who spends all their time in general education is typically considered an itinerant (i.e., consultative) student, where the special education teacher is available to support (i.e., consult with) the general education teacher on an as-needed basis or for scheduled support meetings, depending on the school schedule. For example, the special education teacher may provide support in adapting tests or curriculum materials to facilitate student access to the curriculum, providing suggestions for classroom management, or observing the student to provide suggestions for academic or behavioral accommodations according to student need. The student may also engage in brief, informal check-ins with the special education teacher to discuss grades and behavior in class.

## Co-Teaching

Another aspect of inclusion is **co-teaching**, where the general education teacher and the special education teacher work to provide the instruction and the support in a classroom together. True co-teaching is also often called team teaching, where the teachers are both proficient with the content and can provide instruction while differentiating for the students in the classroom based on a spectrum of needs, from below to above grade level. This requires teachers who are compatible with one another, able to co-plan so they are providing high-quality instruction, as well as provide support to students, regardless of whether that student is a general education student or a student with disabilities, and a high degree of flexibility to allow for student learning and differentiation within lessons (Friend et al., 2010; Stein, 2018).

There are several adaptions to the traditional co-teaching model. One such adaptation is one teach, one support. The versions include one teacher teaching while the second teacher supports students, observes behavior, or circulates the room assisting students. During one teach, one support, one of the teachers is responsible for content, and one is responsible for circulating the room to observe students while the other teacher engages in instruction. Teachers are able to take turns and provide instruction in whatever content they feel more comfortable in, or on agreed-upon parts of the curriculum, while the other teacher is observing or supporting students behaviorally, academically, or both (Friend et al., 2010). Other inclusive co-teaching examples include (a) station teaching, where each teacher runs a station to provide small group and individualized learning; (b) an alternative co-teaching model where one teacher instructs a large group while the other instructs a small group; and (c) a parallel co-teaching model, where each teacher teaches half the class the same thing (Friend et al., 2010; Stein, 2018).

Students with EBD can benefit greatly from inclusion and co-teaching. The students who are fully included receive as-needed support from the co-teachers and can get individualized attention for behavioral or academic support without leaving the general education classroom. Additionally, students who are included for specific subjects receive the support needed to be successful within the general education inclusive classroom with the addition of the special education teacher, who provides an additional layer of reinforcement for appropriate academics and behavior, which leads to student success.

## Resource Room

Students with emotional and behavioral disabilities often spend time in what is commonly referred to as the resource room. This environment provides individualized support that students need to regulate emotions, check in with a special education teacher on academics, take tests in a quiet environment, or work on behavioral plans and supports. The time spent in the resource room looks different for every student but is a time that should be purposeful and planned so that students maximize the time they are spending outside of the general education classroom. Students need targeted individualized support during this time period and should be aware of what they are supposed to be doing as well, since they are also part of their IEP planning. Transparency and student involvement in every setting are necessary for student success.

## Center-Based Schools

Students who require the most behavioral and academic support, whose needs cannot be met within a less restrictive setting, may receive services through center-based, homebased, homebound, or hospital placements. Students with EBD in center-based schools need very structured environments, including level or point systems for earning reinforcement. These environments typically have small classrooms with a small student to teacher ratio to ensure that they are receiving individualized attention for their behavioral and academic needs to be met directly. The students who attend EBD center schools are ones that have been in other settings and those settings were not successful in meeting their needs, nor were they appropriate for the amount of support needed. The students receive intensive intervention services, including counseling, small classrooms for focused academic and behavioral support, mental health supports, and related services (e.g., Applied Behavior Analysis, occupational therapy). A center-based school is not a decision that is made lightly by the IEP team; less restrictive settings must be considered first.

## SPECIALLY DESIGNED INSTRUCTION

**Specially designed instruction** (SDI), often referred to as the *bulk of the IEP*, details the specific services students with disabilities require and that all teachers working with that child need to do to provide the necessary instruction to meet the unique needs of students with disabilities. It is provided at no cost to the family of the child with disabilities. Specially designed instruction is not simply instructional strategies; rather, it is targeted instruction designed to help students master IEP goals and objectives (IDEA, 2004, §300.39). Teachers are legally required to adapt instructional delivery to meet the needs of each student with an IEP in their classroom, which is often called differentiated instruction. The difference between SDI and differentiated instruction is that SDI is provided according to the student's IEP for the purpose of ensuring they progress within the general education curriculum. Specially designed instruction does not replace regular instruction or differentiated instruction; think of SDI as an additional layer of customized instruction.

To implement SDI for students with IEPs in their classrooms, teachers need to change aspects of content, instructional delivery, materials, teaching methods, and instructional settings and environments specific to those students and in accordance with their IEPs (Riccomini, Morano, & Hughes, 2017). For example, students whose IEP goals include becoming more independent during math activities require additional behavioral support in the class during this time, which could include a token board, where the tokens are provided to the student when they complete a number of math problems correctly and with appropriate predetermined behaviors. Requirements for a token may include that the student is seated in the chair with a quiet voice and raising a hand signaling the need for a teacher's assistance. This also needs to be taught, so the SDI for that student includes explicit teaching and rehearsing expectations in each academic setting (i.e., math, language arts, science, and social studies). An example of a token board (elementary) to support a student in math class is provided in Appendix 3–1, and a check sheet for a high school student is provided in Appendix 3–2.

## CLASSROOM MANAGEMENT

The cornerstone of a well-managed classroom is effective instruction, which includes supporting students with disabilities in the general education classroom. If students are not engaged and learning in the classroom in an authentic and meaningful way, students will struggle with academic achievement. Preservice teachers should learn ways to engage students with appropriate instructional materials, use a variety of appropriate teaching strategies, teach students at their instructional level, and provide students a variety of response methods and a plethora of opportunities to respond to increase student participation and support appropriate behavior in the classroom (Oliver & Reschly, 2007). Students who do not receive appropriate instruction, or are taught using inappropriate instructional materials, often display their frustrations through acting-out behaviors, causing disruptions in the classroom. Additionally, students who are engaged in lessons and frequently provided opportunities to respond in class have positive academic and behavioral success in the classroom (Sutherland & Wehby, 2001).

Classroom management is one of the most difficult aspects of teaching, and one where teachers, especially new teachers, struggle the most. Ineffective classroom management and student behavior issues impact teachers' choice to stay in the classroom, thus causing a revolving door of new teachers.

Many new teachers are not equipped or prepared to manage a classroom effectively and may not have the skills to deal with students with behavioral issues in the classroom (Myers et al., 2017). Whole-school behavior management, along with classroom management, should fall under the positive behavior intervention and supports (PBIS) framework utilized at the school level. Teachers should receive training in PBIS in their training programs or their school districts, because PBIS is mentioned in IDEA (2004), where it should be utilized when supporting behavior. Using evidence-based classroom management practices within the PBIS framework appropriately will help to provide structures for positive student behavior within the classroom. The basics of effective classroom management for students with disabilities include effective individualized instruction based on students' emotional, behavioral, or academic needs combined with PBIS and evidence-based classroom management methods (e.g., opportunities to respond, behavior-specific praise, structured teaching routines and expectations), which we will discuss further in the next section. The Office of Special Education Programs (OSEP, 2017) provided guidance on classroom management and suggested four categories of classroom interventions and supports to provide a comprehensive approach to classroom management:

- Foundations—settings, routines, and expectations
- Prevention—supervision, opportunity, acknowledgment, prompts, and precorrections
- Response—error correction, other strategies (e.g., escalation, reinforcement), and additional tools
- Data systems—counting, timing, sampling, ABC cards, incident reports, or office referrals (OSEP, 2017)

## RELATED SERVICES FOR STUDENTS WITH EBD

Approximately 1% of students in special education are identified as having an emotional or behavioral disability. Students with EBD may have a need for additional services outside the scope of traditional related services (i.e., occupational therapy), which can and should be provided within the school context. For example, counseling can be provided at school through either a school guidance counselor or a mental health counselor, depending on the student's need. This looks like a weekly appointment with the counselor at school, in a quiet location, where students work on goals and objectives set forth in their IEP related to counseling (e.g., anger management, organizational skills).

According to the Individuals with Disabilities Act (2004, §300.24), students are entitled to additional services to ensure they access the general education curriculum, referred to as "related services." These services are provided by the school district. Related services that are deemed appropriate and necessary by the IEP team are offered during the school day and ensure that the student receives these services to make academic and behavioral gains necessary to be successful in that environment.

> Related services means transportation and such developmental, corrective, and other supportive services as are required to assist a child with a disability to benefit from special education, and includes speech-language pathology and audiology services, interpreting services, psychological services, physical and occupational therapy, recreation, including therapeutic recreation, early identification and assessment of disabilities in children, counseling services, including rehabilitation counseling, orientation and mobility services, and medical services for diagnostic or evaluation purposes. Related services also include school health services and school nurse services, social work services in schools, and parent counseling and training. (IDEA, 2004, §300.24)

Related services exclude maintaining and monitoring devices that are medically implanted (e.g., cochlear implants; IDEA, 2004). Next, we provide explanations and examples of common related service delivery for students with disabilities.

## Speech-Language Pathology

**Speech-language pathology** services include the identification and diagnosis of speech-language and impairments, referral to medical professionals for additional treatment of speech-language deficits that provide more support than in an educational setting, parent training to provide strategies for using appropriate speech-language in the home and community, and information on supporting and preventing speech-language impairments (IDEA, 2004, §300.113(c)(15)). Audiology services, often linked with speech-language services, help to identify hearing loss through hearing screenings, provide medical referrals to support students with hearing impairments, and offer services to those students to teach them lip reading and other functional accommodations along with parent support (IDEA, 2004, §300.113(c)(1)). Interpreting services are provided to deaf and hard of hearing students to provide access to the general curriculum and include sign language, real-time translation (e.g., C-Print), and oral transliteration (IDEA, 2004, §300.113(c)(4)).

## Physical and Occupational Therapy

**Occupational therapy** services help to improve or restore independent functioning and mobility and are provided or overseen by an occupational therapist (IDEA, 2004, §300.113(c)(6)). **Physical therapy** services are those provided by a physical therapist (IDEA, 2004, §300.113(c)(9)). Orientation and mobility services support blind students or those with visual impairments or low vision, where they learn to navigate spatial and environmental areas utilizing their senses (e.g., learning to cross the street by listening for the traffic sounds) or learn how to use a cane or service animal to navigate the environment (IDEA, 2004, §300.113(c)(7)). Recreation services include therapeutic recreation, as well as adapted physical education for students with physical disabilities and adaptive needs (IDEA, 2004, §300.113(c)(11)). Medical services are provided by a medical professional for students with significant medical needs (IDEA, 2004, §300.113(c)(5)) and may also include school nurse services (IDEA, 2004, §300.113(c)(13)) for students who require additional intensive medical services to access the general education curriculum.

## Counseling Services

**Counseling services** are provided by the appropriate professionals (IDEA, 2004, §300.113(c)(2)). Psychological services are designed to support students with providing and interpreting assessments (e.g., school psychologists), including psychological, academic, and behavioral assessments, where the results are then shared with the IEP team, and the team then helps to develop the positive behavioral intervention plan utilizing the psychologist's recommendations and the data provided by the assessments (IDEA, 2004, §300.113(c)(10)). Social work services are provided by qualified individuals who will research a student's developmental history; provide counseling to groups or individuals, including students and family members; connect families with resources; and provide input for positive behavior support (IDEA, 2004, §300.113(c)(14)). Parent counseling may also be provided as a related service to aid in understanding their child's disability, development, and skills needed to support IEP implementation (IDEA, 2004, §300.113(c)(8)). Remember that this is also an IEP team decision, and the examples are provided to give a global reference.

## Mental Health Services

As mentioned in Chapter 1, the definition and criteria for identifying a student with EBD and therefore deeming them eligible for special education services specifically exclude social maladjustment, which is confusing and unclear (Cloth et al., 2014), yet social maladjustment is not defined in IDEA (2004). When applying these criteria, students who are deemed socially maladjusted are likely to be excluded from special education services and supports. Consequently, the students often continue struggling behaviorally and possibly academically. Denying a student access to special education based on exclusionary criteria adversely affects students and often results in denying access to treatment for students with mental health issues (Cloth et al., 2014).

## RELATED LEGISLATION

One of the critiques of IDEA is that it doesn't include specific provisions (i.e., rules) for mental health services in schools; rather, it is mentioned as a potential related service (IDEA, 2004, §300.24). Local education agencies (i.e., school districts) are responsible for allocating funds to ensure that students receive mental health services if they need them. A proactive approach to mental health is best, but schools must be prepared to support student mental health in every way possible. Typically, students with EBD require a Functional Behavior Assessment (FBA) and (Positive) Behavior Intervention Plan (BIP), which are conducted during the annual IEP process, and it is not clear if behavioral issues are related to mental health or EBD if students do not have a history of receiving mental health services.

Federal law (IDEA, 2004) is considered to be the umbrella by which the states interpret the law. Individual states are able to enhance the requirements of federal law and provide additional protections to students with disabilities by adding additional language (Dalton, 2019). Federal law doesn't define the terms used in the FBA/BIP process and does not require these to be completed when a student with EBD is identified or at their yearly renewal. IDEA does mandate that a Functional Behavior Assessment (FBA) and Behavior Intervention Plan (BIP) be completed when disciplinary procedures occur that result in a change in placement (see Chapters 11 and 12). There are no specific requirements set forth in IDEA (2004) for behavior identification or support, just that the school is required to provide the most appropriate positive behavioral supports, interventions, and modifications to address the most significant behavioral issues (Dalton, 2019). States have the ability to set the bar higher in the FBA/BIP process, and this includes adding supports for mental health into the statutes as a means to proactively provide students and the school communities with a continuum of mental health supports.

It is up to the individual states (and Washington, DC) to create additional language in their statutes adding additional supports and requirements for students with EBD, and this has been done by several states—California, New York, Delaware, Georgia, Florida, Illinois, Indiana, and Iowa (Dalton, 2019). Several states have language that mirrors IDEA—Kansas, Maine, Nevada, New Hampshire, New Jersey, New Mexico, Pennsylvania, South Carolina, Texas, Utah, Washington, and West Virginia (Dalton, 2019). The rest of the states do not have additional language either similar to or expanding on the IDEA, which makes providing additional mental health supports to students with EBD more difficult.

# FAMILY INVOLVEMENT IN THE IEP AND
# SERVICE DELIVERY PROCESS

Parents and families play an especially important role in the lives of their children, and that role should carry over to the school setting, where they are an integral part of the IEP team (Smith, 2001). Parents provide invaluable input during the IEP, Functional Behavior Assessment (FBA), and Positive Behavior Intervention Plan (PBIP) processes where they have the unique advantage of supporting their child from birth to adulthood. This is incredibly important for students with EBD, as the parents can provide their history of behavior supports and interventions, including what has and has not worked for their child in the past and what they believe will work for the child in the future. Additionally, parents can participate in behavior monitoring and provide feedback of impact on the student's life at home. This section will include details on barriers, ways to facilitate parent participation, and suggestions for collaboration with parents for successful outcomes for service delivery for students with EBD.

## Barriers to Collaboration with Parents

Parents and families should be at the center of their child's program development in special education. Often this is not the case, and this is due to many home-school miscommunications or misunderstandings. Examples of issues within the continuum of communication between home and school are provided in the following section.

Schools sometimes infer that there is a lack of parental involvement (Smith, 2001) when parents are unable to attend meetings during the school day, when it is actually a parent's inability to take off work or have other life circumstances that may make them unable to attend meetings. Traditionally, meetings are scheduled by the school and parents attend when they have the ability to schedule time off work, find childcare for their other children, or rearrange their schedule so they can participate in the meetings. In reality, schools are responsible for ensuring that parents participate in their child's team meetings and must provide them that opportunity by:

1. Notifying parents of the meeting early enough to ensure that they will have an opportunity to attend
2. Scheduling the meeting at a mutually agreed-on time and place (IDEA, 2004, §300.322(b)).

Misconceptions can be detrimental to the child meeting success with their program and can cause issues in the relationships between families and the schools. Whether the confusion or miscommunication comes with scheduling, not relaying the importance of meeting attendance to advocate on their child's behalf and their right as a parent, or a lack of communication about the meeting scheduling process, simply communicating with parents in an open and honest manner, which allows enough time to discuss potential roadblocks to meeting attendance and collaboration with the team, is important. Schools need to demonstrate flexibility when scheduling meetings and ensure that all members of the team are there to be courteous and collaborative with the sole purpose of the child flourishing in their programming. If the team can do these things, they help to contribute to facilitating service delivery.

Most parents of students with disabilities are not educators, and teachers, as well as the entire IEP team, need to acknowledge and provide appropriate terminology and information when working with families. Educators tend to talk in educational jargon (Smith, 2001), which is confusing and not clear to individuals who did not go through a teacher training program or work at a school. Parents may not understand specific data collection processes, data analysis, placement options, or related services. It is the school and IEP team's responsibility to make the IEP process clear and easy to understand, while making the decisions as a team and by collaborating with parents and ensuring they understand every part of the process and that they are an integral part of the team decision-making process. Here, parent involvement helps them to understand the education setting and need for home-school communication and fosters their participation in future meetings. It also helps the parents see the importance of home-school communication and partnership.

The school team needs to develop a level of empathy for the student and their family. It is especially important to provide families with the information and tools to support their child. This includes making considerations for **cultural and linguistic diversity**, which includes any student and family who are classified as a race other than White and require accommodation by the IEP team so that these families are included and accommodated in their native language, while considering culture and its impact as part of their program. Additionally, school teams need to be sensitive to culturally and linguistically diverse families' needs (Smith, 2001), by initiating the conversation around advocacy to effectively include **mediators**, individuals who can translate or provide cultural and linguistic assistance, in meetings or wherever parents need them. Specifically stated in IDEA, "the public agency must take whatever action is necessary to ensure that the parent understands the proceedings of the IEP Team meeting, including arranging for an interpreter for parents with deafness or whose native language is other than English" (IDEA, 2004, §300.322(e)).

When it is appropriate, students should attend the meeting to provide support to parents. Students are required to attend meetings once they reach transition age (i.e., 14 and older) and can also serve as mediators for their parents.

As important as it is to have a meaningful, high-quality IEP, like we will discuss in Chapter 11, it is just as important to have parents participate meaningfully in the IEP and service delivery process (Smith, 2001). Their participation in the child's educational programming will create a trusting relationship between the family and the school, and this relationship will lead to continuous positive interactions that will carry the child and family through the child's educational career and beyond.

## Communication with Parents Beyond the IEP

Parents of students with EBD, like all parents of children, appreciate clear, open, and honest communication regarding their children as often as possible. Unfortunately, communication is often limited to negative issues (i.e., discipline or classroom infractions) and can create an adversarial relationship between teachers, schools, and parents. Schools need to make a conscious effort to ensure that parents are a part of their child's education and foster a positive and trusting relationship and environment, not only in school for the student but also for their parents and families. Partnerships between schools and families are incredibly important for student success, yet it is sometimes difficult to engage with students with EBD and their families (Carlson et al., 2019). Family engagement is mandated in the Every Student Succeeds Act (2015).

Schools need to create a mutual relationship of respect and recognize that parents are equal partners in their child's education, and they bear equal responsibility in the process. Schools also need to recognize that parents know their children best and can provide incredible insight into their child's capabilities, strengths, and needs. Additionally, schools should focus on creating that relationship with parents by engaging with parents and children in positive ways, including:

- Positive phone calls home
- Keeping the lines of home-school communication open (see Appendix 3–3)
- Catching students *doing something good* (Figure 3–2)
- Creating a positive school culture
- Welcoming parents into school
- Providing opportunities for participation beyond the school day
- Keeping parents informed (Ferguson & Rodriguez, 2005)
- Documenting communication with parents for accountability (see Appendix 3–4)

There are many intentional activities that schools can orchestrate to create a positive environment for families where they recognize that the school has their child's best interest at heart. Schools can open their doors to parents on

**Figure 3–2.** *Catch students doing something good.*

evenings and weekends and provide activities for families to engage in, especially if the community lacks services. These include providing workshops for parents with free babysitting services, where the school provides different topics monthly that benefit families. Sometimes, schools that receive federal funding (e.g., Title I) are required to engage the community outside of the school day.

Examples of workshops schools can provide include:

- Ways to engage with their children in the digital age
- Families creating something (i.e., a craft)
- Informational sessions about special education and supporting children with disabilities
- Postsecondary-focused topics, where parents learn about financial aid, testing, and the college application process
- Advocacy-focused sessions with guest speakers and veteran parents for parents of younger children
- Engagement options for all parents, including working parents, parents with other children, and working parents
- Opportunities to hear guest speakers from mental health and community agencies for parents to learn about available services in the community (Ferguson & Rodriguez, 2005)

In addition to welcoming parents into schools beyond the school hours, schools should also provide the opportunity for parents to volunteer as they are capable. Volunteering does not need to be limited to the school day; rather, schools can provide opportunities for working parents to volunteer by giving them duties they can fulfill at home (e.g., stuffing envelopes, making phone calls) to facilitate their involvement within the school community. When schools come up with creative solutions to involve all families, the school community becomes more inclusive, diverse, and supportive.

## PROPORTIONAL APPROACHES TO SERVICE DELIVERY

As previously mentioned in Chapter 1, EBD is an identification category in special education that is subjective due to the qualifying inclusion criteria, which are interpreted differently based on different circumstances. Bean (2013) suggests taking a more well-rounded approach to service delivery and understanding student behavior, which is often perceived as negative. This negative perception skews teacher views of children, something commonly referred to as a cultural mismatch (i.e., White teachers and African American children) and often leads to a negative educational outcome. As there is a need for overarching policy guidance and support on mental health, policy recommendations were made by Skiba, Albrecht, and Losen (2013) to reduce disproportionality and encourage federal policy to support proportional services and identification.

Issues that need to be addressed to provide fair and balanced service delivery for students with EBD include reducing testing bias and bias in the referral process, which, as mentioned previously, can be subjective, confusing, and open to interpretation by the individuals conducting the testing as well as members of the team. Inclusive definitions and criteria need to be clear and understood by the entire team, school district, and potentially statewide. The quality of education facilities affects service delivery, where students of color are often transferred to different programs and educational opportunity is disparate; opportunities for students are sometimes based on geography or location, and opportunity shouldn't be defined by ZIP code. Additionally, teacher candidates should learn about service delivery options and providing quality service delivery to students with EBD by utilizing these suggestions.

It's important that special education placement and service delivery provide students access to the general curriculum with the appropriate accommodations and modifications that they require, rather than leading to low expectations, subpar academics, and lack of opportunities (Hibel et al., 2010). It's important to always keep in mind that students deserve the best education that teachers can give, regardless of ability or disability. The following sections contain two vignettes that demonstrate the strategies outlined in this chapter. Read them and see if you can identify the strategies used or others that you could use if you were in a similar situation.

## CASE STUDY—ELEMENTARY

*Mrs. Cameron has a student with EBD in her classroom with a behavior plan who needs consistent reinforcement to stay on task. Bobby's behavior is typically on task, but he works quickly and needs additional tasks or responsibilities so that he does not disrupt other students from working. His annual IEP is coming up, but Bobby's mother has been somewhat standoffish because she does not seem to appreciate it when Mrs. Cameron calls the house to deliver negative news when Bobby isn't having the best day. She hasn't had a student like him in her third-grade general education classroom before, so she consults with the special education teacher, who tells her that the IEP meeting is a great time to discuss this with the team and that parent input is valuable.*

*During the meeting, Mrs. Cameron reports on Bobby's behavior in her class, making sure that she notes how academically talented he is but that his behaviors after completing work can be somewhat disruptive to other students; she provides input on his strengths but listens when the special education teacher, his case manager, discusses strategies to decrease his disruptive behavior that she can implement before starting individual work to remind Bobby that he needs to work slowly, take his time, and then let the teacher know if he needs additional activities or responsibilities to complete during class. The team decides to provide Bobby with some specially designed instruction in his IEP to ensure that he asks for a break when he needs it and uses a token board with specific steps for what to do while working and after he completes his work. They also discussed the best time for Mrs. Cameron to call, as she has been calling Bobby's mom while she is busy is at work (she is a nurse), and she has breaks scheduled throughout the day where she can receive calls to give her full attention. Mrs. Cameron is excited to utilize these in her classroom and looks forward to collaborating with Bobby's mom and the special education teacher.*

## CASE STUDY—SECONDARY

*Mrs. Cassidy is a high school special education teacher who supports students with EBD in their general education inclusion classes. She serves as the co-teacher for math classes and ensures that her students' IEP goals are being met, along with providing structure for students' behavioral needs. She works with a teacher who hasn't had many students with EBD and easily gets rattled when students appear to be frustrated or not listening to her. The general education teacher typically raises her voice and yells at the students for not paying attention and is clearly flustered, which makes all the students laugh, and then they don't complete their work. Mrs. Cassidy sees this happen often and knows that the general education teacher loses credibility with students each time this happens, and it affects all of the students in her classroom.*

*Mrs. Cassidy works with the special education teacher to provide more structure in her classroom. First, they look at her students' IEPs and the SDI listed to support positive classroom behavior. They start with antecedent strategies (e.g., providing expectations, seating in the room, clear and concise directions) and then look at ways to support the students who need additional monitoring. They decided to use a monitoring system that could be implemented all day with students and would benefit both students and teachers, where the students created goals with Mrs. Cassidy, and then had the students check that they did or did not meet their goals for the class period. At the end of each day, Mrs. Cassidy collected the sheet, recorded the percentage of checked "Yes" boxes on a data collection sheet, and then provided incentives when students reached their goals. This arrangement helped the general education teacher with behavior management and provided Mrs. Cassidy with data to show her student behavior and if it was improving.*

## CHAPTER SUMMARY

This chapter introduced different historical legislation that has evolved since 1974 and the subsequent reauthorizations that resulted in IDEA (2004). We discussed an incredibly important part of a student with EBD's school day, service delivery, and the continuum of services for students with disabilities that describe where and when students receive the services they need, which is an IEP team decision, including access to mental health services. Families are an integral part of the IEP process and the school community. Finally, schools need to provide a proportionate, bias-free, culturally relevant approach to service delivery.

 **DISCUSSION QUESTIONS**

1. What important legislation protects students with disabilities?

2. Why is there a continuum of services rather than a one-size-fits-all approach to special education?

3. What are possible related services and their relevance in a student's school day?

4. When should parents be involved in their child's educational programming?

## RESOURCES

https://www.carautismroadmap.org/special-education-placement-options-in-pennsylvania/?print=pdf

https://www.parentcenterhub.org/placement-overview/

https://www.parentcenterhub.org/iep-servicedelivery/

https://www.parentcenterhub.org/iep-relatedservices/

http://www.sedl.org/connections/resources/rb/rb3-Secondary.pdf

http://www.sedl.org/connections/resources/rb/research-brief2.pdf

https://www2.ed.gov/policy/speced/guid/idea/bapr/bmeatab2.pdf

## REFERENCES

Bean, K. F. (2013). Disproportionality and acting-out behaviors among African American children in special education. *Child and Adolescent Social Work Journal, 30*(6), 487–504. doi:10.1007/s10560-013-0304-6

Carlson, R. G., Hock, R., George, M., Kumpiene, G., Yell, M., McCartney, E. D., . . . Weist, M. D. (2019). Relational factors influencing parents' engagement in special education for high school youth with emotional/behavioral problems. *Behavioral Disorders*. Advance online publication. doi:10.1177/0198742919883276

Cloth, A. H., Evans, S. W., Becker, S. P., & Paternite, C. E. (2014). Social maladjustment and special education: State regulations and continued controversy. *Journal of Emotional and Behavioral Disorders, 22*(4), 214–224. doi:10.1177/1063426613487405

Dalton, M. A. (2019). forgotten children: Rethinking the individuals with disabilities education act behavior provisions. *The American University Journal of Gender, Social Policy & the Law, 27*, 137–181.

Every Student Succeeds Act of 2015, Pub. L. No. 114-95 § 114 Stat. 1177 (2015–2016).

Ferguson, C., & Rodriguez, V. (2005). *Engaging families at the secondary level: What schools can do to support family involvement.* Retrieved from http://www.sedl.org/connections/resources/rb/rb3-Secondary.pdf

Friend, M., Cook, L., Hurley-Chamberlain, D., & Shamberger, C. (2010) Co-teaching: An illustration of the complexity of collaboration in special education. *Journal of Educational and Psychological Consultation, 20*(1), 9–27. doi:10.1080/10474410903535380

Hibel, J., Farkas, G., & Morgan, P. L. (2010). Who is placed into special education? *Sociology of Education, 83*(4), 312–332. doi:10.1177/0038040710383518

Individuals with Disabilities Education Act, 20 U.S.C. § 1400 (2004).

Myers, D., Freeman, J., Simonsen, B., & Sugai, G. (2017). Classroom management with exceptional learners. *Teaching Exceptional Children, 49*(4), 223–230. doi:10.1177/0040059916685064

Office of Special Education Programs (OSEP). (2017). *Supporting and responding to behavior: Evidence-based classroom strategies for teachers.* Retrieved from https://osepideasthatwork.org/sites/default/files/ClassroomPBIS_508.pdf

Oliver, R. M., & Reschly, D. J. (2007). *Effective classroom management: Teacher preparation and professional development.* National Comprehensive Center for Teacher Quality. Retrieved from http://www.tqsource.org/topics/effectiveClassroomManagement.pdf

Public Law No. 94-142 S. 6, 94th Congress (1975).

Public Law No. 99-457, 99th Congress (1986).

Public Law No. 101-476, 101st Congress (1990).

Riccomini, P. J., Morano, S., & Hughes, C. A. (2017). Big ideas in special education: Specially designed instruction, high-leverage practices, explicit instruction, and intensive instruction. *TEACHING Exceptional Children, 50*(1), 20–27.

Sayeski, K. L., & Brown, M. R. (2014). Developing a classroom management plan using a tiered approach. *Teaching Exceptional Children, 47,* 119–127. doi:10.1177/0040059914553208

Skiba, R., Albrecht, S., & Losen, D. (2013). CCBD'S position summary on federal policy on disproportionality in special education. *Behavioral Disorders, 38*(2), 108–120. doi:10.1177/019874291303800202

Smith, S. W. (2001). *Involving parents in the IEP process.* ERIC Clearinghouse on Disabilities and Gifted Education.

Stein, E. (2018). *Two teachers in the room: Strategies for co-teaching success.* Routledge and MiddleWeb.

Sutherland, K. S., & Wehby, J. H. (2001). Exploring the relationship between increased opportunities to respond to academic requests and the academic and behavioral outcomes of students with EBD. *Remedial and Special Education, 22*(2), 113–121. doi:10.1177/074193250102200205

## APPENDIX 3–1

# Example of a Token Board for a Student with EBD in an Elementary Math Class

# Did I . . . ?

Yes = 1 ★

| | |
|---|---|
| Keep my hands to myself? | ☐ Yes  ☐ No |
| Raise my hand to answer questions? | ☐ Yes  ☐ No |
| Stay in my area? | ☐ Yes  ☐ No |
| Complete my math problems? | ☐ Yes  ☐ No |
| Use manipulatives (calculator or shapes) if I needed to? | ☐ Yes  ☐ No |

You need 4 stars to earn your chosen reinforcer ☺
5 stars earn you 1 classroom buck.

## APPENDIX 3–2

# Check Sheet for a High School Student with EBD

| Class Period | Did I Meet My Goals? | Teacher Initials = Agreement |
|---|---|---|
| 1 | ☐ Yes<br>☐ No | |
| 2 | ☐ Yes<br>☐ No | |
| 3 | ☐ Yes<br>☐ No | |
| 4 | ☐ Yes<br>☐ No | |
| 5 | ☐ Yes<br>☐ No | |
| 6 | ☐ Yes<br>☐ No | |
| 7 | ☐ Yes<br>☐ No | |
| 8 | ☐ Yes<br>☐ No | |

## APPENDIX 3–3

# Home-School Communication Log

| Date | How Was the Day? | Notes |
|------|------------------|-------|
|      | ☐ Great<br>☐ OK<br>☐ Let's chat |  |
|      | ☐ Great<br>☐ OK<br>☐ Let's chat |  |
|      | ☐ Great<br>☐ OK<br>☐ Let's chat |  |
|      | ☐ Great<br>☐ OK<br>☐ Let's chat |  |
|      | ☐ Great<br>☐ OK<br>☐ Let's chat |  |
|      | ☐ Great<br>☐ OK<br>☐ Let's chat |  |
|      | ☐ Great<br>☐ OK<br>☐ Let's chat |  |
|      | ☐ Great<br>☐ OK<br>☐ Let's chat |  |
|      | ☐ Great<br>☐ OK<br>☐ Let's chat |  |
|      | ☐ Great<br>☐ OK<br>☐ Let's chat |  |

One per student should be kept for documentation.

## APPENDIX 3–4

# Example Documentation for Parent Contact

| Date | Time | Communication Type | Notes |
|------|------|--------------------|-------|
|      |      | ☐ Phone<br>☐ Email<br>☐ In-person |  |
|      |      | ☐ Phone<br>☐ Email<br>☐ In-person |  |
|      |      | ☐ Phone<br>☐ Email<br>☐ In-person |  |
|      |      | ☐ Phone<br>☐ Email<br>☐ In-person |  |
|      |      | ☐ Phone<br>☐ Email<br>☐ In-person |  |
|      |      | ☐ Phone<br>☐ Email<br>☐ In-person |  |
|      |      | ☐ Phone<br>☐ Email<br>☐ In-person |  |
|      |      | ☐ Phone<br>☐ Email<br>☐ In-person |  |
|      |      | ☐ Phone<br>☐ Email<br>☐ In-person |  |
|      |      | ☐ Phone<br>☐ Email<br>☐ In-person |  |

# 4

# Mathematics Strategies and Interventions

## KEY VOCABULARY

Action Response

CRA Sequence

Chalk Talk

Checklist

Choral Response

Classwide Peer Tutoring

Clickers

Cloze/Guided Notes

Cold Call

Computer-Assisted Instruction

Conceptual Understanding

Cooperative Learning

Cover-Copy-Compare

Cross-Age Tutoring

Cross-Curricular Instruction

Cumulative Practice

Developmental Progression

Direct Instruction

Errorless Learning Worksheet

Explicit Instruction

Fidelity

Folding-In Technique

Formative Assessment

Mnemonics

One-to-One Correspondence

Opportunity to Respond

Pair and Write

Peer Guided Pause

Peer Tutoring

Procedural Knowledge

QAR Strategy

Response Cards

Scaffold

Self-Instruction/ Evaluation

Self-Monitoring

Subitizing

Systematic Instruction

Taped Problems

Think-Pair-Share

Visual Representations

## LEARNING OBJECTIVES

By the end of this chapter, you should be able to . . .

- Describe the challenges in teaching math to students with EBD.
- List the components of effective math instruction for students with EBD.
- Explain the differences and similarities between direct and explicit instruction.
- Apply the components of explicit instruction when delivering a math lesson.
- Understand the relationship between time on task, increased opportunities to respond, and improved math achievement.
- Differentiate between verbal and nonverbal responses and list examples of each.
- Locate evidence-based strategies and interventions for teaching math to students with EBD.

## INTRODUCTION

Recent estimates suggest elementary and middle school students with emotional and behavioral disorders perform at least one grade level below their nondisabled peers in math. Outcomes for high school students with EBD are worse, with many students performing at least three grade levels below their nondisabled peers. While factors such as high rates of suspension, absenteeism, and academic avoidance behaviors among students with EBD contribute to their poor academic performance, inadequate, infrequent, or nonexistent math instruction is just as much to blame. Too often, math instruction for these students never goes beyond repetitive practice of basic arithmetic. Some teachers believe students with EBD lack the reasoning skills to engage in rigorous academic content, some teachers want to avoid the conflict they predict will arise when students are presented with challenging material, and other teachers believe arithmetic skills should be mastered before any type of problem solving or higher-level thinking skills are introduced. For these reasons, students with EBD rarely engage in activities that promote higher-level thinking, problem solving, or real-world application of math concepts.

While the ability to accurately and fluently perform computation tasks is important, if students with EBD are expected to make the type of gains in math necessary to perform on level with their same-age peers, calculation interventions alone are not enough. In this chapter, promising practices and strategies for teaching both calculation and problem-solving skills to elementary and secondary students with EBD will be shared.

## CHALLENGES IN TEACHING MATH TO STUDENTS WITH EBD

Consider the following case study that addresses common challenges in teaching math to students with EBD:

### CASE STUDY

*Erica is a fifth-grade student who has been in Ms. Wright's self-contained special education classroom since first grade. At times, Erica is both physically and verbally abusive toward herself, her classmates, Ms. Wright, and other teachers and staff. At other times, she is withdrawn and quiet. Over the past 4 years, her externalizing behaviors have increased in intensity and duration when Ms. Wright starts delivering the math lesson. No matter how fun and engaging Ms. Wright tries to make her math lessons, Erica either refuses to participate or screams and yells to the point of exhaustion, then falls asleep.*

*Erica knows how to add and subtract two- and three-digit numbers, but she doesn't know her math facts fluently, so she uses immature strategies like drawing sticks or dots to calculate the sum or difference of each digit in the problem. Although Ms. Wright has shown Erica how to count on or up when adding and how to count down when subtracting, Erica prefers to use drawings to arrive at her answer. If Ms. Wright can get Erica to participate at all, it usually takes her the entire math period to complete just a few computation problems. She doesn't know how to multiply or divide, and she has very limited understanding of math concepts such as place value, time, money, and measurement. Ms. Wright feels like she's tried everything—token economies, modeling self-calming techniques, praising Erica for on-task behavior, giving edible rewards, and removing privileges like recess—and nothing has worked. She is concerned that Erica may not have the necessary math skills to successfully participate in the prealgebra course she will take next year as a sixth grader, but she's not sure what she can do about it.*

Ms. Wright's dilemma may be like one you've experienced or fear you may experience as a teacher of students with EBD. How can you possibly teach a student about decimals if you can't get her to stay awake? How can a student develop an understanding of place value if he spends the day throwing desks and chairs? Is it reasonable to be expected to implement a math strategy or intervention when a student's behavioral needs are clearly so much more important? Isn't finding an effective behavioral strategy the best way to improve students' math achievement? It's a common misconception that if teachers could just find the right behavioral intervention, students would perform better academically. In fact, little evidence exists to support the implementation of a behavioral intervention alone to improve math achievement. If we want students with EBD to perform well in math, they must be taught in ways that have been shown to be effective for improving math performance.

A major roadblock to implementing effective math interventions and strategies for students with EBDs is the limited research base. In a 2006 review of math intervention studies for students with EBD, Hodge, Riccomini, Buford, and Herbst describe the lack of studies as "alarming and the need for additional research is critical" (p. 305). In fact, there are no interventions for teaching math to students with EBD that can be considered evidence based because none have been attempted in at least five studies with at least 20 participants, a criterion necessary for being considered an evidence-based practice. Instead, math strategies and interventions for students with EBD are categorized as *promising practices* (Mulcahy et al., 2016). Despite their best efforts, researchers using students with EBD as study participants encounter the same difficulties that teachers of students with EBD face when trying to collect consistent and reliable data—high rates of student absenteeism, academic avoidance, and externalizing behaviors. Another serious issue regarding math instruction for students with EBD is the lack of access to standards-based instruction. Many of these students spend most of their school day in self-contained classrooms where the teacher delivers all academic content and may or may not be highly qualified or certified to teach math. Research suggests the rigor of math instruction in special education classrooms does not match that of general education classrooms, and students who receive instruction in special education classrooms do not receive instruction grounded in the principles of effective math instruction outlined by the National Council for Teachers of Mathematics (2003) (Jackson & Neel, 2006; Mulcahy et al., 2014).

Locating and accessing math interventions online is relatively easy; implementing the interventions with fidelity with students with EBD presents a much greater challenge. According to the National Center on Response to Intervention (n.d.), **fidelity** means delivering a program or practice in the same manner it was delivered when it was shown to be effective. For example, a teacher wants to implement an intervention that combines teacher-directed instruction with **computer-assisted instruction** to help improve students' word problem-solving skills. When this intervention was delivered to a group of students with EBD 5 days per week for 50 minutes daily (25 minutes of teacher-directed instruction and 25 minutes of computer-assisted instruction), results indicated the intervention was highly effective. The teacher would like to implement a similar intervention in her classroom, but she only has 30 minutes set aside for math instruction, so she decides to reduce the teacher-directed instruction portion to 10 minutes and the computer-assisted instruction to 20 minutes. Will it be as effective? It's unlikely. To ensure the best possible outcomes for your students, fidelity of implementation is critical; this includes not only the instructional components of the program or practice but also the frequency and duration with which they are implemented.

# COMPONENTS OF EFFECTIVE MATH INSTRUCTION FOR STUDENTS WITH EBD

In a 2009 study, Billingsley, Scheuermann, and Webber highlighted the instructional components found to be most effective for increasing the math achievement of students with EBD: (1) direct, structured, explicit, and systematic teaching; (2) daily review; (3) intensive and extensive support when a topic is introduced, which is slowly decreased as student understanding increases; (4) repeated practice; and (5) multiple opportunities to respond. Each of these instructional components is described in detail in the following section.

## Direct, Explicit, and Systematic

Math instruction should be direct, explicit, and systematic. **Systematic instruction** is instruction that is delivered in a logical and ordered sequence, starting with the simple and concrete and moving to the more complex and abstract. **Direct instruction** is sometimes used to describe a scripted program where teachers are given cues to follow throughout the lesson. It can also be used to describe instruction or teaching practices that have been found to increase student achievement (Brasch et al., 2008). **Explicit instruction**, on the other hand, is a broader term that Archer and Hughes (2011) define as "a series of supports" wherein "students are guided through the learning process with clear statements about the purpose and rationale for learning the new skill, clear explanations and demonstrations of the instructional target, and supported practice with feedback until independent mastery has been achieved" (p. 1). Many characteristics of explicit instruction overlap with the instructional components found to be most effective for teaching students with EBD, including reviewing prior skills before beginning a lesson; providing guidance and support throughout the lesson and throughout guided, cumulative, and independent practice; and requiring frequent responses. Additional resources related to direct and explicit instruction can be found online by visiting the IRIS Center (https://iris.peabody.vanderbilt.edu/).

## CRA Sequence

The **CRA sequence**, a three-step process based on the principles of explicit instruction, is used to develop students' conceptual mathematics knowledge. Students learn the conceptual underpinnings of topics such as factoring equations in algebra, by progressing through stages that include concrete demonstrations or the introduction of physical manipulatives or depictions to represent conceptual properties (holding three apples), followed by representational or pictorial depictions (three tally marks), and concluding with abstract depictions or problems presented in symbolic notation or written form (3 or three) (Figure 4–1). Though many educators believe manipulatives are for primary or elementary grades only, their use has been advocated for and proven effective in higher-level mathematics as well. For example, using algebra tiles in the concrete phase of the CRA teaching sequence allows students to "see" all basic algebraic operations. CRA stages are taught using the principles of explicit instruction, including modeling and identification of critical components, as well as guided and independent practice with examples and nonexamples.

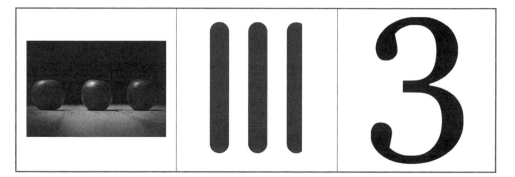

**Figure 4–1.** *CRA sequence for the number 3, moving from a concrete or physical model to a pictorial depiction and then to its abstract written form.*

## Daily Review and Repeated Practice

Effective instruction for students with EBD includes daily review and repeated practice. These instructional components have been grouped together because repeated practice can often be achieved by providing daily review of previously learned concepts. Sometimes referred to as **cumulative practice** or **spiral review**, daily review provides students with increased opportunities to practice previously learned concepts, which, in turn, increases retention of the concepts and helps improve automaticity. Another way to increase practice opportunities is by incorporating the skill you want your students to review into another subject area or instructional block, a method referred to as **cross-curricular instruction**. For example, you might ask students to practice multistep word problems involving addition and multiplication by tallying how many points they earn while playing basketball during gym or recess. Students keep track of how many two- or three-point shots they make, write a number sentence to calculate the total number of points earned from each type of shot, and add the products together to determine their final score. Not only do cross-curricular activities provide students with increased opportunities to practice the skills they are learning, but they also allow students to see the skill used in a real-life context. This is especially important for students with EBD who resist participating in academic activities that don't seem to have any application to their everyday lives.

## Scaffolded Support

When you hear the word **scaffold**, what probably comes to mind is the platform construction workers or painters stand on for support, which allows them to reach places they otherwise wouldn't be able to reach. Instructional scaffolding can be thought of in the same way—it is support that teachers provide to help their students achieve academic success they might otherwise be unable to achieve independently. However, unlike construction scaffolds, instructional scaffolds should be gradually faded as students become more comfortable and skilled with the concepts they're learning. Instructional scaffolds can be increased or decreased in intensity and duration depending on student needs, with the goal being students remembering or performing the concept or skill independently.

Finally, increasing opportunities to respond is frequently cited in the literature as an effective way to improve academic outcomes for students with EBDs (Adamson & Lewis, 2017). **Opportunities to respond (OTR)** increase students' time on task and provide them chances to be active participants in the learning process instead of bystanders who "sit and get" information from the teacher. Providing multiple opportunities to respond increases student engagement, allows the teacher to give immediate and corrective feedback, reduces off-task behaviors, and provides a type of **formative assessment** (checking for understanding) (Levy, n.d.). There are numerous and various ways to provide students with opportunities to respond (Table 4–1), and

**Table 4–1.** Response Types and Example

| Verbal Responses | | Nonverbal Responses | |
|---|---|---|---|
| *Individual* | *Team/Group* | *Written* | *Action* |
| Individual oral response | Choral response | Response Cards/Whiteboards | Clickers |
| Cold call | Partner response | Cloze/guided notes | Touching/Pointing |
| | Think-Pair-Share/Turn and Talk | Pair and Write/Think-Jot-Share | Gestures/Acting Out/Facial expressions |
| | | | Hand signals |

OTR can be used at any time during the lesson cycle—while activating prior knowledge, when stating the learning objective, during teacher modeling, in guided practice, during lesson closure, and during independent practice.

## Verbal Responses

Verbal responses are responses given by individual students, pairs or teams of students, or an entire class of students. One of the simplest ways to elicit a verbal response is by posing a question. It's important to provide about 5 seconds of wait time after asking a question; this gives students time to think and increases the quality of responses. Students with EBD who participate in general education math classes are often reluctant to respond in front of their peers. Consider letting these students know prior to the lesson the specific questions they will be called on to answer. Do not, however, tell them when they will be called on as randomly calling on students increases their engagement and attention. Another individual verbal response strategy that works well with shy, reluctant, or withdrawn students is **cold call**. For this type of response, the teacher poses a question and every student is expected to formulate an answer. Instead of calling on students who raise their hands to provide an answer, the teacher randomly calls on a student to share his or her response, even if that student hasn't indicated he knows the answer. If the chosen student provides an incorrect or incomplete response, the teacher calls on another student to correct or clarify the response. Then, the teacher immediately goes back to the student who provided the incorrect answer and has him restate the correct answer provided by the other student. To ensure all students are provided equal opportunities to respond, use popsicle sticks or strips of paper with students' names on them and draw a name after asking a question. Continue drawing until every student has had an **opportunity to respond**. Or, use a class seating chart and make a tally mark next to a student's name each time you call on her to answer.

## Choral Responses

**Choral responses** are verbal responses given in unison by the entire class. To use choral responses, develop questions in advance that have only one correct answer that is one to three words long. When using choral responses, it's still important to provide students with wait time between asking a question and prompting them to respond. Develop a signal you will use to cue your students to respond and ask questions at a brisk pace. **Partner responses** are choral responses given by a pair of students instead of an entire class. Use partner responses in the same manner as choral responses; give partners 30 seconds to talk to each other and agree on an answer after posing a question. Partner responses help the teacher gauge student understanding and provide time-efficient feedback. Partner responses are particularly helpful for students who might be reluctant to respond individually or who need extra academic support a peer can provide.

### Think-Pair-Share

**Think-Pair-Share** (sometimes called **Turn-and-Talk**) also involves pairs of students, but in this strategy, students share their thinking with each other before sharing it with the entire class. While students talk, the teacher listens in and makes note of pairs whose discussions are especially insightful and might help other students in the class better understand the math concept. Then, the teacher invites those pairs of students to share their thinking with the entire class. When pairing students for this strategy, avoid assigning students to the same partner each time. If classroom size and furniture allow it, consider seating students in groups of four and placing a partner wheel like the one seen in Figure 4–2 in the center of the table or group of desks. Place numbers, shapes, and words on the wheel that are possible answers to math questions that might be posed, then pair students according to the answer. For example, say, "Today, odd numbers will think, pair, share" or "Multiples of seven work together. Multiples of four work together." Numbered heads together (sometimes called numbering off) is a similar, easy-to-use grouping strategy. Either

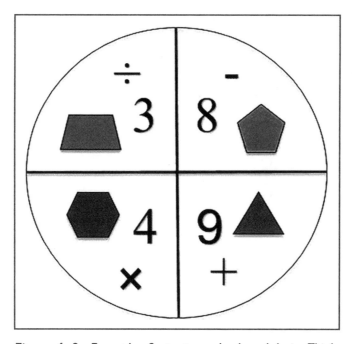

**Figure 4–2.** *Example of a partner wheel used during Think-Pair-Share.*

verbally assign numbers to students or give students a number on a card, then ask students with like numbers to form a group.

## Nonverbal Responses

Nonverbal responses fall into two categories: **written responses** and **action responses**. One of the biggest benefits of using nonverbal responses is that every student in the class responds. When compared with traditional hand raising, nonverbal responses such as response cards provide students with as many as 3,700 additional opportunities to respond (Heward, 1994). Another benefit of nonverbal responses is the teacher can immediately see students' answers. Based on responses, the teacher guides the lesson and incorporates review or reteach as needed. Nonverbal responses are usually more effective than verbal responses for students with EBD because they involve less risk of embarrassment.

## Written Responses

One of the most widely used written response methods is **response cards**. Response cards can be premade by the teacher or made by students prior to or during the lesson. For a lesson on polygons, for example, a teacher provides students with premade response cards that have the word "yes" on one side and the word "no" on the other. The teacher shows students pictures of different shapes and asks, "Is this shape a polygon?" Students hold up the "yes" side of the card if they agree the shape is a polygon and the "no" side if the shape is a nonpolygon. Or, the teacher can make cards containing pictures of polygons, call out the name of a polygon, and ask students to hold up the card with the correct shape on it. Student whiteboards can also be used as response cards; the teacher poses a question, such as "What is the product of 6 and 12?" and each student writes his or her response on a small whiteboard using an erasable marker. On the teacher's signal, students hold up the whiteboards and the teacher scans and checks the boards for accuracy of responses. If a teacher does not have a class set of whiteboards, students can write directly on their desks or tables—if they don't use permanent markers, it's easily wiped away. If using desks or tables instead of white-boards, teachers will need to circulate around the room to check on the accuracy of student responses.

## Guided Notes

**Cloze** or **guided notes** are premade by the teacher and are missing key facts or concepts that students fill in as the lesson progresses. When developing guided notes, consider inserting charts, diagrams, or graphs to help increase student understanding. Also provide students with formatting clues such as blank lines, numbers, or bullets to indicate where responses belong, but be careful not to require too much writing. Figure 4–3 provides an example of guided notes for a lesson on the sums of the interior angles of a polygon (Wilson, 2014).

| Main Ideas/Questions | Notes | | | |
|---|---|---|---|---|
| **Interior Angles Sum** | The sum of the degrees in any polygon can be determined by the number of triangles that can be drawn within the polygon. Complete the table below and look for a pattern to find the sum of the degrees in any polygon. | | | |
| Polygon | Picture | # of Sides | # of Triangles | Sum of Interior ∠'s |
| Triangle | 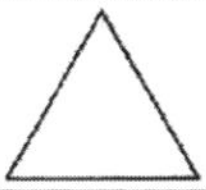 △ | 3 | 1 | 180 |
| Quadrilateral | 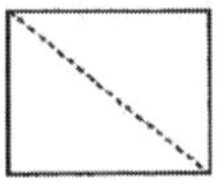 ▢ | 4 | 2 | 360 |
| Pentagon | 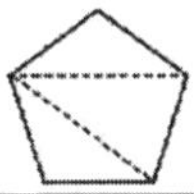 ⬠ | 5 | 3 | 540 |
| Hexagon | 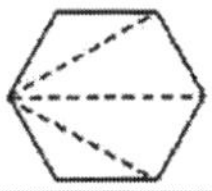 ⬡ | 6 | 4 | 720 |
| Heptagon | X | 7 | 5 | 900 |
| Octagon | X | 8 | 6 | 1080 |
| Nonagon | X | 9 | 7 | 1260 |
| Decagon | X | 10 | 8 | 1440 |
| **Sum of Interior Angles FORMULA!** | If n represents the number of sides of a polygon, then the sum of the interior angles (S) can be found using the formula: $S = (n-2) \times 180$ | | | |
| **INTERIOR ANGLE OF A Regular Polygon** | A regular polygon is one in which all sides are equal; therefore all ___angles___ are equal! To find the measure of an interior angle in a <u>regular polygon</u>, use: △ ▢ $\dfrac{S}{n}$ (sum of interior ∠s ÷ # of sides) | | | |

© Gina Wilson (All Things Algebra), 2014

**Figure 4–3.** *Example of cloze/guided notes for the sum of interior angles. Permission to use given by Gina Wilson.*

## Pair and Write and Peer Guided Pause

Pair and write (sometimes called Think-Jot-Share) involves the same steps as Think-Pair-Share but instead of sharing answers orally, students write their responses. Peer guided pause (Hawkins, Brady, Hamilton, Willams, & Taylor, 1994) is another type of written response that not only provides students with opportunities to respond but also has the added benefit of helping students retain more instructional content. In this method, the teacher pauses at strategic points throughout the lesson so students can work in pairs to complete a worksheet that contains at least one correctly worked example and additional similar problems.

## Chalk Talk

The final written response method, chalk talk, gives students opportunities to share their ideas and learning while also allowing them opportunities to move around the classroom. To use chalk talk, prepare four to six lesson-related questions for students to answer. Write each of the questions at the top of a piece of poster board or large paper and place the boards in various locations throughout the room. Provide students with enough Post-It® notes to write a response to each question and allow them to move around the room to post their notes. Instruct students to write their names on the back of the note, close to the top, so the name is hidden. Once all responses have been collected, read the responses aloud. Only the teacher knows who gave each response, so students are more likely to give honest answers that reflect their true level of understanding without the fear of "looking stupid" in front of their peers.

## Action Responses

Because action responses involve some type of student action—giving a signal, pressing a button, pointing to an answer, moving—students find them highly engaging and motivating. Electronic student response systems, commonly referred to as clickers, have increased in popularity in recent years. These are web-based and/or handheld devices and applications students use to key in answers. Similar to the chalk talk activity, clickers allow students to respond anonymously; only the teacher knows who has given a response. Due to limited financial resources, many schools cannot afford to purchase these types of systems or don't have the Internet infrastructure necessary to run applications on multiple devices. Fortunately, teachers can utilize other action responses such as touching, pointing, gesturing, and movement that are free of charge and easy to implement.

## Touching

A **touching** action response requires students to touch a specific object or part of the body in response to a question or statement. For example, the teacher could show the number 124,379 and say to students, "Touch your nose if you think the 2 is in the hundred thousand place and touch the top of your head if you think the 2 is in the ten thousand place."

## Pointing

**Pointing** responses involve students pointing in the direction of the correct response or answer. A teacher could ask the class, "Where can we look if we want a reminder of the order of operations?" and students point to the anchor chart posted in the classroom showing the order of operations. Gestures, actions, and facial expressions are additional ways to elicit student responses. An action as simple as standing up can indicate a specific response. For example, the teacher says, "If you think a triangle is a type of quadrilateral, stand up. If you think it is not a type of quadrilateral, stay seated." Use a variety of simple gestures and facial expressions such as smiling and frowning, nodding yes or no, snapping fingers, and blinking rapidly to keep student interest high.

## Hand Signals

The final type of action response is **hand signals**. Hand signals allow teachers to easily and quickly visually assess students' understanding of the lesson. One hand signal response called "Thumb It" requires students to indicate how well they understand the lesson concepts by signaling with a thumbs up, sideways thumb, or a thumbs down. A thumbs up indicates the student feels he has a good understanding of the lesson concept. A sideways thumb indicates the student knows or understands some of the lesson's concepts, while a thumbs down indicates she knows or understands very little. Another hand signal response called "Fist of Five" can be used to indicate how well a student knows the information on a scale, with five fingers up indicating knowing it so well they could explain it to someone else and one finger up indicating they are only beginning to understand the information.

## CASE STUDY

Consider this example case study. Ms. Cook's eighth-grade class has been learning about equations and inequalities. Today she begins the lesson by reviewing and assessing her students' understanding of this concept. A portion of her lesson is shown below. Can you identify the number and types of opportunities to respond she provides her students?

*"Today, we will review how to solve two-step equations with variables on both sides of the equal sign or inequality sign. Let's look at our learning objective for today and say it together. 'We will model and write one-variable equations or inequalities with variables on both sides.' Good. Please use your whiteboard to show me an example of an inequality sign. On my signal, hold your whiteboard up so I can see your answer. Great! I can see many of you remember what an inequality sign is. Taylor, would you like to come to the front of the classroom and write the inequality sign you thought of on the big whiteboard? Now everyone, show me with your thumb how comfortable you feel solving two-step equations with variables on both sides of the equal sign or inequality sign. Next, turn and talk with your shoulder partner and answer the questions that are written on the board: (1) What is a variable? (2) What does it mean to isolate a variable? Decide who will talk first. The partner who is not talking needs to write down what the speaking partner says. After 60 seconds, I'll give you the signal and you will switch—the partner who talked first will listen and write her partner's response. While you're talking, I'll be walking around and listening in on your conversations."*

## MATH INTERVENTIONS AND STRATEGIES FOR STUDENTS WITH EBD

Now that we've described the instructional components most effective for teaching math to students with EBDs, let's look at some specific interventions and strategies. Math interventions are divided into five categories: basic numeracy, calculations and math fact fluency, word problem solving, algebra, and geometry. While basic numeracy interventions may seem appropriate only for very young students, some of them might work well for secondary students who are performing significantly below grade level or who need to review foundational skills. Similarly, problem-solving or geometry interventions could benefit elementary-aged learners who have mastered basic numeracy and computation skills. Before deciding on an intervention, it's important to assess students' levels of mathematical knowledge so interventions that best meet student needs can be implemented.

## Basic Numeracy Interventions and Strategies

Basic numeracy skills include one-to-one correspondence, counting, and number-after knowledge. Teaching numbers and operations using a developmental progression is one of five recommendations found to be most effective in teaching math to young children (Frye et al., 2013). A **developmental progression** means that the simplest skills and concepts are taught and built upon as students increase their mathematical understanding. When teaching basic numeracy skills, subitizing is introduced first. **Subitizing** refers to a student's ability to immediately recognize a visual representation for a small number. For example, the teacher might roll a die and ask students to say the rolled number aloud as soon as they see it. Or, the teacher displays pictures of several different items that represent the number 2, such as pictures of eyes, legs, socks, or shoes and pictures of items that do not represent the number 2 (referred to as a **nonexample**), such as the number of legs on a dog, the number of legs on a tripod, or the number of eggs in a half-dozen. Once a child can immediately recognize and name small numbers, move next to counting objects. The goal is for students to demonstrate **one-to-one correspondence**, meaning they assign one number to each object counted. Begin by modeling one-to-one counting, touching each item as it is counted aloud. When counting the final object in the set, say the number word with emphasis so students begin to understand that the last number said is equal to the total number of objects in the set. It's also important for students to understand that the order of the objects does not affect how the objects are counted. If students are counting the beads shown in Figure 4–4, they can count from the first bead to the last or the last bead to the first and still arrive at the same number of objects.

When students master one-to-one correspondence, they are ready to begin comparing two small collections of objects and determining which collection is larger. To practice this skill, a teacher might set out a group of

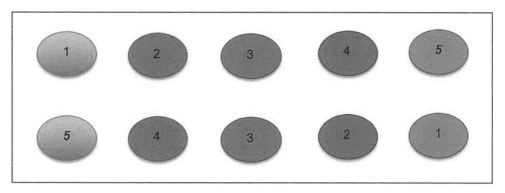

*Figure 4–4. One-to-one correspondence, starting from the front or back of a group of objects.*

three peppermints and a group of four peppermints. The student counts the peppermints in each group and, when asked, tells the teacher which group is larger. The student develops this understanding through counting—the group of four peppermints is larger because the student had to count further than he did when he counted the group of three peppermints. After students establish an understanding of making comparisons between small groups, focus next on building number-after knowledge. This means a student can identify the number that comes after a stated number without counting from 1. For example, the teacher asks, "What number comes after 2?" to which the child with number-after knowledge immediately replies, "Three." Next, students learn to mentally determine which of two numbers is larger. A student shows mastery of this skill when she can answer questions like, "Which number is more, 2 or 3?" mentally, without touching or drawing objects. Last, students develop the knowledge that "any number in the counting sequence is exactly one more than the previous number" (Frye et al., 2013, p. 13). This is a critical skill for students to understand before they begin performing mathematical calculations.

Playing board, card, or dice games is an engaging and effective way to improve students' basic numeracy skills. *The Great Number-Line Race* is a simple board game available free of charge at www.interventioncentral.org. Players take turns rolling a die or spinning a spinner and advance game pieces the number of spaces rolled or spun. Additionally, players are required to call out the names of the numbers on which they land. This type of game reinforces subitizing, one-to-one correspondence, identification of written numbers, and number comparisons. Other games that reinforce numeracy concepts include *Roll a Number!* (see Appendix 4–1) and *Toss It!* (see Appendix 4–2); both can be played individually or in pairs. In *Roll a Value!* students take turns rolling a die, calling out the numbers rolled, and recording them on the recording sheet. The first player to fill in all six boxes above one number is the winner. In *Toss It!* students use counters that are yellow on one side and red on the other (but the game can easily be adapted for use with whatever materials the teacher has on hand). Students take turns tossing the counters or rolling them out of a cup and recording how many counters turn up red and how many counters turn up yellow using tally marks. After a predetermined number of rounds, students count the total number of tally marks in the red column and the total number of tally marks in the yellow column to determine the "winning" color for the game.

Commercially available games such as Uno®, Phase 10®, and Yahtzee® can also help build students' number skills. Other commercially available games such as Candy Land® can be adapted to meet students' needs; use a permanent marker to write numbers on each of the colored spaces and play the game in a manner similar to *The Great Number-Line Race*. Another way to reinforce basic numeracy skills is playing variations of the card game "War" with either cards or dice. Give players counters or tokens and give each player a die (or playing cards with the face cards removed). Students roll their die or turn over a playing card and compare their numbers. The student with the larger number wins the round and receives a counter or token. Once all the counters or tokens have been awarded, the game ends and players count their tokens to determine the winner. Counting tokens provides students with an additional opportunity to practice comparing numbers.

## Computation and Math Fact Fluency Interventions and Strategies

There are numerous benefits to improving computation skills and math fact fluency. Gersten, Jordan, and Flojo (2005) compared the importance of being able to fluently and accurately solve computation problems to the importance of reading fluency on reading comprehension. Students who efficiently and easily perform computation tasks can devote cognitive resources to understanding more complex tasks such as word problem solving. In fact, lack of math fact fluency can impede students' procedural fluency development, "the ability to efficiently remember and apply a series of problem-solving steps" (Riccomini, Stocker, & Morano, 2017). As mentioned previously, computation and math fact fluency interventions for students with EBD far outnumber problem-solving interventions. Select interventions based on your students' needs and remember to introduce skills in a sequential and logical fashion. Providing a fluency intervention before teaching students how to perform the computation isn't logical. Also keep in mind that students need to develop more than just **procedural knowledge**, which is knowing *how* to solve computation problems. They also need to develop **conceptual understanding**, which is knowing *why* they are performing the procedure.

## Self-Mediated Interventions and Strategies

One of the most often used and effective strategies for improving computation skills with both elementary and secondary students is **self-monitoring**. Self-monitoring involves students independently recording whether they are engaged in a task, how well they performed a task, or how long it took them to complete a task (Carr & Punzo, 1993). When teaching students to self-monitor, first establish a target or goal. Goal setting motivates students with EBD to improve academic performance, and teaching students to write down or graph steps toward a goal allows them to easily gauge growth and progress (Bruhn et al., 2016). Model for students each step needed to reach the goal or target, how they will keep track of their progress, and who they can ask for help if needed. Goal and monitoring sheets like the one shown in Appendix 4–3 and Appendix 4–4 can be used to help students establish long- and short-term goals and monitor progress toward goals. When completing the goal monitoring sheet, students write in the date the problems were completed and color in boxes above the date to correspond to the number of problems correctly completed. Alternatively, students can place a dot or x inside the box that corresponds to the number of problems correctly completed and connect the first dot and the last dot to see if they are improving.

## Checklists

Another type of self-monitoring strategy found to be effective for students with EBD is the use of a **checklist**. Checklists outline specific steps needed to complete an algorithm, and teachers can create checklists based on an analysis of student errors (Uberti, Mastropieri, & Scruggs, 2004) or create more generic checklists that outline steps of a common process such as long division (see Figure 4–5). Laminate checklists so they can be used repeatedly with an erasable marker or shrink them so they can be taped directly on students' desks for quick and easy reference. Checklists can be gradually phased out as students commit the steps to memory or as their performance improves.

| Step | Example | Complete ✔ |
|---|---|---|
| **DIVIDE** | $4\overline{)96}$ 2 — 4 goes into 9 → 2 times | |
| **MUTLIPLY** | $4\overline{)96}$ 2, 8 — 2 times 4 is 8 | |
| **SUBTRACT** | $4\overline{)96}$ 2, -8, 1 — 9 minus 8 is 1 | |
| **BRING DOWN** | $4\overline{)96}$ 2, -8↓, 16 — Bring down the 6 | |
| **REPEAT** | $4\overline{)96}$ 24, -8, 16 — Repeat. Begin with Divide. | |

**Figure 4–5.** *Checklist for completing the steps of long division, accompanied by an example for each step.*

## Self-Evaluation/Self-Instruction

In **self-evaluation and self-instruction**, a student compares his performance to an established criterion and receives some type of reinforcement for achieving the criterion (Ryan et al., 2008). To help students increase their accuracy and fluency in solving computation problems, create worksheets containing similar problems (all addition, for example) and a self-monitoring chart with date on the x-axis and number of problems correctly completed on the y-axis. Each student receives a worksheet, a worksheet answer key, and a self-monitoring chart. Before completing the worksheet, students check the self-monitoring chart to determine their most recent score. This gives them a target score to try and exceed. Then, the timer is set for a specified amount of time and students begin completing the worksheet. Once complete, they check their answers against the answer key and graph progress on the monitoring sheet. Bennett and Cavanaugh (1998) suggest allowing students to choose from a reward menu as a type of performance feedback. Develop individual reward menus for students based on their likes and interests. A similar intervention using audio prompts instead of a timer can be implemented to increase computational fluency. Determine how long you would like students to spend practicing problems (no more than 10 minutes) and provide audio prompts at increasing intervals as cues for students to stop and count the number of problems completed. At the end of the intervention period, students total the problems completed at each tone and record the number on a self-monitoring chart (https://www.interventioncentral.org/academic-interventions/math-facts/math-computation-student-self-monitoring-productivity-increase-flu).

### Errorless Learning Worksheet

Caron (2007) describes a self-instruction technique to build computational fluency called an **errorless learning worksheet**. This worksheet contains simple math fact problems for students to solve, each with a number beside it. At the top of the worksheet, an answer key is provided with answers corresponding to the number beside each problem (Figure 4–6). The student sets a timer for a predetermined length of time (2 minutes, for example) and completes the problems as quickly as possible. If the student encounters a problem she doesn't know how to solve, she can find the answer at the top of the worksheet. Errorless learning worksheets motivate reluctant learners, help improve students' visualization skills, and help build math fact fluency.

### Cover-Copy-Compare

**Cover-copy-compare** (CCC) is a self-instruction strategy frequently used to improve spelling accuracy (Darrow et al., 2012; Manfred et al., 2015) that can also be used to improve math fact fluency. The teacher writes several solved math facts on the left side of the CCC worksheet (Figure 4–7). The student studies the math facts, then folds the worksheet to cover the facts and writes the facts from memory in the second column of the CCC worksheet. Next, the student unfolds the worksheet to compare his work against the problems

| | | | |
|---|---|---|---|
| | 1. 6 x 6 = 36 | 2. 6 x 7 = 42 | 3. 6 x 8 = 48 |
| Name: _____ | 4. 6 x 9 = 54 | 5. 7 x 7 = 49 | 6. 7 x 8 = 56 |
| | 7. 7 x 9 = 63 | 8. 8 x 8 = 64 | 9. 8 x 9 = 72 |

6.    7 x 8 = ____          1.    6 x 6 = ____          9.    8 x 9 = ____          4.    6 x 9 = ____

5.    7 x 7 = ____          2.    6 x 7 = ____          8.    8 x 8 = ____          3.    6 x 8 = ____

**Figure 4–6.** *Errorless learning worksheet.*

| COVER | COPY | COMPARE |
|---|---|---|
| 8 x 7 = 56 | | |
| 6 x 8 = 48 | | |
| 7 x 7 = 49 | | |

**Figure 4–7.** *Cover-copy-compare. Fold the "Compare" column back on the second dotted line. After studying the math fact in the "Cover" column, fold it back at the first dotted line and copy the math fact and answer in the "Copy" column. Uncover the original problem and compare it to the response in the "Copy" column. If correct, move to the next problem. If incorrect, copy the math fact and answer from the "Cover" column in the "Compare" column.*

in the first column. If the answer is correct, the student moves to the next problem. If the answer is incorrect, the student uses the third column to copy the correct problem, giving them another opportunity to practice seeing and writing the correct answer. Alternatively, instead of writing the math fact, a student could respond orally (Skinner et al., 1993).

## Taped Problems

**Taped (or recorded) problems** can be used in a manner similar to the cover-copy-compare technique but instead of studying written problems, students listen to recorded problems and answers repeated several times (Bliss et al., 2010). Including recordings with a brief pause after problems are stated allows students to practice "beating the tape" by providing the answer before it's played on the recording. The interval between the recorded problem and the stated answer can be gradually decreased to improve student response rates. Resources for implementing a taped problems intervention can be found at https://www.interventioncentral.org/academic-interventions/math-facts/math-computation-student-self-monitoring-productivity-increase-flu

## Folding-In Technique

The **folding-in technique** approach utilizes flash cards, a checklist, repeated practice, and a performance log to improve math fact fluency. Teachers select the math facts students will practice and create or purchase flash cards with a problem on one side and the solution on the other side of each card. Prior to implementing the intervention, the teacher meets with the student and reviews all the flash cards. Problems the student correctly answers within 3 seconds are placed in a "known" pile and problems answered after 3 seconds, not answered at all, or answered incorrectly are placed in an "unknown" pile. Next, the teacher trains the students to use a self-instruction checklist to implement the intervention and models how to record progress on the performance log.

## Peer-Mediated Interventions and Strategies

Students' math fact accuracy and fluency can be improved using a variety of peer-mediated interventions (Dunn et al., 2017). Spencer (2006) completed a review of peer tutoring interventions for elementary, middle, and high school students with EBD and found these interventions positively affected students' math achievement as well as their social and behavioral functioning. **Classwide peer tutoring** assigns every student in the class the role of tutor or tutee. Tutor and tutee pairs work together to review previously learned concepts. **Cross-age tutoring** uses tutors 2 or 3 years older than tutees. To use **cooperative learning** strategies, teachers create small groups comprising students of various ability levels. All students in the group are responsible for learning the material, but students are graded based on the performance of the group. The most frequently used peer-mediated strategy is peer tutoring. **Peer tutoring** involves explicitly training students to serve as one-on-one tutors who provide instruction and practice to tutees.

Intervention Central (n.d.) outlines a peer tutoring intervention using constant time delay and math fact cards, where students are explicitly taught how to serve as tutors for one another before implementation. Each peer tutoring group uses a set of math fact cards and a progress monitoring form. The teacher serves as an activity supervisor and time keeper. When the timer begins, the tutor shows each card to the tutee for 3 seconds and the tutee provides a response. Correct responses are acknowledged and praised, while incorrect responses require the tutor to state the correct answer and ask the tutee to repeat it. Pairs continue to review cards until the timer sounds. This tutoring session is immediately followed by an assessment session, where the tutor presents each card again but does not provide feedback on the accuracy of the response. Cards are sorted into "correct" and "incorrect" piles, and the tutor records the tutee's progress on a progress monitoring chart.

## Teacher-Mediated Interventions and Strategies

The final set of interventions and strategies for improving computational fluency is teacher mediated. Teacher-mediated interventions and strategies include preventative and predictive steps taken by the teacher before, during, and after the lesson. One type of before-the-lesson teacher-mediated strategy for improving computation accuracy is intermixing easy and challenging computation problems (Hawkins, Skinner, & Oliver, 2005; Skinner, Hurst, Teeple, & Meadows, 2002). Many students with EBD prefer problems that require less time to solve, such as single-digit multiplication or addition, to more complex computation tasks like multidigit multiplication and addition with regrouping (i.e., carrying) (Lee, Lylo, Vostal, & Hua, 2012). Introduce these nonpreferred problems gradually, with just a few items intermixed with many high-preference problems. Select several "easy" and "difficult" problems, interspersed at a specific ratio. Depending on student progress, adjust the ratio to include challenging problems more or less frequently.

## Mnemonics

**Mnemonics** are visual or auditory cues that help students remember the steps needed to perform calculation tasks and are effective for elementary and secondary students with EBD. Cade and Gunter (2002) used a musical mnemonic to teach basic division to students with severe emotional and behavioral disorders. First, students were taught a tapping drill that assigned each finger a number from 1 to 10. For example, the left pinky was assigned the number 1, the next finger the number 2, and so on ending with the right pinky finger, which was assigned the number 10. Next, students were taught a number song one line at a time (Semple, 1992, p. 133).

Seven, fourteen, twenty-one, look at me—I'm having fun!

Twenty-eight and thirty-five, fun-fun-fun—Man alive!

Forty-two and forty-nine—Hey there kids, stand in line!

Fifty-six and sixty-three (what's the time? Don't ask me!)

After learning the song, students watched the teacher sing the song while tapping a finger for each number in the song. Students were next presented with a flashcard with a division problem written in box form (42 ÷ 7 = __). They were taught that the divisor (7) was the name of the song and to envision the box as a mouth. The number in the box (the dividend, 42) was the same number that should be in their mouths when the song was tapped, and the quotient would be the number corresponding to the finger landed on when the dividend was sang. So, for the problem 42 ÷ 7 = __, students would say the number 42 as they tapped their right thumb, which corresponds with the number 6, the answer to the problem.

There are numerous mnemonic strategies and songs that can be used to teach calculation steps that are less complicated than the strategy used by Cade and Gunter. For example, the basic steps of long division are divide, multiply, subtract, and bring down (and, in some mnemonics, remainder or repeat as necessary). Students can use a first-letter **acrostic** mnemonic to remember the order of the steps, such as "<u>D</u>racula <u>M</u>ust <u>S</u>uck <u>B</u>lood" or "<u>D</u>ad <u>M</u>om <u>S</u>ister <u>B</u>rother <u>R</u>over." Acrostic mnemonics use the first letter of a word as the initial letter of another word to form meaningful phrases that are easy for students to remember. There are also a variety of catchy songs available for free on YouTube that can be used to help students remember calculation steps. Websites such as www.onlinemathlearning.com offer mnemonics and songs for a variety of math calculations and concepts, including how to multiply, divide, add, and subtract fractions; how to convert feet to miles; and the order of operations.

## COMPUTER-ASSISTED INSTRUCTION

Included in the National Council of Teachers of Mathematics' (NCTM, 2003) principles for ensuring all students have access to high-quality math instruction is the integration of technology. **Computer-assisted instruction**

(CAI) is a broad term used to describe technology options such as software or web-based programs that can be used on desktop or laptop computers, as well as mobile applications that can be used on tablets and smartphones (Hawkins et al., 2017). Several studies have been conducted examining the effects of computer-assisted instruction on the math calculation and fluency skills of general education students and students with learning disabilities (Berrett & Carter, 2018; Bryant et al., 2015; Zhang et al., 2015); however, limited research of the effects of CAI on students with emotional and behavioral disorders has been conducted. In 2012, Haydon and colleagues compared the use of iPads versus worksheets on the engagement and math fluency skills and of high school students with EBD. They found that students' time on task as well as their number of problems correctly completed per minute were higher using the iPad than using worksheets. One of the major benefits of using the iPad was the provision of immediate feedback. If a student answered a problem incorrectly, the iPad application instructed the student on the correct procedure for solving the problem and then provided them with another similar problem to practice. If a student answered the problem correctly, the application gave them feedback in the form of a sound or words on the screen such as "good thinking" to indicate a correct response.

Why is computer-assisted instruction described in the teacher-mediated strategy section instead of the self-mediated strategy section? A 2009 study by Billingsley et al. compared three instructional methods—direct instruction, computer-assisted instruction, and a combination of direct and computer assisted—on the math skills of high school students with EBD. Results showed that a combination of direct and computer-assisted instruction was most effective. These results are supported by the research on components of effective math instruction for students with EBD that says direct and explicit instruction is essential (Yell, 2009). In other words, for CAI to be effective, it must be used in combination with guided and explicit instruction from the teacher. Teachers who have many students in their classrooms working at a variety of instructional levels might be tempted to use CAI to reduce their preparation and planning time; however, this is not in the best interest of students with EBD who require human interaction to improve their social and academic skills.

## Problem-Solving Interventions and Strategies

Word problem solving poses significant challenges to students because it requires a combination of working memory, language, factual knowledge, and solution execution (Jitendra, Dupuis, & Zaslofsky, 2014). For students with EBD, word problem solving is particularly challenging because teachers allot too much instructional time to computational practice. In their 2011 study on using a strategy-based intervention to improve the word problem-solving skills of students with EBD, Alter, Brown and Pyle noted that "teachers of students with EBD spent up to three times the amount of time teaching algorithms instruction as opposed to conceptually oriented instruction. . . . This is almost the inverse of what is occurring in general education settings in which teachers were observed teaching conceptual" concepts twice as frequently as algorithms (p. 536). Instead of focusing primarily on procedures and basic facts, the National Council of Teachers of Mathematics (NCTM, 2003) recommends using an integrated approach to teach conceptual and procedural math knowledge. This type of instruction incorporates real-world problems and situations that allow students to decide what type of math to use in a given situation.

## Using and Connecting Visual Representations

One of the most effective ways to improve students' conceptual understanding is by introducing and connecting a variety of visual representations (Smith et al., 2018). **Visual representations** are drawings, pictures, or graphic organizers that depict the situation described in a word problem. Teachers can explicitly teach several visual representations for a given problem and ask students to compare the representations for similarities and differences. This strengthens students' analytical thinking and allows them flexibility in problem-solving approaches (Doing What Works, 2012). An example of a worksheet students can use to display multiple visual representations of simple word problems is shown in Table 4–2. Multiple visual representations are especially important when teaching more difficult problem-solving skills, like those used for solving functions in algebra. When students create visual representations, encourage them to share them with one another. It's often more helpful and impactful for students to see how their peers represented a problem than for the teacher to do all of the modeling.

**Table 4–2.** Multiple Representations

| Problem | Drawing | Mathematical Procedure | Solution as a Sentence |
|---|---|---|---|
| Jessie has five balloons and Julie has four balloons. How many balloons do they have in all? | | $5 + 4 = 9$ | Jessie and Julie have 9 balloons in all. |

## Mnemonics

Acrostic or first-letter mnemonics are frequently used to help students remember the steps involved in solving math word problems. Some commonly used four- and five-step problem-solving approaches include RICE (Read and restate the problem, Illustrate the problem, Calculate the answer, and Explain the answer; retrieved from www.teacherspayteachers. com/Product/Math-Mnemonic-RICE-for-Problem-Solving-2690284), RUNS (Read the problem, Underline and draw a diagram, Number sentence, and State the answer; Codding et al., 2017, p. 195, Figure 4–8), and CUBES (Circle important numbers, Underline the question you need to answer, Box key math words, Evaluate and eliminate, and Solve and double-check your work; retrieved from https://www.scholastic.com/teachers/blog-posts/ genia-connell/2017/cubes-strategy-to-tackle-tough-word-problems-/). Be extremely cautious when using the B step in the CUBES mnemonic. Math problem solving requires a level of comprehension that goes beyond locating "keywords" or math terms. When students are taught to look for keywords, it often results in a rigid view of terms such as *more* meaning addition or *product* meaning multiplication.

For problem-solving mnemonics to be effective, teachers should follow these steps: (1) Introduce the mnemonic and tell students this is a way to help them remember the steps needed to solve a problem, (2) explicitly model and explain each of the problem-solving steps using multiple examples, and (3) provide guided practice to students, helping them learn each step until they can perform them independently (retrieved from http://www.ldonline. org/article/13717/). Create small cards with the problem-solving mnemonic printed on it that can be taped to student desks for easy reference. Reinforce the mnemonic by creating a poster or anchor chart and hanging it in a location where it can be seen by all students.

| | R | Read the problem |
| --- | --- | --- |
| | U | Underline and draw a diagram |
| | N | Number sentence |
| | S | State the answer |

*Figure 4–8.* The RUNS problem-solving mnemonic.

## Metacognitive Strategies

Metacognitive strategies refer to strategies students use to understand their own learning. Examples of metacognitive strategies include planning for a task, evaluating task success, and monitoring for mistakes. Intervention Central outlines a three-part metacognitive strategy called Say-Ask-Check that is used in conjunction with a problem-solving checklist. First, the student states the purpose of the step (e.g., "I will create a visual representation of this problem"). Second, the student questions herself or himself about how to complete the step (e.g., "Does my drawing depict what the problem is asking?"). Third, the student answers the question he or she posed in the Ask step (e.g., My drawing does represent the problem).

## Schema-Based Instruction

Schema-based instruction (SBI) emphasizes the structure of problems and is used to help students solve various problem types using semantic cues and schematic diagrams (Jitendra et al., 2010). Problems are first categorized into one of two structures: additive or multiplicative. Additive problems involve addition and subtraction while multiplicative problems involve multiplication and division. There are three types of additive problems—change, compare, or group—and two types of multiplicative problems—equal groups (sometimes referred to as vary problems) and comparison. Next, a schematic diagram for each problem type is taught. Appendix 4–5 and Appendix 4–6 provide examples of schematic diagrams for each of the additive and multiplicative problem types. In the next section, each problem type is explained and examples given. Adapt these examples for use with your students by replacing the names and activities with the names and interests of your students. Problem difficulty can be adjusted by using larger numbers, fractions, or decimals.

### Change (Additive Problem Type)

In a change problem, an initial amount is increased or decreased, resulting in a new amount (Griffin & Jitendra, 2009). The schematic diagram for a change problem has three parts: the beginning, the change, and the ending, and the unknown can be in any of these positions. Examples of change problems are (a) unknown in the ending position (*Jill had 14 cookies. She gave 4 cookies to her sister. How many cookies does Jill have now?*), (b) unknown in the change position (*Jill had 14 cookies. She gave some to her sister. Now she has 10 cookies left. How many cookies did Jill give to her sister?*), and (c) unknown in the beginning position (*Jill had some cookies. After giving 4 cookies to her sister, she had 10 cookies left. How many cookies did Jill have to begin with?*).

### Group (Additive Problem Type)

Group problems, which involve combining two separate groups to form a new group, focus on part-part-whole relationships where either the whole or one of the parts is unknown. This problem type is the easiest for students to solve because combining groups is a concept introduced as early as prekindergarten. Although students that young may not be able to write a number sentence to match the problem situation, they are able to develop a conceptual understanding that putting two or more smaller groups together forms a larger group (Jitendra et al., 2013). Examples of group problems: (1) part unknown (*Patrick and Peter have 15 baseball cards. Peter has 8 baseball cards. How many cards does Patrick have?*) or (2) whole unknown (*Patrick has 7 baseball cards. Peter has 8 baseball cards. How many cards do Patrick and Peter have altogether?*).

### Compare (Additive Problem Type)

Compare problems involve the comparison of two sets that have no elements in common and tend to be the most difficult for students to solve. Compare problem types include words related to magnitude, such as *fewer* and *more than*, that students often have trouble understanding (Jitendra et al., 2010). Compare problems are typically worded in one of three ways: (1) *Adam has 45 toy cars. Alex has 23 toy cars. How many more toy cars does Adam have than Alex?* (2) *Adam has 23 more toy cars than Alex. If Alex has 22 toy cars, how many cars does Adam have?* (3) *Adam has 22 toy cars. Alex has 10 fewer cars than Adam. How many toy cars does Alex have?*

### Equal Groups/Vary (Multiplicative Problem Type)

An equal-groups or vary problem describes equal sets. The unknown in this problem type can be the unit rate (the number of items or cost per unit), the number of units, or the product (Xin, 2008). An example of an equal groups problem with the unit rate as the unknown would be *9 friends want to buy concert tickets. The total cost of the tickets is $216. How much did each concert ticket cost?* The same problem with the number of units unknown would be *Amy spent $216 on concert tickets. If each ticket costs $24, how many people can attend the concert?* An example with the product as the unknown would be *Amy bought 9 concert tickets for $24 each. How much money did Amy spend on concert tickets?*

### Compare (Multiplicative Problem Type)

Like additive-type comparison problems, multiplicative compare problems involve the comparison of one quantity to another and describe "one quantity (the *compared*) as a multiple or part (the *scalar*) of the other quantity (the *referent*) (Xin, 2008, p. 533). Just as with equal groups problems, the unknown can be in any position in the problem. For example, a multiplicative problem with the compared quantity as the unknown would be: *The zoo has 8 tigers. The zoo has three times as many elephants as tigers. How many elephants does the zoo have?* The unknown can also be in the referent position. For example: *The zoo has 24 elephants. This is three times as many tigers as the zoo has. How many tigers does the zoo have?*

## QAR Strategy

Students frequently encounter math problems accompanied by tables, charts, pictures, and graphs, and many students have trouble analyzing and interpreting these graphics. Mesmer and Hutchins (2002) suggest several factors that contribute to students' difficulties: (1) inattention to details in the graphic, (2) attention to irrelevant information in the graphic, (3) not reading the question that accompanies the graphic, (4) not applying prior knowledge to the graphic, and (5) assuming the answer to the problem will be "right there" in the graphic. One suggestion for helping students overcome their difficulties solving problems containing graphics is a reading comprehension strategy called **Question-Answer Relationships**, or **QARs**. The QAR strategy uses four questions to help students decide how to answer a problem. To implement this strategy, students first look for similarities and differences between the most common types of math graphics and practice identifying and categorizing graphics presented by the teacher. Then, students work in pairs to examine various graphics, asking questions such as, "Why was this type of graphic used to display this information?" Next, students practice identifying which QAR question would best help them solve a teacher-provided, solved problem accompanied by a graphic. Finally, students independently solve problems with graphics, using a checklist to help them remember the QAR strategy steps.

## Enhanced Anchored Instruction

The anchored instruction (AI) model asserts that learning should be anchored around a case study or real-life problem and presented using instructional media (Bransford et al., 1990). For example, students view a video showing a group of friends attempting to build a skateboard ramp and consider how they would read or develop building plans, calculate the cost of supplies, and measure the materials. Enhanced anchored instruction (EAI) extends AI, involving students in applied projects based on the video problems. Students might construct an actual skateboard ramp or design a car from recycled materials that can travel the greatest distance. Bottge, Rueda, and Skivington (2006) implemented an EAI intervention with 17 high school students, 10 of whom were identified as having EBD. Students were highly motivated to participate in problem solving related to the video and were even more excited to engage in the hands-on activities related to the video. Results of the study indicated an increase in scores on problem-solving tests of the concepts directly related to those taught during the EAI lessons; however, there was no improvement in scores on standardized tests.

## ALGEBRA AND GEOMETRY INTERVENTIONS AND STRATEGIES

Not surprisingly, the number of studies related to higher-level mathematics involving students with EBD is practically nonexistent. In a search of the literature, only one study focusing on geometry concepts and students with EBD was located; no studies focusing on algebra concepts and students with EBD were found. Despite this lack of research, some strategies for teaching algebra and geometry based on the principles of explicit instruction discussed earlier in the chapter can be utilized to help students with EBD experience success with algebra and geometry.

Mulcahy and Krezmien (2009) studied the effects of an intervention designed to improve the area and perimeter problem-solving ability of secondary students with EBD. The intervention included (1) instruction situated in a real-world context, (2) self-monitoring of academic performance and behavior, and (3) the use of manipulatives and cue cards. Students practiced area and perimeter problem solving by "building" dog pens, patios, and playgrounds on paper and by measuring objects in the classroom like the top of their desks and the chalkboard. During problem solving, students referred to cue cards when they needed help remembering a formula and used manipulatives such as Geoboards, inch tiles, and paperclips to help them visualize the problem and build conceptual knowledge.

### Mnemonics

Conderman, Hedin, and Bresnahan (2013) include several useful mnemonics for geometry and algebra problem solving in their book *Strategy Instruction for Middle and Secondary Students with Mild Disabilities*. Create cue cards or anchor charts for these strategies and model using each strategy using numerous and varied examples. The **SET** strategy (S—Substitute each letter with its value, E—Execute the operation, T—try the problem again to double-check) can be used to help students evaluate algebraic expressions. **CAP** (Mercer, Jordan, & Miller, 1996) is another strategy students can use for solving basic algebra problems. C stands for combine like terms, A stands for ask yourself how you can isolate the variable, and P stands for put the values of the variables in the original equation and see if the equation is balanced. Mnemonics for remembering geometry concepts include "At 90 degrees, one angle is tight. We will remember it is right," and "Each angle is the same at 60 degrees. That's how to remember an equilateral with ease" (Conderman et al., 2013, p. 231). You and your students can create your own rhymes, raps, and songs to reinforce algebra and geometry concepts.

## CHAPTER SUMMARY

Teaching mathematics to students with emotional and behavior disorders presents numerous challenges. Provide engaging, creative, and hands-on math activities situated in real-world contexts as often as possible. Utilize the principles of effective instruction for teaching math to students with EBD, including increasing their opportunities to respond and providing guided practice after introducing a new concept or skill.

### DISCUSSION QUESTIONS

1. What are the differences and similarities between direct and explicit instruction?

2. Why are increased opportunities to respond particularly important for students with emotional and behavioral disorders?

3. A seventh-grade student with ADHD and anxiety is experiencing difficulty solving word problems involving multiplication and division. What are some of the strategies or interventions her teacher could implement to increase her motivation and attention while simultaneously strengthening her problem-solving skills?

4. How could the self- and peer-mediated strategies and interventions presented in this chapter be applied to other subject areas such as reading, history, or science?

## RESOURCES

http://www.bestevidence.org/math/elem/elem_math_2018.htm

https://www.centeroninstruction.org/topic.cfm?k=ST

https://www.centeroninstruction.org/topic.cfm?k=SE

https://www.wested.org/project/doing-what-works/

https://ies.ed.gov/ncee/wwc

https://iris.peabody.vanderbilt.edu/resources/iris-resource-locator/

https://www.interventioncentral.org/response-to-intervention

https://charts.intensiveintervention.org/chart/instructional-intervention-tools

https://www.nctm.org/

https://ceedar.education.ufl.edu/

https://education.nsw.gov.au/teaching-and-learning/curriculum/literacy-and-numeracy/teaching-and-learning-resources/numeracy/resources/dice-games

https://dataworks-ed.com/blog/2016/03/how-to-learn-better-part-5-metacognitive/

www.ldonline.org/article/5678

http://www.ldonline.org/article/13717/

https://www.abss.k12.nc.us/cms/lib02/NC01001905/Centricity/Domain/2091/LongDivisionDeskCards.pdf

## REFERENCES

Adamson, R. M., & Lewis, T.J. (2017). A comparison of three opportunity-to respond strategies on the academic engaged time among high school students who present challenging behavior. *Behavioral Disorders, 42*(2), 41–51. doi:10.1177/0198742916688644

Alter, P., Brown, E. T., & Pyle, J. (2011). A strategy-based intervention to improve math word problem-solving skills of students with emotional and behavioral disorders. *Education and Treatment of Children, 34*, 535–550. doi:10.1353/etc.2011.0028

Archer, A. L., & Hughes, C. A. (2011). *Explicit instruction: Effective and efficient teaching.* Guilford.

Bennett, K., & Cavanaugh, R. A. (1998). Effects of immediate self-correction, delayed self-correction, and no correction on the acquisition and maintenance of multiplication facts by a fourth-grade student with learning disabilities. *Journal of Applied Behavior Analysis, 31*(2), 303–306. doi:10.1901/jaba.1998.31-303

Berrett, A. N., & Carter, N. J. (2018). Imagine math facts improves multiplication fact fluency in third-grade students. *Journal of Behavioral Education, 27,* 223–239. doi:10.1007/s10864-017-9288-1

Billingsley, G., Scheuermann, B., & Webber, J. (2009). A comparison of three instructional methods for teaching math skills to secondary students with emotional/behavioral disorders. *Behavioral Disorders, 35*(1), 4–18.

Bliss, S. L., Skinner, C. H., McCallum, E., Saecker, L. B., Rowland-Bryant, E., & Brown, K. S. (2010). A comparison of taped problems with and without a brief post-treatment assessment on multiplication fluency. *Journal of Behavioral Education, 19*(2), 156–168. doi:10.1007/s10864-010-9106-5

Bottge, B., Rueda, E., & Skivington, M. (2006). Situating math instruction in rich problem-solving contexts: Effects on adolescents with challenging behaviors. *Behavioral Disorders, 31,* 394–407. doi:10.1177/019874290603100401

Bransford, J. D., Sherwood, R. D., Hasselbring, T. S., Kinzer, C. K., & Williams, S. M. (1990). Anchored instruction: Why we need it and how technology can help. In D. Nix & R. Spiro (Eds.), *Cognition, education and multimedia: Exploring ideas in high technology* (pp. 115–141). Lawrence Erlbaum.

Brasch, T. L., Williams, R. L., & McLaughlin, T. F. (2008). The effects of a direct instruction flashcard system on multiplication fact mastery by two high school students with ADHD and ODD. *Child and Family Behavior Therapy, 30,* 50–59. doi:10.1300/J019v30n01_04

Bruhn, A. L., Mcdaniel, S. C., Fernando, J., & Troughton, L. (2016). Goal-setting interventions for students with behavior problems: A systematic review. *Behavioral Disorders, 41,* 107–121. doi:10.17988/0198-7429-41.2.107

Bryant, B. R., Ok, M., Knag, E. Y., Kim, M. N., Lang, R., Bryant, D. P., & Pfannestiel, K. (2015). Performance of fourth-grade students with learning disabilities on multiplication facts comparing teacher-mediated and technology-mediated interventions: A preliminary investigation. *Journal of Behavioral Education, 24,* 255–272. doi:10.1007/s10864-015-9218-z

Cade, T., & Gunter, P. L. (2002). Teaching students with severe emotional or behavioral disorders to use a musical mnemonic technique to solve basic division calculations. *Behavioral Disorders, 27*(3), 208–214.

Caron, T. A. (2007). Learning multiplication the easy way. *The Clearing House, 80*(6), 278–282. doi:10.3200/TCHS.80.6.278-282

Carr, S. C., & Punzo, R. P. (1993). The effects of self-monitoring of academic accuracy and productivity on the performance of students with behavioral disorders. *Behavioral Disorders, 18*(4), 241–250.

Codding, R. S., Volpe, R. J., & Poncy, B. C. (2017). *Effective math interventions: A guide to improving whole-number knowledge.* Guilford.

Conderman, G., Hedin, L., & Bresnahan, V. (2013). *Strategy instruction for middle and secondary students with mild disabilities: Creating independent learners.* Corwin.

Darrow, D., McLaughlin, T. F., Derby, K. M., & Johnson, K. (2012). Using cover, copy, and compare spelling with and without timing for elementary students with behavior disorders. *International Electronic Journal of Elementary Education, 4*(2), 417–426.

Doing What Works. (2012, February). *Effective problem-solving instruction part 1: Visual representations.* Retrieved from https://ies.ed.gov/ncee/wwc/Docs/Practice Guide/wwc_mps_pg_vr.pdf

Dunn, M. E., Shelnut, J., Ryan, J. B., & Katsiyannis, A. (2017). A systematic review of peer-mediated interventions on the academic achievement of students with emotional/behavioral disorders. *Education and Treatment of Children, 40*(4), 497–524. doi:10.1353/etc.2017.0022

Frye, D., Baroody, A. J., Burchinal, M., Carver, S. M., Jordan, N. C., & McDowell, J. (2013). *Teaching math to young children: A practice guide* (NCEE 2014-4005). National Center for Education Evaluation and Regional Assistance (NCEE), Institute of Education Sciences, U.S. Department of Education. Retrieved from http://what works.ed.gov

Gersten, R., Jordan, N. C., & Flojo, J.R. (2005). Early identification and interventions for students with mathematics difficulties. *Journal of Learning Disabilities, 38*, 293–304. doi:10.1177/00222194050380040301

Griffin, C. C., & Jitendra, A. K. (2009). Word problem-solving instruction in inclusive third-grade mathematics classrooms. *The Journal of Educational Research, 102*(3), 187–201. doi:10.3200/JOER.102.3.187-202

Haydon, T., Hawkins, R., Denune, H., Kimener, L., McCoy, D., & Basham, J. (2012). A comparison of iPads and worksheets on math skills of high school students with emotional disturbance. *Behavioral Disorders, 37*(4), 232–243.

Hawkins, J., Brady, M., Hamilton, R., Willams, R., & Taylor, R. (1994). The effects of independent and peer guided practice during instructional pauses on the academic performance of students with mild handicaps. *Education and Treatment of Children, 17*(1), 1–28.

Hawkins, J., Skinner, C.H., & Oliver, R. (2005). The effects of task demands and additive interspersal ratios on fifth-grade students' mathematics accuracy. *School Psychology Review, 34*(4), 543–555.

Hawkins, R. O., Collins, T., Hernan, C., & Flowers, E. (2017). Using computer-assisted instruction to build math fact fluency: An implementation guide. *Intervention in School and Clinic, 52*, 141–147. doi:10.1177/1053451216644827

Heward, W. L. (1994). Three "low tech" strategies for increasing the frequency of active student response during group instruction. In R. Gardner, D. M. Sainato, J. O. Cooper, & T. E. Heron (Eds.), *Behavior analysis in education: Focus on measurably superior instruction* (pp. 283–320). Brooks/Cole.

Hodge, J., Riccomini, P. J., Buford, R., & Herbst, M. H. (2006). A review of instructional interventions in mathematics for students with emotional and behavioral disorders. *Behavioral Disorders, 31*(3), 297–311. doi:10.1177/019874290603100304

Jackson, H. G., & Neel, R. S. (2006). Observing mathematics: Do students with EBD have access to standards-based mathematics instruction? *Education and Treatment of Children, 29*, 593–614.

Jitendra, A. K., Dupuis, D. N., Rodriguez, M. C., Zaslofsky, A. F., Slater, S., Cozine-Corroy, K., & Church, C. (2013). A randomized controlled trial of the impact of schema-based instruction on mathematical outcomes for third-grade students with mathematics difficulties. *The Elementary School Journal, 114*(2), 252–276. doi:10.1086/673199

Jitendra, A. K., Dupuis, D. N., & Zaslofsky, A. F. (2014). Curriculum-based measurement and standards-based mathematics: Monitoring the arithmetic word problem-solving performance of third-grade students at risk for mathematics difficulties. *Learning Disability Quarterly, 37*(4), 241–251. doi:10.1177/0731948713516766

Jitendra, A. K., George, M. P., Sood, S., & Price, K. (2010). Schema-based instruction: Facilitating mathematical word problem solving for students with emotional and behavioral disorders. *Preventing School Failure, 54*(3), 145–151. doi:10.1080/10459880903493104

Lee, D. L., Lylo, B., Vostal, B., & Hua, Y. (2012). The effects of high-preference problems on the completion of nonpreferred mathematics problems. *Journal of Applied Behavior Analysis, 45*(1), 223–228. doi:10.1901/jaba.2012.45-223

Levy, M. (n.d.). *Opportunities to respond: Learning is not a spectator sport. Many responses, many responders.* Retrieved from http://www.pent.ca.gov/mt/opportunities respond.pdf

Manfred, A., McLaughlin, T. F., Derby, K. M., & Everson, M. (2015). The effects of a modified cover, copy, compare on spelling tests and in written compositions for three students with specific learning disabilities. *Educational Research Quarterly, 38*(3), 3–31.

Mercer, C.D., Jordan, L., & Miller, S.P. (1996). Constructivist math instruction for diverse learners. *Learning Disabilities Research & Practice, 11,* 147-156.

Mesmer, H. A. E., & Hutchins, E. J. (2002). Using QARs with charts and graphs. *The Reading Teacher, 56*(1), 21–27.

Mulcahy, C. A., & Krezmien, M. P. (2009). Effects of a contextualized instructional package on the mathematics performance of secondary students with EBD. *Behavioral Disorders, 34*(3), 136–150.

Mulcahy, C. A., Krezmien, M. P., & Travers, J. (2016). Improving mathematics performance among secondary students with EBD: A methodological review. *Remedial and Special Education, 37*(2), 113–128. doi:10.1177/0741932515579275

Mulcahy, C. A., Maccini, P., Wright, K., & Miller, J. (2014). An examination of intervention research with secondary students with EBD in light of common core state standards for mathematics. *Behavioral Disorders, 39*(3), 146–163. doi:10.1177/019874291303900304

National Center on Response to Intervention (n.d.). *Using fidelity to enhance program implementation within an RTI framework.* Retrieved from https://rti4success.org/sites/default/files/Using%20Fidelity%20to%20Enhance%20Program%20Imple mentation_PPTSlides.pdf

National Council of Teachers of Mathematics. (2003). *Principles and standards for school mathematics.* Author.

Riccomini, P. J., Stocker, J. D., & Morano, S. (2017). Implementing an effective mathematics fact fluency practice activity. *Teaching Exceptional Children, 49*(5), 318–327. doi:10.1177/0040059916685053

Ryan, J. B., Pierce, C. D., & Mooney, P. (2008). Evidence-based teaching strategies for students with EBD. *Beyond Behavior, 17*(3), 22–36.

Semple, J. (1992). *Semple math.* Attleboro Falls, MA: Stevenson Learning Skills.

Skinner, C. H., Bamberg, H. W., Smith, E. S., & Powell, S. S. (1993). Cognitive cover, copy, and compare: Subvocal responding to increase rates of accurate division responding. *Remedial and Special Education, 14*(1), 49–56.

Skinner, C. H., Hurst, K. L., Teeple, D. F., & Meadows, S. O. (2002). Increasing on-task behavior during mathematics independent seat-work in students with emotional disturbance by interspersing additional brief problems. *Psychology in Schools, 39*(6), 647–659. doi:10.1002/pits.10058

Smith, M., Bill, V., & Raith, M. L. (2018). Promoting a conceptual understanding of mathematics. *Mathematics Teaching in the Middle School, 24,* 36–43.

Spencer, V. G. (2006). Peer tutoring and students with emotional or behavioral disorders: A review of the literature. *Behavioral Disorders, 31*(2), 204–222. doi:10.1177/019874290603100206

Uberti, H. Z., Mastropieri, M. A., & Scruggs, T. E. (2004). Check it off: Individualizing a math algorithm for students with disabilities via self-monitoring checklists. *Intervention in School and Clinic, 39*(5), 269–275.

Wilson, G. (2014). *All things algebra: Sum of interior angles.* Retrieved from allthings algebra.com

Xin, Y. P. (2008). The effect of schema-based instruction in solving mathematics word problems: An emphasis on prealgebraic conceptualization of multiplicative relations. *Journal for Research in Mathematics Education, 39*(5), 526–551.

Yell, M. (2009). Teaching students with EBD I: Effective teaching. In M. Yell, N. Meadows, E. Drasgow, & J. Shriner (Eds.), *Evidence-based practices for educating students with emotional and behavioral disorders* (pp. 320–241). Merrill/Pearson Education.

Zhang, M., Trussell, R. P., Gallegos, B., & Asam, R. R. (2015). Using math applications for improving student learning: An exploratory study in an inclusive fourth grade classroom. *TechTrends, 59*(2), 32–39.

# APPENDIX 4–1

## Roll a Number! Recording Sheet

If playing the game in pairs, each student will need his or her own recording sheet.

| Roll a Number! | 1 | 2 | 3 | 4 | 5 | 6 |
|---|---|---|---|---|---|---|
| | | | | | | |
| | | | | | | |
| | | | | | | |
| | | | | | | |
| | | | | | | |

# Toss It! Recording Sheet

Recording sheet can be adjusted for longer games or for use with different-colored counters.

## Toss It!

| Player 1 | | Player 2 | |
|---|---|---|---|
| Red | Yellow | Red | Yellow |
| | | | |
| | | | |
| | | | |
| | | | |
| | | | |

**APPENDIX 4–3**

# Generic Goal-Setting Worksheet

Goal:
_____

_____

_____

Steps I will take to reach my goal:

1. _____

2. _____

3. _____

Who can help me reach my goal?

1. _____

2. _____

3. _____

## APPENDIX 4–4

# A Blank Goal-Monitoring Worksheet

Skill: _____

| | | | | | | | | | |
|---|---|---|---|---|---|---|---|---|---|
| 15 | | | | | | | | | |
| 14 | | | | | | | | | |
| 13 | | | | | | | | | |
| 12 | | | | | | | | | |
| 11 | | | | | | | | | |
| 10 | | | | | | | | | |
| 9 | | | | | | | | | |
| 8 | | | | | | | | | |
| 7 | | | | | | | | | |
| 6 | | | | | | | | | |
| 5 | | | | | | | | | |
| 4 | | | | | | | | | |
| 3 | | | | | | | | | |
| 2 | | | | | | | | | |
| 1 | | | | | | | | | |
| 0 | | | | | | | | | |
| Date | | | | | | | | | |

**APPENDIX 4–5**

# Schematic Types for Additive Problems

**Group**

|  |  |  |
|---|---|---|
| Part | Part | Whole |

Part + Part = Whole

**Change**

Beginning → Change → Ending

**Compare**

Bigger - Smaller = Difference

## APPENDIX 4–6

# Schematic Diagrams for Four Problem Types

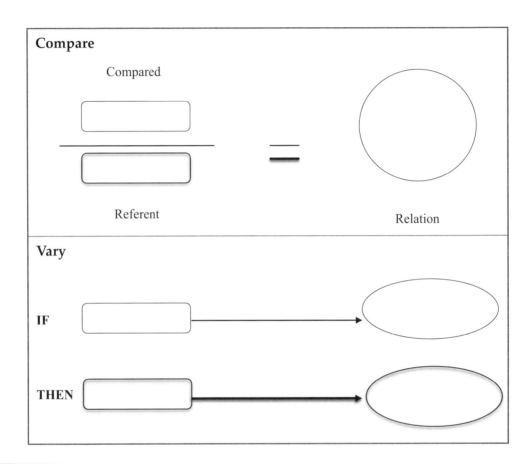

# 5

# Writing Interventions

*With Contributions from Nelly Kaakaty*

# INTRODUCTION

For students with emotional and behavioral disabilities, writing in particular presents a unique set of challenges. In order for students to be considered successful writers, they have to sit still, often for extended periods of time; focus on a specific task; and have the mental stamina and motivation to carry the task to completion. Students with EBD are consistently one to two grade levels behind their same-aged peers in writing and score lowest on writing assessments overall (Trout et al., 2003); therefore, the need for targeted writing interventions for students with EBD is critical.

The majority of interventions for students with EBD focus on social skills and behavior, while the least amount of studies, approximately 10% of them, focus on writing specifically (Mooney et al., 2003). Ideally, writing interventions for students with EBD must be both academic and behavioral: They must teach writing in a way that improves the quality of students' writing and they must address the internalizing and externalizing behaviors that make writing in particular difficult for students with EBD.

A multifaceted approach is necessary to target writing performance, and one of the most effective ways to do this is through a structured framework called Self-Regulated Strategy Development (SRSD).

# SELF-REGULATED STRATEGY DEVELOPMENT

**Self-Regulated Strategy Development (SRSD)** is an evidence-based instructional framework used to teach writing to students with EBD. It involves six stages that work to teach students a strategy through explicit instruction while embedding self-regulatory practices like positive self-talk and goal setting throughout the process (Harris et al., 2008). The six stages are (1) develop it and activate background knowledge, (2) discuss it, (3) model it, (4) memorize it, (5) support it, and (6) independent practice. This framework can be used with any strategy chosen to assist students with EBD in writing and can be utilized to teach any type of writing: persuasive, descriptive, expository, or narrative writing. We will explore the SRSD framework through a persuasive writing strategy.

# PERSUASIVE WRITING

**Persuasive writing** aims to convince readers or influence their opinion on a given topic (Guillain, 2016). Persuasive writing prompts can range from specific to a content area (math, science, history-related questions) to general prompts (often social topics or conversation starters) to more fun topics for low-stakes writing assignments, such as warm-ups, that aim to get students in the mindset for writing. Table 5–1 contains a few examples of persuasive writing prompts.

**Table 5–1.** Persuasive Writing Sample Prompts

| *Persuasive Writing Sample Topics* |
|---|
| Should all schools require uniforms? |
| Should students be allowed to have lunch off campus? |
| Is a hotdog a sandwich? |
| Should daylight saving time exist? |
| Should college athletes be paid? |
| Which is better: a Mac or a PC? |
| Should there be term limits for politicians? |

Though we know all types of writing can be taught through the SRSD framework, a strategy has to be selected first. For instance, persuasive writing can be taught through a variety of strategies depending upon students' grade level, and many of these strategies involve mnemonics. Mnemonic devices are techniques used to improve memorization by associating words with other words/phrases, mental images, or stories (Atkinson, 1975). To use a mnemonic device, students must assign meaning to a word or phrase they are trying to learn, then create a mental image that relates to it, as adding a visual component to information increases memory retrieval and retention (Atkinson, 1975).

**Mnemonics** are powerful for assisting students with writing, and many evidence-based writing strategies are based in mnemonics. An example of this would be a writing strategy used for persuasive writing called POW+TREE. We will use POW+TREE as our example of a writing strategy to be taught through the SRSD framework.

## POW+TREE

The mnemonic device **POW+TREE** stands for Pick an idea, Organize your notes, Write and say more, Topic, Reasons (three), Explanation, and Ending. Students are taught the POW+TREE through an SRSD framework to demonstrate how to use this strategy and maintain using it over time. As you may recall, the SRSD framework involves six steps (1) develop it and activate background knowledge, (2) discuss it, (3) model it, (4) memorize it, (5) support it, and (6) independent practice. Table 5–2 explains how POW+TREE can be taught through the SRSD framework at each step of the process. Appendix 5–1 contains a POW+TREE organizer.

**Table 5–2.** SRSD

| SRSD Step | What It Means | How to Do It |
|---|---|---|
| **Step 1:** Develop it and activate background knowledge | Assess if students have the necessary skills to learn POW+TREE (note: the teacher should already have assessed students' writing and have an idea of where their writing skills currently are) | Ask students what they know about writing: What do they currently use to stay organized, on task, etc.? |
| **Step 2:** Discuss it | Talk about what makes a good persuasive essay and introduce students to POW+TREE | • Give students graphic organizers and sample essays to help them begin to learn POW+TREE<br>• Describe goal-setting procedures<br>• Provide students with transition word chart |
| **Step 3:** Model it | Demonstrate how to use POW+TREE | • Provide sample essays<br>• Write sample essay with class, using each step of POW+TREE<br>• Verbalize thoughts to give students examples of positive self-talk |
| **Step 4:** Memorize it | Help students memorize the components of POW+TREE and when to use which parts of the strategy<br>Note: Students do not have to have POW+TREE memorized in order to move to the next step | • Create mini-quizzes or activities to encourage committing POW+TREE to memory<br>• Use prompts or cue cards to help practice memorization |
| **Step 5:** Support it | Help students as they work with POW+TREE | • Collaborative practice —work with students to write essays<br>• Students label the number of essay parts |
| **Step 6:** Independent practice | The goal is that students are able to use POW+TREE on their own | • Students write essays with POW+TREE without feedback from teacher<br>• Teacher monitors progress and charts improvement |

### Goal Setting and Self-Regulation

Goal setting and **self-regulation** are vital components of the SRSD framework. In many ways, this is what sets it apart from other writing practices, as students are actively working to keep themselves engaged in the writing process and tracking their own progress, which is something usually left to teachers (Harris et al., 2008).

Goal setting and self-regulation can be done in a few different ways. Self-monitoring checklists are often used and can be made for each student so that it targets specific behaviors or areas of growth (Mastropieri et al., 2009). Students should also be encouraged to work with teachers to create their own goals. Examples of this could be writing five sentences per paragraph or using at least one transition word before switching topics. The key is that students' goals be meaningful to the student. They should be clear, attainable, and still a stretch for the student; the goal should be a challenge, a push. It is up to teachers to help model this goal setting and help students meet their goals (Graham, 2012). The key is to help hold students accountable for these practices so that they understand it is just as fundamental to the writing process as writing itself.

Teaching students to create their own goals and a plan to achieve them is a skill that transcends the writing process and helps in all classes (Harris et al., 2006). To teach goal setting, it must be embedded in the writing process and fostered through encouragement. SRSD interventions use self-statement sheets that give students space to complete the phrases like "To think of good ideas," "While I work," and "To check my work." Teachers encourage students to ultimately think "This is hard, but I can do this. I am capable of meeting my goals" and model different kinds of **positive self-talk** (Harris et al., 2006). Appendix 5–2 contains a positive self-statement sheet.

## EXPOSITORY WRITING

**Expository writing** is writing that explains or provides information about a topic. Expository writing is also nonfiction writing or writing that seeks to explain, such as writing found in a news article, textbook, or instructional manual. In an educational setting, expository writing is used across disciplines.

### Writing in Content Areas

Writing in content areas is the idea that writing can be used outside of English and language arts classes. Traditionally, science and math classes do not incorporate many writing activities outside of assignments such as lab reports; however, writing in content area classes can be a useful tool for teachers when implemented consistently. Writing in content areas helps to check student comprehension and understanding by asking them to make connections between concepts (Fang, 2012). It also allows students to draw connections between different classes and across disciplines.

## Journal Writing

**Journal writing** assignments can be used in content areas in a number of ways. Often, journal writing is reserved for expressive or narrative assignments that are inherently personal, but journal writing can also be used to document ideas to plan essays or as a dialogue journals for writing assignments and receiving feedback from a teacher or peer (Christenbury, 2000).

## Learning Logs

**Learning logs** are a simple way of incorporating writing outside of an English classroom. Learning logs are short writing assignments where students are given a content-specific question and asked to write an answer to the question using evidence to support their answer (Olson, 2003). This can be used as a "exit ticket," where teachers will give students a question to answer at the end of each class that students must submit a written response to before leaving class for the day.

Providing sentence stems can help facilitate writing in the content areas, as it may not come naturally to students. Example sentence stems are:

Evidence for this can be found _____.

This connects to what we learned about _____ because _____.

See Table 5–3 for sample topics for writing in the content areas.

**Table 5–3.** Expository Writing Sample Prompts

| *Expository Writing Sample Topics* |
| --- |
| Math:  Explain how you solved for x. |
| Math:  Tell me everything you know about multiplication. |
| Science:  Discuss the life cycle of a plant. |
| Science:  Imagine you're on an island, what tools would you need to survive and why? |
| History:  Summarize the Gettysburg address. |
| History:  Describe a period in history that you would visit if you could time travel. |

## NARRATIVE WRITING

**Narrative writing** is writing that tells a story. Narratives can be personal (also known as a personal essay) and share information about the author's life or explore possibilities and center on fictional characters. Table 5–4 contains samples of narrative writing prompts.

## DESCRIPTIVE WRITING

**Descriptive writing** is writing that uses imagery to show rather than tell a story. Writers of descriptive stories should use all five senses as they craft their narratives. See Table 5–5 for descriptive writing sample prompts.

**Table 5–4.** Narrative Prompt Samples

| *Narrative Writing Sample Prompts* |
| --- |
| Write a story about how a moment from your childhood helped shape who you are today. What was this moment? How did it impact you? How do you see your current self in that moment from your past? What is similar and different about you? |
| Write about a time you had to make a difficult decision involving people close to you. What was the decision you made? How did it affect the people in your life? |

**Table 5–5.** Descriptive Writing Sample Prompts.

| *Descriptive Writing Sample Prompt* |
| --- |
| Describe your favorite place in detail without revealing what your place is until the end of the paper. What does this place look like? What it does it sound like and smell like? |
| Describe the perfect day. Where would you go? What would you do? Who would be there? |

## CASE STUDY

Kendrick is an 11th grade student who receives special education and related services as a student with an EBD due to anxiety and Obsessive Compulsive Disorder (OCD). Each middle and high school student enrolled in Deer Creek Independent School District has an email account. The 11th grade writing curriculum includes drafting professional emails. Kendrick is struggling to meet writing standards; often omitting greetings and sharing unkind remarks (e.g., "no one wants to work with you") when emailing peers. Kendrick fails to respond to almost 55% of email requests from teachers.

What strategies should Mrs. Smithson, Kendrick's English teacher, and Mr. Kermit, his case manager, use to support Kendrick?

## CHAPTER SUMMARY

Writing is often challenging for students with EBD. SRSD is an evidence-based practice that has been shown to help students. Within the SRSD framework, keyword mnemonics are effective writing strategies that help support students' written language development.

## DISCUSSION QUESTIONS

1. How do the components of SRSD work to facilitate learning for students with EBD?

2. What are two writing strategies to support students with EBD?

3. Define at least three types of writing and provide a sample prompt.

## RESOURCES

https://srsdonline.org/

https://www.ldatschool.ca/srsd/

https://www.thinksrsd.com/

https://iris.peabody.vanderbilt.edu/module/srs/

# REFERENCES

Atkinson, R. C. (1975). Mnemotechnics in second-language learning. *American Psychologist, 30*(8), 821–828.

Christenbury, L. (2000). *Making the journey: Being and becoming a teacher of English language arts* (2nd ed.). Boynton/Cook.

Fang, Z. (2012). Language correlates of disciplinary literacy. *Topics in Language Disorders, 32*(1), 19–34. doi:10.1097/tld.0b013e31824501de

Graham, S. (2012). *Putting evidence-based practices into play in your classroom.* Workshop for Region 10 Educational Service Center.

Guillain, C. (2016). *What is persuasive writing?* Raintree.

Harris, K., Graham, S., Mason, L., & Friedlander, B. (2008). *Powerful writing strategies for all students.* Paul H. Brookes.

Mastropieri, M. A., Scruggs, T. E., Mills, S., Cerar, N. I., Cuenca-Sanchez, Y., Allen-Bronaugh, D., . . . Regan, K. (2009). Persuading students with emotional disabilities to write fluently. *Behavioral Disorders, 35,* 19–40.

Mooney, P., Epstein, M. H., Reid, R., & Nelson, J. (2003). Status of and trends in academic intervention research for students with emotional disturbance. *Remedial & Special Education, 24*(5), 273–287. doi:10.1177/07419325030240050301

Trout, A., Nordness, P. D., Pierce, C. D., & Epstein, M. H. (2003). Research on the academic status of children and youth with emotional and behavioral disorders: A review of the literature from 1961–2000. *Journal of Emotional and Behavioral Disorders, 11*(4), 198–210. doi:10.1177/10634266030110040201

# POW+TREE

# POW+TREE
# Organizer

**P Pick an idea**
What side of the topic are you on?

_____

**O Organize your notes**
What helps you gather your thoughts? Write an outline, make a t-chart, use a graphic organizer. Whatever helps you organize your ideas!

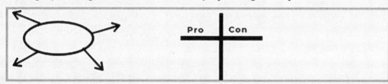

**W Write and say more**
This is where the TREE part comes in--you'll need your topic sentence, 3 (or more!) reasons, explanation, and ending.

**Topic sentence:**

**Reason #1:**
Answer: Why do I believe this? Will my readers believe this?

**Reason #2:**
Answer: Why do I believe this? Will my readers believe this?

**Reason #3:**
Answer: Why do I believe this? Will my readers believe this?

**Explanation:** Each of your reasons should have an explanation--go back and make sure you have explained the WHY behind each of your reasons and use evidence.

**Ending:** Wrap it up--use at least one sentence to restate your reasons and sum up your position on the topic. Go back and examine to make sure you have all of your parts!

## Positive Self-Statement Sheet

# POSITIVE SELF-STATEMENTS

### FILL IN YOUR OWN ENCOURAGEMENT-- YOU CAN DO IT!

**To think of good ideas, I..**

☐ _____
☐ _____
☐ _____
☐ _____
☐ _____
☐ _____
☐ _____

**While I work, I...**

☐ _____
☐ _____
☐ _____
☐ _____
☐ _____
☐ _____
☐ _____

**To check my work, I...**

☐ _____
☐ _____
☐ _____
☐ _____
☐ _____
☐ _____
☐ _____

**To motivate myself, I...**

☐ _____
☐ _____
☐ _____
☐ _____
☐ _____
☐ _____
☐ _____

# 6

# Reading Strategies and Interventions

Accuracy

Alliteration

Alphabetic Principle

Alphabetics

Comprehension

Concept Map

Corrective Reading

Decoding

Essential Five

Expository

Fluency

Grapheme

Listening-While-Reading

Multisensory Instruction

Narrative

Onset

Peer-Assisted Learning Strategies

Phoneme

Phoneme Change

Phoneme Deletion

Phoneme Identification

Phoneme Segmentation

Phonemic Awareness

Phonics

Phonogram

Phonological Awareness

Prosody

Rapid Naming

Rate

Repeated Reading

Story Mapping

Student-Teacher Learning Game

TWA-WS

Vocabulary

Word Boxes

Word Map

## LEARNING OBJECTIVES

By the end of this chapter, you should be able to . . .

- Describe the challenges in teaching reading to students with EBD.
- Identify the five major components of reading instruction.
- Understand effective interventions for improving student achievement in each of the five component areas.

- Locate evidence-based strategies and interventions for teaching reading to students with EBD.

## INTRODUCTION

Reading is central to many of the academic tasks in which students participate while in school and plays a significant role in an almost endless array of daily activities and interactions. But the process of learning to read is complex and multifaceted, and not every student develops reading skills at the same rate or with the same level of expertise. To learn to read, children need to develop phonemic awareness (understanding that speech is made up of individual sounds), alphabetic awareness (understanding that letters and letter combinations represent sounds), and an understanding that printed words convey meaning. Students with EBD often lack these essential reading skills due to academic avoidance behaviors that result in fewer opportunities for instruction and practice. To make matters worse, the limited instruction students with EBD receive is often of poor quality, with students spending a disproportionate amount of time completing seatwork instead of participating in direct reading instruction or reading for pleasure (Burke et al., 2015). The most effective reading instruction for students with EBD involves explicit, teacher-directed instruction using a balanced approach that allows students to simultaneously develop listening, speaking, reading, and writing skills. In this chapter, evidence-based strategies and promising practices for teaching the five major components of reading to students with EBD will be shared.

## CHALLENGES IN TEACHING READING TO STUDENTS WITH EBD

### CASE STUDY

*This year marks Mrs. Cones's sixth as the teacher in a classroom for students with emotional and behavioral disorders. She's excited about this school year because she feels comfortable assessing and addressing the social, emotional, and behavioral needs of her students. She also understands how to complete required paperwork in a minimal amount of time and effectively communicate with her students' parents and other service providers. But she does have one major worry: How can she can help her students become better readers? All 10 of her students read at least 1 year below grade level. Three of them will move on to junior high school at the end of the year, and she wants to help improve their vocabulary, comprehension, and fluency skills before they move on. For her younger students, Mrs. Cones wants to find some effective and engaging ways to improve their phonological awareness, phonics, and oral reading skills. She can access and utilize materials from the district's adopted reading curriculum, but she would like to supplement those materials with interventions and practices that have been shown effective in improving reading outcomes for elementary-aged students with EBD.*

*Mr. Callahan is a high school special education teacher whose students with EBD are experiencing some of the same difficulties as Mrs. Cones's elementary-aged students. All his students perform several years below grade level on measures of reading achievement and two of his students are not able to read at all. These two students don't routinely and regularly attend school due to suspensions, expulsions, or arrests. Mr. Callahan has spent countless hours looking for reading interventions specific to adolescent students with EBD. He's also searched for articles specific to reading interventions for adjudicated youth, but he's had little success. He's beginning to wonder if he should implement some of the strategies he knows are effective for improving the reading skills of younger students with EBD and try to tailor them to more closely match the needs of his older students.*

Both Mrs. Cones and Mr. Callahan have good reason to be concerned about their students' below-average reading skills. Poor literacy skills are the most common characteristic among students with EBD, and as these students age, their reading achievement gaps tend to widen and become more resistant to intervention. This is particularly problematic because students in middle and high school use reading as their primary means of accessing information. Many older students with EBD lack the foundational literacy skills necessary to read efficiently; by the time they reach secondary school, they may be as far as 4 years behind their nondisabled peers on measures of reading achievement (Benner et al., 2010). Compounding the problem is the almost nonexistent literature base related to reading interventions for secondary students with EBD. There are several published studies that examine spelling interventions but few that involve more complex literacy skills such as vocabulary and text comprehension (Griffith et al., 2008). In general, the number of published studies on reading interventions for students with EBD of *any* age remains alarmingly small. Interventions for this population are frequently delivered for only a short time, and high attrition rates translate into fewer participants completing research studies.

What we have been able to determine from research are several of the key factors that contribute to the poor reading performance of students with EBD. These include limited instructional time, few opportunities to practice skills, low response rates, disruptive behaviors, negative student-teacher interactions, and frustration due to numerous learning and school failures (Wills et al., 2010). The most detrimental of these factors on reading performance is disruptive behaviors; in fact, Benner et al. (2010) contend these behaviors negatively impact reading performance more significantly than weak phonological processing skills, memory deficits, low IQ, and demographic variables including race and gender. Additionally, students with EBD often have difficulty forming mental models, have limited academic vocabulary, have limited background experiences, and have difficulty making connections between school and the real world, all skills necessary for becoming an efficient and successful reader (Vannest et al., 2009).

## COMPONENTS OF EFFECTIVE READING INSTRUCTION FOR STUDENTS WITH EBD

In 2000, the National Institute of Health and Human Services formed a National Reading Panel to examine the existing research literature on reading instruction. The panel identified three major components of reading instruction: alphabetics, which includes phonemic awareness and phonics; fluency; and comprehension, which includes vocabulary instruction, text comprehension, and comprehension strategies. Today, these instructional components are commonly referred to as the **essential five**. **Alphabetics** (or the **alphabetic principle**) is the understanding that sounds can be represented by symbols. Phonemic awareness and phonics are subsets of alphabetics. **Phonemes** are the smallest unit of sound, such as /r/, /o/, and /sh/. **Phonemic awareness** involves the ability to both recognize and manipulate phonemes through identification, isolation, segmentation, blending, deleting, or substitution. **Phonics** is the study of the connection between sounds and the letters that represent those sounds. There are numerous instructional approaches for teaching phonics (synthetic, analytic, embedded, analogy, onset-rime), but the goal of all phonics instruction is to allow learners to gain meaning from the printed word.

**Fluency** focuses on three aspects of oral or silent reading: rate, accuracy, and prosody. **Rate** is the time it takes to read a passage or story. **Accuracy** is the number of words correctly pronounced when reading the passage or story. **Prosody** includes the expression, rhythm, tone, and intonation used when reading. Fluency is a critical component of reading instruction because it directly impacts how well a reader comprehends. There are two major approaches to teaching fluency skills: repeated reading-type techniques and encouraging students to increase the amount of time they spend reading independently through efforts such as Sustained Silent Reading (SSR) and Drop Everything and Read (DEAR). Research suggests that encouraging students to read more has little positive effect on their reading achievement; only fluency studies involving explicit modeling of oral reading through guided repeated reading result in improvements in students' word recognition, reading rate and accuracy, and comprehension skills (National Reading Panel & National Institute of Child Health and Human Development [NICHD], 2000).

Reading **comprehension** involves a person's ability to understand what he or she reads. The National Reading Panel divides comprehension instruction into three categories. The first is **vocabulary** instruction that can be delivered in various ways: explicitly, implicitly, using multimedia, and using associations between what learners do know and words they don't know. The second is text comprehension instruction. Text comprehension strategies include self-monitoring of understanding, the use of graphic organizers, asking and answering questions about what was read, and summarization. The final category of comprehension instruction included in the National Reading Panel's report is teacher preparation for teaching comprehension strategies. These suggestions provide teachers a wide range of instructional strategies they can use flexibly based on student need.

Students with EBD don't need reading instruction that is drastically different from what other students receive (Bruhn & Watt, 2012). In fact, explicit and systematic instruction, shown to be one of the most effective approaches for improving academic achievement in students with EBD, is mentioned in the report as the most effective method for teaching reading to *all* students. Characteristics of explicit instruction that are most effective for students with EBD include a focus on critical content, introduction of concepts in a logical and sequential order, ensuring student understanding of each step involved in a complex skill before moving to the next step, accessing students' prior knowledge, avoiding the use of complicated or vague language, the inclusion of frequent low-level questions, providing examples and nonexamples, requiring frequent responses, monitoring student performance and providing immediate feedback, and utilizing simple instructional strategies (Archer & Hughes, 2011).

Students with EBD also require multiple opportunities to read all types of literature that they enjoy and is written at their instructional reading level. They need relevant, engaging, and creative lessons that incorporate self-monitoring and teacher monitoring of progress. Students with EBD benefit from primary interventions using the core reading curriculum as well as secondary or supplementary programs that are fast-paced, are carefully sequenced, and incorporate letter-sound practice, sound blending and segmenting, sight word practice, fluency building, and comprehension strategies such as sequencing and retelling (Nelson et al., 2005; Wills et al., 2010). Interventions that provide multiple opportunities to respond (discussed in detail in Chapter 4), include mastery criteria, and use correction procedures are also promising practices.

## Peer-Mediated Interventions

**Peer-mediated interventions** such as **Peer-Assisted Learning Strategies** (PALS) are particularly efficacious for students with EBD who may not respond to teachers. Problematic relationships between teachers and students with EBD result in low rates of positive teacher attention, such as academic talk, teacher praise, and opportunities to respond (Sutherland & Snyder, 2007).

Peer-mediated interventions can also be used in conjunction with teacher-mediated instruction to improve student reading outcomes. Wehby et al. (2003) examined the effects of combining a teacher-delivered, commercial reading program—Open Court Reading (Adams et al., 2000)—with PALS on students' nonsense word fluency, sound naming, blending, and segmenting skills. Results indicated a moderate improvement in skills, with variability in performance noted among the four study participants, which is common for studies involving students with EBD as participants.

## Reading Interventions and Strategies for Students with EBD

Some studies have shown that improved literacy skills result in a decrease in disruptive classroom behaviors (Cook et al., 2012); however, the exact relationship between problem behaviors and poor literacy skills is unclear. Do poor literacy skills result in increased behavior problems or do behavior problems result in poor literacy skills? Whatever the relationship, we know that EBD and reading difficulties often coexist and that improving one may have some influence on improving the other. Unfortunately, as previously mentioned, there is very little information available on precisely how to best incorporate rigorous literacy instruction with effective behavioral interventions. A recently published meta-analysis of reading interventions for students with coexisting reading and behavioral difficulties (including EBD and ADHD) yielded only 11 studies; 6 of the studies included instruction on a specific reading component in conjunction with some type of behavioral support (Roberts et al., 2019). The most common behavioral support provided was positive reinforcement, followed by behavior management techniques intended to increase engagement for students with ADHD such as frequent reminders and visual prompts. Throughout the remainder of this chapter, we'll provide evidence-based strategies and promising practices for improving the phonemic awareness, phonics, fluency, vocabulary, and comprehension skills of students with EBD. For maximum effectiveness, use these interventions in conjunction with the behavioral interventions introduced in Chapters 8, 9, and 10.

## STRATEGIES AND INTERVENTIONS FOR ALPHABETICS

### Phonemic Awareness

Before we examine interventions and strategies related to phonemic and phonological awareness, it's important to clarify some of the jargon used when discussing these skills. The terms *phonemic awareness* and *phonological awareness* are frequently used interchangeably even though the words represent different units of language. **Phonemic awareness** involves the individual sounds in spoken language, called **phonemes**. Students with phonemic aware-ness can manipulate individual sounds within words through segmentation, blending, and deletion. According to Kilpatrick (2016), phonemic awareness is "a critical cognitive/linguistic skill needed to store words for immediate, effortless retrieval" (p. 27). Phonemic awareness skills play a critical role in improving sight word memory and bolstering reading fluency, and deficits in these skills often predict future reading problems (Kostewicz & Kubina, 2008). Appendix 6–1 summarizes the National Reading Panel's suggestion of the order in which teachers should introduce phonemic awareness tasks, ordered from easiest to most difficult.

## Phonological Awareness

**Phonological awareness**, on the other hand, is the ability to distinguish larger units of language, including syllables and words. Students with phonological awareness recognize and produce rhymes, clap out syllables in words, and identify and name words with the same initial sounds. Explicit instruction in phonemic and phonological awareness beginning in kindergarten can prevent students from needing more intensive intervention in later grades and helps students remain on target for subsequent reading development. Activities for developing phonological awareness include taking apart and blending syllables, rhyming, alliteration, and other word play using songs like "Willoughby, Wallaby, Woo" by children's entertainer Raffi Cavoukian; the "Name Game" (Dan, Dan, Bo-Ban, Banana Fanna, Fo-Fan, Me-My Mo Man, Da-an); nursery rhymes such as Jack Splat; and books such as *There's a Wocket in My Pocket!* by Dr. Seuss. Teachers can also emphasize these skills during transition times such as lining up to go to the cafeteria or dismissal at the end of the school day. For example, the teacher might say, "Everyone whose name begins with the /m/ sound can get in line. That's Mary, Mark, Manuel, and Melissa." In a search of the literature for interventions designed to improve the phonemic or phonological awareness of students with EBD, three main interventions were identified: Phonological Awareness Training for Reading (Torgesen & Bryant, 1994), Stepping Stones to Literacy (Nelson et al., 2005), and Peer-Assisted Learning Strategies (PALS; Fuchs et al., 2000). Phonological Awareness Training for Reading (PATR) refers to a general practice aimed at improving phonological awareness skills or to a prepackaged curriculum developed by Torgesen and Bryant (2014; PATR-2). Stepping Stones to Literacy (SSL) is a 25-lesson curriculum intended to be used as a supplement to the core reading curriculum. SSL does not include word reading; instead, the lessons focus on six foundational literacy skills, including listening compre-hension, phonological awareness, sentence meaning, alphabet knowledge, phonemic awareness, and rapid automatic naming. Peer-Assisted Learning Strategies (PALS) is a peer tutoring strategy originally designed to strengthen the fluency and comprehension skills of students in Grades 2 to 6. Extensions for kindergarten and first grade were later developed with activities focusing on phonological awareness, letter-sound correspondence, and fluency (Fuchs et al., 2001). One of the most important components of PALS is the provision of immediate corrective feedback, which is first modeled by the teacher and then implemented by students during peer-mediated activities. This practice has been shown to be highly effective for students with or at risk for EBD (Garwood, 2017).

## Phonological Awareness Training for Reading

Phonological Awareness Training for Reading (PATR) includes four parts: rhyming, sound blending, sound segmenting, and reading and spelling, and it takes approximately 20 minutes of instructional time. PATR supplements core reading programs such as Scott Foresman (Wehby et al., 2005) and has been implemented effectively by both paraprofessionals (Lane et al., 2007) and teachers of students with EBD (Lane et al., 2007). The goal of PATR is to improve students' phonological awareness skills so they are able to benefit from literacy instruction provided during the literacy block, which typically includes reading, writing, and spelling activities. Utilizing PATR in conjunction with group contingency plans has been shown effective in motivating young students with EBD to participate in PATR activities (Lane et al., 2001). For students with EBD receiving PATR instruction in the general education classroom, use systematic accommodations as well as frequent assessment to chart student academic progress (Wehby et al., 2003).

A PATR lesson begins with a warmup activity during which students practice rhyming (listening for or creating words with the same **rime** or ending sound) and **alliteration** (listening for or creating words with the same **onset** or beginning sound). After the warmup activity, students practice blending sounds to form words. Next, they learn how to segment the sounds in words, first by identifying words with the same initial sounds, then the same final sounds, then the same medial sounds. Children learn to identify the position (first, middle, or last) of sounds in words and to generate the individual sounds at the beginning and ending of words. Once students acquire the skill of segmenting, they can begin to analyze words more completely. In the final lessons, students use letters to represent the sounds in words and participate in reading and spelling activities.

## Stepping Stones to Literacy

Stepping Stones to Literacy (SSL) consists of 25 lessons delivered daily in sessions lasting between 10 and 20 minutes. Lessons consist of six prereading activities: parallel phonemic awareness tasks, letter names, sentence meanings, phonological awareness, phonemic awareness, and rapid naming. Parallel phonemic awareness tasks focus on the identification, manipulation, and memory of environmental sounds using five instructional activities: sounds in isolation, sound relationships, sounds in sequence, sound expectations, and omit a sound. Nursery rhymes, animal names, and environmental sounds such as a dog barking are used in these lessons because they are familiar to most young children. Letter naming and sentence meaning activities include sentence recognition, sentence generation, letter names, and letter naming practice and/or letter name cumulative review. During phonological awareness activities, nursery rhymes are used to help students identify individual words and generate rhyming words. Students also practice blending to make new words, either by combining two or more syllables or by combining onsets and rimes. Four instructional activities are used to teach phonemic awareness: phoneme deletion, phoneme identification, phoneme segmentation, and phoneme change. **Phoneme deletion** involves students saying the word that remains after the initial phoneme is deleted. During **phoneme identification**, students identify each phoneme in a word said orally by the teacher. **Phoneme segmentation** requires students to state the initial, initial and final, or initial, medial, and final phonemes in a word said orally by the teacher. The last phonemic awareness task is **phoneme change**, wherein students generate new words by changing the first, middle, or last sound in a word said orally by the teacher. For example, the teacher says the word *can*. The teacher instructs students to change the /c/ in *can* to /t/. Students say the resulting new word, *tan*. The final foundational literacy skill included in all 25 SSL lessons is serial processing or rapid naming practice. **Rapid naming** is important because it is a prerequisite to automatic word retrieval and oral reading fluency. During serial processing practice, children are presented with a variety of randomly ordered, familiar visual stimuli, including colors, numbers, and known objects.

## K- and First-Grade PALS

Kindergarten Peer-Assisted Learning Strategies (K-PALS) utilizes classwide peer tutoring to supplement the core reading curriculum and is typically implemented at least three times per week (Falk & Wehby, 2001). Sessions last between 20 and 30 minutes and consist of two main activities: Sound Play and Sound and Words. Sound Play involves a 5- to 10-minute teacher-directed phonological awareness activity—either identifying beginning or ending sounds, rhyming, blending, or segmenting—using a game format. Sound and Words is also included in First-Grade PALS and involves both phonological awareness and decoding activities (in this section, we'll look only at phonological awareness activities). It begins with a 5-minute teacher-led activity that includes blending and segmenting as well as the introduction of new sounds and words. Students then work in pairs throughout the remainder of the 20-minute Sound and Words portion of First-Grade PALS, taking turns acting as the reader or the coach. Wehby and colleagues (2003) implemented K- and First-Grade PALS with eight kindergarten and first-grade students with EBD. Results showed an improvement in students' ability to blend and segment words and to read nonsense words.

A fantastic resource for phonological awareness activities can be found at https://pals.virginia.edu/tools-activities.html. The site provides free, printable lesson plans for helping students identify beginning sounds, blending, segmenting, and rhyming. Each printable lesson includes the grade levels for which the activity was intended, the materials needed to implement the activity, and the procedures for implementing the activity. One idea the website includes for helping students identify beginning sounds is taking pictures of each student, labeling the pictures with student names, and allowing students to organize the pictures in groups according to the first letter in each name. Pictures could also be sorted according to the number of syllables in the person's name, the number of consonants, or the number of vowels.

## Phonics

Phonics involves learning to match sounds (phonemes) with the letter or letters that represent those sounds (**graphemes**). A suggested sequence for introducing phonics elements is shown in Figure 6–1. Other terms used synonymously with phonics are **decoding** or the **alphabetic principle**. We know that mastery of the alphabetic principle is instrumental in developing reading proficiency; once readers can automatically make the connection between letters and sounds, they can spend cognitive resources attending to more complex literacy tasks. We also know that deficits in phonics skills are a common characteristic among adolescent students with reading difficulties as well as students with emotional and behavioral difficulties.

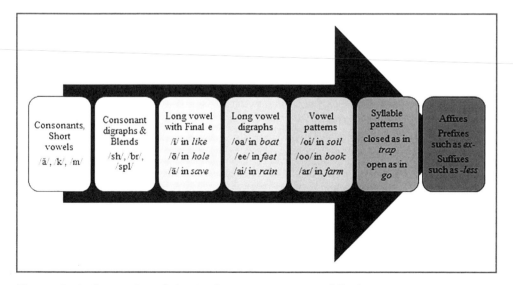

**Figure 6–1.** *Progression of phonics from easiest to most difficult.*

## Multisensory Instruction

One promising approach to teaching phonics to students with EBD is multisensory instruction. **Multisensory instruction** involves the simultaneous use of one or more modalities, including tactile-kinesthetic (what we feel or how we move), visual (what we see), and auditory (what we hear). The use of these modalities, based in part on the Orton-Gillingham approach, enhances memory and plays an important role in learning to read and spell. Warnick and Caldarella (2016) examined the effects of a multisensory phonics intervention on the word identification, word attack, passage comprehension, and global reading ability of adolescent students with a variety of emotional and behavioral difficulties who were housed in a long-term treatment facility. Students received lessons from *Spelling and Reading with Riggs* (McCulloch, 1995), chosen in part because it is inexpensive, requires no formal teacher training, and can be administered in short sessions. The program includes instruction on the 71 "Orton" **phonograms**, which are the letters or letter combinations that make up the 45 sounds of English speech. Sight (seeing the phonogram), sound (hearing the phonogram), voice (saying the phonogram), and touch (writing the phonogram or tracing the shape of the letter with a finger) are used simultaneously to establish sound-symbol correspondence. Students then apply this knowledge to write, spell, and read words using a memory-device marking system called the *Writing and Spelling Road to Reading and Thinking* (McCulloch, 2000). Results indicated significant gains in overall reading scores for all intervention participants.

## Peer-Assisted Learning Strategies

The K-PALS Sound and Words component focuses on decoding and word recognition. After a brief introduction of the Sound and Words lesson by the teacher, students work in pairs for the remainder of the 20-minute session, taking turns acting as the reader or the coach. Two activities students engage in during this time are "What Sound?" and "What Word?" In the "What Sound?" activity, students practice the sounds of newly learned and previously taught letters. The coach points to a letter and asks the reader, "What sound?" If the reader responds incorrectly, the coach says, "Stop. That sound is. . . . " In the "What Word?" activity, the same corrective procedure is used, but this time students practice reading sight words or decoding words by singing the sounds. Keep in mind that although this strategy includes the word *kindergarten*, it may be appropriate for use with older students who need additional decoding and word recognition practice.

Another activity students may complete during the Sounds and Words portion of PALS is Sound Boxes, sometimes referred to as **Word Boxes** (Figure 6–2). The student acting as the coach reads a CVC word (consonant-vowel-consonant, such as *cat* or *pen*), then says the word sound by

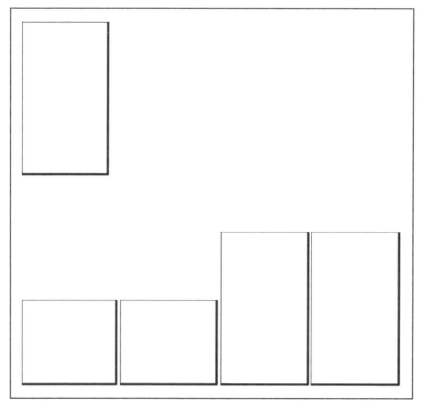

**Figure 6–2.** *Examples of sound/word boxes used to practice phonics skills. These sound boxes could be used to practice the word "apple."*

sound. As the coach says the first sound, the reader slides a counter (e.g., coin, poker chip) into the first box. Working from left to right, the reader continues placing counters in the boxes one at a time as each sound is given. Finally, the reader blends the sounds he or she heard to "read" the word. Variations of this activity involve students moving magnetic or cut-out letters instead of counters, students writing in the letters representing each sound, boxes for each letter drawn according to the letter's orientation (such as a tall box for "tall letters" like t, k, and h or a long box for "long letters" such as g, q, or p), or boxes already filled in with letters. Results of studies involving students with or at risk for EBD indicate K-PALS is an effective intervention for improving their letter-sound identification and sound blending skills (Falk & Wehby, 2001).

First-Grade Sound and Words begins with a 5-minute, whole-group, teacher-led lesson that introduces new sounds and words and reviews blending and segmenting. Students spend the remainder of the 20-minute Sound and Words session in pairs, completing phonological awareness and decoding games and tasks. In the decoding activity "Sound it Out," peer groups practice blending sounds to read words introduced by the teacher during the whole-group lesson. For each word, the coach prompts the reader to "sound it out" and then "read it fast." If the reader makes an error, the coach says, "Stop," then models how to say each sound in the word and how to read the word quickly. The coach then prompts the reader to try again. Lane and colleagues (2007) implemented First-Grade PALS with seven students at risk for behavioral disorders as well as reading difficulties in a general education classroom. In the study, the general education teacher acted as the coach during the peer-assisted portions of lessons. This teacher-led reading intervention resulted in improvements in students' nonsense word reading fluency, which measures students' understanding of the alphabetic principle.

Barton-Arwood et al. (2005) examined the effects of a commercial reading program designed to improve letter naming and decoding skills—Horizon Fast Track A-B (McGraw-Hill, 1996)—paired with Peer-Assisted Learning Strategies on the reading achievement and behavior of third-grade students at risk for EBD. Horizon Fast Track uses direct, systematic instruction to target phonemic awareness, letter-sound knowledge, word reading, story reading, comprehension, handwriting, spelling, and sentence writing. First-Grade PALS activities were used as a supplement to the Horizons program and provided students with additional opportunities to segment and blend sounds. Like the Lane et al. study, the peer-assisted portion of PALS in the study by Barton-Arwood and colleagues was modified to include more teacher-directed instruction throughout, an important consideration when implementing interventions for students with EBD.

There are several characteristics of PALS that make it an effective intervention for students with EBD. Immediate corrective feedback procedures are embedded throughout PALS lessons. In addition, many teachers incorporate a behavioral reinforcement system based on the Student-Learning Game when implementing PALS (Harris et al., 2009). In this system, students earn points for correctly naming letter sounds, blending sounds, and reading words or sentences. They also earn points for appropriate academic social behaviors such as hand raising and eye contact. Teachers earn points when students engage in off-task behaviors but not when students make errors in reading skills. At the end of each session, points are totaled and stickers awarded if students have more points than the teacher. When students collect a predetermined number of stickers, they exchange them for a small prize.

## Systematic Instruction in Phonological Awareness, Phonics, and Sight Words

Shelfelbine and Newman (2001 developed a decoding intervention called Systematic Instruction in Phonological Awareness, Phonics, and Sight Words (SIPPS) that can be used as a stand-alone or supplementary intervention for struggling readers in Grades K–12. Students engage in activities such as oral blending, learning new sight words and reviewing previously learned sight words, reading chapter books, and dictation and writing. Lane et al. (2002) used Shelfelbine's Phonics Chapter Books as the intervention for seven first-grade students with or at risk of EBD. The intervention consists of a teacher's manual with explicit guidelines for implementing phonics lessons, as well as six decodable books students use to practice the phonics skills introduced during the teacher-directed lessons. Results indicated an improvement in students' nonsense word fluency and a decrease in disruptive behavior. Texts similar to those developed by Shelfelbine are available for purchase on sites such as https://dogonalogbooks.com and https://shop.scholastic.com. While decodable texts are a promising practice for improving the decoding skills of students with EBD, they should only be used as one very small part of instruction. Students with EBD require exposure to a wide range of literature, not just texts containing words they can "sound out."

## STRATEGIES AND INTERVENTIONS FOR FLUENCY

Fluent reading—the ability to read with speed, accuracy, and proper expression—is crucial to improving overall reading ability (Al Otaiba & Rivera, 2006). To increase reading fluency, students need to effortlessly decode words and rapidly recognize sight words. This allows them to spend their energy and attention constructing meaning from what they are reading, a critical literacy skill known as comprehension. Students with reading difficulties tend to have problems reading text fluently and in turn have difficulty comprehending text (Oakes et al., 2010). Because of their close relationship, fluency and comprehension strategies and interventions often overlap. Some researchers argue that a measure of reading comprehension should always be included when measuring a student's reading fluency (Rasinski et al., 2011).

In 2014, Garwood et al. synthesized the research conducted between 2004 and 2012 for improving the reading comprehension and fluency outcomes of students with EBD. Five interventions were identified, including Repeated Reading (Samuels, 1979), choice with antecedent instruction and reward (Daly et al., 2006), Listening-While-Reading (LWR; Daly & Martens, 1994), Corrective Reading (Engelmann et al., 1999), and Peer-Assisted Learning with self-graphing (PALS; Sutherland & Snyder, 2007). Many of these strategies overlap; for example, Listening-While-Reading and self-graphing are important components of Repeated Reading, and Listening-While-Reading and Repeated Reading are both utilized during PALS.

### Repeated Reading

Repeated Reading (RR) is a widely used reading fluency intervention for students with reading difficulties. RR can be implemented at little to no cost and with just a few materials. During Repeated Reading, a student rereads a short text (usually 200 words or less) until a preestablished criterion is met. The criterion may be related to the student's reading rate, reading accuracy, or a combination of both. When selecting texts to use for Repeated Reading, carefully consider both the student's instructional reading level and the student's interests. Look for texts that have a large number of common words that are repeated and fewer unfamiliar words. As the student's reading level increases, more difficult texts with larger numbers of unfamiliar words can be introduced.

RR can be implemented as either a teacher- or peer-mediated intervention. Regardless of who delivers the intervention, it's important to provide a model of fluent reading before expecting students to read the text for the first time. This strategy is referred to as **Listening-While-Reading** (LWR; Hale et al., 2005). During LWR, a fluent model of the text is read aloud by an adult, a peer tutor, or technology such as text-to-speech software or an audio recording. At the same time, the student reads the passage aloud or silently. The benefit of using technology is it allows students to listen to the text as many times as needed until they feel comfortable reading it independently. Each time the recording is played, students might listen for a different aspect of fluent reading—the first time, they may listen for expression and emphasis, the second time they may listen for reading speed and tone of voice, and so on.

When it's time for the student to read the passage independently, both the student and the teacher or peer helper will need a copy of the text. As the student reads, the teacher or peer helper uses a scripted correction procedure when the student makes a reading error. The student continues to practice reading the story as many times as possible for a set amount of time (usually 8–10 minutes). When the practice session ends, the teacher or peer helper sets a 1-minute timer and the student reads the passage one more time. The resulting rate and accuracy are recorded by the student using a graph such as those available at https://buildingrti.utexas.org/instructional-materials/fluency-graphs-for-progress-monitoring

## Choice with Antecedent Instruction and Reward

The key to becoming a fluent reader is to practice fluent reading. Students with EBD often lack the motivation to engage in academic tasks, resulting in decreased opportunities for practice. Providing students with choices during instruction increases their motivation and engagement, leading to more time on task. Daly and colleagues (2006) examined the effect of instructional choice on the oral reading fluency of two middle school students with EBD. Students were told they could earn tangible rewards such as candy, pens, and so on if they met predetermined fluency goals. Students were then given the choice of receiving instruction or not receiving instruction. If they chose to be instructed, they could also choose the type of instruction they would receive—teacher modeling, practice, error correction, or performance feedback, all shown to be effective strategies for improving oral reading fluency (Chard et al., 2002). Both students in the study chose instruction, and both students demonstrated an increase in reading fluency and a decrease in word reading errors from baseline. A similar intervention can be easily and inexpensively implemented in your classroom. Offer students a choice menu like the one in Table 6–1. Devote 10 to 15 minutes of the daily reading block for reading fluency practice, giving students enough time to engage in at least two of the menu choices.

**Table 6–1.** A Reading Choice Menu to Use During Reading Fluency and Comprehension Practice

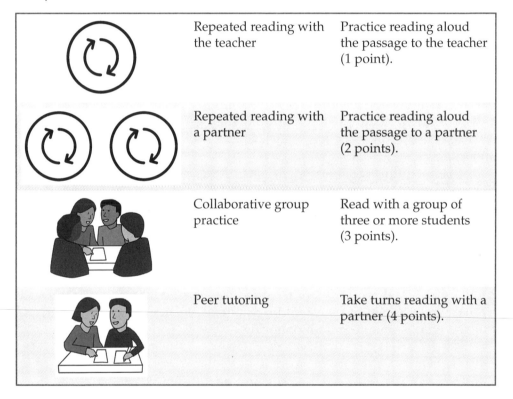

| | Repeated reading with the teacher | Practice reading aloud the passage to the teacher (1 point). |
| | Repeated reading with a partner | Practice reading aloud the passage to a partner (2 points). |
| | Collaborative group practice | Read with a group of three or more students (3 points). |
| | Peer tutoring | Take turns reading with a partner (4 points). |

## Corrective Reading

**Corrective Reading** (CR; Englemann et al., 1999) is a fast-paced, systematic, scripted phonics-based reading program designed to improve the oral reading fluency and accuracy of older students. CR lessons consist of three parts: word attack (10 minutes), group reading (15 minutes), and workbook exercises or oral reading fluency probes (5 minutes). During word attack, students practice word reading and also practice sounding out words with different ending sounds and vowel combinations. In the group reading portion, students read a story that is divided into sections. After each section, students orally answer questions about what they've read. During the final part of CR, students complete teacher-directed and independent workbook exercises that review the words practiced during the first two parts of CR. Alternatively, teachers can conduct oral reading fluency probes to measure students' oral reading rate.

## Peer-Assisted Learning with Self-Graphing

Sutherland and Snyder (2007) implemented a study to reduce disruptive behavior while simultaneously increasing reading fluency and active responding using peer-assisted learning (PALS) and self-graphing. Peer dyads were created by the teacher with one student in the dyad being a higher-performing reader and the other student in the dyad being a lower-performing reader. The intervention lasted approximately 20 minutes daily and consisted of three activities: partner reading, paragraph shrinking, and prediction relay. During partner reading, the higher-performing reader reads aloud for 5 minutes while the lower-performing student listens and follows an error correction procedure such as the one outlined at https://iowareadingresearch .org/sites/iowareadingresearch.org/files/oral_reading_fluency_error_ correction_procedure.pdf. Then students switch roles—the lower-performing student reads while the higher-performing student listens. In paragraph shrinking, the higher-performing student reads the text aloud again, this time stopping at the end of each paragraph to identify the main idea. After reading the entire selection, the reader tries to summarize the main idea in 10 words or less. Then students switch roles. The last activity in PALS is prediction relay. During this activity, the higher-performing student predicts what will happen in the next half-page of text. After reading the next half-page of text, the reader summarizes it and the tutor judges if the prediction made prior to reading was correct. Finally, students are taught to self-graph words read correctly per minute and errors per minute on the practiced texts. Results indicated a decrease in disruptive behaviors, an increase in active responding, an increase in words read correctly per minute, and a decrease in word reading errors per minute.

## Great Leaps

Great Leaps (greatleaps.com) is a commercial program used to supplement core reading programs. There are two sets of materials available, one for emerging readers in Grades K–2 and one for low-performing students in Grades 3–5. Great Leaps requires approximately 10 minutes of instructional time and includes modeled reading, goal setting, and performance feedback. In addition to traditional packages that include an instructor and a student manual with alphabet, phonics, sight word phrases, and stories for fluency practice, a one-on-one online tutoring program is also available. A limited number of reading fluency samples are available for download free of charge at https://greatleaps.com/pages/resources.

## Helping Early Literacy with Practice Strategies

Helping Early Literacy with Practice Strategies (HELPS; Begeny et al., 2010) is a multicomponent program developed by Dr. John Begeny at North Carolina State University to strengthen students' reading fluency skills. A typical HELPS session lasts between 10 and 12 minutes and includes peer-mediated repeated reading of instructional-level texts as well as immediate corrective feedback, verbal cues, goal setting, and a structured reward system. Staubitz et al. (2005) implemented the HELPS curriculum with six fourth- and fifth-grade students with or at risk for EBD. Results showed a mean increase in words read correctly per minute from 71 to 133. HELPS materials are available in both English and Spanish and can be downloaded free of charge by creating an account at www.helpsprogram.org

## Read Naturally

Read Naturally (Hasbrouck et al., 1999) was developed to improve students' oral reading fluency using high-interest, nonfiction stories that contain words most commonly used in the English language. Similar to HELPS and Great Leaps, Read Naturally includes three components: teacher modeling, repeated reading, and progress monitoring. Several versions of Read Naturally are available. Read Naturally Live is a web-based version of the original Read Naturally program that can be accessed using a computer or tablet; Read Naturally Encore utilizes print materials and audio CDs; the One-Minute Reader iPad app allows students to engage in the three Read Naturally instructional components at their own pace, either while at school or at home; the Read Naturally Masters Edition is designed specifically for English language learners; and the Read Naturally GATE program is designed to be used with small groups of students. A 60-day free trial of Read Naturally Live is available by registering at https://www.readnaturally.com/rn-live-trial

## STRATEGIES AND INTERVENTIONS FOR COMPREHENSION

Comprehension skills include vocabulary knowledge, story grammar, and general knowledge. Vocabulary refers to the words a person knows and uses to communicate with others. Story grammar refers to characteristics or components of a story such as characters, setting, main idea, and sequence.

General knowledge includes the reader's background experiences and understanding of the world. These comprehension skills can be enhanced by reading both **narrative** (fiction) and **expository** (nonfiction) texts aloud to students, including students in middle and high school. Keep in mind that comprehension is also heavily influenced by students' attention, motivation, and memory.

## Vocabulary

Vocabulary plays an important role in learning to read. When a student decodes and pronounces a printed word, he or she searches through the list of words he knows to check that the pronunciation makes sense. If it doesn't make sense, the student goes back and rereads the word until its pronunciation and meaning match. This meaning-matching process is also important for comprehension of text. The greater the number of words in a student's vocabulary, the easier it is for the student to understand increasingly complex texts.

Vocabulary can be conceptualized in levels or tiers (Beck et al., 2005). Tier 1 words are common labels that can be illustrated, such as *table*, *cat*, and *swim*. Tier 2 words focus on more abstract concepts like *embarrassment* or *honesty*. Tier 3 words are content specific, such as words used in math, science, and social studies. While not specific to students with EBD, the IRIS Center offers evidence-based activities for Tier 3 vocabulary instruction during English language arts, science, and social studies. Other evidence-based strategies for vocabulary instruction include repetition of words in various contexts; using enactive (doing something), iconic (concrete objects), and symbolic (letters or numbers) modes; and talking about words as they arise in texts (Jalongo & Sobolak, 2011).

In a search of the literature for vocabulary interventions specific to students with emotional and behavioral disorders, the use of concept maps was the only intervention located (Reed et al., 2017). **Concept maps** are graphic organizers used to illustrate the relationship between concepts. One type of concept map—a **word map**—is used specifically for vocabulary instruction (Figure 6–3). The map is divided into four sections and the vocabulary word is written in the center of the map. One section of the map is a space for writing the definition of the word, one section is for synonyms of the word, one section is for using the word in a sentence, and one section is for antonyms of the word. A section for an illustration or picture of the word could also be included if it is a Tier 1 word.

## Text Comprehension

Comprehension is the ultimate goal of reading. For a reader to understand a text, he or she must be able to decode the words on the page and draw from

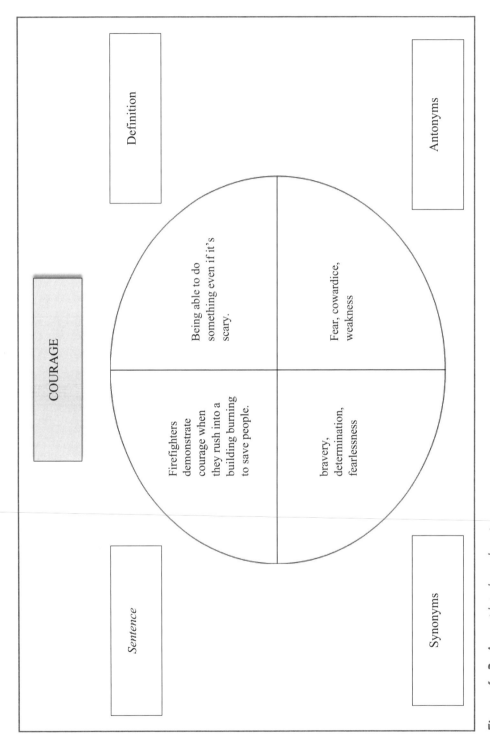

**Figure 6–3.** A completed word map.

his or her background knowledge and vocabulary to make meaning out of what is being read. For students with reading difficulties, including students with EBD, direct instruction on text structure is essential for building comprehension. Students should be taught to recognize elements of narrative texts such as characters, setting, and plot and types of expository texts, including cause and effect and problem and solution. As previously mentioned, many of the text comprehension interventions and strategies used to improve reading fluency have also shown to be effective in improving students' comprehension. Throughout the remainder of this section, text comprehension strategies that were not introduced in the fluency section will be discussed.

## Story Mapping

Story mapping—sometimes referred to as text mapping, cognitive mapping, concept mapping, or semantic mapping—is a tool used to help students of all ages organize and understand information in a narrative text. Story maps help students attend to key story elements during reading and help facilitate text summarization after reading. When using story maps, Garwood et al. (2017) suggest previewing the text with students, helping them read unfamiliar proper nouns such as character or city names, providing definitions for several vocabulary words, and showing pictures or concrete objects to support understanding of vocabulary.

Babyak et al. (2000) implemented a story mapping intervention with fourth- and fifth-grade students with EBD by teaching the five elements of a story, including characters, setting, problem, outcome, and major events. Students participated in guided practice by reading as story and completing a blank story map like the one in Appendix 6–2. Once students were able to identify story elements with 90% accuracy over two consecutive sessions, they completed story maps independently. To measure students' reading comprehension after independent completion of story maps, students were asked to retell the story, answer comprehension questions based on the story, and select one of four statements that best described the story's main idea. Results of the study indicated an increase in the percentage of correct answers to comprehension questions from baseline to independent practice.

Two studies examining the effects of story maps on the reading comprehension of high school students with EBD have been conducted. Blankenship et al. (2005) implemented a cognitive mapping strategy for three high school students with EBD but instead of using paper and pencil to complete maps, students used a computer software program, Inspiration. The researchers theorized that completing maps using the computer would increase students' engagement and motivation, leading to increased time on task and improved scores on chapter tests and quizzes. Results indicated a sharp increase in the number of correctly answered test questions from preintervention to independent practice for all three students. Stone et al. (2008) examined the use of text maps to improve the reading comprehension skills of four high school students with EBD. In this study, students constructed their own story maps and reported enjoying using them in their language arts classes. Results indicated an improvement in students' comprehension of narrative texts and an increase in student attention.

## TWA-WS

A self-regulated strategy used for the comprehension of expository texts is <u>T</u>hinking before reading, <u>W</u>hile reading, and <u>A</u>fter reading with <u>W</u>ritten <u>S</u>ummarization (TWA-MS; Mason, 2004; Rogevich & Perin, 2008). To implement TWA-MS, the teacher explicitly teaches students the nine steps of the TWA strategy (Appendix 6–3) and then models each step using a sample text. Students practice self-monitoring by checking off each step as it is modeled by the teacher. Next, the teacher and students work together to write a summary of the text. Guided practice of the strategy continues, with the teacher gradually reducing the amount of support provided until students are able to implement each step and write a summary independently. Rogevich and Perin (2008) included five rules for students to use when writing an expository summary: (1) cross out information that isn't important, (2) cross out information that is repeated, (3) substitute lists of words with a single word, (4) locate and rephrase the topic sentence, and (5) make up your own topic sentence if you can't find one in the text. Place these rules on an anchor chart, poster, or cue card for easy student reference.

TWA-WS isn't the only **mnemonic device** that can be used to help students comprehend text. Intervention Central describes a similar intervention using the mnemonic ART—Ask, Read, Tell. During Ask, students read the title of the passage, asking themselves what the topic may be and generating two questions about the topic they will ask themselves after reading. During Read, students read the passage, pausing intermittently to check their understanding of the text. reading. During Tell, students answer the questions they created during Ask and then share their questions and answers with a partner. You may use TWA-WS, ART, or some other mnemonic to help your students comprehend text; whichever one you choose, make sure you explicitly teach and model each step before expecting students to use it independently.

## MISCELLANEOUS STRATEGIES AND INTERVENTIONS

While we know that students with emotional and behavior disorders often have comorbid reading difficulties and have particular difficulties with higher-level literacy skills such as comprehension, only a limited number of studies have explored interventions specific to this population. So where can teachers of students with EBD find evidence-based reading practices and interventions for improving students' text comprehension skills? Intervention Central outlines reading comprehension interventions for students with a variety of disabilities; many of these interventions are based on the principles of direct instruction, which have shown to be highly effective for improving the academic performance of students with EBD. Another resource for locating evidence-based practices is the Florida Center for Reading Research (https://www.fcrr.org/). Reading center activities for Grades K–1, Grades 2–3, and Grades 4–5 can be downloaded free of charge from the website, and each activity includes a teacher resource guide. Finally, the National Council of Teachers of English's website (http://www.readwritethink.org/) offers lesson plans, interactive online graphic organizers for summarizing and analyzing text, and printable graphic organizers, grading rubrics, and information sheets explaining technology such as podcasts, Movie Maker, and PowerPoint.

Many of the strategies and interventions introduced in this chapter have focused on a single aspect of literacy instruction such as phonics or vocabulary. You may find that many of these interventions are effective for addressing multiple literacy components. For example, some phonemic awareness strategies such as blending and segmenting may improve students' spelling or phonics skills. Fluency interventions such as repeated reading may increase both students' oral reading fluency as well as their text comprehension.

## Read 180

Bruhn and Watt (2012) examined the effects of embedding a self-management strategy within a reading program called Read 180. Read 180 (Houghton Mifflin Harcourt, 2005) is designed for students in Grades 3 through 12 who read 2 or more years below grade level. Instruction is divided into three blocks: Block 1 is 20 minutes of whole-group instruction in reading, writing, and vocabulary; Block 2 consists of three 20-minute small-group rotations, including time with the teacher, computer software, and structured independent reading time; and Block 3 is 10 minutes of whole-group instruction.

## SELF

Daunic et al. (2013) explain that the executive functioning skills used for the self-regulation of emotions are the same as those used to comprehend oral and written language. The University of Florida Cognitive Behavioral group piloted a program with kindergarten and first-grade students at risk for EBD that integrated social-emotional learning foundations with literacy instruction. The SELF lessons cover five social-emotional components: self-awareness, self-management, social awareness, relationships, and decision making. Each topic is introduced through books read aloud by the teacher.

Then, students and teachers discuss four or five prompts related to the social-emotional objective. Last, students engage in a variety of activities to practice the skill, including role-play and vocabulary practice. More information about the SELF program can be found by visiting https://education.ufl.edu/cognitive-behavioral-research-group/self/

## Sonday System

The Sonday System is a commercially available, two-part system that includes reading, writing, and spelling practice. The Sonday System 1 focuses on prereading skills using a multisensory approach. Harris and colleagues (2009) implemented a three-part supplemental reading intervention using the Sonday System, the Great Leaps Reading Program for fluency, and a behavioral reinforcement system based on the **Student-Teacher Learning Game** with first-grade students exhibiting comorbid reading and behavioral difficulties. Groups met four times per week for 30 minutes and practiced skills such as letter-sound correspondence, phonics, and word reading through choral-response activities, songs, and games. The intervention resulted in moderate gains in oral reading fluency and nonsense word fluency.

## CHAPTER SUMMARY

Students with emotional and behavioral disorders frequently exhibit comorbid reading difficulties. It is crucial for students with EBD to improve their literacy skills so they can access and understand content-area subject matter. Provide explicit teacher-mediated interventions for each of the five components of reading as well as peer-mediated interventions such as Peer-Assisted Learning Strategies and self-mediated interventions such as self-graphing of fluency progress. Students should be given ample time each day to practice improving their phonemic awareness, phonics, fluency, vocabulary, and text comprehension skills.

## DISCUSSION QUESTIONS

1. Why is it important for students to develop both phonemic and phonological awareness?

2. What are the four phonemic awareness activities used in Stepping Stones to Literacy, and how do you think each activity helps foster strong phonemic awareness skills?

3. Peer-Assisted Learning Strategies (PALS) are mentioned throughout the chapter as an effective method for teaching literacy skills. What components of PALS make it a particularly effective reading intervention for students with EBD?

4. What methods can be used to help improve students' oral reading fluency? What are some online resources students can utilize to track their fluency progress?

## RESOURCES

http://www.bestevidence.org/reading/elem_read/elem_read.htm

http://www.bestevidence.org/reading/mhs/mhs_read.htm

http://www.bestevidence.org/reading/strug/strug_read_2011.htm

http://www.bestevidence.org/reading/strug/strug_read_2019.htm

https://www.ldatschool.ca/teaching-the-brain-to-read-strategies-for-enhancing-reading-decoding-fluency-and-comprehension/

https://nysrti.org/files/statewide_trainings/2012/new_york_rti_11-2-12_part_1_handouts.pdf

http://ebi.missouri.edu/?page_id=981

https://www.readingrockets.org/teaching

https://ies.ed.gov/ncee/wwc/Docs/PracticeGuide/adlit_pg_082608.pdf

https://ies.ed.gov/ncee/wwc/Docs/PracticeGuide/rti_reading_pg_021809.pdf

https://ceedar.education.ufl.edu/wp-content/uploads/2014/12/IC-12_FINAL_12-15-14.pdf

# REFERENCES

Adams, M. J., Bereiter, C., Carruthers, I., Case, R., Hirshberg, J., McKeough, A., . . . Treadway, G. H. (2000). *Open court reading*. SRA/McGraw-Hill.

Al Otaiba, S., & Rivera, M.O. (2006). Individualizing guided oral reading fluency instruction for students with emotional and behavioral disorders. *Intervention in School and Clinic, 41*(3), 144–149.

Archer, A. L., & Hughes, C. A. (2011). *Explicit instruction: Effective and efficient teaching.* Guilford.

Babyak, A. E., Koorland, M., & Mathes, P. G. (2000). The effects of story mapping instruction on the reading comprehension of students with behavioral disorders. *Behavioral Disorders, 25,* 239–258.

Barton-Arwood, S. M., Wehby, J. H., & Falk, K. B. (2005). Reading instruction for elementary-age students with emotional and behavioral disorders: Academic and behavioral outcomes. *Exceptional Children, 72,* 7–27.

Beck, I. L., McKeown, M. G., & Kucan, L. (2005). Choosing words to teach. In E. H. & M. L. Kamil (Eds.), *Teaching and learning vocabulary.* Lawrence Erlbaum.

Begeny, J. C., Laugle, K. M., Krouse, H. E., Lynn, A. E., Tayrose, M. P., & Stage, S. A. (2010). A control-group comparison of two reading fluency programs: The helping early literacy with practice strategies (HELPS) program and the great leaps K-2 reading program. *School Psychology Review, 39,* 137–155.

Benner, G. J., Nelson, J. R., Ralston, N. C., & Mooney, P. (2010). A meta-analysis of the effects of reading instruction on the reading skills of students with or at risk of behavioral disorders. *Behavioral Disorders, 35*(2), 86–102.

Blankenship, T. L., Ayres, K. M., & Langone, J. (2005). Effects of computer-based cognitive mapping on reading comprehension for students with emotional behavior disorders. *Journal of Special Education Technology, 20*(2), 15–23.

Bruhn, A., & Watt, S. (2012). Improving behavior by using multicomponent self-monitoring within a targeted reading intervention. *Behavioral Disorders, 38*(1), 3–17.

Burke, M. D., Boon, R. T., Hatton, H., & Bowman-Perrott, L. (2015). Reading interventions for middle and secondary students with emotional and behavioral disorders: A quantitative review of single-case studies. *Behavior Modification, 39,* 43–68. doi:10.1177/0145445514547958

Chard, D. J., Vaughn, S., & Tyler, B. (2002). A synthesis of research on effective interventions for building reading fluency with elementary students with learning disabilities. *Journal of Learning Disabilities, 35,* 386-406.

Cook, C. R., Dart, E., Collins, T., Restori, A., Daikos, C., & Delport, J. (2012). Preliminary study of the confined, collateral, and combined effects of reading and behavioral interventions: Evidence for a transactional relationship. *Behavioral Disorders, 38,* 38–56.

Daly, E. J., Garbacz, A., Olson, S. C., Persampieri, M., & Ni, H. (2006). Improving oral reading fluency by influencing students' choice of instructional procedures: An experimental analysis with two students with behavioral disorders. *Behavioral Interventions, 21,* 12–30. doi:10.1002/bin.208

Daly, E. J., & Martens, B. K. (1994). A comparison of three interventions for increasing oral reading performance application of the instructional hierarchy. *Journal of Applied Behavior Analysis, 27,* 459–469.

Daunic, A., Corbett, N., Smith, S., Barnes, T., Santiago-Poventud, L., Chalfant, P., Pitts, D., & Gleaton, J. (2013). Brief report: Integrating social-emotional learning with literacy instruction: An intervention for children at risk for emotional and behavioral disorders. *Behavioral Disorders, 39*(1), 43–51.

Englemann, S., Hanner, S., & Johnson, G. (1999). *Corrective reading series guide.* SRA/McGraw-Hill.

Falk, K. B., & Wehby, J. H. (2001). The effects of peer-assisted learning strategies on the beginning reading skills of young children with emotional or behavioral disorders. *Behavioral Disorders, 26,* 344–359.

Fuchs, D., Fuchs, L. S., & Burish, P. (2000). Peer-assisted learning strategies: An evidence-based practice to promote reading achievement. *Learning Disabilities Research and Practice, 15*(2), 85–91.

Fuchs, D., Fuchs, L. S. Thompson, A., Svenson, E., Yen, L., Al Otaiba, S., . . . Saenz, L. (2001). Peer-assisted learning strategies in reading: Extensions for kindergarten, first grade, and high school. *Remedial and Special Education, 22,* 15–21.

Garwood, J. D. (2017). Literacy interventions for secondary students formally identified with emotional and behavioral disorders: Trends and gaps in the research. *Journal of Behavioral Education, 27,* 23–52. doi:10.1007/s10864-017-9278-3

Garwood, J. D., Brunsting, N. C., & Fox, L. C. (2014). Improving reading comprehension and fluency outcomes for adolescents with emotional-behavioral disorders: Recent research synthesized. *Remedial and Special Education, 35,* 181–194. doi:10.177/074193251351-4856

Garwood, J. D., Ciullo, S., & Brunsting, N. (2017). Supporting students with emotional and behavioral disorders' comprehension and reading fluency. *Teaching Exceptional Children, 49,* 391–401. doi:10.1177/0040059917707434

Griffith, A. K., Trout, A. L., Hagaman, J. L., & Harper, J. (2008). Interventions to improve the literacy functioning of adolescents with emotional and/or behavior disorders: A review of the literature between 1965 and 2005. *Behavioral Disorders, 33,* 124–140.

Hale, A. D., Skinner, C. H., Winn, B. D., Oliver, R., Allin, J. D., & Mollowy, C. C. M. (2005). An investigation of listening and listening-while-reading accommodations on reading comprehension levels and rates in students with emotional disorders. *Psychology in Schools, 42,* 39–51. doi:10.1002/pits.20027

Harris, P. J., Oakes, W. P., Lane, K. L., & Rutherford, R. B. (2009). Improving the early literacy skills of students at risk for internalizing or externalizing behaviors with limited reading skills. *Behavioral Disorders, 34,* 72–90.

Hasbrouck, J. E., Ihnot, C., & Rogers, G. H. (1999). "Read Naturally": A strategy to increase oral reading fluency. *Reading Research and Instruction, 39,* 27–38. doi:10.1080/19388079909558310

Jalongo, M. R., & Sobolak, M. J. (2011). Supporting young children's vocabulary growth: The challenges, the benefits, and evidence-based strategies. *Early Childhood Education Journal, 38,* 421–429. doi:10.1007/s10643-010-0433-x

Kilpatrick, D. A. (2016). *Equipped for reading success: A comprehensive, step by step program for developing phonemic awareness and fluent word recognition.* Casey & Kirsch Publishers. Retrieved from https://www.cec.sped.org/~/media/Files/Professional%20Development/Webinars/Handouts/Excerpts%20from%20Equipped%20for%20Reading%20Success.pdf

Kostewicz, D. E., & Kubina, R. M. (2008). The national reading panel guidepost: A review of reading outcome measures for students with emotional and behavioral disorders. *Behavioral Disorders, 33,* 62–74.

Lane, K. L., Fletcher, T., Carter, E. W., Dejud, C., & DeLorenzo, J. (2007). Paraprofessional-led phonological awareness training with youngsters at risk for reading and behavioral concerns. *Remedial and Special Education, 28*, 266–276.

Lane, K. L., Little, A. M., Redding-Rhodes, J., Phillips, A., & Welsh, M. T. (2007). Outcomes of a teacher-led reading intervention for elementary students at risk for behavioral disorders. *Exceptional Children, 74*, 47–70.

Lane, K. L., O'Shaughnessy, T. E., Lambros, K. M., Gresham, F. M., & Beebe-Frankenberger, M. E. (2001). The efficacy of phonological awareness training with first-grade students who have behavior problems and reading difficulties. *Journal of Emotional and Behavioral Disorders, 9*, 219–231.

Lane, K. L., Wehby, J. H., Menzies, H. M., Gregg, R. M., & al, e. (2002). Early literacy instruction for first-grade students at-risk for antisocial behavior. *Education & Treatment of Children, 25*(4), 438.

Learning Point Associates. (2004). *A closer look at the five essential components of effective reading instruction: A review of scientifically based reading research for teachers.* Naperville, IL: Author. Retrieved from https://files.eric.ed.gov/fulltext/ED512569.pdf

Mason, L. H. (2004). Explicit self-regulated strategy development versus reciprocal questioning effects on expository reading comprehension among struggling readers. *Journal of Educational Psychology, 96*, 283–296.

Mastropieri, M. A., Emerick, K., & Scruggs, T. E. (1988). Mnemonic instruction of science concepts. *Behavioral Disorders, 14*, 48–56.

McCulloch, M. (1995). *Spelling and reading with Riggs: Daily/weekly lesson plans, study guide and syllabus.* The Riggs Institute Press.

McCulloch, M. (2000). *Writing and spelling road reading and thinking: A neurolinguistics approach to cognitive development and English literacy.* The Riggs Institute Press.

National Reading Panel & National Institute of Child Health and Human Development. (2000). *Report of the National Reading Panel: Teaching children to read: An evidence-based assessment of the scientific research literature on reading and its implications for reading instruction: reports of the subgroups.* National Institute of Child Health and Human Development, National Institutes of Health.

Nelson, J. R., Benner, G. J., & Gonzalez, J. (2005). An investigation of the effects of a prereading intervention on the early literacy skills of children at risk of emotional disturbance and reading problems. *Journal of Emotional and Behavioral Disorder, 13*, 3–12.

Oakes, W. P., Mathur, S. R., & Lane, K. L. (2010). Reading interventions for students with challenging behavior: A focus on fluency. *Behavioral Disorders, 35*, 120–139.

Rasinski, T. V., Reutzel, C. R., Chard, D., & Linan-Thompson, S. (2011). Reading fluency. In M. L. Kamil, P. D. Pearson, E. B. Moje, & P. Afflerback (Eds.), *Handbook of reading research* (Vol. 4, pp. 286–319). Routledge.

Reed, D. K., Miller, N., & Novosel, L. C. (2017). Vocabulary instruction to support the career readiness of juvenile offenders. *The Journal of Correctional Education, 68*, 32–51.

Roberts, G. J., Cho, E., Garwood, J. D., Goble, G. H., Robertson, T., & Hodges, A. (2019). Reading interventions for students with reading and behavioral difficulties: A meta-analysis and evaluation of co-occurring difficulties. *Educational Psychology Review.* Advance online publication. doi:10.1007/210648-017-09485-1

Rogevich, M. E., & Perin, D. (2008). Effects on science summarization of a reading comprehension intervention for adolescents with behavior and attention disorders. *Exceptional Children, 74*, 135–154.

Samuels, S. J. (1979). The method of repeated readings. *Reading Teacher, 32,* 376–381.

Shefelbine, J. L., & Newman, K. K. (2001). *SIPPS: Systematic instruction in phoneme awareness, phonics, and sight words.* Developmental Studies Center.

Sonday, A. (1997). *Sonday System learning to read: Beginning and intervention.* Windsor Learning.

Staubitz, J. E., Cartledge, G., Yrick, A. L., & Lo, Y.-Y. (2005). Repeated reading for students with emotional or behavioral disorders: Peer- and trainer-mediated instruction. *Behavioral Disorders, 31,* 51–64.

Stone, R. H., Boon, R. T., Fore, C., Bender, W. N., & Spencer, V. G. (2008). Use of text maps to improve the reading comprehension skills among students in high school with emotional and behavioral disorders. *Behavioral Disorders, 33,* 87–98.

Sutherland, K. S., & Snyder, A. (2007). Effects of reciprocal tutoring and self-graphing on reading fluency and classroom behavior of middle school students with emotional or behavioral disorders. *Journal of Emotional and Behavioral Disorders, 15,* 103–118.

Torgesen, J. K., & Bryant, B.R. (1994). *Phonological awareness training for reading.* Pro-Ed.

Vannest, K. J., Temple-Harvey, K. K., & Mason, B. A. (2009). Adequate yearly progress for students with emotional and behavioral disorders through research-based practices. *Preventing School Failure, 53,* 73–83.

Warnick, K., & Caldarella, P. (2016). Using multisensory phonics to foster reading skills of adolescent delinquents. *Reading & Writing Quarterly, 32,* 317–335. doi:10 .1080/10873569.2014.962199

Wehby, J. H., Falk, K. B., Barton-Atwood, S., Lane, K. L., & Cooley, C. (2003). The impact of comprehensive reading instruction on the academic and social behavior of students with emotional and behavioral disorders. *Journal of Emotional and Behavioral Disorders, 11,* 225–238.

Wehby, J. H., Lane, K. L., & Falk, K. B. (2005). An inclusive approach to improving literacy skills of students with emotional and behavioral disorders. *Behavioral Disorders, 30,* 155–169.

Wills, H., Kamps, D., Abbott, M., Bannister, H, Kaufman, J., & Juniper Garden's Children's Project, University of Kansas (2010). Classroom observations and effects of reading interventions for students at risk for emotional and behavioral disorders. *Behavioral Disorders, 35,* 103–119.

## APPENDIX 6–1

# Progression of Phonemic Awareness Tasks in Order from Easiest to Most Difficult

| | | | | |
|---|---|---|---|---|
| **First-sound comparison** ⬇ | | | | |
| **Blending onset-rime (real words)** ⬇ | | | | **c + at = cat** |
| **Blending phonemes (real words)** ⬇ | **/p/ + /i/ + /n/ = pin** | | | |
| **Deleting phonemes** ⬇ | | **–** | | **clap – /l/ = cap** |
| **Segmenting words into phonemes** ⬇ | **/f/ × /r/ × /0/ × /g/** | | | |
| **Blending phonemes (fake words)** | **/f/ + /e/ + /m/ = fem** | | | |

**APPENDIX 6–2**

# A Story Map for Use with a Narrative Text

| | | |
|---|---|---|
| | Characters | |
| | Setting | |
| | Problem | |
| | Solution | |
| | Events | |

## APPENDIX 6–3

# A Checklist for Students to Use When Implementing the TWA-WS Strategy

| TWA Checklist | | |
| --- | --- | --- |
| **When** | **What** | **Complete?** |
| Before reading | is the author's purpose? | |
| Before reading | do I already know? | |
| Before reading | do I want to find out? | |
| While reading | is my reading speed? | |
| While reading | information can I connect to what I'm reading? | |
| While reading | do I need to read again? | |
| After reading | is the main idea? | |
| After reading | is a good summary for what I've read? | |
| After reading | did I learn from what I read? | |

# 7

# Study Skills

## KEY VOCABULARY

Conditional Knowledge
Direct Instruction
Declarative Knowledge
Explicit Instruction
Procedural Knowledge
SAFMEDS
Strategy Instruction

## LEARNING OBJECTIVES

By the end of this chapter, you should be able to . . .

- Identify the importance of explicit instruction.
- Create SMART goals for the continuum of supports in special education.
- Identify study skills strategies to learn new material.
- Teach and utilize study skills strategies.
- Identify ways to determine if a practice is evidence based.

## INTRODUCTION

This chapter will discuss different aspects of study skills for students in the classroom. Explicit instruction is the cornerstone of engaging, effective, and efficient teaching and can be implemented across the school day when teaching behavioral expectations, academics, and strategies. Managing a classroom is difficult, and providing students explicit instruction in all areas alleviates the struggles that many new teachers have in the classroom management realm because they are essentially telling students what is expected of them. Study skills are reviewed in relation to organizational skills for academics. Finally, evidence-based practices will be discussed, along with the importance of using evidence to identify practices in schools.

The first thing that a teacher needs to do every school year is provide a structure for students to maximize learning opportunities in their classroom. Most students grasp this structure quickly by learning the daily routines, typically requiring little instruction. Many teachers assume that students know how to act in every situation they encounter during the school day and are surprised when students struggle with classroom and school routines.

## EXPLICIT INSTRUCTION

Students with EBD and other disabilities often struggle and do not infer classroom routines without **explicit instruction**, which is "instruction that is systematic, direct, engaging, and success oriented" (Archer & Hughes, 2011, p. vii). Explicit instruction is beneficial for all students, especially those with learning and behavioral challenges, and can be used to teach behavioral expectations and academic content, along with strategies to support learning the content, study skills, and strategies that support both academics and behavior. Explicit instruction provides a scaffolded structure, where students receive multiple levels of supports based on their needs, and then the supports are faded as they meet mastery with the skills they are learning (Archer & Hughes, 2011). Explicit instruction should be utilized when teaching students skills and strategies for learning academic and behavioral skills for success in the classroom and beyond.

Teaching students systematically, breaking activities into small steps or chunks, is best practice in education, specifically in special education with students with disabilities. This makes learning new skills, strategies, or content accessible to students who may need to learn this way in order to retain and apply these skills and strategies in the future. Archer and Hughes (2011) developed explicit instruction techniques which included 16 elements that were then categorized into six principles of effective teaching:

- Time on task
- Success
- Content
- Instructional grouping
- Scaffolded instruction
- Knowledge

Additional information is provided with detailed explanations of each teaching function along with examples and suggestions to use for providing academic and behavior instruction and study skills support for students with EBD in the next section.

## Time on Task

Time that students spend on task is incredibly important, and there are two important elements to how time is spent—teaching and learning. The important thing to remember with time on task is that both quantity and quality of teaching are equally important, and there must be a balance of quantity and quality to ensure that students learn (Archer & Hughes, 2011). Students must be engaged for a reasonable amount of time—a specific percentage of the school day—in meaningful, engaging instruction, and learning must be balanced with other activities (both instruction and noninstructional) as well as a social-emotional component of instruction for students with EBD. The amount of time students are engaged in meaningful instruction is important, specifically when students are listening, taking notes, problem solving, or working with peers. Students should be engaged in the academic learning time where elements of explicit instruction are utilized to appropriately differentiate for them, tasks that are designed for them to learn effectively, and their social/emotional needs are also met (Archer & Hughes, 2011).

## Success

Students should meet a degree of success when they are learning. Engagement in a task is important, but celebrating successes is often forgotten and can be frustrating for students who need feedback about successes to stay motivated and engaged in the task and academics as a whole, especially students with EBD, as they benefit from the positive feedback and positive interaction with peers and adults. Task engagement becomes counterproductive when students are making errors and receiving negative feedback (e.g., wrong answer), and they often spend time practicing errors that are not corrected (Archer & Hughes, 2011). Errors should be corrected as soon as students make them, which does not allow them to practice something an incorrect way (i.e., inappropriate grouping in addition with regrouping). Delayed feedback, or no feedback, delays error correction and promotes the possibility of error practice, which is detrimental to learning. As Scheeler and Lee (2002) noted, "Precise, immediate, frequent feedback increases efficacy and efficiency . . . if feedback is delayed, it allows learners to practice errors, especially in the acquisition phase of learning and when learners are allowed to repeat errors" (p. 232). Receiving feedback can lead to higher success rates for students with EBD who receive little to no feedback in the academic setting, because feedback is sometimes focused on behavior, and academics are often secondary to ensuring that students are displaying appropriate behavior. Teachers can increase the feedback provided for student success by teaching easier skills first and by providing specific praise and feedback heavily, especially for already mastered skills, working through more difficult skills with students to ensure that they are learning and practicing them appropriately, and then carefully monitoring students when they are independently practicing skills or strategies (Archer & Hughes, 2011).

## Content

The more effectively a teacher presents content, the more a student will retain and apply (Archer & Hughes, 2011). If teachers spend time planning quality content delivery, students benefit from this, and then are able to learn and apply content while receiving more individualized time on skills that may need additional support. A more global approach to instruction, such as teaching students strategies for decoding rather than spending time on decoding a specific word, provides students with a skill set to utilize in more than one academic situation, and they can apply it toward a variety of words (Archer & Hughes, 2011). This is especially applicable with study skills, as they can be applied toward a number of academic areas, where a broad strategy, such as creating note cards, can be used for spelling words and for studying vocabulary. Keeping the focus broad covers more than one area, and ensuring it is applicable across a spectrum helps to set the student up for success.

## Instructional Grouping

Teacher instruction is directly linked to student achievement, meaning that the more time students spend learning from the teacher, the more they learn, and the higher they achieve (Archer & Hughes 2011). Basic skills are typically taught during group instruction, where the educator is able to teach skills and strategies explicitly, using best practices (e.g., modeling, opportunities to respond, feedback), and is most effective if delivered in a small group (Archer & Hughes, 2011). Students are typically broken into smaller groups in classrooms to allow for targeted instruction, which allows for **direct instruction** time, skill practice, and targeted remediation, if needed. This is especially helpful when student groups are created specifically to address skill deficits for students with similar learning needs and abilities, so teachers can address skill deficits explicitly and directly. Homogeneous grouping should be flexible and will change over time based on skills addressed in teaching (Archer & Hughes, 2011).

## Scaffolding

Like the scaffold used in building, scaffolding is a strategy used in education in a similar way. Scaffolding starts with a highly supportive structure—teaching a skill or strategy explicitly, then slowly fading those supports until a student demonstrates mastery with the skill or strategy (Archer & Hughes, 2011). Scaffolding instruction builds on basic skills (e.g., learning letters and sounds) and leads to higher-level skills (e.g., word blends, complex words). Scaffolding can be used to address memory, attention, and learning difficulties, where a teacher provides graduated guidance, providing more support at first and then decreasing the amount of support depending on the student need and ability. As the teacher decreases the support, the student becomes more independent in skill acquisition and application, until they can perform the skill independently (Archer & Hughes, 2011). Figure 7–1 provides an example of a scaffolded lesson. Scaffolding uses explicit instruction in the following ways:

- Break down (i.e., chunk) skills into smaller, more manageable units.
- Teach skills in sequence to build upon previous knowledge.
- Move from easier to more difficult tasks.
- Provide multiple examples and opportunities to practice at all stages of learning.
- Provide multiple hints and prompts for skill practice.
- Provide visual tools (e.g., cards, checklists) to support student learning for multistep processes and problem solving (Archer & Hughes, 2011).

## Knowledge

Students need to acquire and understand at several levels of knowledge to learn, recall, and use information. Ellis and Worthington (1994) describe the levels as declarative, procedural, and conditional. **Declarative knowledge** is at the fact level—naming or identifying things—identifying *what* something is; **procedural knowledge** is at the application level and involves knowing *how* to do something; and **conditional knowledge** is knowing under what provisions—*when* or *when not*—to use a skill or strategy (Ellis & Worthington, 1994).

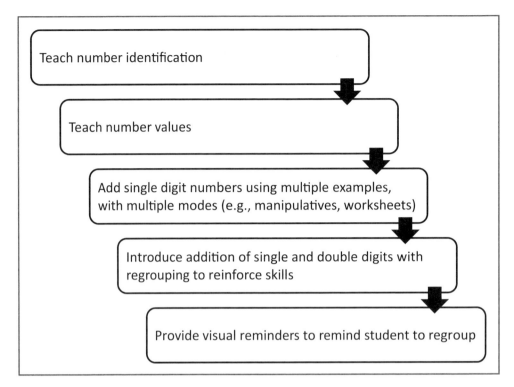

**Figure 7–1.** *Scaffolded example for math.*

Archer and Hughes (2011) recommend both teaching about something and encouraging application at all three knowledge levels (Ellis & Worthington, 1994) to ensure that students learn independently. Instruction is especially useful if applied in the following format: I do, we do, you do (Archer & Hughes, 2011), also called Model-Test-Lead, where students learn the skill through direct instruction, apply the skill side-by-side with the teacher and classmates, and then practice the skill independently observed by the teacher.

## TEACHING AND LEARNING ROUTINES

**Explicit instruction** (Archer & Hughes, 2011) in academics is effective and efficient, where the ultimate goal is student mastery. Explicit instruction is also helpful for students to learn routines in the classroom, starting with behavioral expectations. Students need to know what teachers expect of them and how they expect them to do it. However, teachers should not assume students know what teachers expect from them if they do not provide explicit instruction with classroom routines and behavioral expectations (Myers et al., 2017). Students should be explicitly taught *how* they are expected to do all things at all points in their school day, including:

- Morning routines, including lockers, cubbies, or how to check in
- Transitioning from one activity, academic subject, or class to another
- Turning in assignments and homework
- Who to talk to when they need help in the classroom or outside of it
- Volume levels during different types of work (e.g., CHAMPS)
- Restroom requests or how to get a pass to the restroom (Myers et al., 2017)

Teachers who set up the expectations in their classroom at the beginning by using explicit instruction to teach *what* they expect and *how* students should behave in each situation they encounter will have students who are capable learners that navigate academic and behavioral situations appropriately. Students with EBD benefit from explicit behavioral expectation instruction, because they are often left to guess what the teacher would like for them to do in a given situation. Students will encounter different expectations in the same school with different teachers and should not be expected to infer what a teacher means when they provide a student with directions without providing them with explicit instruction on how to follow those directions. Similar to an academic area, where teachers use a lesson plan, teachers should use behavioral expectation lesson plans (Myers et al., 2017; Simonsen et al., 2012) to deliver instruction with the *I do, We do, You do* format (Archer & Hughes, 2011) discussed in the explicit instruction section of the chapter. As with academics, students may require remediation, and this should be assessed across environments to address any skill deficit areas that students may display. Additionally, Simonsen et al. (2012) recommend implementing a behavior (i.e., social skills) matrix to teach schoolwide behavior supports for students.

According to Simonsen et al. (2012, p. 260), the matrix should meet specific criteria:

- Be developed collaboratively by all team members
- Be given to all faculty and staff members for feedback
- Incorporate existing schoolwide behavioral expectations
- Identify the most important settings in a school
- Use developmentally, culturally, and contextually relevant language and examples

Behavioral and social skills fluency leads to success in school settings where students are able to navigate the moment-to-moment encounters with adults and peers. Table 7–1 provides an example of a behavior matrix with examples and nonexamples to utilize when an educator explains to students what to do and what not to do during the school day.

**Table 7–1.** Example of a Classroom Behavior Expectation Matrix with Examples and Nonexamples

| Expectation | Morning Routine | Transitions | Independent Work |
|---|---|---|---|
| Respect | Come into class quietly and get your morning folder.<br><br>Example: Student walks into class using quiet feet, picks up his morning folder from the bin, and starts working quietly.<br><br>Nonexample: Student stomps loudly into the classroom, grabs his morning folder, throws it on his desk, and yells everyone's name as he walks around his desk. | During transitions between classes, quietly gather necessary materials and line up at the door.<br><br>Example: Student picks up appropriate folder for the next class and places current class folder in desk and then lines up at the door.<br><br>Nonexample: Student throws folders, yells, and refuses to line up at the door. | Work quietly and raise your hand if you have a question.<br><br>Example: Student works diligently to write spelling words and raises hand when they do not know a word.<br><br>Nonexample: Student sits and talks to other students around them, while yelling that they need help on a word. |
| Responsible | Place your belongings in your cubby.<br><br>Example: Student places all belongings in the correct cubby and in the appropriate way.<br><br>Nonexample: Student's belongings are thrown near the cubby. | Bring necessary items (e.g., folder and pencil) to the next class with you.<br><br>Example: Student brings a folder and pencil to the next class.<br><br>Nonexample: Student brings nothing to the next class. | Store all items in their appropriate place.<br><br>Example: Student stores pencils in their pencil pouch and easily retrieves them when needed.<br><br>Nonexample: Student's belongings are strewn about, and they cannot find a pencil when needed. |

**Table 7–1.** *continued*

| Expectation | Morning Routine | Transitions | Independent Work |
|---|---|---|---|
| Safe | Keep hands and feet to self in the cubby area.<br><br>Example: Student places belongings in cubby and stays in area while doing so.<br><br>Nonexample: Student runs around, pushes other students, and drops items in the cubby area in the process. | Walk quietly in a line and follow the hallway arrows.<br><br>Example: Students walk using quiet feet in the hallway and follow arrows.<br><br>Nonexample: Students walk next to each other in the hallway on the incorrect side. | Stay in your area and keep items in your desk unless you are using them.<br><br>Example: Student stays in area and retrieves items from desk when needed.<br><br>Nonexample: Student is out of seat, is walking around classroom, and has trouble locating items as they are not in the correct location. |

## Setting Goals

Explicit instruction can be applied in several different areas, including goal setting for students. One type of goal setting teachers can use is the SMART (Lazarus, 2004) acronym for routines and goal setting, and this should be utilized in the continuum of writing Individualized Education Program goals, as well as creating lesson plans, to the formulate daily academic and behavioral goals for students (Hedin & DeSpain, 2018; Jung, 2007). The SMART acronym stands for:

- Specific
- Measurable
- Attainable or Action verbs
- Results oriented or Routines based
- Time bound or Tied to a functional priority

Much like writing IEP goals, goals for behavior should meet the criteria spelled out above. Figure 7–2 provides an outline for writing SMART goals.

Written goals should be able to be met by students, as opposed to lofty goals where students will not make progress. This is especially important

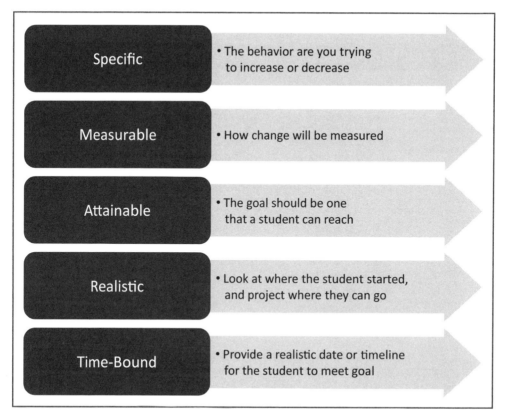

**Figure 7–2.** *Tips for writing SMART goals.*

given the recent U.S. Supreme Court decision on minimum progress and the need for IEP goals to be both measurable and achievable (U.S. Department of Education [USDOE], 2017). Based on the *Endrew F. v. Douglas County* decision, the Supreme Court ruled that merely meeting more than the minimum (i.e., *de minimus*) does not satisfy the standard of progress and that schools must do more than provide students an education to make minimum progress; they should strive for more than the minimum (USDOE, 2017).

As teachers, it is our job to ensure that students succeed, and this is even more important for special education teachers, especially teachers of students with EBD. Students should be given the appropriate instruction needed to ensure that they progress in a way that they are able, but they must also be sufficiently challenged, and teachers should not be satisfied with minimal progress. Students need to be given ample instruction, whether that is academic instruction or behavioral skills instruction, and the teachers need to ensure that it is appropriate and meaningful and that they make sufficient progress.

# TEACHING STUDENTS HOW TO STUDY

Students with EBD and other disabilities often have difficulty with test-taking skills, and this may be due in part to a lack of instruction provided to students in study skills, specifically in independent study skills (Minskoff & Allsopp, 2003). Students with disabilities are sometimes dependent on their special education teacher because of the level of support they provide in the resource room setting, and that dependence does not create efficient learners with study skills that translate beyond the special education setting. In the home setting, this translates to students' parents, who assist them in the learning and study process, as well as provide a high level of assistance that does not lead to independence. Learning effective independent study skills and strategies will foster the ability to study and successfully take tests, which benefits them through their K–12 schooling and through postsecondary training.

Students with disabilities are typically *passive learners*, as a lot of their programming is prescribed, and they spend the majority of their school day learning through passive means (e.g.., direct instruction, whole-group and small-group instruction). They are not taught to create a plan for studying, engage in breaking down units of study independently or specific study skills (e.g., create notecards—SAFMEDS—or outlines), or take data on their studying to see if they are making progress in their knowledge and application (Minskoff & Allsopp, 2003). Rather, they engage in readings and activities that may or may not encourage comprehension, and they often use little to no study skills or strategies learned along the way; the goals are simply survival and work completion.

It's important for students to learn strategies for studying with different organizational aspects. When students are studying from books, they should look at context clues within the book to determine what information is important. Students should use whatever strategy works for them, and they need study strategy instruction to learn what that means.

Minskoff and Allsopp (2003) categorized study skills into three interrelated subsets: attention, cognitive processes, and memory; the areas of the three subsets of study skills are broken down below.

- Attention
  - Coming to attention
  - Sustaining attention
  - Overcoming distraction (Minskoff & Allsopp, 2003, p. 129)
- Cognitive processes
  - Studying from notes
  - Studying from books
  - Organizing information (Minskoff & Allsopp, 2003, p. 129)

- Memorization
    - ○ Meaningful memorization—memorizing information (Minskoff & Allsopp, 2003, p. 129)

Students need to utilize each subset area of study skills to develop efficient and effective independent study skills. Therefore, they need cohesive instruction in each study skill subset. Minskoff and Allsopp (2003) use several acronyms to teach students how to study. The first one, CHECK, helps to get the study process started:

- **C**hange environments
  This helps students identify a distraction-free environment where they can effectively study—this is up to the individual. For example, they can choose whether it has noise or is quiet, alone or with others, or well-lit or dim lights.

- **H**ave all equipment nearby
  This helps students identify what they need to prepare for a study session, so they aren't leaving the study area to retrieve items or supplies.

- **E**stablish rewards for yourself
  This helps students see that accomplishments should be rewarded, and it is important to reward yourself for achieving goals.

- **C**reate a checklist of tasks to be done
  This helps students keep track of tasks they already completed, as well as those that still need to be completed, and minimizes off-task behavior.

- **K**eep a worry pad
  This allows students to write down anything they are struggling with during studying, and rather than perseverating on these things and getting distracted from studying, they can write them down, move on with studying, and revisit them at a later time (Minskoff & Allsopp, 2003).

Getting started and creating a study plan are important steps in setting up study skills, but students also need focusing skills that keep them from distractions when studying. Minskoff and Allsopp (2003) suggest utilizing a timer, making yourself aware of what you're doing in the moment, taking a second to organize thoughts, and pressing on once thoughts are organized. They recommend utilizing the CHECK acronym to start the process and utilizing a system to avoid distraction involving the environment, reducing distractions, eliminating noise, and using self-talk to remove any distractions that are internal (Minskoff & Allsopp, 2003).

## Notecards

Many students find the process of creating and utilizing notecards in their studying to be an effective method for learning, reviewing, and retaining information. Students should use organizational strategies during this process. First, students should be taught to look at the headings and subheadings in the chapter to create a structure to group the main ideas. Second, they should organize and number the notecards according to their chapter or content. For example, Notecard 1–3 would indicate that it was from Chapter 1 and the third card completed. Third, create a storage system for the notecards. For example, they can be bundled together using rubber bands; students can use binder rings to store notecards so they can be accessed easily and then studied in the classified grouping. Finally, students should graph their progress using notecards as they master the vocabulary and concepts they are studying, and they should continue to revisit the notecards, so they retain the information. These strategies can be applied for creating and maintaining notecards related to outlining information from books, readings assigned in class, or notes taken during class.

One notecard strategy students can use to build fluency is **SAFMEDS**, which stands for Say-All-Fast-Minute-Every-Day-Shuffled. SAFMEDS is a concept introduced by Ogden Lindsley in the 1970s and is frequently used by students researching Applied Behavior Analysis. Students use SAFMEDS to do timed mastery trials daily (e.g., Lindsley, 1992). First, they write the vocabulary word or concept on the front of the card and the definition on the back of the card. Second, they set a time for 1 minute. Third, they practice by looking at the definition and stating the vocabulary word, then flipping the card to see if they were correct or incorrect. Corrects are placed in one pile, and incorrects are placed in a separate pile. If a student isn't sure of the answer, they can pass and place that card in the incorrects pile. When the timer goes off at the end of 1 minute, students count the total correct cards and graph it. Students should also graph incorrect answers. Once students have reached their goal, 100% mastery of all terms, they can move on to the next set of SAFMEDS. Students continue to do this during courses and will likely see improvement in term recognition and recall in a short period of time. Figure 7–3 shows an example of how to create SAFMEDS for successful studying.

## Note-Taking

Taking notes is an ongoing skill that students will utilize throughout their education, from elementary school to college. It is also a skill that takes practice and, like notecards, requires organization and time. Students must be able to pick out the important content, record it live, and recall why it was important when they revisit notes to highlight important items or create

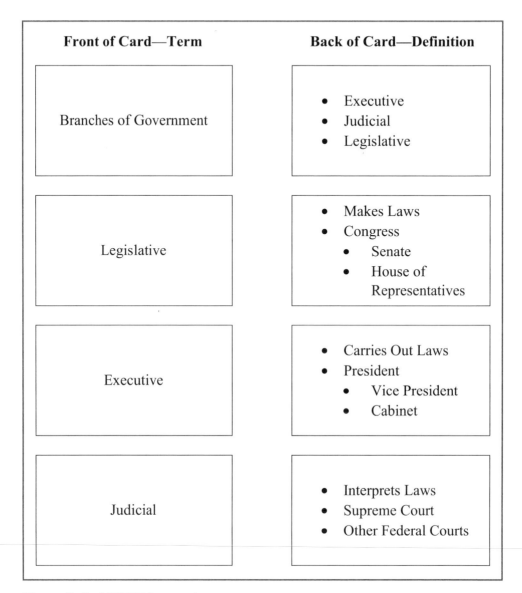

***Figure 7–3.*** *SAFMEDS example.*

notecards. Note-taking for students with disabilities may be a difficult skill to master, so accommodations are made to create more efficient and effective ways to take notes. For example, students may take notes using graphic organizers with headings to provide structure for students to record important items. Figure 7–4 has an example of a graphic organizer with headings for a social studies class. Students can also have access to a computer to take notes, receive guided notes with blanks to fill in, or receive structured notes with headers.

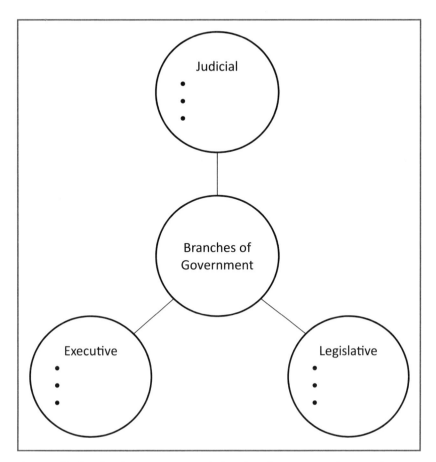

**Figure 7–4.** *Graphic organizer with headers for structured note-taking.*

## Study Groups

Students may benefit from study groups with peers. Study groups provide additional opportunities for practice with the test materials, as well as conversation about the content. Students may find this to be beneficial for them, because talking about the content helps them to become more fluent with the material they are learning and may help them to learn the content faster. They may also come up with different ways to learn concepts while discussing them and working with other students, as well as fill in any gaps in knowledge by processing information with other students verbally and in writing. Study groups promote a more proactive approach to studying, where students meet at a scheduled time, often more than once, to study together. Students also learn effective study methods from each other and utilize their social and interpersonal skills when studying in a group, which helps them succeed in more than just the educational setting.

Once students have gone through the process of creating notecards and utilizing study aids that work for them, they can set up a study schedule, where they plan out when, how, and where they plan to study. Students can create a plan but change it as they go, which allows for them to change the schedule if they need more or less time to master a concept. Figure 7–5 is an example of a study schedule, with a timeline and plan for students to complete before and during their studying for small and large tasks or units.

There are several online platforms to aid in studying that students use more often and can use to accommodate disabilities and support organizational needs. Bringing studying into the digital age may also make it more accessible to individuals with disabilities. The digital applications are available in several forms and can be accessed across platforms and on mobile devices. This makes studying more available and accessible to everyone, and it may provide different ways to access the information, including those that provide auditory prompting, where the application will read the material. Table 7–2 provides additional detail on several online platforms available online to organize, share, and use study materials posted by others.

| Test Name | Due By | Activities | | |
|---|---|---|---|---|
| *Social Studies* | *January 19th* | *Make notecards by 1/3* | *Complete guided notes by 1/10* | *Complete Quizlet by 1/15* |
| | | | | |
| | | | | |
| | | | | |
| | | | | |
| | | | | |
| | | | | |
| | | | | |

**Figure 7–5.** *Studying schedule with deadlines.*

## Strategy Instruction

Teachers need to possess basic knowledge about student learning, so they are able to facilitate the learning process effectively and efficiently, which is more than just teaching the content (Reid et al., 2013). Before attempting to teach **strategy instruction**, students should learn that having a disability means that they need to learn and apply information in a way that works for them

**Table 7–2.** Examples Online Platforms for Studying and Organization

| Name | Website | Contents |
|------|---------|----------|
| Evernote | https://evernote.com/ | Take notes, share projects, create lists. |
| Hippocampus | https://www.hippocampus.org/ | Videos on different subjects to help students study. |
| Khan Academy | https://www.khanacademy.org/ | Videos on different subject areas for studying and learning concepts. |
| Quizlet | https://quizlet.com/ | Online flash cards, practice tests, share content. |
| Schooltraq | http://schooltraq.com/p/home/ | Digital academic planner to help organization homework, assignments, and tests. |
| StudyBlue | https://www.studyblue.com/ | Study, locate materials for specific courses by content and location. |
| Study Guides and Strategies | http://www.studygs.net/ | Provides study guides for all content areas, grade levels, and concepts. |
| StudyStack | https://www.studystack.com/ | Make, share, or download online flashcards. |
| Tinycards | https://tinycards.duolingo.com/ | Flashcards on different subjects to learn concepts. |

and become comfortable with advocating for themselves. It is the teacher's job to ensure that the disability is not a hurdle but a part of them and their learning process. Students with EBD may display frustration or seem to lack motivation and may need additional supports to incentivize and facilitate the learning process, such as token economies or group contingencies. Teachers must possess proactive classroom management skills to engage students in learning and provide explicit (Archer & Hughes, 2011) strategy instruction so that students can apply what they learn.

Strategies are used by individuals in everyday life and are often things we don't think twice about. In short, a strategy is "a series of ordered steps that helps a student perform a task" (Reid et al., 2013). For example, to remember an appointment, someone might write it down in a planner or add it to the electronic calendar on a smartphone, which serves as a prompt or reminder to go to the appointment when the time comes. Other strategies, such as ones for remembering how to spell the word Mississippi, the alphabet song, and using a mnemonic device to remember a mathematical process, like using PEMDAS for order of operation, which signifies that the learner should complete mathematical processes in the following order—parentheses, exponents, multiplication, division, addition, and then subtraction—to solve a problem given those parameters, are also helpful. Figure 7–6 provides sample math strategies for math using mnemonic devices. By using explicit instruction to teach strategies and processes, it takes the guessing away and give students specific ways to solve problems, read, or behave in specific situations. Strategy instruction focuses on equipping students with the tools they need for whatever they may encounter along the way. It works because it uses memory and cognition to learn and then retrieve the strategy when needed (Reid et al., 2013). Strategy instruction is directly related to study skills in that teachers provide the strategies when teaching study skills (e.g., notecards, online applications) and students go forward and apply those strategies to studying to ensure that they are successful.

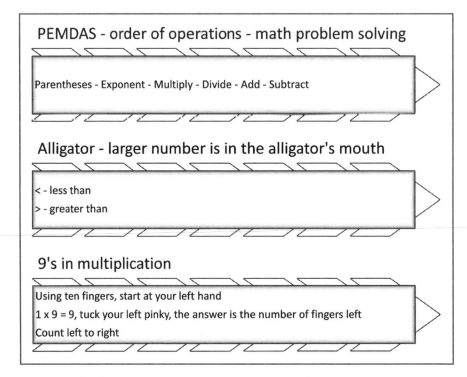

**Figure 7–6.** *Examples of mnemonic devices for mathematics.*

## EVIDENCE-BASED PRACTICES

Standards proposed for Evidence-Based Practice (EBP) vary somewhat across disciplines and research methods. For experimental research using single subject designs (e.g., Cook et al., 2008; Horner et al., 2005), as single subject (or single case) is utilized frequently in special education research. Standards for single-case design include:

- An experimental design study has the goal of showing a causal relationship between the independent (i.e., experimental) and dependent variables.
- The participants, typically three to eight per study, serve as their own control.
- All aspects of the study are operationally defined.
- Dependent variables are measured repeatedly, assessed for social validity, and constantly assessed for change.
- Independent variables under investigation are actively manipulated and evaluated for fidelity.
- Baseline condition exists as the comparison condition, where the dependent variable is measured.

Standards for determining an intervention is an EBP using a single-case design involves conducting a review of peer-reviewed research in scientific journals in specific practice areas. The National Professional Development Center on Autism Spectrum Disorder (NPDC) determines if an intervention was effective through a review of peer-reviewed research in scientific journals based on the specific criteria:

- two high-quality experimental (randomized) or quasi-experimental group design studies conducted by at least two different researchers or groups of researchers, or
- five high-quality single-subject design studies conducted by three different researchers or groups of researchers with at least 20 a total of participants total across those studies, or
- one high-quality randomized (experimental) or quasi-experimental group design study *combined with* at least three high-quality single-subject design studies conducted by at least three different researchers or groups of researchers, between the group and single-subject design studies (NPDC, n.d.).

## Learning Styles—A Myth

Educators across the nation have heard the old adage about learning styles, and many of them talk about the type of learner they are when in a classroom. What may come as a surprise to these individuals is that learning styles are a myth. Simply put, learning styles are not real, there is no evidence to support them, and teachers need to focus on the science of teaching and learning, so that they can effectively teach children. The issue with perpetuating the learning style myth is that there is no science to back it up, yet many schools are utilizing *learning style assessments* and teaching particular learning styles, and their use in public school continues (Travers, 2017). Travers (2017) noted common reasons for teachers' continued use of pseudoscience, or unproven theories and concepts, in schools, including stereotyping students with disabilities as unable to express their wants and needs, stating that they lack motivation, or claiming positive reinforcement is bribery. The following sections contain two case studies that address topics covered in this chapter.

## CASE STUDY—ELEMENTARY

*Mrs. Scott is a fourth-grade special education emotional support teacher who works directly with the fourth-grade general education teacher. They co-plan and co-teach and Mrs. Scott supports her students and other students in the classroom when the other teacher teaches and then vice versa. While they were planning a social studies lesson, Mrs. Scott noticed that the general education teacher had a learning style preference assessment in the lesson plan, students would separate into groups by learning style to talk about strategies to use with their learning style, and that students would spend the class period discussing their learning style in those groups. This concerned Mrs. Scott, since she earned her Master of Special Education degree at a nearby university, and they emphasized evidence-based practices. She knows that learning styles is a myth, that it isn't evidence based, and that she needs to step in and prevent this lesson from happening but is concerned about stepping on the general education teacher's toes and that he may still do the lesson anyway.*

*During their meeting, Mrs. Scott reviewed the lesson plan with the general education teacher and shared her concerns. She came prepared to the meeting with a few different articles, as well as some links to blog posts debunking the learning styles myth, and she planned to stand her ground so that the students didn't buy into learning styles as a solution for why they struggled with academics and use it as a crutch or excuse, like so many of her students in the past did. She calmly explained the issue with the general education teacher and shared her resources with him. He listened to her, asked her some questions, and agreed not to do the lesson. The teachers came up with a more appropriate lesson about using PEMDAS as a mnemonic device and creating different ways to remember and use it in practice, where they would be creating songs, poems, and plays about the concept. Mrs. Scott was pleased that it went so well.*

**CASE STUDY—SECONDARY**

*Mr. Bender is a high school social studies teacher who minored in special education, and his class rosters typically comprise around half of the students having Individualized Education Programs (IEPs). While his teacher prep program did prepare him to teach students with disabilities, his students don't come to him prepared for learning, let alone taking tests and quizzes. They don't seem to study, and he knows that they need to learn the material to pass the end-of-course assessment so they can graduate from high school.*

*Mr. Bender thinks back to his teacher prep program, where he learned about explicit instruction and study skills. He knows that the students need to learn exactly how to study for tests, so he reviews some literature and devises a plan. He starts with notecards and has the students develop notecards in class for each chapter with the vocabulary words and important concepts. He also recalls his Introduction to Behavior Analysis class where the professor required them to use notecards called SAFMEDS, and students graphed their incorrect and correct answers daily. He introduces the students to SAFMEDS, has them create their first set based on the vocabulary and content in the current chapter, and provides them with graphs where they can easily graph their incorrect and correct answers daily. The students grumble a bit, but once he lets them know that this is a weekly grade and will be an easy way to earn points, they quickly change their tune and class ends.*

*Mr. Bender saw dramatic improvement in student scores from the pretest to the posttest on the next weekly unit quiz. He also had nearly 100% participation in SAFMEDS for the remainder of the semester, with students graphing their scores daily and making major gains from pretest to posttest on the weekly unit quizzes! He decided that he would continue using this strategy to support student learning and make them accountable for their education while helping them pass the end-of-course exam.*

## CHAPTER SUMMARY

The chapter emphasized the importance of explicit instruction and the reasons teachers should apply the principles of explicit instruction to academic and behavioral instruction. The need for creating SMART goals for the continuum of supports in special education was introduced. Ways to identify study skills strategies to learn new materials and teach and utilize new study skills strategies were discussed. Finally, ways to determine if a practice is evidence based, the importance of using evidence-based practices, and strategies for avoiding pseudoscientific common practices were provided.

## DISCUSSION QUESTIONS

1. Identify multiple ways that explicit instruction can be used.

2. Why is it important to teach students study and organizational skills?

3. Explain the three types of knowledge that students need to learn, recall, and use information.

4. Discuss the methods listed for studying. What would work best for you?

5. Why is it important to use evidence-based practices in your classroom?

## RESOURCES

https://www.angelesinstitute.edu/thenightingale/benefits-of-group-study

https://www.lynchburg.edu/academics/tutoring-academic-support/top-10-study-skills/

https://www.theatlantic.com/science/archive/2018/04/the-myth-of-learning-styles/557687/

https://blog.mindresearch.org/blog/learning-styles-myth

## REFERENCES

Archer, A. L., & Hughes, C. A. (2011). *Explicit instruction: Effective and efficient teaching.* Guilford Press.

Ellis, E. S., & Worthington, L. A. (1994). *Research synthesis on effective teaching principles and the design of quality tools for educators* (Technical Report No. 5). University of Oregon National Center to Improve the Tools for Educators. Retrieved from https://files.eric.ed.gov/fulltext/ED386853.pdf

Hedin, L., & DeSpain, S. (2018). SMART or not? Writing specific, measurable IEP goals. *TEACHING Exceptional Children, 51*(2), 100–110. doi:10.1177/0040059918802587

Horner, R. H., Carr, E. G., Halle, J., McGee, G., Odom, S., & Wolery, M. (2005). The use of single subject research to identify evidence-based practice in special education. *Exceptional Children, 71*(2), 165–179. doi:10.1177/001440290507100203

Jung, L. A. (2007). Writing SMART objectives and strategies that fit the routine. *Teaching Exceptional Children*, *39*(4), 54–58. doi:10.1177/004005990703900406

Lazarus, A. (2004). Reality check: Is your behavior aligned with organizational goals? *The Physician Executive*, *30*(5), 50–52.

Lindsley, O. R. (1992). Precision teaching: Discoveries and effects. *Journal of Applied Behavior Analysis*, *25*(1), 51–57. doi:10.1901/jaba.1992.25-51

Minskoff, E., & Allsopp, D. (2003). *Academic success strategies for adolescents with learning disabilities and ADHD*. Brookes.

Myers, D., Freeman, J., Simonsen, B., & Sugai, G. (2017). Classroom management with exceptional learners. *Teaching Exceptional Children*, *49*(4), 223–230. doi:10.1177/0040059916685064

National Professional Development Center on Autism Spectrum Disorder (NPDC). (n.d.). *What criteria determined in an intervention was effective?* Retrieved from https://autismpdc.fpg.unc.edu/what-criteria-determined-if-intervention-was-effective

Reid, R., Lienemann, T. O., & Hagaman, J. L. (2013). *Strategy instruction for students with learning disabilities*. Guilford.

Scheeler, M., & Lee, D. (2002). Using technology to deliver immediate corrective feedback to preservice teachers. *Journal of Behavioral Education*, *11*(4), 231–241. doi:10.1023/A:1021158805714

Simonsen, B., Myers, D., Everett, S., Sugai, G., Spencer, R., & LaBreck, C. (2012). Explicitly teaching social skills schoolwide: Using a matrix to guide instruction. *Intervention in School and Clinic*, *47*(5), 259–266. doi:10.1177/1053451211430121

Sprick, R. (n.d.). *CHAMPS—Classwide positive behavior support (PBS)*. Retrieved from http://www.safeandcivilschools.com/services/classroom_management.php

Travers, J. C. (2017). Evaluating claims to avoid pseudoscientific and unproven practices in special education. *Intervention in School and Clinic*, *52*(4), 195–203. doi:10.1177/1053451216659466

Urbina, T., Cihon, T. M., & Baltazar, M. (2019). Exploring procedural manipulations to enhance student performance on SAFMEDS in undergraduate introduction to behavior analysis courses. *Journal of Behavioral Education*. Advance online publication. doi:10.1007/s10864-019-09359-0

U.S. Department of Education (USDOE). (2017). Questions and answers on U.S. Supreme Court case decision *Endrew F. v Douglas County School District Re-1*.

Yell, M. L., & Bateman, D. F. (2017). Endrew F. v. Douglas County School District (2017) FAPE and the U.S. Supreme Court. *Teaching Exceptional Children*, *50*(1), 7–15. doi:10.1177/0040059917721116

# Teacher-Directed Behavioral Interventions

*With Contributions from Brianna Joseph*

---

## KEY VOCABULARY

Behavior Contracts

Behavior Specific Praise

Data Collection

Differential Reinforcement
of Alternative Behaviors

Differential Reinforcement
of Incompatible Behaviors

Differential Reinforcement
of Low Rates of Behavior

Differential Reinforcement
of Other Behaviors

Duration

Event Recording

Extinction

Force

Frequency

Functions of Behavior

Group Contingencies

Interval Recording

Latency

Noncontingent Reinforcement

Opportunities to Respond

Punishment

Rate

Response Cost

Replacement Behaviors

Scatterplot

Time-Out

Token Systems

Topography

## LEARNING OBJECTIVES

By the end of this chapter, you should be able to . . .

- Understand the importance of effective data collection.
- Discriminate between data collection methods.

- Identify functions of behavior.
- Emphasize the importance of evidence-based interventions.
- Recognize evidence-based interventions to increase and decrease behaviors.
- Locate the difference between differential reinforcement procedures.
- Identify considerations when using time-out procedures.
- Apply classroom-wide behavior support interventions.

## INTRODUCTION

Before implementing interventions in the classroom, teachers must be aware of the extent of the behavior. Behavior is observable, measurable, and learned (Skinner, 1953; Spence, 1956). For a behavior to truly be considered a problem behavior, the teacher needs to define and describe the behavior explicitly. Problem behavior impacts the teacher's ability to teach, impedes peer learning within the environment, creates an unsafe psychological or physical environment, and destroys property (Levin & Nolan, 2011). When behavior interferes with the teaching process and prevents students from learning effectively and systematically, this affects the teacher's capability to teach students.

Although the student's behavior can be distracting for their own learning environment, the behavior can also be distracting to the other students in the classroom. Meaning, if the behavior is manifesting in the same environment with other students, they may be influenced to display the same behavior, which impacts teaching. The behavior can also be psychological and physically unsafe for the classroom environment. The student or students may have some mental health deficits that needs to be addressed or display aggressive behaviors to students and staff in the classroom or themselves (e.g., self-injurious behaviors; Epstein et al., 1998). The student may destroy property in the classroom, which impacts safety and welfare of others within the environment. A problem behavior may continuously repeat in the same environment or environments. When a problem behavior arises, effective data collection measures, behavior change procedures, and interventions must be put in place. Problem behaviors are measured by multiple data collection procedures, where teachers and other school team members analyze data and implement evidence-based teacher-directed behavior interventions.

## DATA COLLECTION

Interventions should be based on the results from data. Collection of data (i.e., **data collection**) that measures behavior can determine the extent of the target behavior(s), which then can be used to apply interventions that may assist with increasing or decreasing the behavior (Alberto & Troutman, 2013). A target behavior is the problem behavior that is identified and needs to change. In order for the target behavior to be changed, assessments are needed to analyze and evaluate the data. There are two types of assessments that can be used to collect data: informal and formal assessments. Informal assessments collect data on the behavior that is not observable. Some examples are anecdotal behavior scales, questionnaires, interviewing the student (if possible) and/or guardian(s), and work samples (i.e., permanent product). Appendix 8-1 provides an example of a parent and teacher questionnaire.

## Formal Assessments

Formal assessments require the teacher to observe the behavior directly. When observing the behavior, the teacher will need to have knowledge of the dimensional components of behavior, including:

- **Rate**—measures the frequency of the behavior based on a given period of time that the behavior is observed. Rate also allows the teacher to determine if the behavior should be increased or decreased the amount of time a student engages in the behavior or a task/ activity in the classroom.
- **Frequency**—number of times the behavior occurs.
- **Duration**—the period of times that the behavior is illustrated from beginning to end.
- **Latency**—the length of time between a given direction/instruction/ command and the occurrence of the behavior.
- **Topography**—description of the actual behavior. For example, if the teacher described the behavior as the student having a tantrum, the teacher will need to describe explicitly what the behavior looks like. Does the student scream, hits others, cry, etc.? This information must be stated to concretely define the behavior that is being displayed.
- **Force**—the intensity of the behavior. For example, data can be collected on the extent of the aggression, inappropriate verbal responses, noises, or body movements (Cooper et al., 2020).

Within formal assessment dimensions, the teacher will need to collect observable data using various data collection sheets. Examples of data collection documents include scatterplot, event recording, interval recording, latency, duration, and antecedent-behavior-consequence (ABC) functional assessment. **Scatterplot** data collection provides information about patterns of behavior. Scatterplot can indicate data patterns such as times of the day, settings, or activities in which the behavior is occurring.

### Event Recording

Event recording is used to record discrete behaviors, those that have a clear beginning and end, during a given time. For example, a teacher can record the number of occurrences that a student yells during a specific period within the day in which the behavior usually occurs. However, event recording should not be used when behaviors occur at a high frequency, those that are difficult to decipher when they begin and end, or behaviors that are displayed for long periods of time (i.e., tantrums).

### Interval Recording

Interval recording involves recording behavior during an interval of time (e.g., 30 seconds, 10 minutes). The teacher should be able to observe and collect data on whether the targeted behavior occurs or not. There are four types of interval recording: time sampling, partial-interval, whole interval, and momentary time sampling (Alberto & Troutman, 2013; Cooper et al., 2019).

### Time Sampling

Time sampling data collection requires the observer to record if a behavior happened or not at the end of each specified interval.

### Interval Recording

Partial-interval recording refers to recording if the behavior happened any time during the interval. Partial-interval recording is recommended as a form of data collection when the target behavior needs to be decreased. Whole-interval recording involves recording the occurrence of the behavior throughout the entire interval. When the objective is to increase a behavior, the use of whole-interval recording is recommended. Momentary time sampling can be used for high-frequency behaviors that the teacher can record at the end of preset intervals. Momentary time sampling is not recommended for low frequency and short duration of behaviors. Appendix 8–2 provides an example of a form for partial interval data collection.

## Antecedent-Behavior-Consequence

An ABC (antecedent-behavior-consequence) functional assessment is a systematic method of generating information of events proceeding (antecedent/before) a behavior, the behavior itself, and those following the behavior (consequence/after). This is an attempt to determine what antecedents and consequences have a strong correlation with the occurring target behavior. This process can be used to determine the function of behavior. This information is gathered on an ABC chart. ABC recording can be recorded in different sessions and intervals throughout the day (i.e., during science, math, reading, circle time, recess, etc.). Table 8–1 is an example of a tool for ABC data collection. Table 8–2 provides an example of a targeted time-period ABC data collection.

The ABC data collection process helps to form a hypothesis, leads to determining the individual's function of behavior, and helps to create the possible

**Table 8–1.** Example Antecedent-Behavior-Consequence (ABC) Recording Form

Setting: <u>Classroom time from 8:05–10:00 a.m.</u>

Target Behavior: <u>Yelling at teacher and peers</u>

| Antecedent | Behavior | Consequence |
|---|---|---|
| Bethany is asked to go to the independent reading station. | Bethany tells the teacher "make me." | Teacher tells Bethany if she does not do her work then she will not have recess. |
| Teacher tells Bethany if she does not do her work then she will not have recess. | Bethany wanders around the class with a smile on her face. | Teacher tells Bethany that she has lost her recess time. |
| Bethany is asked to match CVC words to pictures. | Bethany completes her work. | Bethany is given a break. |
| Teacher comes over to Bethany in independent math station. | Teacher reprimands Bethany in front of peers that her work is wrong. | Bethany yells at teacher. |
| Bethany yells at teacher. | Teacher tells Bethany that she will eat her lunch with the teacher and not in the cafeteria. | Bethany yells even louder. |
| Bethany is asked to redo her work. | Bethany throws her assignment from the station on the floor and yells at teacher. | Teacher tells Bethany that she has afterschool detention. |

*Note.* The ABC recording during the period of time in which Bethany was in the classroom was conducted in the morning. Based on the data, if Bethany is given a consequence in which reinforcers her escape from peer interaction, she will display the challenging behavior. Also based on the ABC recording, when Bethany is given work that she does not find challenging and is given a break, Bethany's challenging behavior is not displayed.

**Table 8–2.** Targeted Time ABC Recording Form

Setting: <u>Lunch from 10:20–10:50 a.m.</u>

Target Behavior: <u>Yelling at teacher and peers</u>

| | | |
|---|---|---|
| Bethany gets in the lunch line. | A classmate says "hi" to Bethany. | Bethany yells, "Leave me alone or I will punch you!" |
| Bethany yells, "Leave me alone or I will punch you." | The classmate turns around in line. | The classmate leaves Bethany alone. |
| Some of Bethany's classmates sit near Bethany to eat lunch. | Bethany yells, "Move away from me now!" | The classmates move away from Bethany. |
| The classmates move away from Bethany. | Bethany smiles. | Bethany sits by herself during lunch time. |

*Note.* Based on the ABC recording, Bethany will display the challenging behavior in order to have her peers not interact with her. Bethany enjoys the isolation from her peers.

rationale as to why the behaviors occur, along with a way to change the environment variables that are causing the behavior to occur (Kearney, 2015). **Functions of behaviors** include sensory, escape, attention, and tangible (i.e., SEAT). Examples of behaviors and the connection to function are provided as follows:

- Sensory—a student is displaying behaviors because it is stimulating one or more senses (i.e., touch, smell, sound, taste, or is visually appeasing).
- Escape—a student is trying to escape or avoid a situation, which could be due to certain individuals (staff or peers in the classroom), a nonpreferred task, the environment, or noises.
- Attention—a student may display the behavior in order to get *attention* from the teacher and/or peers, such as calling out repeatedly during a lesson, or the student may stop calling out for a short period of time, where the function of their behavior is teacher attention.
- Tangible—a student wants to engage in a specified preferred item or activity, and the behavior is functioning to gain access to something obtainable within the environment.

To analyze and provide interventions that are based on the results of the data, teachers should collect data consistently for a given period of time (e.g., daily for 6 weeks). The teacher should also consider if the student is on any medications or has any medical issues that that may influence behavior. Accurate data can increase the reliability and fidelity of the data to drive the implementation of the intervention. Observing and taking data in the environment in which the behavior occurs is necessary for accurate data collection and analysis. For example, if the behavior only occurs during reading instruction time, the teacher should collect data during that specific time of the day. When analyzing the data, it is crucial to understand functions of the behavior and why the student displays the behavior, so a hypothesis is formed, and interventions are developed.

## POSITIVE BEHAVIORAL INTERVENTIONS AND SUPPORTS

Positive Behavioral Interventions and Supports (PBIS) is a hands-on, practical educational approach for decreasing and eliminating unwanted behaviors. It is based on far-reaching research as well as principles regarding the rights of all students to be treated given the same opportunities as other students. In Section 1414(d)(3) of the Individuals with Disabilities and Education Act (IDEA) of 2004, considerations should be made when determining "interventions and supports, and other strategies, to address that behavior" for students with Individualized Education Programs and behavioral directed plans, including functional behavior assessments and behavior intervention plans. Implementing PBIS is crucial and needed in these plans and in the classroom (Horner et al., 1999). When using PBIS in the classroom with students with EBD, consider what stakeholders must be involved and their roles to ensure that the students' needs and concerns are being represented by the correct designated individual. This also includes the implementation and monitoring of the interventions, supports, and strategies, as well as use of evidence-based assessments that are culturally sensitive. Develop proactive and reactive strategies that are designed to target the function of the behavior, and employ interventions that are evidence-based practices and monitor the intervention to evaluate the effectiveness and delivery of the intervention (Hart, 2009; Horner, 1994; Horner et al., 1999; Scott & Alter, 2017).

### Replacement Behaviors

Teaching functional behaviors to replace problem behaviors within their current environment gives students opportunities to display the behavior and allows the students to meet continuous and systematic expectations daily (Trussell et al., 2008). A **replacement behavior** is taught to a student and serves the same function of the challenging behavior. The replacement behavior is suitable and typically appropriate to use across settings. Teaching replacement behaviors is important. For a problem behavior to be decreased or eliminated, another behavior needs to put in place of that problem behavior to replace it (State et al., 2017). If the problem behavior is not replaced by socially acceptable desired behaviors, the challenging behavior will persist. It is also important that goals, objectives, and proactive and reactive strategies are aligned with the schoolwide behavior support plan. Examples of replacement behaviors include:

- Asking for attention
- Raising hand
- Asking for help
- Requesting an item or activity
- Asking questions
- Seeking peer help
- Requesting a break
- Requesting an alternative activity
- Appropriately communicating a protest response
- Requesting movement to address sensory needs (e.g., stretch break, squeeze stress ball, move to an empty desk, stand while working, sit on an exercise ball, go for a walk; Wright-Gallo et al., 2006)

## Environmental Arrangements

Structure in the learning environment is imperative for all students, especially students with EBD, because structure provides predictability throughout the environment for the individual (Levin & Nolan, 2011). Unstructured environments may increase inappropriate behaviors. Teachers can use tools such as individual visual schedules and communication devices with visual pictures tailored to each specific student. Schedules should be based on the environment and can function successfully within the environment. Other environment arrangements include providing access to materials, preferential seating arrangements, entrances and exits in zones/centers, and transitional space throughout the classroom to prevent physical contact between students and lessen the chance of someone in the classroom getting injured.

## Classroom Expectations

Setting expectations in the classroom is the first thing that teachers do every new school year. Expectations (i.e., classroom rules) should be realistic and appropriate for the setting. **Behavior expectations** in the classroom are set based on the students' current level of following and illustrating rule-governed behavior. Set expectations for the student(s) based on the appropriate behavior that is in the repertoire and then increase the measure of expectations over time. Levin and Nolan (2011) recommend no more than five rules. Expectations, like *rules*, are governed based on the behavior that is expected in the classroom environment. Therefore, expectations are written in active voice, using positive language, without negative terminology (e.g., *don't*). When developing the expectations, the teacher must consider learning integrity and safety in the learning environment and include stating acceptable and appropriate behaviors. Teachers should involve their students when creating the expectations in the classroom, typically during the first days of school. Allowing students to assist when developing expectations creates a personal investment for students and may increase their willingness to follow the rules. Table 8–3 provides examples of effective and ineffective expectations.

Teachers can increase student desire to meet behavioral expectations by using the Premack principle. The **Premack principle** helps to provide motivation for nonpreferred behaviors and includes explaining the expected behavior to the student first, and if (and only if) the behavior is followed through by the student, then the student is able to receive a designated preferred outcome or reinforcer (Banks, 2014). Using the *if-then* statement creates various opportunities to have the student or students understand the pragmatics of how demonstrating the deemed appropriate behavior is important as well as to be reinforced. For example, a student's target behavior is running out of the classroom to escape a nonpreferred task, and the school team wants to target this behavior for reduction and eventually elimination. When the student sits down at their desk and is given math problems, the student proceeds to run out of the classroom. Since the student is able to communicate their needs and wants verbally, the teacher can teach, model, and provide opportunities for the student to practice the replacement behavior of asking for a break. When the student has mastered asking for a break, the teacher can then increase the

**Table 8–3.**  Effective and Ineffective Classroom Expectations

| Effective Rules | Ineffective Rules |
|---|---|
| 1. Follow directions the first time given | 1. No fighting |
| | 2. Don't yell in class |
| 2. Use walking feet in the classroom | 3. No cursing |
| 3. Keep all body parts to yourself | 4. Love yourself and others |
| 4. Raise hand and wait to be called on by teacher | 5. Work hard and be obedient |
| | 6. Don't steal. It's not nice |
| 5. Only use items that belong to you | 7. Leave others alone |

contingency of getting a break by using the Premack principle. The teacher tells the student, "If you sit down and complete one math problem correctly, then you can ask for a break." After the student follows the Premack principle consecutively for a given period of time with this specific behavior, the teacher can then increase the *if* contingency by gradually increasing the amount of math problems that the student will need to complete in order to get a break. The Premack principle can also be generalized across people and settings, including other teachers, staff members, and classrooms. The Premack principle also teaches real-world situational events that the student will need to understand to be productive members of society.

## Procedures and Routines

Effective procedures and routines are key in the classroom. A classroom behavior management system will not function effectively without a systematic structure, where the teacher develops, implements, maintain, and monitors classroom routines and procedures that are effective at producing behaviors expected in the classroom. Procedures are routines within the classroom where expected behaviors are illustrated by students during specific times/activities. These procedures must be taught to students through modeling, where the teacher models the expected behavior in each procedure within the classroom. The teacher then gives students multiple opportunities to practice the procedures and provide feedback when necessary. Some examples of procedures are:

- Entering the classroom
- Exiting the classroom
- Asking to the use the bathroom
- Transitioning within and outside of the classroom
- Following classroom schedule
- Sharping pencils
- Turning in homework and classwork
- Walking in the halls

## Behavior Contracts

A **behavior contract** is a written, agreed-upon contingency document between a teacher and student. The purpose of a behavior contract is to reinforce appropriate behaviors that are agreed on by the teacher and student. The student is included in developing the contract, and it is written in terminology that the student can read and comprehend to make sure that all parties fully understand the meaning and information within the contract. The contract states the appropriate behavior, emphasizes under what conditions the behavior should be displayed, and allocates realistic reinforcers that can be provided to the student within the classroom. All parties including the parent/guardian should sign the contract.

## Behavior Specific Praise

**Behavior specific praise** alerts the student to the desired behaviors that the teacher expects to see in the classroom. Praise statements such as *good job* and *great job* are not specific enough for students, because they do not provide the student with specific feedback on what they did well at that moment. Behavior specific praise directs the student to the appropriate behavior they are displaying with praise from the teacher. For example, a student who usually calls out the answer during whole-group science raises their hand and waits to be called upon. Before the teacher calls on the student, the teacher can use specific praise to acknowledge the student's desired behavior of raising their hand and waiting to be called upon. The teacher may then say to the student, "Great job, Bobby, sitting, raising your hand quietly, and waiting for me to call on you. Now that's the behavior I like to see! What's the answer?" The teacher gives the student praise while acknowledging the correct behavior that the student displayed.

## Opportunities to Respond

**Opportunities to respond** (OTR) help a teacher engage students during instructional time through questioning, statements, and gestures to increase student responses. Studies have shown that students with EBD receive fewer OTR than other students without disabilities (Mooney et al., 2003). High rates of OTR improve academic and behavioral performance for students with EBD (Tennessee Behavior Supports Project, 2019) and should include several types of OTR: individual responding, choral responding, and response cards (Haydon et al., 2012). The teacher provides a signal to students and then they respond. Students can answer questions verbally individually; all students respond in unison to a question (i.e., choral responding) or use response cards (e.g., pictures, pointing to words, or writing the answer on paper). For example, the teacher will state, "There are three types of state of matter, solid. . . . " The teacher then signals the students (e.g., claps twice) and the class responds in unison, "Liquid and gas." It is recommended that teachers provide three to five OTRs per minute for drill-type instruction and a minimum of one OTR per minute for other intervals (MacSuga-Gage & Simonsen, 2015).

## Negative Reinforcement

Negative reinforcement involves removing an aversive stimulus within the environment following a response to increase the response (Cooper et al., 2019). Often, teachers confuse negative reinforcement with punishment, but negative reinforcement is not punishment. Negative reinforcement is used to increase behaviors, not decrease behaviors. An example of effectively using negative reinforcement for a student who does not like answering reading comprehension questions from passages is as follows: The student can read the passage and answer 25% to 50% of the questions and turn in the assignment versus answering all of the questions and get a break. The teacher then increases the percent criterion contingency over time while allowing the student to take a break after completing the entire passage questions. If implemented correctly, negative reinforcement also teaches students naturally recurring reinforcers in the environment completing assignments on time to avoid consequences such as getting points off, studying to not get a bad grade, and displaying appropriate behaviors to not get in trouble.

## Levels of Reinforcement

Differential reinforcement procedures are used to decrease target behaviors by reinforcing the appropriate behavior on contingencies (Cooper et al., 2019). There are five types of differential reinforcement procedures (1) **differential reinforcement of low rates of behavior (DRL)**, (2) **differential reinforcement of other behaviors (DRO)**, (3) **differential reinforcement of alternative behaviors (DRA)**, (4) **differential reinforcement of incompatible behaviors (DRI)**, and (5) **noncontingent reinforcement**. See Table 8–4 for terminology definitions and examples. Implementing differential reinforcement can be effective based on the behavior that is targeted. Although interventions are based on trial and error, it is important to note that each procedure provides different outcomes. Applying the wrong procedure and/or applying the procedure inconsistently can have negative and possibly aversive effects on the target behavior (i.e., increasing the target behavior). Table 8–4 provides additional details on the types of differential reinforcement.

## Extinction

Extinction reduces behavior by withholding or eliminating the positive reinforcer that correlates with the undesired behavior. Before extinction is implemented, the teacher will need to teach, model, and shape replacement behaviors to add to the student's repertoire. The student may display the undesired behavior, but demonstrate that they are aware of the appropriate behavior to receive the reinforcer. When implementing extinction, the target behavior may intensify because the behavior is being ignored. When the rate of the undesired behavior increases immediately after implementing extinction, this is called an **extinction burst**.

**Table 8–4.** Reinforcement Definitions and Examples

| Differential Reinforcement | Example |
|---|---|
| Differential reinforcement of low rates of behavior (DRL)<br><br>DRL is used to decrease the rate of a behavior. | Rachel calls out in class during whole- and small-group instruction six times every 10 minutes. The teacher uses DRL to decrease the amount of times Rachel calls out. If Rachel calls out three or fewer times every 10 minutes, the teacher reinforces Rachel. If Rachel calls out four or more times every 10 minutes during instructional time, she is not reinforced. |
| Differential reinforcement of other behaviors (DRO)<br><br>DRO is used to provide reinforcement when the behavior is not displayed based on a specified interval of time. | Christian is constantly out of his seat during whole-group instructional time in the classroom. The teacher uses DRO and sets a timer for 2 minutes during instructional time. Every 2 minutes that Christian is sitting in his seat, he is reinforced. Over time, the teacher can increase the allocated time for Christian to remain seated. |
| Differential reinforcement of alternative behaviors (DRA)<br><br>DRA is used to reinforce the replacement behaviors that are an alternative to the inappropriate behavior. | Jeffery uses profanity to get teacher and peer attention. The teacher implemented DRA to only reinforce socially acceptable desired behaviors in the classroom such as raising a hand and, when called on, using acceptable language in the classroom. |
| Differential reinforcement of incompatible behaviors (DRI)<br><br>DRI is used to only reinforce behaviors that are incompatible to the problem behavior. DRI is not given when the student is displaying the problem behavior. | Keshia always runs in the classroom when transitioning from one location to the next. The teacher implements DRI. The teacher only reinforces when Keisha is walking in the classroom and does not reinforce when Keisha is running in the classroom. |
| NCR is used to reinforce behaviors based on scheduled intervals. | The teacher builds in reinforcers within the student's schedule. For example: The student has the word *computer* on their individual day schedule after completing nonpreferred tasks. |

For example, a student's target behavior is screaming for 3 to 5 seconds to get the teacher's attention. To stop the student from screaming in the classroom, the teacher inadvertently positively reinforces the undesired behavior by telling the student to stop screaming. After the teacher notices that the student's behavior is continuing due to the attention that is given, the teacher then implements extinction and ignores the behavior. After the fourth scream from the student and the student notices that the teacher has not responded, the student then increases the length of screaming to 7 seconds. The teacher ignores the behavior and gives specific praise to students who are on task (i.e., pivot praise). Although the teacher wants the screaming to stop, if the teacher responds to the target behavior, the behavior will now be under the contingency that screaming for 3 to 5 seconds does not get the teacher's attention, but screaming for 7 seconds does. Some behaviors that may lead to an extinction burst include a student physically harming others or themselves; however, these behaviors should be taken in to careful consideration to determine if extinction is the most effective intervention to implement. The student may display the behavior that was previously extinct (**spontaneous recovery**), other new undesirable behaviors (**novel behaviors**), and the extinction procedure not being followed by others who come in contact with the student (**limited generalization**).

## Punishment

**Punishment** is a consequence administered immediately following a problem behavior. In order for punishment to be effective, the punishment must have a negative effect on the behavior (i.e., reduces the occurrence of behavior in the future). Punishment can be paired with replacement behaviors that are deemed appropriate, so the student is presented with opportunities to demonstrate the desired behavior. Punishment can also be used with overcorrection procedures. Overcorrection procedures teach the desired behavior by implementing an undesirable inflated experience. For example, if a student continuously throws paper on the floor and not in the garbage, the teacher may have the student pick up all of the paper that the student threw on the floor and all other paper that is also the classroom floor. Behaviors where punishment can be effective include reprimanding the student and blocking the student to engage in the problem behavior (**response blocking**). Punishment should be used as a last resort and only after positive interventions have been discussed.

## Response Cost

Some behaviors can be decreased by using response cost. **Response cost** withdraws a specified amount of a reinforcer contingent upon an individual displaying inappropriate behaviors. For example, students can earn their tokens to be exchanged for prizes at the end of the day. However, tokens can also be taken away. If a student displays the incorrect behavior, the teacher will take a token. Although response cost demonstrates real-world contingencies of negative consequences of not following rules and expectations within an environment, it can also cause a concern. In order for response cost to be effective, the teacher must be able to withdraw the reinforcer immediately following the inappropriate behavior. Teachers must also consider the amount of reinforcer that can be withdrawn, and if all of the reinforcers are withdrawn, there may be a potential for the target behavior to intensify. Response cost should be used sparingly and cautiously.

## Time-Out

Denying a student access to reinforcement for a specified period of time within the environment is called **time-out**. Time-out should have an adverse effect on the behavior in order for the behavior to decrease. There are two types of time-out procedures: non-exclusion and exclusion. During **non-exclusion time-out**, the student remains in the environment but is not allowed access to a reinforcer for a specified time. The student can be relocated to another part of the classroom and can visually view peers engaging in the reinforcer or the student is visually blocked from seeing the reinforcer (i.e., chair is turned around and vision is blocked with furniture in the classroom). During **exclusion time-out**, a student is removed from the environment where the reinforcer is taking place. Exclusion time-out can also be referred to as exclusionary time-out, as a student is isolated from the environment due to an increase in verbal and/or physical aggression to others or self or destroying property within the environment. Teachers need to consider when using time-out procedures that the problem behavior may increase during the implementation of the procedure (i.e., extinction burst), the procedure is not consistently decreasing the behavior, or the procedure may have no effect on the target behavior (Costenbader & Reading-Brown, 1995; Musser et al., 2001). For example, if the student is trying to escape the environment, the student may display the undesired behavior that results in their removal. When this happens, the teacher is positively reinforcing the behavior and the behavior may increase.

Teachers should also consider the amount of time a student is placed in time-out. Although there is little research that states longer time-out periods are more effective than short-term time-out periods, a rule of thumb for short intervals is 3 to 5 minutes (Intervention Central, 2019; Yell, 1994). Other considerations include nonpreferred activities the student should complete in time-out, determining when the student can rejoin the rest of the classroom, how to handle outbursts of the problem behavior in time-out, and so on (Intervention Central, 2019).

## Token Systems

Token systems allow for students to receive a reinforcer that can be exchanged at a later time for a backup reinforcer. Backup reinforcers are items and activities that can be used with a designated number of tokens. Token systems shape students' behavior by using a delayed reinforcement to increase the repetition of a desired behavior over time while attempting to decrease undesired behaviors. This type of system assists students in monitoring and regulating their behaviors while working for a reinforcer. When establishing a token system, the teacher needs to be aware of activities and items that are reinforcing for students in the classroom (Weeden et al., 2016). Tokens can be individualized for all students in the classroom. Examples of these tokens include coins, tickets, stars, or a sticker chart and should be socially appropriate for the age group of students. The teacher can set the measurement of each reinforcer for the predetermined number of tokens, which can vary per student. Some highly desired reinforcers should be worth more than others. This can teach the students to increase desired behavior, and then they can save tokens for a highly preferred reinforcer. When the token is exchanged for the reinforcer, the reinforcer should be immediately given to the student following the exchange. To decrease instant gratification, the teacher can increase the length of time between earning tokens and exchange for backup reinforcement (Weeden et al., 2016). The teacher can also pair the token system with natural reinforcers within the environment, such as specific praise, break time, and access to an item or activity so that it can be generalized into other settings.

## Group Contingencies

Group contingencies are consequences that the teacher sets using students in the classroom and may involve the entire class or specific students (or groups of students) in the classroom. Contingencies are based on set criteria from the teacher, which can be based on the action/performance of one or more pretaught behaviors. There are three types of group contingencies, with different requirements for students to meet each contingency. Independent contingency features reinforcement when any student who meets the set criterion then receives the reinforcer. Dependent contingency is when a student or a group of students follows a set criterion, and the entire group (in this case, the class) is provided with a reinforcer. Interdependent contingency is when all students must follow the set criterion in order for all students to receive the reinforcer. Before implementing interdependent contingencies, teachers need to evaluate if all students can understand and demonstrate the target behavior or behaviors (Alberto & Troutman, 2013). If not, the interdependent contingency may not be suitable for the entire class until the behaviors are observed and illustrated by each student. It is important to note that group contingencies also follow the Premack principle guideline and should be stated as such. Table 8–5 provides details on group contingencies.

## CASE STUDY—ELEMENTARY

*Chien is a fourth-grade student with EBD who receives instruction in a self-contained classroom, and his level of reading, math, and writing is at the first grade. Chien displays disruptive behaviors of throwing away nonpreferred independent assignments, biting himself, or biting the teacher on the arm. When asked to complete assignments with peers in a small group, he does not present the target behaviors. Mr. Smith has difficulty assisting Chien because of the constant biting.*

**Table 8–5.** Group Contingencies

| Group Contingency | Definition | Example |
|---|---|---|
| Independent | The reinforcer is only given to individuals who meet the criterion. | All students who complete today's math assignment in their seats quietly will receive three extra tokens for the classroom store. |
| Dependent | The reinforcer is dependent upon an individual or group of individuals to meet the criterion in order for all to receive the reinforcer. | If Group 2 completes all of their task on their checklist for the science project, the entire class will get an additional 10 minutes of recess. |
| Interdependent | All members must meet the criterion in order to receive the reinforcer. | All students must follow directions in art class to get free computer time or no students will get free computer time. |

## CASE STUDY—SECONDARY 1

*Antoine is a seventh-grade student with EBD. He is currently in a self-contained classroom, but he attends electives in a general education classroom. Antoine is on reading and math grade level. Mrs. Jackson, Antoine's special education teacher, wants to increase his instructional time in the general education classroom for math. When he is anxious, has high anxiety, or is in stressful situations in school such as working with peers and given writing assignments, he will get out of his seat and jump around the classroom, run in place, and rock back and forth in his seat. Mrs. Jackson is concerned that if Antoine's behaviors do not decrease, he will not be allowed to transition with his peers to a general education classroom. Mrs. Jackson wants to figure out how to improve his target behaviors in order to begin the process of fading his instructional time in her class and increasing time in the general education classroom.*

## CASE STUDY—SECONDARY 2

*Jasmine is a tenth grader who receives special education and related services as a student with EBD in the second grade. She is currently in a general education inclusion classroom. Jasmine receives itinerant special education services in the general education classroom. Jasmine is on grade level and likes to help the teacher and her peers. However, Jasmine calls out during instructional time, talks over the teacher, and tells jokes to make her classmates laugh. She often demonstrates these behaviors during any whole-group and small-group math lessons. Jasmine's teacher, Mr. Raymond, is upset and would like for Jasmine to be in a self-contained classroom. Mr. Raymond has taken data but very sporadically and implements interventions that do not improve Jasmine's target behaviors.*

## CHAPTER SUMMARY

Teacher-directed behavior interventions that are implemented effectively can increase desired behaviors and decrease problem behaviors. Interventions must be evidence based and implemented according to the behavior and the function of that behavior. Before implementing any intervention, the intervention must be based on the results of data that have been collected thoroughly over a given period of time. Teachers need to provide opportunities for students to demonstrate replacement behaviors that can be generalized across settings and people. Teachers need to also monitor the interventions and fade when necessary.

**DISCUSSION QUESTIONS**

1. What are some considerations when taking data?

2. Why is it important to understand the rationale of the behavior?

3. How can teachers increase generalization of desired behaviors across settings and people?

4. What are some ways that teachers can increase their knowledge of implementing evidence-based positive behavior support interventions?

5. What data collection options are available to the teacher? Which data collection method would you recommend? Why?

6. Does the target behavior(s) need to be increased or decreased? Why?

7. What are some interventions that can be implemented for the student?

8. After reviewing data, the teacher determines that the intervention is not effective. What are the next steps?

 **RESOURCES**

http://www.apbs.org/files/PBSwhole.pdf

https://challengingbehavior.cbcs.usf.edu/Pyramid/pbs/index.html

https://www.interventioncentral.org/behavioral-interventions/challenging-students/time-out-reinforcement

https://www.interventioncentral.org/sites/default/files/pdfs/pdfs_interventions/beh_contract_example.pdf

http://tennesseebsp.org/wp-content/uploads/2016/12/OTRs-Tips.pdf

## REFERENCES

Alberto, P., & Troutman, A. (2013). *Applied behavior analysis for teachers* (9th ed.). Merrill/Prentice Hall.

Banks, T. (2014). Creating positive learning environments: Antecedent strategies for managing the classroom environment & student behavior. *Creative Education*, 5(7), 519. doi:10.4236/ce.2014.57061

Cooper, J., Heron, T., & Heward, W. (2019). *Applied behavior analysis* (3rd ed.). Pearson.

Costenbader, V., & Reading-Brown, M. (1995). Isolation timeout used with students with emotional disturbance. *Exceptional Children*, *61*(4), 353–363.

Epstein, M. H., Kutash, K. E., & Duchnowski, A. E. (1998). *Outcomes for children and youth with emotional and behavioral disorders and their families: Programs and evaluation best practices*. Pro-Ed.

Facilitator's Guide: Positive Behavior Support. (1999). Retrieved from http://www .apbs.org/files/PBSwhole.pdf

Hart, J. (2009). Strategies for culturally and linguistically diverse students with special needs. *Preventing School Failure*, *53*(3), 197. doi:10.3200/PSFL.53.3.197-208

Haydon, T., MacSuga-Gage, A. S., Simonsen, B., & Hawkins, R. (2012). Opportunities to respond: A key component of effective instruction. *Beyond Behavior*, *22*(1), 23–31. doi.org/10.1177/107429561202200105

Horner, R. H. (1994). Functional assessment: Contributions and future directions. *Journal of Applied Behavior Analysis*, *27*(2), 401–404. doi:10.1901/jaba.1994.27-401

Horner, R. H., Albin, R. W., Sprague, J. R., & Todd, A. W. (1999). Positive behavior support. In M. E. Snell & F. Brown (Eds.), *Instruction of students with severe disabilities* (5th ed., pp. 207–243). Merrill/Prentice Hall.

Intervention Central. (2019). *Time out from reinforcement*. Retrieved from https://www .interventioncentral.org/behavioral-interventions/challenging-students/time-out-reinforcement

Intervention Central. (2011). *How RTI works series*. Retrieved from https://www.inter ventioncentral.org/sites/default/files/pdfs/pdfs_interventions/beh_contract_ example.pdf

Kearney, A. J. (2015). *Understanding applied behavior analysis: An introduction to ABA for parents, teachers, and other professionals*. Jessica Kingsley Publishers.

Levin, J., & Nolan, J. F. (2011). *Principles of classroom management: A professional decision-making model* (7th ed.). Pearson/Allyn & Bacon.

MacSuga-Gage, A., & Simonsen, B. (2015). Examining the effects of teacher directed opportunities to respond on student outcomes: A systematic review of the literature. *Education and Treatment of Children*, *38*(2), 211–240. doi:10.1353/etc.2015.0009

Mooney, P., Epstein, M. H., Reid, R., & Nelson, J. R. (2003). Status of and trends in academic intervention research for students with emotional disturbance. *Remedial and Special Education*, *24*(5), 273–287. doi:10.1177/07419325030240050301

Musser, E. H., Bray, M. A., Kehle, T. J., & Jenson, W. R. (2001). Reducing disruptive behaviors in students with serious emotional disturbance. *School Psychology Review*, *30*(2), 294.

Scott, T. M., & Alter, P. J. (2017). Examining the case for functional behavior assessment as an evidence-based practice for students with emotional and behavioral disorders in general education classrooms. *Preventing School Failure: Alternative Education for Children and Youth*, *61*(1), 80–93. doi:10.1080/1045988X.2016.1196645

Skinner, B. F. (1953). *Science and human behavior*. Simon and Schuster.

Spence, K. (1956). *Behavior theory and conditioning*. Yale University Press.

State, T. M., Harrison, J. R., Kern, L., & Lewis, T. J. (2017). Feasibility and acceptability of classroom-based interventions for students with emotional/behavioral challenges at the high school level. *Journal of Positive Behavior Interventions*, *19*(1), 26–36. doi.org/10.1177/1098300716648459

Tennessee Behavior Supports Project. (2019). *Opportunity to respond tip sheet*. Retrieved from http://tennesseebsp.org/wp-content/uploads/2016/12/OTRs-Tips.pdf

Trussell, R. P., Lewis, T. J., & Stichter, J. P. (2008). The impact of targeted classroom interventions and function-based behavior interventions on problem behaviors of students with emotional/behavioral disorders. *Behavioral Disorders, 33*(3), 153–166. doi:10.1177/019874290803300303

Weeden, M., Wills, H. P., Kottwitz, E., & Kamps, D. (2016). The effects of a class-wide behavior intervention for students with emotional and behavioral disorders. *Behavioral Disorders, 42*(1), 285–293. doi:10.17988/BD-14-12.1

Wright-Gallo, G. L., Higbee, T. S., Reagon, K. A., & Davey, B. J. (2006). Classroom-based functional analysis and intervention for students with emotional/behavioral disorders. *Education and Treatment of Children, 29*(3), 421–436.

Yell, M. L. (1994). Timeout and students with behavior disorders: A legal analysis. *Education and Treatment of Children, 17*(3), 293–301.

## APPENDIX 8–1

# Example Parent and Teacher Questionnaire

1. What areas are your child's (student's) strengths?

   _____

   _____

   _____

2. What types of things (reinforcers) work best for your child (student) in terms of rewards and motivation?

   _____

   _____

   _____

3. Do changes in routine or transitions to new activities affect your child's (student's) behavior? Circle one.

   Always        Frequently        Never

4. Briefly describe your child (student) challenging behavior at home/school.

   _____

   _____

   _____

5. What do you think triggers your child's (student's) challenging behavior (why do you think he or she engages in this kind of behavior(s)?)

   _____

   _____

   _____

## APPENDIX 8–2

# Partial-Interval Recording

Directions: Circle whether the behavior occurred. If no behavior occurred, circle zero in the last column.

Student Name: _____ Date: _____

| Time | Activity | Self-Injurious Behavior | Screaming | Dropping to the Floor | No Behaviors |
|------|----------|-------------------------|-----------|-----------------------|--------------|
| 7:15– | Cafeteria breakfast | SIB | SCRM | DROP | 0 |
| 7:45–8:05 a.m. | Calendar | SIB | SCRM | DROP | 0 |
| 8:05–8:20 a.m. | Skills center | SIB | SCRM | DROP | 0 |
| 8:20–8:35 a.m. | 1:1 with teacher (math) | SIB | SCRM | DROP | 0 |
| 8:35–8:50 a.m. | Computer | SIB | SCRM | DROP | 0 |
| 8:50–9:05 a.m. | Independent work | SIB | SCRM | DROP | 0 |
| 9:05–9:25 a.m. | Read aloud | SIB | SCRM | DROP | 0 |
| 9:25–9:50 a.m. | 1:1 with teacher (reading) | SIB | SCRM | DROP | 0 |
| 9:50–10:15 a.m. | Sensory | SIB | SCRM | DROP | 0 |
| 10:15–10:40 a.m. | Computer | SIB | SCRM | DROP | 0 |
| 10:40–11:05 a.m. | Sensory | SIB | SCRM | DROP | 0 |
| 11:05–11:30 a.m. | Science | SIB | SCRM | DROP | 0 |

*continues*

**APPENDIX 8–2.** *continued*

| Time | Activity | Self-Injurious Behavior | Screaming | Dropping to the Floor | No Behaviors |
|------|----------|-------------------------|-----------|-----------------------|--------------|
| 11:30 a.m.–12:00 p.m. | Lunch | SIB | SCRM | DROP | 0 |
| 12:00–12:30 p.m. | Recess | SIB | SCRM | DROP | 0 |
| 12:30–1:00 p.m. | Specials | SIB | SCRM | DROP | 0 |
| 1:00–1:15 p.m. | Snack | SIB | SCRM | DROP | 0 |
| 1:15–1:35 p.m. | Getting ready for dismissal | SIB | SCRM | DROP | 0 |

# 9

# Student-Directed Behavioral Interventions

*With Contributions from Lauren Berlingo*

---

## KEY VOCABULARY

Check-In, Check-Out

Choice Board

Emotion Identification

Emotion Regulation

Fading

Goal Setting

Independence

Positive Self-Talk

Self-Management

Self-Monitoring

Tracking

## LEARNING OBJECTIVES

by the end of this chapter, you should be able to . . .

- Define self-management.
- Identify emotion identification, emotion regulation, and self-monitoring.
- Identify strategies and interventions that can be used for students with emotional and behavioral disabilities to identify emotions.
- Support students in self-monitoring behavior.
- Identify appropriate goals for students.

# INTRODUCTION

Students with emotional and behavioral disabilities (EBD) display an inability to learn, an inability to build or maintain relationships with peers and teachers, inappropriate behaviors or feelings under normal circumstances, a general mood of unhappiness, and a tendency to develop fear associated with school and personal problems. However, students with EBD can become independent in managing their own behavior and emotions with explicit instruction and appropriate interventions in place. This chapter will introduce you to student-directed behavioral strategies that will assist these students in self-management, emotion identification, emotion regulation, self-monitoring, and goal setting. Interventions having to do with each area are explained for elementary school, middle school, and high school. Examples of each strategy are provided.

# SELF-MANAGEMENT

**Self-management** consists of a collection of techniques used to change one's own behavior and actions (Cooper et al., 2007). Students with weak self-management skills often react to challenging situations with impulsive and socially inappropriate behavior in the attempt to get the result they want (Bambara et al., 2015). Students with EBD often have difficulty managing aggression and impulsivity within the classroom (Patton et al., 2006).

Teaching and encouraging students to self-manage different aspects of their lives, specifically in behavior self-management, teaches and fosters independence. Self-management includes self-monitoring, goal setting, self-evaluation, and self-reinforcement (Cooper et al., 2007). This chapter covers strategies that focus on identifying and regulating emotions, as well as self-monitoring and goal-setting strategies. These skills are essential for students with EBD to be successful in school. Elementary school students with EBD perform academically and function behaviorally at least a year below grade level, and when they get to high school, these students typically perform about 3.5 years below grade level (Dunn et al., 2017). Using self-management strategies can make a significant impact on their academic and behavioral programming and make a positive impact on life beyond school-age years.

## Emotion Identification

Understanding one's emotions is a confusing process for children. Emotions can be very overwhelming and hard to regulate. Before students are able to regulate emotions, they must be able to identify how they are feeling, as well have knowledge of strategies they can turn to when needed; students need to be equipped with a toolbox of strategies, which support **emotion iden-**

**tification** and regulation. According to Havighurst and colleagues (2015), "School-based interventions that build emotional awareness and social competencies have been found to produce significant changes for children with behavior problems and learning difficulties" (p. 750). Starting at the beginning and teaching students how to recognize their emotions can make other areas of self-management more manageable. The following sections provide examples of simple school-based interventions that can be used to help students build emotional awareness based on grade level.

### Elementary

For elementary-age students, self-management interventions can be paired with visuals so independence in identifying and managing one's emotions and behaviors can be increased (Bambara et al., 2015). Emojis are images that can be inserted into text messages or emails via an electronic device. They are extremely popular, trendy versions of the original smiley face. Emoji popularity is world known, with a movie made about them; they are seen on clothing items and made into stuffed animals and pillows. They are everywhere, and children know them well. Emojis can be used to teach students how to identify how they are feeling because they are descriptive and relatable. Teachers can implement a *Today I Feel* . . . classroom board used for students to identify how they are feeling at the beginning of each day. For example, during a morning meeting, the teacher asks each student to come to the board and show the class how they are feeling today by moving the emoji picture next to their name and/or picture, one at a time. Doing this gives the teacher insight to how each student is starting their day and allows the them to step in and use strategies that work best with each student. As students get comfortable with this each morning, teachers can use it as needed throughout the day. When students are more fluent, accurate, and independent in identifying their emotions this way, teachers fade themselves out, making each student an independent board so they identify how they are feeling when needed. This intervention is useful for young students learning to work with their emotions, students with challenging behaviors who might have limited verbal ability, and students with challenging behaviors who might be shy or are not confident in asking for help when frustration sets in.

### Charts

Smiley faces are a simple and constructive way of teaching students to identify emotions, especially with younger students (i.e., kindergarten through second grade). They are universal symbols for showing happiness and sadness, which make them fairly easy to teach. Figure 9–1 shows an example of a smiley face chart that can be used in the classroom to allow students to monitor how they are feeling throughout the school day. The visual chart can be laminated and attached to students' desks. Students can be taught how to mark their emotion if it changes throughout the academic day with a dry-erase marker or an identifier attached with Velcro. This is a tool that introduces primary-age students with EBD to the skill of appropriately identifying their own emotions and feelings and builds emotional awareness.

**Figure 9–1.** *Smiley face desk chart. Students indicate how they are feeling on their desk using a marker or an arrow with Velcro.*

## Traffic Light Strategy

One common way many elementary school special education teachers teach emotions and how to recognize emotions is by using a traffic light. Many teachers use the traffic light because it is a simple visual, it utilizes colors, and meaning is already applied to the colors, so teachers do not have to reinvent the wheel. As many know, a standard traffic light has three colors, green, yellow, and red. Teaching emotions is relatable to a traffic light. This strategy should be used as an teaching tool and not posted publicly or used as a consequence.

### Green

When a traffic light is green, it means that it is okay to go. Transferring this to emotions is similar, meaning that a student is feeling good, calm, and is ready to learn. A student has their most successful day when they are considered *green* emotionally. Typically, students do not need to utilize strategies when they are feeling good, but it is important to keep them feeling this way. When they are relaxed and ready to learn, they are in a stable condition. Some strategies to keep students green, or *feeling good*, include drinking water, helping a friend, and other individual strategies previously known to keep the student focused.

### Yellow

When a traffic light is yellow, it means that the person driving the car needs to slow down because the light is about to turn red. Emotionally, this means that an individual might be excited, nervous, overwhelmed, or upset. When students are considered *yellow*, they are usually about to lose control. It is important that they are able to recognize this feeling and use the appropriate strategies to calm down. Strategies that can be taught when students are about to lose control are to stop and think (i.e., what can I do to get back to feeling good?), use self-talk to get back on track (i.e., *I'm a little off, I can sit in the calm corner for a minute and get focused*), or use fidget toys to keep give their body the movement it may need at the time (i.e., fidget spinner or clicker). When a student is feeling this way, it is imperative that they use the strategies taught to them. The last thing the student or teacher wants is for the student to escalate into the next level. The main goal is to have the student back into a calm, focused state and return their stoplight to green.

### Red

Individuals with drivers' licenses know that when driving, red on a traffic light means to STOP. This is the same with emotions. When a student starts yelling, is angry, or is becoming verbally and physically aggressive, they are considered to be feeling *red*. This means that a student has lost control and is in need of de-escalation. There is no teaching going on when a student is feeling this way; therefore, strategies that need to be in place for students who become this way include, but are not limited to, exercising (i.e., going to the basketball court, walking laps, or taking a few sprints outside of the classroom/building) or taking a break in a different room (usually a preferred teacher or school personnel that is "on board" with this).

An easy, nonstigmatizing way to teach students to track how they are feeling while using this idea of the traffic light is to provide a desk tracker. On their desk, provide a horizontal traffic light with an indicator that can be moved and seen easily (Figure 9–2). Teachers often have a large version of this posted on a wall and either have students move a clip showing where they are in terms of behavior and/or emotions or move the clip themselves, often in front of the entire class. This can be very stigmatizing for a student who is learning how to regulate their emotions and can cause them to stand out from their peers in a negative way. Having this on students' desks makes it more personal, less embarrassing, and less likely to cause an increase in maladaptive behaviors. The goal is to teach rather than to punish. Teachers must be attentive to students who move their desk tracker to yellow or red so prompting and/or intervention can occur if needed.

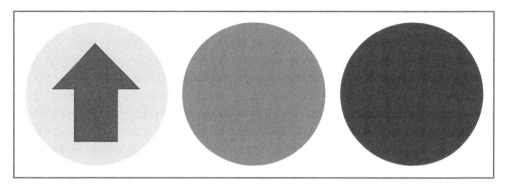

**Figure 9–2.** *Traffic light desk tracker. This tool enables students to identify their emotions throughout the day by moving the arrow to the correct color on the traffic light to describe how they are feeling.*

## EMOTION REGULATION

**Emotion regulation** focuses on individuals modifying their feelings to feel a certain way (Tamir, 2009). This is influenced by the need or want for instant gratification (e.g., pleasure). Often times, when the need for instant gratification arises, long-term benefits and usefulness are not thought of, which can produce negative behaviors. Students with EBD lack the ability to select emotions that are useful in particular situations. With repetitive explicit instruction, these students can learn that emotions are more useful for situations that increase positive outcomes and lessen destructive behaviors. The following are useful tools to assist students with EBD and increase independence in regulating their emotions.

### Choice Board

Students need opportunities to make choices, often provided by the teacher, where they are allowed two (or more possibilities) depending on the situation (Jolivette et al., 2001). Student choice is an antecedent intervention. For example, the student could choose materials, assignment type, order of completion, and reward (Skerbetz & Kostewicz, 2013). Providing students with choice decreases challenging behaviors and increases on-task behavior. Choice making can be modified and utilized for emotional regulation as well. A **choice board** can be differentiated depending on age, grade, and social appropriateness.

For the elementary and early middle school grades, individual choice boards are often effective. These can be used to promote self-management with two key elements included. First, smiley faces are provided for students to track how they are feeling. This is similar to the smiley face chart provided earlier, but this can be a key part in regulating one's emotions once a student is able to accurately identify how they are feeling without teacher assistance. Next, two or more situational choices are provided. These choices are partnered with the smiley face; for example, if a student displays that they are angry, they would be able to select from two choices to calm down, for example, one choice to go to the calm corner and the other to take a walk with a preferred adult.

Figure 9–3 is an example of a choice board that could be used in elementary school. This example is meant to be interactive, allowing the students to move the correlating face that accurately describes how they are feeling and the strategy they choose to remain *feeling good* or to move from being anxious, silly, overwhelmed, angry, or upset to feeling calm and focused. Planning and explicit instruction must occur prior to implementation in order to have immediate consequences based on choice.

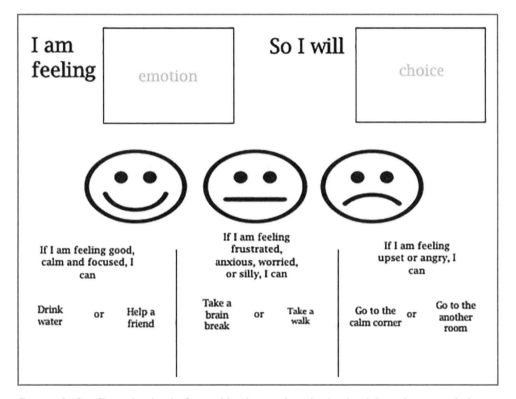

**Figure 9–3.** *Choice lap book. Created by the teacher, this lap book has alternative behavior choices that are correlated with emotion. These choices are what the student is expected to do instead of the problem behavior.*

In late middle school and high school, students with or at risk of EBD should still be provided choices to maximize academic success. A smiley chart is inappropriate for students of this age. Instead, it is useful in a menu format. Older students can play a part in creating this menu with their special education and general education teachers. Choices on the menu can be about assignment completion, seating preference, preferred testing setting, and any other predetermined item that will make the student regulated and successful.

Table 9–1 is an example of a student- and teacher-created choice menu for older students. In this particular example, behaviors include completing one's assignment, asking for help with classwork, and getting frustrated with work and/or others. This should be kept by the student so when they face an obstacle in their day, the student can look to the chart to track and resolve it.

**Table 9–1.** Choice Menu

| Topic | Choice 1 | Choice 2 |
|---|---|---|
| I want to complete my assignment . . . | Handwritten | Typed |
| To complete my work, I need . . . | Flexible seating (i.e., stability disc) | Listen to music |
| If I need help, I can . . . | Ask my peer buddy | Ask the teacher |
| If I get frustrated with my work, I can . . . | Drink some water and refocus | Stretch break |
| If I get angry with another student, my teacher, or myself, I can . . . | Use my pass to leave the room and go to a preferred place to cool down | Go to the track and run one lap with _____ |

*Note.* A choice menu is created by the teacher with student assistance and input. Choices that are on this menu should have been previously discussed and agreed upon with all school personnel that are involved with the student.

## Hot Card

Students with EBD may have difficulty managing their aggression and impulsivity within the classroom (Patton et al., 2006). Impulsivity often increases when a student is angry, and they may act out in a physical manner such as taking their aggression out on other students and adults in the classroom or on the classroom furniture, which are both very dangerous. When there are students who are unpredictable when upset, students need explicit instruction on what to do when they feel that way, which is crucial to classroom operations and the safety of everyone within the room. Explicit instruction needs to occur when they are in stable functioning (i.e., their light is on green).

Teachers can provide an easily accessible *Hot Card*, which helps create a different outlet when students start to feel frustrated, prior to displaying aggression. Instead of acting on physical aggression, the card serves as a pass to go to the calm corner or a previously approved area in the classroom or school. Use of the card is pretaught, with the student involved in the planning portion of the card (i.e., where the student can go when using the card). At initial implementation, the student will need practice, as well as verbal and nonverbal cues and prompting to understand complete use of the card. For example, when a teacher notices a student starting to get angry, the teacher can prompt the student by saying, "Use your card," or by simply holding it up for the student to see. Figure 9–4 is an example of a hot card used within the classroom to promote emotion regulation.

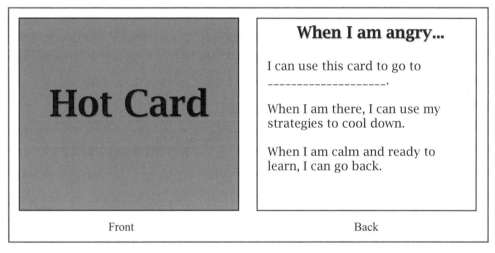

**Figure 9–4.** *Hot Card.This card is used to get a student out of a situation that makes them angry. It is used to go to another place until they are ready to return.*

### Whoops! Card

Different from a *Hot Card*, a *Whoops! Card* serves as a prompt and reminder to that student that they need to make a quick fix on a mistake without teacher redirection or consequence. Students with EBD may struggle with taking ownership of mistakes in the school setting because they are sometimes seen as the students who misbehave, possibly causing behavior to escalate. A *Whoops! Card* serves as a way for teachers to empower students by self-correcting errors without teacher and student attention, decreasing behavior escalation. Implementation involves the card placed at the corner of the desk so if a student acts impulsively, breaks classroom rules, or does not follow individualized, predetermined behaviors, students can say *Whoops!* and put a tally mark on the card. For example, a student with EBD in a fourth-grade classroom swears very loudly due to his excitement for a field trip his class going on. Rather than the teacher addressing the student, potentially creating a scene and escalation in behavior, the student can use the card and correct the behavior. Prompting is needed in the beginning, which can be verbal or in the form of a gesture. The teacher might hear the student swear or start getting agitated from making a mistake on their work and tell them to mark a *Whoops!* and move on with the lesson, averting behavior issues. As the student's behavior recovers, the teacher can point to the card next time something happens and then eventually fade out any type of prompting. **Fading** something means it is removed gradually. This promotes student accountability. Students displaying more severe behaviors may not benefit from this tool right away, but a progressive prompting and fading system can be used until students can use it independently.

Figure 9–5 shows an example of a *Whoops! Card*. The front of the card has a visual and a place to tally mistakes and the back lists individualized coping strategies, reminding the student that everyone makes mistakes. The coping strategies vary from child to child due to their individualized needs. It is important to continuously remind the student that no one is perfect and making mistakes happens to everyone, thus including this as a part of the classroom culture.

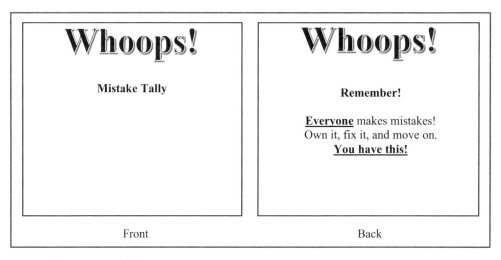

**Figure 9–5.** *Whoops! Card. Using this card, students are expected to own, track, and be okay with their mistakes throughout the day. This is to avoid teacher reprimand for miniscule problems.*

## Pass

In the secondary grades, having a *Hot Card* or a "*Whoops! Card* would not be age appropriate or socially appropriate. If a high school student struggles regulating emotions, that student can benefit from having an *escape* pass. This pass has similar uses to other cards (i.e., *Hot Card* or *Whoops! Card*), allowing the student to go to a place that can be used to de-escalate appropriately. The special education teacher, the student, and the team of professionals that are involved with the student set guidelines for the pass, its uses, and preferred places and adults the student can go to and access if the pass is needed. Teachers track student uses to avoid inappropriate use (i.e., avoiding academic and nonpreferred tasks).

## Positive Self-Talk

Each day, students are faced with academic, emotional, and social tasks that can be difficult to navigate if they have never been taught how to. Students with EBD have difficulties navigating peer relationships and coping with adversity, which can be an indicator of low self-esteem. Students may act out due to insecurity and negative self-perception (Barrett et al., 1999). Teaching students to use **positive self-talk**, or *talk themselves up*, rather than *talk themselves down*, is a hard task when it seems that every relationship is a negative or a failed one, or when they try hard on an academic activity and perceive it as subpar work. Because of this, students automatically shut down and say "I can't" when they are presented with an academic task. Others might speak negatively about themselves and say that they are stupid or lame and/or react abruptly or physically if a social situation with another individual fails. The use of positive self-talk can help these students get through the daily struggles they encounter.

Students can use positive self-talk to coach themselves through situations they encounter throughout the school day and even outside of school. For instance, a student might be hesitant to work with partners in science class because they might not be strong in that subject. Instead of refusing to work with partners that class period, the student can begin by using positive self-talk. This may cause social anxiety because the student may not know how to interact with their classmates in this setting. If the student feels like they are not strong in a subject, the last thing they would want to do is show others they are not confident. Positive self-talk can also be used in order to demonstrate prosocial behaviors. In the situation described above, the student might want to remind themselves of their capabilities. Table 9–2 is an example of a table that is printed out and given to students to refer back to. It includes negative comments that students say to themselves and how they can change what they are saying to be more positive. These can be somewhat generic, but teachers can create these types of tables based on their students' needs and comments they have made about themselves. Coaching examples and reflective statements are provided in the table.

Not only can they coach themselves, they can also give themselves feedback after a situation that occurred, whether it be academic or social. If the situation went well and was overall positive, they can coach themselves. If the situation or interaction did not go well, the feedback can be more constructive while still positive. Being able to reflect on how a situation was handled is a skill that can have a great impact on one's self-management.

No matter whether it is to offer themselves encouragement or to give themselves feedback, students with EBD need to learn how to use positive self-talk to help their self-esteem. Unfortunately, many of these students have not heard positive words directed at them often, making it difficult for them to come up with statements or thoughts to tell themselves in certain situations. Providing a list of potential positive things to say to oneself would be a helpful start for these students. The attempt to change the way they think about themselves is crucial for their in-school and postschool success.

**Table 9–2.** Positive Self-Talk

| Coaching Statements | | Reflective Statements | |
|---|---|---|---|
| *The student says . . .* | *Replace with . . .* | *The student says . . .* | *Replace with . . .* |
| "I'm not good at this." | "I'm getting better with practice." | "My work is never good enough." | "I did the best I could do." |
| "I give up." | "Keep trying, you've got this!" | "I should have never raised my hand." | "My teacher and classmates appreciated my input." |
| "I'm so dumb." | "There is so much that I CAN do!" | "I bombed that test." | "I will study better next time." |
| "I can't do anything." | "I can do anything with hard work and focus." | "I made a fool of myself in front of everyone!" | "Everyone makes mistakes, next time will be better." |
| "I just can't do this work." | "I can keep trying and ask for help if I need it." | "I really messed up." | "I struggled today, but I will learn from it and make better choices tomorrow." |
| "She is so smart. I will never be like that." | "I can do it too!" | | |
| "This math is stupid." | "I can learn this!" | | |

*Note.* Students can refer back to this to change the way they think and talk to themselves.

## Self-Monitoring

**Self-monitoring** is the process of observing and recording one's own behavior (Hunter et al., 2017; Patton et al., 2006). The student should record a number of instances a target behavior is being decreased or increased (Menzies et al., 2009). For example, a target behavior that a student and teacher would want to decrease is the number of callouts (i.e., shouting the answer out without raising their hand) within a class period or the number of times the student gets out of their seat. An example of a behavior that the student and teacher would want to increase would be raising a quiet hand to be called on or time spent on a task. After the target behavior is chosen, the student and teacher decide on an appropriate criterion, or agreed-upon number, that the student would have to meet for reinforcement (Menzies et al., 2009). When self-monitoring is implemented, the student first needs to determine if the target behavior did or did not occur, followed by recording some aspects of the target behavior (Mace et al., 2001). Below are examples of different ways students throughout elementary, middle, and high school can monitor their own behaviors.

## Tracking System

Self-management is an effective way to bring about change in multiple behaviors (Cullinan, 2002). The purpose of students self-managing their own behavior is to encourage independence while promoting appropriate behavior, which can then lead to academic success (Patton et al., 2006). Vargas (2013) noted, "One of the best consequences students can put into place for their own behavior is a record of progress" (p. 324). By having students track their own behavior, it enables them to be more intrinsically motivated. Motivation is associated with engagement, learning, and educational achievement (Hulleman & Barron, 2016). By allowing these students to take part in tracking their own behavior, motivation will increase, which will then positively impact their academic and behavioral achievement.

### Primary Grades

Students in the early elementary school grades—kindergarten, first grade, and second (and sometimes third) grade—are considered to be in the primary grades (U.S. Department of Education, 2008). With explicit instruction and initial teacher guidance, these students can participate in their own behavior tracking. Students should track behavior in a smaller window of time, such as 10 minutes, rather than an entire class period. In elementary school, the use of visual aids for beginning and struggling readers will assist students in the independence portion of self-monitoring their behavior throughout the day. Having visuals makes for accessibility for students with reading difficulties.

Table 9–3 is an example of a simple paper/pencil system that students can use to track their behavior. Though this figure shows that it is for reading time, it can be edited and used for any time slot that fits the classroom schedule. This chart has four positively stated target behaviors, leaving no question as to what the student should be doing during the allotted time. For this example, students are also asked to total the amount of *yes* check marks they circled. If the student obtains at least three out of four check marks, that student would meet their goal for that time and given reinforcement. In the beginning stages of implementation and use, this requires teacher assistance. This also serve as a quick check-in on student behavior.

**Table 9–3.**  Self-Monitoring Chart for Primary

| Name: | Date: | |
|---|---|---|
| **Reading Time** | | |
| **Behavior** | **Yes** **Circle One** | **No** |
| I kept my hands to myself by not touching anyone else or anything. | Yes ✓ | No X |
| I stayed on task by doing my work. | Yes ✓ | No X |
| I used nice words. | Yes ✓ | No X |
| I stayed in my area. | Yes ✓ | No X |
| Total "Yes": Goal: 3 | | |

*Note.* Students are meant to track four target behaviors by hour, circling the green check mark indicating that they displayed the behavior or circling the red X indicating that they did not successfully display the target behavior. Students' goal should be to get three out of four check marks, showing that their total accuracy for the allotted time is 75% or more.

### Intermediate/Middle Grades

Just like the younger students, with explicit instruction and teacher guidance, older students can track their own behavior, sometimes for a longer duration of time. Although at this age, the goal is for students to be independent readers and on grade level, it is important to keep in mind that teachers might have to differentiate self-monitoring charts for those who are still struggling readers. Some may begin with a few visuals to foster independence with the intention of fading them out eventually.

Appendix 9–1 shows an example of a paper/pencil monitoring system that students can use to track their daily behavior. Just like the primary chart, this one shows four target behaviors that students should aim to demonstrate for the allotted time, which in this case is in 1-hour intervals. If the student accurately demonstrates the behavior (e.g., the student used appropriate language the entire hour), that student would put a check in that box. At the end of each hour, the student will mark whether they were able to get at least three out of four (75%) check marks for the time slot. Similarly, at the end of the day, the student will see how many times they were able to reach their goal throughout the academic day by counting how many times they achieved 75%. A big difference in this chart from the primary chart is that there is a chance for a *bonus check*. The bonus comes from the teacher, if he or she feels a student did something exemplary during the hour, such as a random act of kindness toward a classmate. It is important to tell the students that the bonus section will not preclude them from earning their points; it only helps and adds encouragement. At the bottom of the chart, there is a teacher comment section that allows the teacher to have daily communication with home.

### High School

Students who are in high school may already be more cognizant of this process. These students usually benefit from a system where they have a quick and easy tracking sheet of their target behaviors and can record behaviors. At the end of each period, the student adds up the points they received and continues adding points throughout the day. At the end of the day, the student conferences with the special education teacher and receives feedback and reinforcement. Appendix 9–2 provides an example of a student self-tracking sheet for middle and high school students. This figure illustrates five target behaviors to be demonstrated by the student each period. If demonstrated, the student checks the corresponding box. At the end of each period, students add up points they received for that period. In this example, it is expected that the teacher checks to make sure the student completed the chart for their class period accurately. At the end of the day, the teacher and the student review the chart, and the student continues with this for the week.

## Check-In, Check-Out

Check-In, Check-Out (CICO) is an intervention that involves a coordinator that is assigned to a particular student, which is usually the special education teacher that works with the student who is getting this intervention or a preferred adult that is involved with the student (Hawken et al., 2014). During check-in, the student and coordinator meet at the beginning of each school day to ensure the student has what they need to be successful that day. Additionally, the coordinator provides them with their Daily Progress Report (DPR), which usually lists the target behaviors for the student or the schoolwide expectations. The DPR is where students can track their progress to show if they are meeting behavioral expectations and includes a section where teachers can comment on the student's day. Check-out consists of the student and coordinator debriefing about the student's day, as well as adding up points that are associated with the behaviors listed on the DPR. This is when the coordinator provides previously agreed-upon reinforcement or, in the instance of an "off" day, corrective feedback and next steps based on the day that is documented (Hawken et al., 2014). Parents are expected to sign the DPR and return it the following day, ensuring parental involvement and open communication with the home.

CICO is a useful tool for all ages and grade levels, elementary through high school. If implementing CICO, it is imperative that daily points are documented for tracking purposes. Coordinators for elementary-age students should document points themselves on a spreadsheet or chart. However, students in middle and high school are able to document their own behavior by saving an electronic file (e.g., Excel, Google Sheets) that is easily accessed by all members of the CICO team, including the student, coordinator, and teachers. Tracking daily points is beneficial for the student, teacher(s), and parents to see student behavioral progress. These point values can be graphed, weekly, monthly, quarterly, or by trimester.

## Goal Setting

**Goal setting** is related to self-management and self-regulation and is a commonly used self-management intervention (Mooney et al., 2005). Setting goals involves "establishing a standard or objective to serve as the aim of one's actions" (Schunk, 2001, p. 1). Goal setting increases self-regulation by having positive effects on learning and motivation (Schunk, 2001) and is targeted toward a specific goal, which is a part of becoming a self-regulated learner (Arslan, 2014). Individuals who set goals regularly stay focused on the task at hand, are able to select strategies that are appropriate for the task, apply the strategy that best fits the task, and then monitor their work and progress toward meeting the goal (Schunk, 2001). For students with EBD, goal setting is extremely important. Many of these students may require intensive instruction in this skill set so they obtain the skills needed for learning (Bruhn et al., 2016). This skill set can encourage behavioral success, which can then lead to successful academic work. Students who set "realistic and relevant goals" (Morrison, 2010) have a better chance of achieving them. Though students may need assistance with this skill in the beginning, it is important that they are always involved in setting their goals (Palmer et al., 2004). Bruhn and colleagues (2016) conducted a systematic review of literature that looked at goal-setting interventions for students with behavior problems. Studies that they investigated found that having student input produces positive perceptions about setting goals, as well as positive outcomes. Having student involvement at any level promotes accountability in one's own work and achievement, as well as provides a sense of achievement, which is crucial for these students. This feeling can produce a positive sense of self and increase confidence and commitment to school (Bruhn et al., 2016). The following sections provide examples of school-based interventions that can be used to help students build their emotional awareness. Each example seeks to follow the guidelines that call for a specific measurable goal that can be achieved by the student in a reasonable amount of time (Lawlor & Hornyak, 2012).

### Kindergarten

Goal setting might be difficult in the early grades of elementary school, such as kindergarten, because of the limited experience students have with school. Providing them with prewritten goals is an effective way to introduce goal setting. When goals are prewritten, expectations are already in place. Students should still have a part in the goal-setting process. Students are a part of the decision-making portion of it. For example, students can pick a goal from the menu or bank that corresponds with their needs and help set a reasonable time frame to accomplish the goal. Additionally, they can be taught to monitor and track their progress toward meeting it. Although kindergarten students might be choosing from a teacher-written goal, this process allows students to learn how to plan and problem solve how they will be meeting these goals, which provides students with deficits in self-regulating their emotions with practice in goal setting (Blair, 2002).

Appendix 9–3 provides an example of a menu of goals, or a prewritten *goal bank*. This example has a mixture of academic and behavioral goals for a kindergarten student. Some students might be able to have yearly, monthly, or trimester or quarterly goals, but others may need goals for shorter amounts of time or goals that are more specific to their individualized needs. Though this example shows a menu of prewritten goals, teachers should be aware of what works best for each student. Child involvement with the use of a menu, such as this one, should be high and consistent. Students should know exactly what they are working on and when the date is for potential mastery, along with being the lead in the process of tracking their progress.

If a goal menu is too much for a particular child, it might be beneficial to provide a student with up to five prewritten, achievable goals per day. Each goal corresponds with a subject area and one target behavior based on student need. Similar to the menu, goals are accompanied by visuals so there is a push for **independence**, which ensures that the student can do things by themselves. Where appropriate, student involvement in the creation of daily goals should be used. Allowing students with or at risk for EBD at a young age to start setting goals and expectations for themselves with teacher support can significantly impact student achievement both academically and behaviorally.

### Elementary Grades

For other elementary grades, goal setting can be done more independently. For Grades 1, 2, and possibly 3, students can create their own behavioral and academic goals, but they may require a sentence starter and lines to fill in certain criteria of the goal to make sure it is complete. Students in Grades 4 and 5 may be able to complete the goal with limited teacher assistance.

Although these students are older, it is important to understand that when working with students with or at risk for EBD, behavioral goals may take precedence over academic goals (Bruhn et al., 2016). Additionally, the period in which the goal should be accomplished may vary with these students. For example, a student who reacts to difficult situations with physical aggression every day may need to start with setting a behavioral goal that focuses on responding to difficult situations in a more safe, appropriate manner (i.e., using a hot card) and is monitored every class period. Since the aggression is said to happen every day, this student may start with setting a goal for class periods, 1 day, or 1 week, and then as progress is being made, the allotted time can be extended until the goal is no longer needed. The point is for students to understand what they need to work on, put it into words and on paper, operationally define it so that it is clear, and be accountable in utilizing strategies that can aid in meeting the goal and tracking their progress.

Appendix 9–4 provides an example of a chart that can be used in for students to set goals and track their progress. In this example, students set academic and/or behavioral weekly goals and create an action plan, which states how they are going to meet that goal. At first, students may need assistance with creating an action plan. This chart also asks students to describe how they will know if they meet their goal, providing a criterion for mastery. Students will monitor their progress daily. Under *progress monitoring*, the students will track their progress for the day, taking their own data. The data they take are driven by the action plan they create. At the end of each day, the teacher and student conference to look at their progress for the day on their goal(s). During this meeting, students can transfer their data for the day onto a graph (teacher discretion). This meeting will also give teachers the opportunity to discuss the student's day, deciding whether their action plan is working toward meeting their goal. Additionally, it has an accountability measure to be completed on the day the goal was set for, asking the student if they met their goal and why or why not.

An academic example is the goal to master the *2 times tables*. This student's action plan might be to study flashcards for 10 minutes each day during independent work. The criteria for mastery may involve getting at least an 80% on some type of a timed worksheet or timed flash card test. Each day, the student would record how they did on a similar task and record their daily result in the progress-monitoring box next to the appropriate day. At the end of the week, the student will write if they met their goal or if they did not and why.

A behavior example might focus on raising a quiet hand for a student who is impulsive and calls out numerous times throughout the day. This student's goal would be to raise their hand 15 times during the school day when they have something to say. When a goal is like this, using tally marks might be an easy way for the student to track how many times they raised their hand, which is recorded in the progress-monitoring section. Similar to the academic goal, at the end of the week, the student will comment on whether they met their goal or not.

A roadmap can be a beneficial way to provide elementary-age students with a goal-setting tool. This can be done in the form of a board game or a poster. Each fifth *stop* can be a goal that the student and teacher set together. This can be based on unit, trimester, and so on. Each time the student meets a goal on the roadmap, they can move to the next goal on the board. After meeting each goal, the student gets a small reward. Upon completion of the *map*, students receive a slightly larger reward and get to switch out their goals with their teacher. A roadmap is a fun and interactive way to set goals and track student progress toward meeting them.

### Middle and High School

At the **secondary**, or high school, level, students are setting goals that are more focused on their life after school, for instance, transition goals for college or career paths (Carter et al., 2011). Students with EBD need short-term behavioral and academic goals to get significant immediate outcomes. It is often difficult for students to plan far in advance when each day can be a struggle. For them, the focus should be on behavior and/or academic goals that can allow them to have a feeling of accomplishment. There are many different ways to have students with EBD in middle and high school set realistic goals, track them, and work to achieve them.

A vision board is a great way to have students document their goals in a different, unique way. Depending on student need, vision boards can be created to set goals for the year, each quarter, monthly, or every other week. Vision boards can be completed with magazine pictures, drawings or writing, printouts, or actual pictures the students bring in. Visuals must be relevant to what the student wants to accomplish for the allotted time. They should also be partnered with a system to track their progress toward that goal. Progress monitoring can be done on the back of the board, keeping everything in one spot. Depending on the time selected, each board can be redone with new goals once the initial ones were achieved.

Many apps are used to set goals and track student progress toward meeting those goals. If your classroom has the technology and the means to do so, this may be a more time-savvy way for students to set and track goals. There are many different apps that are geared toward setting and tracking goals. Some apps require more extensive data collection, and others require a tally mark, or a frequency count. Teachers can search "goal setting" on the Apple App Store or the Microsoft Store and browse through results that will best fit the needs of their students. Table 9–4 provides an example of applications for goal setting. The following sections contain two vignettes that outline concepts covered in this chapter.

**Table 9–4.**  Goal-Setting Apps

| Name | Description |
|------|-------------|
| Goal-Setting Tracker Planner | This app allows you to set and plan long-term and short-term goals. The goal-setting process used in this program is the SMART process, ensuring individuals focus on their important goals. Goal-Setting Tracker Planner allows for daily journaling so the individual can reflect about their progress toward their goal(s). |
| Strides: Habit Tracker | This app has multiple means to build and track goals throughout daily activities and longer periods. It not only uses the SMART to create goals but also helps individuals build a daily routine list, keep data of progress, and send reminders to the person's device. |
| Tally: The Anything Tracker | This program is user-friendly in nature, just requiring frequency counts toward meeting one's goals. It allows you to choose what you want to tally, how often it needs to reset data (i.e., daily, weekly, monthly, etc.), and the target amount. If there are multiple goals, they can be color coded. |

*Note.* These are just three examples of apps that can be used with electronic devices to have students set goals for themselves. Each one allows students to track their progress and to take notes to reflect upon their work.

*Source.* These apps are the result of an Apple App Store search, "Goal Setting." This information was taken and summarized from the App Store.

## CASE STUDY—ELEMENTARY

*John is a fourth-grade student with emotional and behavioral difficulties who is in a general education inclusive setting. He feels that he stands out because there are times when he gets overwhelmed or frustrated and cannot control his verbal and aggressive outbursts. He feels embarrassed after an outburst because he thinks his classmates are judging him and that they do not want to be around him. At lunch, John sits in the seat at the very end of the table, and there is usually an empty seat next to him. He also thinks that his teacher does not want to be around him because she constantly calls the office to get him removed from the classroom, even if he is not being aggressive. It is now December and John is 3 to 4 months behind in his academic work with either very low passing or failing grades and has no friends. This makes him even more frustrated, not wanting to come to school because he thinks there is no point if he cannot do the work and if there is no one to talk to about it. His special education teacher has attempted to do Check-In, Check-Out with him, but he has seen a decrease in his motivation to be at school and an increase in his outbursts in the classroom.*

*To make an impact on John's social inclusion, academic achievement, and self-worth, his special education teacher thinks he would benefit from a self-*

*management intervention. It is clear that he knows he has outbursts but does not know how to control them. It can be concluded that he has weak self-management skills and reacts inappropriately to situations he may find challenging. Now, just physically being in school is a challenge for him. Due to his aggressive outbursts, caused by being overwhelmed and/or frustrated, John would benefit from a choice board or a choice menu. Having loud aggressive outbursts is not appropriate and is causing him to feel ostracized within his class. He needs alternative behaviors to cope with potential challenges that come about within the classroom. A choice board can direct John to take a break, take a walk, stretch, or, if possible, get some help from the teacher or a peer. Decreasing John's outbursts and increasing other skills that he can utilize instead will significantly influence John's experience at school and attitude toward going to school and will allow him to have a sense of belonging within his class again.*

## CASE STUDY—SECONDARY

*Mr. White is a special education teacher in a Title I high school. He sees his students one period a day on his own and then pushes into reading and math classes the rest of the day. He sees each of his special education students that he services every morning and every afternoon to implement the Check-In, Check-Out intervention. In the afternoon, he sits with the students and reflects on their day and their behavior reports from their teachers, talking about what went well and what they could have done better. Then they make a plan to stay consistent or to improve for the following day. In the mornings, Mr. White and the students sit with him and eat breakfast in the cafeteria, go over their plans from the previous day, and talk about what they will accomplish today.*

*One day, Mr. White noticed that one of his newer students, Alyssa, was struggling for a few weeks with her behavior reports from her teachers. After his morning check-in with the group, he asked her to stay back for a little while to talk. When he asked her what was going on, she said she did not know what she was doing wrong. Mr. White went through generic behavioral expectations that are expected throughout high school classrooms. Alyssa was able to acknowledge that those were the expectations but was unsure how to display those behaviors. Mr. White soon realized that Alyssa needed to monitor herself with specific target behaviors so she knew exactly what needed to be done to meet classroom expectations. He set her up with a self-monitoring chart that listed the behaviors needed for each class that will allow her to have a successful class period. In collaboration with the teachers, he told them to still write a daily report, but Alyssa was to complete her monitoring chart independently and report back to Mr. White so they would be able to compare the self-monitoring chart and the teacher reports. After 2 weeks of implementation, Alyssa's received reports changed drastically and each teacher reported a significant improvement in behavior.*

## CHAPTER SUMMARY

In this chapter, we discussed interventions and strategies that students with or at risk for EBD can use to monitor their own behavior and different strategies used for students to set goals. With explicit instruction, students can begin to accurately identify their own emotions throughout the day, apply strategies that can be used to regulate their emotions in a socially appropriate way, and monitor their expected behaviors. Although interventions vary based on grade level and age range, the concept of having a strategy for promoting more useful emotions per situation and four to five target behaviors to successfully get through the school day is consistent throughout grade levels. Similarly, the ability to set realistic and relevant goals that can be tracked accordingly may look different based on grade level but is similar in construct and end goal. This chapter shows that each aspect of self-management can significantly impact student behavior and produce academic achievement.

## DISCUSSION QUESTIONS

1. What is self-management and why is it important for students with EBD?

2. Why is it important to teach young children who have or are at risk for emotional and behavioral problems to identify their emotions?

3. Name and describe an intervention that is suitable to teach young children how to identify their behavior. How would you utilize the intervention in your classroom?

4. What intervention can a general educator implement in his or her classroom if a student berates himself or herself daily? What would this intervention look like?

5. Why should teachers focus on teaching high school students to set short-term goals rather than transitional goals?

**RESOURCES**

https://www.counseling.org/resources/library/eric%20digests/2001-08.pdf

https://www2.ed.gov/about/offices/list/ous/international/usnei/us/edlite-structure-us.html

https://www.interventioncentral.org/node/961544

https://www.pbisworld.com/tier-2/self-monitoring/

https://rapidbi.com/history-of-smart-objectives/

## REFERENCES

Arslan, S. (2014). An investigation of the relationships between metacognition and self-regulation with structural equation. *International Online Journal of Educational Sciences, 6*(3), 603–611.

Bambara, L. M., Janney, R., & Snell, M. E. (2015). *Teachers' guide to inclusive practices: Behavior support* (3rd ed.). Paul H. Brookes.

Barrett, P. M., Webster, H. M., & Wallis, J. R. (1999). Adolescent self-esteem and cognitive skills training: A school-based intervention. *Journal of Child and Family Studies, 8*(2), 217–227. doi:10.1023/A:1022044119273

Blair, C. (2002). School readiness. *American Psychologist, 57*(2), 111–127. doi:10.1037/0003-066X.57.2.111

Bruhn, A. L., McDaniel, S. C., Fernando, J., & Troughton, L. (2016). Goal-setting interventions for students with behavior problems: A systematic review. *Behavioral Disorders, 41*(2), 107–121. doi:10.17988/0198-7429-41.2.107

Carter, E. W., Lane, K. L., Crnobori, M. E., Bruhn, A. L., & Oakes, W. P. (2011). Self-determination interventions for students with or at risk for emotional and behavioral disorders: Mapping the knowledge base. *Behavioral Disorders, 36*(2), 100–116.

Cooper, J. O., Heron, T. E., & Heward, W. L. (2007). *Applied behavior analysis* (2nd ed.). Pearson Merrill Prentice Hall.

Coutinho, M. (1986). Reading achievement of students identified as behaviorally disordered at the secondary level. *Behavioral Disorders, 11*(3), 200–207. doi:10.1177/019874298601100305

Cullinan, D. (2002). *Students with emotional and behavioral disorders: An introduction for teachers and other helping professionals.* Upper Saddle River, NJ: Merrill/Prentice Hall.

Dunn, M. E., Shelnut, J., Ryan, J. B., & Katsiyannis, A. (2017). A systematic review of peer-mediated interventions on the academic achievement of students with emotional/behavioral disorders. *Education and Treatment of Children, 40*(4), 497–524.

Falk, K. B., & Wehby, J. H. (2001). The effects of peer-assisted learning strategies on the beginning reading skills of young children with emotional or behavioral disorders. *Behavioral Disorders, 26*(4), 344–359. doi:10.1177/019874290102600404

Havighurst, S. S., Duncombe, M., Frankling, E., Holland, K., Kehow, C., & Stargatt, R. (2015). An emotion-focused early intervention for children with emerging conduct problems. *Journal of Abnormal Child Psychology*, *43*(4), 749–760. doi:10.1007/s10802-014-9944-z

Hawken, L. S., Bundock, K., Kladis, K., O'Keeffe, B., & Barrett, C. A. (2014). Systematic review of the check-in, check-out intervention for students at risk for emotional and behavioral disorders. *Education and Treatment of Children*, *37*(4), 635–658.

Hunter, W., Williamson, R. L., Jasper, A. D., Casey, L. B., & Smith, C. (2017). Examining self-monitoring interventions for academic support of students with emotional and behavioral disorders. *Journal of International Special Needs Education*, *20*(2), 67–78.

Jolivette, K., Wehby, J. H., Canale, J., & Massey, N. G. (2001). Effects of choice-making opportunities on the behavior of students with emotional and behavioral disorders. *Behavioral Disorders*, *26*, 131–145. doi:10.1177/019874290102600203

Lawlor, K. B., & Hornyak, M. J. (2012). SMART goals: How the application of SMART goals can contribute to achievement of student learning outcomes. *Developments in Business Simulation and Experiential Learning*, *39*, 259–267.

Mooney, P., Ryan, J. B., Uhing, B. M., Reid, R., & Epstein, M. H. (2005). A review of self-management interventions targeting academic outcomes for students with emotional and behavioral disorders. *Journal of Behavioral Education*, *14*(3), 203–221. doi:10.1007/s10864-005-6298-1

Morrison, M. (2010). *History of SMART objectives*. Rapid Business Improvement. Retrieved from https://rapidbi.com/history-of-smart-objectives/

Palmer, S. B., Wehmeyer, M. L., Gipson, K., & Agran, M. (2004). Promoting access to the general curriculum by teaching self-determination skills. *Exceptional Children*, *70*(4), 427–439.

Patton, B., Jolivette, K., & Ramsey, M. (2006). Students with emotional and behavioral disorders can manage their own behavior. *Teaching Exceptional Children*, *39*(2), 14–21.

Schunk, D. H. (2001). *Self-regulation through goal setting*. Retrieved from https://www.counseling.org/resources/library/eric%20digests/2001-08.pdf

Skerbetz, M. D., & Kostewicz, D. E. (2013). Academic choice for included students with emotional and behavioral disorders. *Preventing School Failure: Alternative Education for Children and Youth*, *57*(4), 212–222.

Tamir, M. (2009). What do people want to feel and why? Pleasure and utility in emotion regulation. *Current Directions in Psychological Science*, *18*(2), 101-105.

U.S. Department of Education. (2008). *Organization of U.S. education: The school level*. Retrieved from https://www2.ed.gov/about/offices/list/ous/international/usnei/us/edlite-structure-us.html

Vargas, J. S. (2013). *Behavior analysis for effective teaching* (2nd ed.). Routledge.

# APPENDIX 9–1

## Self-Monitoring Chart for Intermediate

Students are meant to track four target behaviors by hour, putting a check indicating that they displayed the behavior for the hour time slot or an X in the correlating box indicating that they did not successfully display the target behavior. The goal is for students to get three out of four check marks each hour and five out of six for the whole day.

Name:

Date:

| Behavior → Time Slot ↓ | Hands to self ✓ or X | On task ✓ or X | Appropriate language ✓ or X | In assigned area ✓ or X | Bonus (from teacher) | 75%? (at least 3/4) Yes or No |
|---|---|---|---|---|---|---|
| 8:00–9:00 a.m. | | | | | | |
| 9:00–10:00 a.m. | | | | | | |
| 10:00–11:00 a.m. | | | | | | |
| 11:00–12:00 p.m. | | | | | | |
| 12:00–1:00 p.m. | | | | | | |
| 1:00–2:00 p.m. | | | | | | |
| | | | | Total "Yes": Goal = 5 out of 6 | | |

Teacher Comments:

# Self-Monitoring Chart for Middle School and/or High School

This tool can be taken class to class for students to easily monitor their behavior.

| | Period 1: | Period 2: | Period 3: | Period 4: |
|---|---|---|---|---|
| **Monday** | ☐ I was on time to class. <br><br> ☐ I was prepared for class (i.e., correct books, pencil, etc.). <br><br> ☐ I stayed in the classroom. <br><br> ☐ I stayed on task. <br><br> ☐ I kept my hands and comments to myself. <br><br> **Total:** _____ | ☐ I was on time to class. <br><br> ☐ I was prepared for class (i.e., correct books, pencil, etc.). <br><br> ☐ I stayed in the classroom. <br><br> ☐ I stayed on task. <br><br> ☐ I kept my hands and comments to myself. <br><br> **Total:** _____ | ☐ I was on time to class. <br><br> ☐ I was prepared for class (i.e., correct books, pencil, etc.). <br><br> ☐ I stayed in the classroom. <br><br> ☐ I stayed on task. <br><br> ☐ I kept my hands and comments to myself. <br><br> **Total:** _____ | ☐ I was on time to class. <br><br> ☐ I was prepared for class (i.e., correct books, pencil, etc.). <br><br> ☐ I stayed in the classroom. <br><br> ☐ I stayed on task. <br><br> ☐ I kept my hands and comments to myself. <br><br> **Total:** _____ |
| | Period 1: | Period 2: | Period 3: | Period 4: |
| **Tuesday** | ☐ I was on time to class. <br><br> ☐ I was prepared for class (i.e., correct books, pencil, etc.). <br><br> ☐ I stayed in the classroom. <br><br> ☐ I stayed on task. <br><br> ☐ I kept my hands and comments to myself. <br><br> **Total:** _____ | ☐ I was on time to class. <br><br> ☐ I was prepared for class (i.e., correct books, pencil, etc.). <br><br> ☐ I stayed in the classroom. <br><br> ☐ I stayed on task. <br><br> ☐ I kept my hands and comments to myself. <br><br> **Total:** _____ | ☐ I was on time to class. <br><br> ☐ I was prepared for class (i.e., correct books, pencil, etc.). <br><br> ☐ I stayed in the classroom. <br><br> ☐ I stayed on task. <br><br> ☐ I kept my hands and comments to myself. <br><br> **Total:** _____ | ☐ I was on time to class. <br><br> ☐ I was prepared for class (i.e., correct books, pencil, etc.). <br><br> ☐ I stayed in the classroom. <br><br> ☐ I stayed on task. <br><br> ☐ I kept my hands and comments to myself. <br><br> **Total:** _____ |

| | Period 1: | Period 2: | Period 3: | Period 4: |
|---|---|---|---|---|
| **Wednesday** | ☐ I was on time to class.<br>☐ I was prepared for class (i.e., correct books, pencil, etc.).<br>☐ I stayed in the classroom.<br>☐ I stayed on task.<br>☐ I kept my hands and comments to myself.<br><br>**Total:** _____ | ☐ I was on time to class.<br>☐ I was prepared for class (i.e., correct books, pencil, etc.).<br>☐ I stayed in the classroom.<br>☐ I stayed on task.<br>☐ I kept my hands and comments to myself.<br><br>**Total:** _____ | ☐ I was on time to class.<br>☐ I was prepared for class (i.e., correct books, pencil, etc.).<br>☐ I stayed in the classroom.<br>☐ I stayed on task.<br>☐ I kept my hands and comments to myself.<br><br>**Total:** _____ | ☐ I was on time to class.<br>☐ I was prepared for class (i.e., correct books, pencil, etc.).<br>☐ I stayed in the classroom.<br>☐ I stayed on task.<br>☐ I kept my hands and comments to myself.<br><br>**Total:** _____ |
| | Period 1: | Period 2: | Period 3: | Period 4: |
| **Thursday** | ☐ I was on time to class.<br>☐ I was prepared for class (i.e., correct books, pencil, etc.).<br>☐ I stayed in the classroom.<br>☐ I stayed on task.<br>☐ I kept my hands and comments to myself.<br><br>**Total:** _____ | ☐ I was on time to class.<br>☐ I was prepared for class (i.e., correct books, pencil, etc.).<br>☐ I stayed in the classroom.<br>☐ I stayed on task.<br>☐ I kept my hands and comments to myself.<br><br>**Total:** _____ | ☐ I was on time to class.<br>☐ I was prepared for class (i.e., correct books, pencil, etc.).<br>☐ I stayed in the classroom.<br>☐ I stayed on task.<br>☐ I kept my hands and comments to myself.<br><br>**Total:** _____ | ☐ I was on time to class.<br>☐ I was prepared for class (i.e., correct books, pencil, etc.).<br>☐ I stayed in the classroom.<br>☐ I stayed on task.<br>☐ I kept my hands and comments to myself.<br><br>**Total:** _____ |
| | Period 1: | Period 2: | Period 3: | Period 4: |
| **Friday** | ☐ I was on time to class.<br>☐ I was prepared for class (i.e., correct books, pencil, etc.).<br>☐ I stayed in the classroom.<br>☐ I stayed on task.<br>☐ I kept my hands and comments to myself.<br><br>**Total:** _____ | ☐ I was on time to class.<br>☐ I was prepared for class (i.e., correct books, pencil, etc.).<br>☐ I stayed in the classroom.<br>☐ I stayed on task.<br>☐ I kept my hands and comments to myself.<br><br>**Total:** _____ | ☐ I was on time to class.<br>☐ I was prepared for class (i.e., correct books, pencil, etc.).<br>☐ I stayed in the classroom.<br>☐ I stayed on task.<br>☐ I kept my hands and comments to myself.<br><br>**Total:** _____ | ☐ I was on time to class.<br>☐ I was prepared for class (i.e., correct books, pencil, etc.).<br>☐ I stayed in the classroom.<br>☐ I stayed on task.<br>☐ I kept my hands and comments to myself.<br><br>**Total:** _____ |

# Kindergarten Premade Goal Menu

The menu is meant to help kindergarten students set and track goals having to do with academics and behavior.

| My Kindergarten Goals | | | | | |
|---|---|---|---|---|---|
| **Academics** | | | | | |
| I can recognize my name. | I can write my first name. | I can write my last name. | I can say the alphabet. | I can recognize all lowercase letters. | I can recognize all capital letters. |
| Date: | Date: | Date: | Date: | Date: | Date: |
| I can recognize all letter sounds. | I can make all letter sounds. | I can write letters a to z onto paper. | I can write a sentence | I know all of my sight words. | I can read a book by myself. |
| Date: | Date: | Date: | Date: | Date: | Date: |
| I can count to 100. | I know numbers to 100. | I can match the amount to the number up to 20. | I can count by 5s and 10s to get to 100. | I know all of my plane shapes. | I can fluently add within 5. |
| Date: | Date: | Date: | Date: | Date: | Date: |
| I can tell which group is greater. | I can tell which group is less. | I know all of my 3D shapes. | I can write numbers 0 to 20. | I can fluently subtract within 5. | I can make a ten by adding more to a group. |
| Date: | Date: | Date: | Date: | Date: | Date: |
| **Behavior Skills** | | | | | |
| I can raise my hand when I need help or know an answer. | I can stay in my area. | I can do my work. | I can use kind words to my friends. | I can keep my hands to myself. | I can listen to the teacher. |
| Daily | Daily | Daily | Daily | Daily | Daily |

# Intermediate Goal Setting Weekly Chart

This chart is used for students to set and monitor academic and behavioral goals, create a plan, and reflect on their outcome.

| Name: | Week Of: | Progress Monitoring |
|---|---|---|
| **Academic Goal:**<br>I will | **Action Plan:** | **M-**<br>**T-**<br>**W-**<br>**Th-**<br>**F-** |
| **How will I know if I met my goal?** | | |
| **Did I meet my goal? What worked? What did not work?**<br>I met my goal because<br><br><br>I did not meet my goal because | | |

# 10

# Peer-Directed Behavioral Interventions

*With Contributions from Kelly B. Kearney*

## KEY VOCABULARY

Cross-Age Peer Tutoring

Data Sheet

Fidelity

Literacy-Based Behavioral Intervention (LBBI)

Opportunities to Respond

Peer-Assisted Learning Strategies (PALS)

Peer Initiation Training

Peer-Mediated Instruction and Intervention (PMII)

Peer Modeling

Peer Tutoring

Social Skills

Social Validity

Video Modeling

## LEARNING OBJECTIVES

By the end of this chapter, you should be able to . . .

- Describe various peer-directed behavioral interventions.
- Identify the advantages of peer-directed behavioral interventions over traditional instructional methods.
- Determine which peer-directed behavioral interventions would be beneficial in your classroom.
- Develop a peer-directed behavioral intervention to target an acquisition skill.

## INTRODUCTION

This chapter will discuss peer-directed behavioral interventions. Peer-directed interventions, also referred to as **peer-mediated instruction and intervention (PMII)**, are a collection of peer-driven, classroom-based interventions that are used to teach students with disabilities, including those with emotional and behavioral disabilities, various acquisition skills (Maheady et al., 2001). Peer-directed interventions use other students in the classroom as the instructional agent for the target student, allowing the teacher's role to shift to facilitator of learning and monitor of the intervention.

Peer-directed interventions have been used to effectively teach academic tasks, social skills, and behavioral skills. Peer-directed interventions are one way to break the cycle of challenges many students with EBD face throughout their school career. These challenges are academic, behavioral, social, and authoritarian, and their impact can be felt long after the student exits the school system. Figure 10–1 shows the cycle of challenges students with EBD encounter in school.

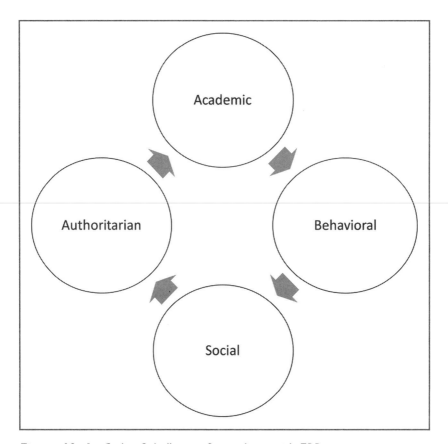

***Figure 10–1.*** *Cycle of challenges for students with EBD.*

Most students with EBD spend the majority of their school time in a general education classroom but often have difficulties with behavioral and interpersonal interactions, engaging in a variety of avoidance and escape behaviors in the classroom, such as disruption and noncompliance (Maheady et al., 2001), which create a distracting learning environment and cause friction, tension, or conflict between themselves, teachers, and peers. Students with EBD experience low rates of positive teacher attention and praise and limited opportunities to respond to academic requests (Sutherland & Snyder, 2007). Conflict makes peer-directed behavioral interventions particularly poignant, since these interventions have been shown to enhance peer social relationships and are designed to increase opportunities for response and praise in order to facilitate learning (Kaya et al., 2015; Sutherland & Snyder, 2007).

## SOCIAL SKILLS

Many peer-directed behavioral interventions can be used to work on social skills. **Social skills** are a class of skills that enable those who have mastered them to navigate their environment successfully (Quinn et al., 1999). Students with EBD are typically identified and labeled due to their lack of interpersonal, peer, and social skills (Quinn et al., 1999). Social skills involve interacting with peers and adults appropriately, communicating emotional and physical needs appropriately, following social rules and manners, and an ability to appraise social situations (Quinn et al., 1999). Students who are successful in the classroom know how to cooperate, problem-solve, and compromise with other students as needed to effectively navigate social situations. They can communicate their wants and needs effectively with both peers and adults, are assertive and able to advocate for themselves, and have the self-control needed to appropriately handle rejection or conflict. These four skills—cooperation, communication, assertiveness, and self-control—are integral social skills for classroom integration. Figure 10–2 illustrates the social skills students need to be successful in the classroom.

Peer-directed behavioral interventions may include strategies such as tutoring, modeling, counseling, and mentoring to improve the social skills and behavioral outcomes of a student with EBD (Kaya et al., 2015). Since these interventions are peer driven, using them creates an environment that enables students with EBD to remain in the general education classroom and witness their peers successfully navigating their surroundings. This also leads to an increased likelihood of positive social interactions with peers outside of school.

Many studies using peer-directed behavioral interventions have used typically developing peer trainers to facilitate the intervention (Blake et al., 2000), and the peer trainers should ideally be members of the targeted peer group, experiencing the same environmental challenges and sharing similar experiences. This is particularly true for adolescent males, who hold their peers in high esteem (Blake et al., 2000). Peer trainers should share a similar background as the target peer. Using peer trainers that are a part of the target peer's natural environment increases the likelihood that the skills will maintain and generalize to other environments (Blake et al., 2000). Also, the peer trainers themselves benefit from the interaction, often expressing feelings of pride in the role of the instructional agent (Blake et al., 2000). Teachers have the ability to harness the power of peer influence to improve behavioral outcomes for students with EBD.

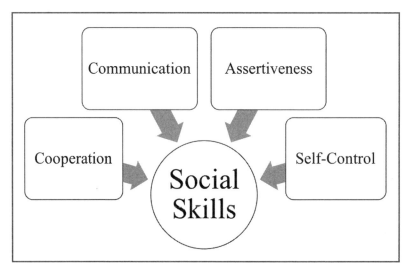

**Figure 10–2.** Social skills.

## ADVANTAGES OF PEER-DIRECTED
## BEHAVIORAL INTERVENTIONS

There are many different reasons for teachers to use peer-directed behavioral interventions in their classrooms. First and foremost, a well-run peer-directed behavioral intervention can help to free up a teacher's time during the day. Having a peer provide social and behavioral support to a struggling student means that the teacher does not need to spend that designated time directly supporting said student, enabling the teacher to engage in other teaching activities during that block of time. These interventions provide one-on-one support and individualized attention to target students, increasing their task engagement and lowering the chance of them engaging in disruptive or off-task behaviors. This ensures the teacher spends less time managing behaviors and more time engaging in other teaching activities (Kaya et al., 2015).

Students receive immediate feedback more frequently when participating in peer-directed interventions. This immediate feedback prevents students from practicing new skills incorrectly (Heward, 1997). Students participating in peer-directed interventions are also provided more opportunities to respond. **Opportunities to respond** are the resulting interactions that occur from a teacher's (or in this case a peer's) direct prompt to a student and the student's response (Randolph et al., 2019). Increasing the amount of opportunities to respond that each student has often increases student engagement and increases the frequency of appropriate student behavior (Randolph et al., 2019). Involving multiple peer partners across school settings can also promote generalization of skills to new people, environments, and behaviors and improves maintenance of new skills over extended periods of time (DuPaul et al., 1997).

Peer-directed behavioral interventions may be particularly reinforcing for students in older grades. Older students tend to prefer peer interaction to adult interaction, and teachers who implement peer-directed interventions may witness increased levels of target student engagement when compared to teacher-directed interventions. Peer-directed interventions are also beneficial to both students participating in the partnership. Peers who act as the instructional agent in the dyad are also more likely to engage in desired behaviors (DuPaul et al., 1997), making peer-directed interventions particularly beneficial in classrooms with diverse learner needs.

## TYPES OF PEER-DIRECTED BEHAVIORAL INTERVENTIONS

There are many types of peer-directed behavioral interventions. This chapter will discuss the following interventions (1) peer modeling, (2) peer initiation training, (3) video modeling, (4) peer tutoring, (5) peer-assisted learning strategies, and (6) literacy-based behavior intervention. Table 10–1 provides steps of video-modeling peer-directed interventions.

### Peer Modeling

Peer modeling is the foundation of many other peer-directed interventions. **Peer modeling** involves a competent peer accurately displaying or engaging in a targeted skill, allowing the student an opportunity to observe the skill completed correctly. Pairing a trained, competent peer with a less-skilled peer creates opportunities for observational learning to occur. Educators can create opportunities for the target student to observe the peer model engage in successful social interactions with peers, enact positive classroom behaviors, or complete tasks in the classroom appropriately. However, just creating opportunities for observation is not enough. Observational learning alone using peer models may not be a strong enough intervention on its own to see substantial change in the target student's behavior. Peer models need to be trained by the teacher to ensure that the models are engaging appropriately in targeted behaviors (Utley et al., 1997). Teachers should pair peer modeling with direct instruction, role-playing, adult reinforcement, or some other intervention for the most impact.

**Table 10–1.**  Steps of Video Modeling Peer-Directed Behavioral Interventions

| Intervention | Description |
|---|---|
| Peer Modeling | Target student observes a highly skilled peer engage in a targeted skill (social, behavioral, academic). |
| Peer Initiation Training | Peer is trained to evoke and maintain intended social behaviors from a target student. |
| Video Modeling | Target student watches a previously recorded video of a peer model demonstrating a targeted skill. |
| Peer-Assisted Learning | A highly structured version of peer tutoring that pairs target students with peers to deliver academic instruction multiple times a week, with each student alternating role of coach and pupil. |
| Peer Tutoring | Target students are paired with select peer tutors, often reversing role of tutor and tutee (dyads could comprise novice student/proficient student, older student/younger student, or novice student/younger student). |
| Cross-Age Peer Tutoring | Older students matched with younger students. Tutors are often at least 2 years older than the target students. |
| Literacy-Based Behavioral Intervention (LBBI) | Storybook that has text and pictures, each page demonstrating the next step in a chained skill. Read by a peer to the target student. |

## Peer Initiation Training

**Peer initiation training** involves a teacher training a peer to evoke and maintain the intended social behaviors from a target student (Utley et al., 1997). Some of the behaviors that peers have been taught to facilitate include engaging in eye contact, initiating play activities, starting a conversation, offering help, and showing affection (Utley et al., 1997). There has been some evidence to indicate this intervention has generalization effects to nontargeted students in nontargeted settings (Strain et al., 1977). Although this is a peer-directed intervention, it is still very labor intensive for the educator. Educators need to spend a lot of time training the peers to appropriately evoke and reinforce the desired behavior from the target student. Additionally, teachers must provide opportunities for peers to practice before implementing the intervention with the target student to ensure fidelity of the intervention.

### Video Modeling

**Video modeling** involves the target student watching a video of a peer model demonstrating a new behavior or promoting the occurrence of a known behavior (Seok et al., 2018). Video modeling allows educators to create targeted individualized interventions, and students are able to watch the peer demonstrate the desired skill on the playground, in the classroom, in the cafeteria, or whatever setting the target student may be struggling in (Baker et al., 2009). Video modeling also enables the use of multiple stimulus and response exemplars and ensures the skill is taught with fidelity each time it is presented (Clinton, 2016). The most effective peer models for this intervention should be very similar to the target student in age, gender, and personality (Seok et al., 2018). Figure 10–3 is the process used for video modeling.

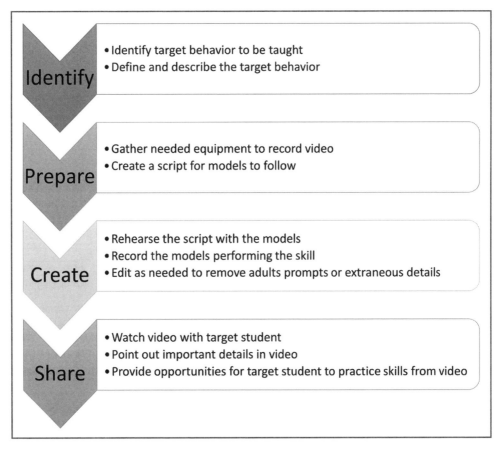

**Figure 10–3.** *Steps of video modeling.*

Video modeling capitalizes on Bandura's concept of social learning theory, positing that individuals learn skills through observation (Bandura, 1997). Some researchers have suggested that video modeling may be effective for resistant learners because watching television and viewing video footage is associated with fun and leisure (Goodwyn et al., 2013). Pairing a preferred activity (watching a video) with a nonpreferred activity (social skills instruction) may lessen resistance in some reluctant learners while increasing levels of compliance.

## Peer Tutoring

Peer tutoring involves trained peers of a similar age and background providing academic tutoring services to targeted peers. The roles of tutor and tutee may shift arbitrarily for the purpose of "promoting academic achievement and social competence" (Foot, Shute, Morgan, & Barron, 1990, p. 65). Shifting student roles of tutor and tutee periodically allows each student the opportunity to shine, highlights each individual's abilities, and increases their social status in the classroom (Tournaki & Criscitiello, 2003). Role reversal gives the target student something to be responsible for and proud of (Tournaki & Criscitiello, 2003). The student acting as the tutor is likely to see an academic gain by achieving a deeper understanding of the material in order to synthesize it and teach it to another individual. The tutor is also likely to experience an increase in self-esteem and self-confidence, leading to more frequent prosocial behaviors exhibited in the classroom. The tutee is likely to be more engaged in the instruction with a peer tutor rather than with adult-directed instruction and therefore is less likely to engage in disruptive or distracting behaviors during instruction.

Peer tutoring has been used to increase proficiency in the academic areas of math (Franca et al., 1990), reading (Locke & Fuchs, 1995), and social studies (Spencer et al., 2003). All the above-mentioned peer tutoring studies, regardless of what academics were targeted, had an increase in prosocial behaviors in the classroom setting, such as positive social interactions with peers, positive peer-to-peer comments, and increased on-task behavior. The increase in prosocial behaviors was compounded with a significant decrease in display of disruptive and off-task behaviors during instruction.

Using peer tutors as one-to-one instructional agents provides students with individualized instruction, frequent opportunities to respond, and extra practice of academic concepts (Utley et al., 1997). A popular dyad that is used in peer tutoring is the pairing of a novice student with a proficient student. The proficient student may be more proficient in the academic task or with a social/behavioral skill. The proficient student is able to serve as a model for the novice student. Other popular dyads pair students of different ages together. When there is a significant age disparity between the tutor and tutee (of 2 or more years), this is referred to as cross-age peer tutoring.

Cochran and colleagues (1993) demonstrated that **cross-age peer tutoring** has a positive impact on academic achievement as well as prosocial behaviors. Cross-age peer tutoring utilizes peers with an age difference of 2 or more years than the target students (Utley et al., 1997). Cross-age peer tutoring has a different dynamic than peer tutoring, expanding the social skills required by each student. Caretaking roles become more defined in older students when cross-age peer tutoring is utilized (Utley et al., 1997). Cochran and colleagues (1993) found an increase in student cooperation, assertion, and self-control after 8 weeks of peer tutoring, as well as an increase in academic competence and a decrease in maladaptive behaviors.

There are two dyads frequently used in cross-age peer tutoring: the older student/younger student dyad and the novice student/younger student dyad. The older student/younger student dyad will partner a student 2 or more years older with a younger student. In this dyad, the older student typically serves as a model for the younger student. The novice student/ younger student dyad pairs a target student who is struggling academically or socially/behaviorally with a younger student, creating a definitive "care-taker" role for the older novice student in the classroom during the tutoring time. Figure 10–4 includes examples of dyads.

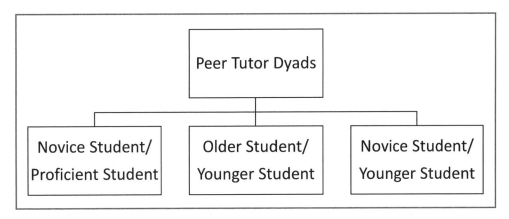

**Figure 10–4.** *Peer tutoring dyads.*

Cross-age peer tutoring can be highly effective, but it takes considerable scheduling on the effort of multiple educators. Tutors may be students from the same school or nearby middle schools or high schools, increasing the complexity of determining appropriate days and times for all students. The complex scheduling needs of this intervention should be taken into consideration before implementation of this peer-directed intervention.

### Peer-Assisted Learning Strategies (PALS)

As discussed throughout this chapter, researchers have found that remediation of academic skills has a positive impact on student behavior in the classroom (Falk & Wehby, 2001), although it is contested what should be addressed first—poor academic skills or poor behavior skills. Some researchers have long argued that early deficits in reading create future behavioral problems (Fitzsimmons et al., 1969; Williams & McGee, 1994). Conversely, other researchers argue behavioral difficulties make it more likely for students to suffer academically (Cornwall & Bawden, 1992; Patterson et al., 1989).

Regardless of which came first, peer-directed interventions that target academics, such as **Peer-Assisted Learning Strategies (PALS)**, have shown positive outcomes for prosocial behavior. PALS is a highly structured version of peer tutoring that pairs students with peers to deliver instruction multiple times a week, each student alternating the role of coach and pupil (Falk & Wehby, 2001). PALS has demonstrated that it improves reading achievement in all levels of readers, from low achievers to high achievers (McMaster et al., 2006). Highly structured peer tutoring strategies, such as PALS, have been shown to be more effective than teacher's creating tutoring dyads and allowing the tutor and tutee to interact at their own discretion. However, the more structured the intervention, the more time-intensive it is for the teacher.

PALS was originally created as a reading intervention for elementary-aged students. Educators paired a high-achieving student with a low-achieving student. The dyads conduct highly structured activities designed to increase reading fluency and comprehension. All students are trained to use specific prompts and feedback when interacting in their dyads (McMaster et al., 2006). Students engage in frequent verbal interaction, increasing opportunities to engage and respond (Ramsey et al., 2007). Students take turns switching roles from tutor to tutee, giving each student an opportunity to be the instructional agent. PALS is very structured and involves scripted lessons and activities. McMaster et al. (2006) provide thorough information regarding the implementation of PALS overview. The frequent verbal interaction encouraged in PALS leads to positive social outcomes for students with EBD. Fuchs and colleagues (2002) demonstrated that students with disabilities enjoyed greater social acceptance in a classroom implementing PALS than in a control classroom that was not implementing PALS, furthering the idea that academic interventions have a positive impact on student behaviors and social interactions in the classroom.

### Literacy-Based Behavioral Intervention (LBBI)

Literacy-based behavioral interventions (LBBIs) encompass an array of interventions that use text and pictures as the instructional medium to teach a skill (Bucholz & Brady, 2008). Teachers can create an LBBI to teach students the skills needed in a particular situation, giving them an opportunity to engage in repeated readings, look at the visual cues on each page, and practice the skill in real time. The teachers can easily create LBBIs using Microsoft Word or PowerPoint. LBBIs should be individualized for the target student, using person-first language that is comprehensible to the target student. Table 10–2 outlines an example of what an LBBI storybook might look like using simple, person-first language (plus the accompanying picture on each page) to teach a student what other behaviors he could engage in instead of leaving the classroom when he feels frustrated.

**Table 10–2.** Content of Example LBBI

| Page | Story Content | Photograph |
|------|--------------|------------|
| 1 | My name is _____. | Photo of individual |
| 2 | Sometimes I feel angry. | Photo of individual looking angry |
| 3 | When I feel angry, I should stay in my seat. | Photo of a chair |
| 4 | When I feel angry, I can raise my hand and ask to take a break. | Photo of individual sitting at desk and raising hand |
| 5 | When I feel angry, I can put my head down. | Photo of individual putting head on desk |
| 6 | When I feel angry, I can take a deep breath. | Photo of individual sitting at desk and taking a deep breath |
| 7 | It's important for me to stay in the classroom when I am angry. | Photo of individual's classroom |
| 8 | My teacher and friends are happy when I stay in the classroom. | Photo of teacher and classmates smiling |

Figure 10–5 depicts an example page from the LBBI storybook a teacher used to teach one of her students with EBD what other behaviors that individual could engage in when he is frustrated instead of running out of the classroom.

LBBIs historically were presented by a job coach or a teacher to target students, but recently researchers have begun to have peers implement LBBIs. Peers have used LBBIs to teach target students employment skills (Honsberger et al., 2019), safety skills (Kearney et al., 2018), and daily living skills (Brady et al., 2016). Each page of the LBBI provides a step in the task, providing the information needed to complete the step (verbalized by the peer reading the storybook) and an accompanying picture as a visual model. The peer points to each picture while reading the accompanying text on the page, then directs the target student to practice the skill on that page. Once the peer finishes reading the storybook, the peer can direct the target student to complete the entire skill sequence, providing prompts and feedback as needed. This provides more opportunities

When I feel angry, I should stay in my seat.

**Figure 10–5.** *Page from a literacy-based behavioral intervention.*

for practice of the skill and increases the amount of immediate feedback the target student receives while learning a new skill. Creating an LBBI is simple for educators to do; see Figure 10–6 for the steps required to create an LBBI.

## I'VE PICKED A PEER-DIRECTED BEHAVIORAL INTERVENTION—NOW WHAT?

Once you have decided which peer-directed behavioral intervention you want to try, it's time to implement it! Familiarize yourself with how to run the intervention. Choose a peer that has strengths you'd like the target student to emulate. Train the peer one-on-one until you're sure the peer is implementing the intervention with **fidelity**, or with 100% accuracy.

Before implementing the peer-directed intervention, create a **data sheet** outlining each step in the skill the student should be performing and take some baseline data on how often the target student is implementing the skill

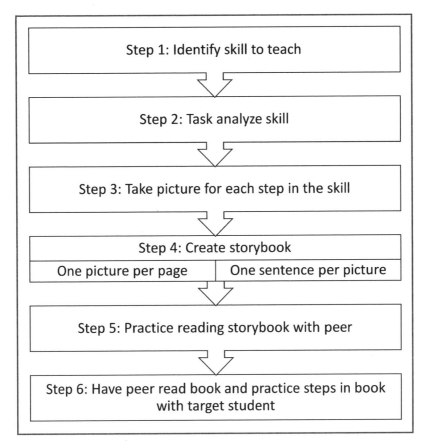

**Figure 10–6.** *How to create an LBBI.*

prior to receiving any intervention. After 3 or 4 days of baseline data, you're ready to begin the peer-directed intervention. Make sure to continue to use your data sheet to collect data on how well the target student is performing the new skill with the peer-directed intervention.

Consider collecting fidelity data on the peer's implementation of the intervention. A generic fidelity data sheet available for you to customize is in Appendix 10–1. Retrain the peer as needed to ensure the target student is receiving a well-implemented intervention.

Once the target student has reached your predetermined mastery criteria of the new skill, collect some social validity data. **Social validity** data will tell you as the teacher how acceptable the intervention was for the target student and how satisfied they were with what they've learned and how they've learned it.

As we are teaching students skills we want them to use throughout their lives, we need to make sure that the skills we target are appropriate and we use fair and reasonable interventions to teach these skills (Wolf, 1978). Adjust your interventions as needed based on the data you collect. The following section contains a vignette that outlines topics covered in this chapter.

## CASE STUDY

*Richard is a 13-year-old seventh-grade student diagnosed with an emotional/ behavioral disorder. He is enrolled in a general education classroom at his local middle school. Richard's special education teacher supports him and other students with special needs during the reading block in his general classroom. He has a full-scale IQ of 90 (verbal = 85 and performance = 95) according to the Wechsler Intelligence Scale for Children. Richard enjoys interacting with his peers in the classroom but experiences difficulties initiating social exchanges appropriately, often resulting in frustrating peer interactions.*

*Richard's teachers report he performs below grade level in reading. He is inattentive during class, often looking out the window or being disruptive by trying to talk to peers or saying things like "this is boring" or "I hate this." He is noncompliant when asked to read out loud. He has slammed books on the table, used loud profane language, and stormed out of the classroom during reading. Richard is rated in the clinical range for the areas of hyperactivity, impulsivity, and conduct problems on the Behavior Assessment System for Children (BASC; Reynolds & Kamphaus, 2002).*

*Richard's teacher, Ms. Smith, is concerned he will fail the upcoming state assessment. Ms. Smith has tried numerous interventions to no avail, including calling his parents, taking away classroom privileges (computer time, music time), and moving his seat away from peers. He is now regularly sent to the office for disruptive behavior, which results in a momentarily quieter classroom, but he continues to fall further behind academically when he leaves the classroom. This puts him at greater risk of failing the upcoming assessment and being prevented from moving on to the next grade.*

*Ms. Smith realizes she needs to teach Richard strategies to engage in when he feels frustrated instead of cursing loudly and running out of the classroom. Since Richard is so driven by peer attention, Ms. Smith decides to record a popular student, Alex, acting out how to ask for help on video. She records Alex asking a teacher for help and then shares the video with Richard. She also pairs Richard with Alex for peer tutoring during reading. In the past, Richard had not received much positive feedback during reading class, but with Alex as a tutor, Richard receives individualized feedback much more frequently than before. Ms. Smith has each boy switch tutor/tutee roles every few days, instilling a sense of responsibility in each of them.*

*Over the next few weeks, Richard has made some gains in reading and is now more motivated to try new tasks. Since he is now interacting with his peers more appropriately, Ms. Smith has been able to praise his positive behavior. Since he has been receiving positive peer and teacher attention for attempts at new or difficult tasks, he is much less frequently slamming his books on the desk and storming out of the classroom. He has learned how to ask for help appropriately and has improved his interactions with his peers at the same time.*

## CHAPTER SUMMARY

Peer-directed behavioral interventions create a lower pupil-teacher ratio, freeing the teacher for other teaching activities. This ratio also allows target students to receive more frequent error correction and reinforcement from their peers than they would be able to receive from their teacher. Peer-directed interventions give students with EBD more opportunities to respond followed by immediate peer feedback, increasing rates of learning (Utley et al., 1997). Peer-directed behavioral interventions increase student engagement, increase task completion, and increase positive peer interactions. Using peers as instructional agents is powerful, capitalizing on childhood and adolescent desire for peer acceptance and interaction. Teachers working with students with EBD will find the strategies outlined in this chapter to be beneficial to all the students in their classrooms.

## DISCUSSION QUESTIONS

1. What are the benefits of peer-directed behavioral interventions?

2. Think of a skill you would use video modeling to teach. Following the steps in Figure 10–3, write out how you would create the video and how you would use the video to teach the skill.

3. Give arguments for and against peer initiation training.

4. What acquisition skills could you use a peer-directed intervention for? Describe what that would look like.

5. Why is social validity important?

## RESOURCES

https://www.fau.edu/education/centersandprograms/card/documents/lbbidirectionsforcard.pdf

http://www.polyxo.com/socialstories/

https://vkc.mc.vanderbilt.edu/assets/files/resources/psiPeermedstrategies.pdf

http://www.readwritethink.org/materials/comic/

http://www.specialconnections.ku.edu/?q=behavior_plans/classroom_and_group_support/teacher_tools/peer_assisted_interventions

# REFERENCES

Baker, S. D., Lang, R., & O'Reilly, M. (2008). Review of video modeling with students with emotional and behavioral disorders. *Education and Treatment of Children, 32*(3), 403–420. https://www.jstor.org/stable/42900030

Bandura, A. (1997). *Self-efficacy: The exercise of control.* W. H. Freeman and Company.

Blake, C., Wang, W., Cartledge, G., & Gardner, R. (2000). Middle school students with serious emotional disturbances serve as social trainers and reinforcers for peers. *Behavioral Disorders, 25*(4), 280–298.

Brady, M. P., Hall, K., & Bielskus-Barone, K. (2016). Literacy-based behavioral interventions delivered by peers: A teaching strategy for students with severe disabilities. *Educational Psychology in Practice, 32*, 424–434. doi:10.1080/02667363.2016.1206848

Brady, M. P., Honsberger, C., Cadette, J., & Honsberger, T. (2016). Effects of a peer-mediated literacy-based behavioral intervention on the acquisition and maintenance of daily living skills in adolescents with autism. *Education and Training in Autism and Developmental Disabilities, 51*, 122–131.

Browder, D. M., & Spooner, F. (2011). *Teaching students with moderate and severe disabilities.* Guilford.

Bucholz, J., & Brady, M. P. (2008). Teaching positive work behaviors with Literacy-Based Behavioral Interventions: An intervention for students and employees with developmental disabilities. *Teaching Exceptional Children, 41*(2), 50–55. doi:10.1177/004005990804100206

Clinton, E. (2016). A meta-analysis of video modeling interventions for children and adolescents with emotional/behavioral disorders. *Educational Research Quarterly, 40*(2), 67–88.

Cochran, L., Feng, H., Cartledge, G., & Hamilton, S. (1993). The effects of cross-age tutoring on the academic achievement, social behaviors, and self-perceptions of low-achieving African-American males with behavioral disorders. *Behavioral Disorders, 18*(4), 292–302. doi:10.1177/019874299301800402

Cornwall, A., & Bawden, H. N. (1992). Reading disabilities and aggression: A critical review. *Journal of Learning Disabilities, 25*(5), 281–288. doi:10.1177/002221949202500503

DuPaul, G. J., McGoey, K. E., & Yugar, J. M. (1997). Mainstreaming students with behavior disorders: The use of classroom peers as facilitators of generalization. *The School Psychology Review, 26*, 634–650.

Falk, K. B., & Wehby, J. H. (2001). The effects of peer-assisted learning strategies on the beginning reading skills of young children with emotional and behavioral disorders. *Behavioral Disorders, 26*(4), 344–359. doi:10.1177/019874290102600404

Fitzsimmons, S. J., Cheever, J., Leonard, E., & Macunovich, D. (1969). School failures: Now and tomorrow. *Developmental Psychology, 1*(2), 134–146. doi:10.1037/h0027088

Foot, H. C., Shute, R. H., Morgan M. J., & Barron, A. M. (1990). Theoretical issues in peer tutoring. In H. C. Morgan, M. J. Shute, & R. H. Shute (Eds.), *Children helping children* (pp. 65–92). John Wiley & Sons.

Franca, V. M., Kerr, M. M., Reitz, A. L., & Lambert, D. (1990). Peer tutoring among behaviorally disordered students: Academic and social benefits to tutor and tutee. *Education & Treatment of Children, 13*(2), 109–128.

Fuchs, D., Fuchs, L. S., Mathes, P. G., & Martinez, E. (2002). Preliminary evidence on the social standing of students with learning disabilities in PALS and no-PALS classrooms. *Learning Disabilities Research and Practice, 17*(4), 205–215. doi:10.1111/1540-5826.00046

Goodwyn, F. D., Hatton, H. L., Vannest, K. J., & Ganz, J. B. (2013). Video modeling and video feedback interventions for students with emotional and behavioral disorders. *Beyond Behavior, 22*(2), 14–18. doi:10.1177/107429561302200204

Heward, W. L. (1997). Four validated instructional strategies. *Behavior and Social Issues, 7*(1), 43–51. doi:10.5210/bsi.v7i1.298

Honsberger, T., Brady, M. P., Honsberger, C., & Kearney, K. B. (2019). Peer-mediated literacy-based behavioral interventions: A job coaching strategy for secondary students with ASD. *Career Development and Transition for Exceptional Individuals, 42*(2), 99–110. doi:10.1177/2165143418808508

Kaya, C., Blake, J., & Chan, F. (2015). Peer-mediated interventions with elementary and secondary school students with emotional and behavioural disorders: A literature review. *Journal of Research in Special Educational Needs, 15*(2), 120–129. doi:10.1111/1471-3802.12029

Kearney, K. B., Brady, M. P., Hall, K., & Honsberger, T. (2018). Using peer-mediated literacy-based behavioral interventions to increase first aid safety skills in students with developmental disabilities. *Behavior Modification, 42*(5), 639–660. doi:10.1177/0145445517725866

Locke, W. R., & Fuchs, L. S. (1995). Effects of peer-mediated reading instruction on the on-task behavior and social interactions of children with behavior disorders. *Journal of Emotional and Behavioral Disorders, 3*, 92–99.

Maheady, L., Harper, G. F., & Mallette, B. (2001). Peer-mediated instruction and interventions and students with mild disabilities. *Remedial and Special Education, 22*(1), 4–14. doi:10.1177/074193250102200102

McMaster, K. L., Fuchs, D., & Fuchs, L. S. (2006). Research on peer-assisted learning strategies: The promise and limitations of peer-mediated instruction. *Reading & Writing Quarterly, 22*(1), 5–25. doi:10.1080/10573560500203491

Patterson, G. R., DeBaryshe, B. D., & Ramsey, E. (1989). A developmental perspective on antisocial behavior. *American Psychologist, 44*(2), 329–335. doi:10.1037/0003-066X.44.2.329

Quinn, M. M., Kavale, K. A., Mather, S. R., Rutherford, R. B., & Forness, S. R. (1999). A meta-analysis of social skill interventions for students with emotional or behavioral disorders. *Journal of Emotional and Behavioral Disorders, 7*, 54–64.

Ramsey, M. L., Jolivette, K., & Patton, B. (2007). Peer-Assisted Learning Strategies (PALS) for reading in the EBD classroom. *Beyond Behavior, 17*(1), 2–6.

Randolph, K. M., Duffy, M. L., Brady, M. P., Wilson, C. L., & Scheeler, M. (2019). The impact of iCoaching on teacher-delivered opportunities to respond. *Journal of Special Education Technology, 35*(1), 15–25. doi:10.1177/0162643419836414

Reynolds, C. R., & Kamphaus, R. W. (2002). *The clinician's guide to the Behavior Assessment System for Children (BASC).* Guilford Press.

Seok, S., DaCosta, B., McHenry-Powell, M., Heitzman-Powell, L. S., & Ostmeyer, K. (2018). A systematic review of evidence-based video modeling for students with emotional and behavioral disorders. *Education Sciences, 8*(4), 170–187. doi:10.3390/educsci8040170

Spencer, V. G., Scruggs, T. E., & Mastropieri, M. A. (2003). Content area learning in middle school social studies classrooms and students with emotional or behavioral disorders: A comparison of strategies. *Behavioral Disorders, 28*(2), 77–93. doi:10.1177/019874290302800208

Strain, P. S., Shores, R. E., & Timm, M. (1977). Effects of peer social initiations on the behavior of withdrawn preschool children. *Journal of Applied Behavior Analysis, 10*(2), 289–298. doi:10.1901/jaba.1977.10-289

Sutherland, K. S., & Snyder, A. (2007). Effects of reciprocal peer tutoring and self-graphing on reading fluency and classroom behavior of middle school students with emotional or behavioral disorders. *Journal of Emotional and Behavioral Disorders, 15*(2), 103–118. doi:10.1177/10634266070150020101

Tournaki, N., & Criscitiello, E. (2003). Using peer tutoring as a successful part of behavior management. *Teaching Exceptional Children, 36*(2), 21–25. doi:10.1177/004005990303600203

Utley, C. A., & Mortweet, S. L., Greenwood, C. R. (1997). Peer-mediated instruction and interventions. *Focus on Exceptional Children, 29*(5), 1–23.

Williams, S., & McGee, R. (1994). Reading attainment and juvenile delinquency. *Journal of Child Psychology and Psychiatry, 35*(3), 441–459. doi:10.1111/j.1469-7610.1994.tb01733.x

Wolf, M. M. (1978). Social validity: The case for subjective measurement or how applied behavior analysis is finding its heart. *Journal of Applied Behavior Analysis, 11*(2), 203–214. doi:10.1901/jaba.1978.11-203

## APPENDIX 10–1

# Generic Fidelity Sheet

| For each session, in the appropriate column:<br><br>• Record the date of the session<br>• Indicate initials of target student<br>• Record + if the peer successfully performs intervention step<br>• Record – if the peer does not successfully perform intervention step | Date | Date | Date | Date | Date |
|---|---|---|---|---|---|
| | Student | Student | Student | Student | Student |
| Step 1: | | | | | |
| Step 2: | | | | | |
| Step 3: | | | | | |
| Step 4: | | | | | |
| Step 5: | | | | | |
| Step 6: | | | | | |
| Step 7: | | | | | |
| Step 8: | | | | | |
| Step 9: | | | | | |
| Step 10: | | | | | |
| Step 11: | | | | | |
| Step 12: | | | | | |
| Step 13: | | | | | |
| Step 14: | | | | | |
| Step 15: | | | | | |
| **Number of steps correct** | | | | | |
| **Number of total steps** | | | | | |
| **Percent correct** | | | | | |

# 11

# Functional Behavior Assessment

*With Contributions from Sarah Heiniger*

---

**KEY VOCABULARY**

| | |
|---|---|
| Antecedent | Methods of Data Collection |
| Applied Behavior Analysis | • Frequency |
| Behavior | • Duration |
| Consequence | • Latency |
| Functional Behavior Assessment | • Intensity |
| Function | Operational Definition |
| Functional Analysis | Reinforcement |

**LEARNING OBJECTIVES**

By the end of this chapter, you should be able to . . .

- Determine whether an FBA is warranted.

- Gather information through record reviews, interviews, assessment, and observation.

- Analyze and interpret information and baseline data to develop hypotheses for behavioral function.

- Read and analyze FBAs to determine integrity.

## INTRODUCTION

**Functional Behavior Assessment** (FBA) is one of those official-sounding special education acronyms that really just describes a best practice. At its essence, an FBA is the process identifying the relationship between behavior and the environment to develop a behavior support plan linked to the function of the behavior (O'Neill et al., 1997). It could also "be defined as a collection of methods for gathering information about antecedents, behaviors, and consequences in order to determine the reason (**function**) of behavior" (Gresham et al., 2001). Although the permanent product of an FBA is a written document, it really is a process, not just a piece of paper or an event in time. Observation, assessment, records reviews, and interviews inform that actual document and can take place over days or weeks to create an accurate depiction of the situation. The FBA then informs the Behavior Intervention Plan (BIP), which will be discussed more fully in the next chapter. The FBA can be included in a student's IEP and is sometimes required. It can also be a part of a Response to Intervention (RtI) or eligibility for special education and related services process for a student.

The process of conducting an FBA is a step in the larger problem-solving process. Whether it is called a multitiered system of support, response to intervention, problem behavior intervention system, or something else entirely, the overarching series of events is typically the same and is couched in best practice. The starting point is the problem behavior itself. A referral is made because of a challenging behavior. Next is where the FBA comes in. That behavior is identified by crafting an observable definition and then the problem is analyzed. The pieces of the FBA are designed in order to fully pull apart the behavior in order that the next step will hopefully be more successful. That next step is developing the plan (i.e., the BIP), implementing the plan, and, finally, evaluating the plan by examining the data. If needed, the process is begun again, or the plan is continued as set.

Typically, the formal FBA does not come into play until Tier 3 level service is reached. Think about the interventions that are in place in a typical school building at this time. Tier 1 includes supports that are provided to all students. Schoolwide Social Emotional Learning curricula; schoolwide expectations, rules, procedures, and visuals; and building or district culture all are all essential components of this tier. The second tier is provided only for some students, because those students are in need of additional support beyond the typical. Examination at this level can and should be function based but may not necessarily require a "formal" functional behavior assessment and behavior intervention plan. Some of the strategies that are typically found at Tier 2 could include social skills group, a check-in/check-out plan, group counseling, or a mentoring program. It could also be a quick "sticker chart" that the classroom teacher uses to provide positive **reinforcement** for one specific behavioral skill. Tier 3, on the other hand, ought to resemble the support a student would get through special education. At this level, there are many options, including one-on-one counseling with a social worker, counselor, or school psychologist to teach behavior skills that are missing; a more involved classroom plan that requires multiple people to implement; and specialized training for staff, among others.

Some of the questions commonly heard in response to recommendation for an FBA include: Why is it important to determine the function of a behavior before designing a behavior plan? Why can't we just skip ahead to a plan to get the kid the help they need? Isn't this just another hoop to jump through?

Because all **behavior**, no matter how complex or how simple, serves a function or a purpose. The practices and principles of **Applied Behavior Analysis** (ABA) should be the grounding for all FBA/BIPs. Baer and colleagues (1968) definitively defined ABA as "the process of systematically applying interventions based upon the principles of learning theory to improve socially significant behaviors to a meaningful degree, and to demonstrate that the interventions employed are responsible for the improvement in behavior." Essentially, this means taking what is known to work based on the scientific literature and using it to change behavior in the environment in which it occurs. In this case, the school setting in which the child with the EBD label learns. Failure to base interventions on functions often results in ineffective and unnecessarily restrictive procedures, and the inverse is also true (Steege et al., 2019). Students with EBD engaging in a challenging behavior need a behavior plan based on function, which is precisely the purpose of an FBA. An FBA also enhances the "effectiveness, efficiency, and relevance" of the subsequently developed BIP (Sugai et al., 2010). Students who are eligible for special education under the Emotional and Behavioral Disorder (EBD) category should have an FBA and BIP as a part of their Individualized Education Plan. By its very nature, this disability category is defined by behaviors that are problematic in the school setting (among others) and should therefore include a structured plan to address those. Ineffective interventions can lead to resistance to intervention by further reinforcing problem behaviors, which then makes it even more difficult to meet student outcomes. A strong behavior plan designed based on a functional behavior assessment will lead to stronger academic outcomes for these students.

The guidelines for when to conduct an FBA can fall into the "might want to," "should do," and "necessary by law" categories. In general, you should be considering an FBA when (1) what's happening at Tier 1 and Tier 2 levels is insufficient to eliminate challenging behaviors, and (2) behaviors are impacting the student performance. You *might want* to do an FBA when you are seeing resistance to intervention and an increase in problem behavior, your team is unclear about the intervention that should be developed even after informal data collection, or what is happening in the classroom is insufficient to eliminate challenging behavior. You *should* conduct an FBA when behavior is impacting the student's performance because of extended avoidance, extended refusal, and aggressive behavior or when Tier 1 and Tier 2 level supports are not resulting in a reduction of the problem. You *absolutely must* conduct an FBA when it's necessary by law, which is when one of the following has occurred (1) a manifestation determination review has taken place (Walker & Hott, 2015), (2) a student is suspended for more than 10 consecutive school days, (3) there is a pattern of short-term suspensions totaling more than 10 school days in a year, (4) the student is placed in an interim alternative educational setting for not more than 45 days, or (5) it is relevant as part of an Individualized Education Plan evaluation process. To the fifth point, Section 300.324 of the special education regulations states that "in the case of a child whose behavior impedes the child's learning or that of others, consider the use of positive behavioral interventions and supports, and other strategies, to address that behavior." In this case, "interventions and support, and other strategies," should be preceded by an FBA (Gable et al., 1998). To further the point about students eligible for EBD services, those whose behaviors manifest through internalizing, emotional difficulties rather than easily observable externalizing behaviors should not be forgotten. While these events might not be as easily distinguished by a third party, internal emotions are still behaviors and can be managed through behavioral interventions. In behavior analysis, these are referred to as "private events" but have **antecedent** events (what occurs immediately before) and maintaining **consequences** (what occurs immediately after), just like their external brethren.

This chapter will use two case studies to illustrate FBA development in a classroom situation.

## CASE STUDY—ELEMENTARY

*Xavier is a 5-year-old kindergarten student. He is new to the school district this year, as his family moved from South Carolina over the summer. His classroom teacher, Mrs. Elizabeth, recently reached out to the problem-solving team because his behaviors have become increasingly difficult to manage. She describes general defiance, yelling, and refusal to complete work, all of which have continued to escalate, culminating most recently in property destruction of the classroom supplies and other student work. She is at a loss of what to try with him, as he does not seem to be responding to praise when he performs well or the classroom behavior plan (which is a "caught being good" jar of marbles for the class to earn an activity of their choosing). He is also demonstrating impulsive behaviors and a lot of negative self-talk, as well as difficulty explaining himself when he becomes agitated. Xavier gets along well with peers who continue to seek him out during unstructured times but who appear to be wary of sitting close to him in the classroom because of the explosive-type behavior he is demonstrating and on the carpet because of how much he moves around (he often accidentally hits or kicks other students). When asked, Mrs.*

*Elizabeth is not sure what is triggering the behavior because overall, he seems to be a smart student and academically within the average range and should not have a problem with the work. She has tried a superhero sticker chart (because Xavier loves superheroes) but that got ripped up the day before after he was asked to complete a math worksheet.*

### CASE STUDY—SECONDARY

*Lily is in the seventh grade at her local public middle school. She has historically been a really great student, earning As and Bs, but recently her grades have been dropping. She is appearing withdrawn, not turning in her work, and is in danger of failing her classes. Lily's attendance has also become sporadic lately, and she has not been participating in her usual activities. Her teachers have all started to notice the change in her behavior and are becoming concerned.*

Xavier, Lily, and their teachers, clearly need additional supports. We will circle back to Xavier and Lily throughout this chapter as an example at each stage of the FBA process.

## WHAT MAKES A GOOD FBA?

The importance of conducting an FBA has been established, but there is also a difference between a thorough, well-done assessment and one that is less than stellar. Van Acker and colleagues (2005) found that school teams who received training related to FBA/BIP development and utilized a self-monitoring tool for high-quality FBAs and BIPs were found to produce better results.

A rigorous FBA relies upon validated information and helps to determine the underlying function that is maintaining the challenging behavior. Applied Behavior Analysis has identified four functions that govern the continuance of every behavior: (1) escape from something aversive, (2) seeking attention from others, (3) seeking a sensory or other internal physical or emotional experience, or (4) seeking a tangible item.

If a student is engaging in a challenging behavior, it is because they do not have the more socially appropriate means to get what they want or need. Possibly this is due to a disability, that "learned behavior component" to which they have had wants and needs met more expediently by engaging problem behavior, never learning the skills necessary to communicate or engage in their environment, or that appropriate behavior is not being reinforced. There are several myths that many individuals hold about behavior. First, challenging behavior does *not* occur because the student is trying to get under someone's skin, is lazy, or is doing it purposefully to cause problems. Another commonly held false belief is that the student will never be able to change. Behavioral change is always possible but often takes a very precise and methodological approach to do so. Enter the FBA.

As noted, functional assessment covers the first two steps in the problem-solving process—identification and analysis of the problem. If functional analysis is a familiar term, do note that it is different from functional assessment and not an interchangeable term. A **functional analysis** should only be conducted under experimental conditions by a trained behavior analyst. It involves creating experimental conditions to test hypotheses and actually eliciting the challenging behavior to confirm those hypotheses. This is not typically a practice easily engaged in within the school setting, nor should it be conducted by those without training (Gresham et al., 2001).

## THE FUNCTIONAL ASSESSMENT PROCESS

A good FBA is also thorough and accurate. Functional assessment can be thought of as a series of steps that must be thoroughly examined before moving on. The first step of functional assessment is to begin gathering information about the student's strengths, the environment in which the behavior occurs, antecedents, consequences, environmental variables, and a more in depth description of the target challenging behavior. Multiple informants and multiple methods of data collection should be considered.

Using a framework like the ICEL/RIOT matrix helps to organize the process and ensure thoroughness and quality of data collection. It also helps to keep the focus on the environment that can be modified rather than on factors internal to the student. ICEL is an acronym for the key domains of learning: Instruction, Curriculum, Environment, Learner. *Instruction* is the methodology for communicating the curriculum to the students and can vary in many ways. *Curriculum* is the content of what is being taught, including the scope, sequence, pace, material, rigor, and format. *Environment* is the physical context in which the instruction takes place and includes all of the nontangible variables like school culture and beliefs or attitudes. *Learner* is the student, and components of the person are only considered a variable to be modified when it is determined that all other domains are appropriate and accommodating. When combined with RIOT, which is an acronym for potential sources of information (Review, Interview, Observe, Test), the matrix provides information on the gathering portion of the FBA. See Appendix 11–1 for an example of the ICEL/RIOT matrix.

### Gathering Information

A record review is an excellent starting point to learn more about the student (see Appendix 11–2 for a sample record review template). When thinking about challenging behaviors, ruling out potential biological or physical causes is very important. Trying to intervene on a behavior that is caused by illness or physical pain is just going to be an exercise in frustration. Look through the permanent and temporary files for any previously documented diagnoses, illnesses, patterns in behavior, or patterns in attendance or any red flag social or emotional variables. Look at any IEPs or response to intervention documentation. Record any interventions that have been tried in the past and responses to those. Check for health histories or behavioral referral/ incident documentation. Some questions to ask yourself could include the following: (1) Is there a regular pattern of absences? (2) Does the student have any academic deficits that could be playing a role? (3) Are they any medical diagnoses that manifest as behavior problems? Summarizing the student's history is a helpful practice that is often overlooked and is a crucial method to help the team identify patterns.

## CASE STUDY—ELEMENTARY— RECORD REVIEW

*Upon reviewing Xavier's records, it was found that he moved to the area just 2 weeks prior to the start of school. Before that, he lived in Nevada for 2 months and in Florida prior to that. He does not have any diagnoses or other health problems as reported by parents. His hearing and vision have not yet been assessed by the district as he is a new student and it is relatively early in the school year. Benchmark reports from the fall assessment period indicate early reading and early math scores within the high-average range.*

## CASE STUDY—SECONDARY— RECORD REVIEW

*Lily's records indicate a student who received academic intervention for reading early in elementary school but since that time has been maintaining grades either in the average to above-average range. In middle school, she has been receiving A or B grades every semester. In addition to receiving intervention through the elementary problem-solving process for academics, teachers also described some concerns with "nervousness and perfectionism" around turning in assignments and testing situations. It appears that at the beginning of this school year, a new address is reported for her and her mother, but the address remains the same for her father. In her health history, it was noted that Lily suffers from asthma that is maintained by an inhaler she carries with her and uses only on an as-needed basis.*

After conducting a thorough record review, the next step is to talk to the relevant parties involved with the student. Interview those who have been involved with the student either directly or on the periphery. The idea is to get a complete picture of the student's history of challenging behavior and everything that has been tried previously. Often talking to previous teachers, parents, or interventionists will give you a better picture of the behavior that what was recorded in records. Talk to the student themselves if possible (again, an often-overlooked piece in the process when the student often has good insight into their own needs). Both current and past general and special education teachers who have worked with the student will have excellent insights. And do not forget about the paraeducators or instructional assistants who may see the student under other conditions. The principals or administrators who have dealt with the student during disciplinary referrals will have an additional different perspective. Parents can also be a good source to rule out any other medical or biological conditions or any extracurricular life events that might be contributing to the problem behavior. Related service team members, behavior specialists, or outside private providers may also have very valuable information to contribute.

Interviews can range from highly structured to much less so, depending upon the experience of the interviewer. See Appendix 11–3 for a structured interview tool to assist in this process. Other interview tools that are helpful in this process look at the interviewee's experience with the problem behavior in question and their hypothesis about why those behaviors are occurring. Tools like the Questions About Behavior Function (QABF; Matson et al., 2012), the Functional Assessment Screening Tool (FAST; Iwata & DeLeon, 1995), the Motivation Assessment Scale (MAS; Duker & Sigafoos, 1998), and the Problem Behavior Questionnaire (PBQ; Lewis et al., 1994) are quick and easy to conduct interview tools to help quickly identify possible behavioral functions. The PBQ is especially conducive to use in schools as the questions

## CASE STUDY—ELEMENTARY— INTERVIEW

*Xavier's classroom teacher and parents were interviewed. His classroom teacher did describe a few more details about what is happening in the classroom, including a few students whose behavior seem to set him off, and any activity that involves "creativity" typically results in more problem behavior. She continued to express concerns that Xavier does not seem to want to listen to her and responds better to adult males. The parent interview resulted in a description of a lot of hyperactive and impulsive behaviors at home, as well as parents who both work full-time in alternating schedules. Xavier looks up to his dad, who travels a lot for work, and his behavior appears to be worse at home when the dad is home than when he is not.*

## CASE STUDY—SECONDARY— INTERVIEW

*Interviews with Lily's teachers did not reveal much more information than what was written into the referral. None of her teachers had been able to get any additional comments from Lily. Her mother revealed that she and Lily's father had divorced early in the year and that Lily has not been taking it well. Additionally, her older sister had moved out to college this fall. Lily's mother is also concerned about Lily's current behavior, as at home she tends to lock herself in her room and is not very communicative. Lily was pulled by the social worker for an interview as well. It took several sessions, but Lily finally opened up about how she is feeling and how English and writing class have gotten much harder lately. She also reported feeling "short of breath" in those classes and in PE and is having difficulty managing her emotions most of the time. She did not know what to do and was unable to change the patterns of behavior, so she started skipping afterschool activities and not participating in class to avoid the increased feelings of anxiety.*

are based on the school context. The Functional Assessment Interview (FAI; O'Neill et al., 1997) is a longer tool that encompasses all parts of the interview process. A tool that can help guide an interview with the student themselves is the Student-Directed Functional Assessment Interview (Student-FAI; O'Neill et al., 1997).

Observing the student and systematically gathering information around the challenging behavior comes next. Conduct observations in the locations in which the target behavior is already occurring and make sure to observe the same events more than once for purposes of comparison. In this stage, look to validate the information gathered through interviews and assessment tools in the previous steps. While observing, do not forget to look for strengths that the student demonstrates in the different school environments. Make sure to record any schoolwide, classwide, and more individual interventions that are in place in the classroom setting already.

Begin data collection with ABC. Antecedent, behavior, and consequence (ABC) data are always important. Knowing what happens directly before the challenging behavior in question occurs can give the team ideas for environmental variables that can be easily modified or skills that potentially need to be taught. The focus of observation should be on environmental triggers and contexts that others might overlook. Where does the behavior happen? With whom does the behavior occur? When does the behavior happen? What activity is surrounding the behavior? What are other students doing? What are the adults in the room doing?

And, on the opposite end, knowing what happens directly after the behavior occurs provides information about what is acting to maintain the behavior. Is the student getting attention from other students directly after engaging in the behavior? Is he escaping an assignment that he does not want to do? Is he relieving some sort of sensory need? Is he receiving a snack? Often staff are not even aware of how they are maintaining problems that occur in the classroom setting because there is so much else going on, so having a third party observe and document can be helpful. The observer should focus on maintaining consequences that might have been overlooked. See the ABC Data Collection form in Appendix 11–4.

In addition to anecdotal data gathered on the ABC chart, additional data on frequency, duration, latency, or intensity might be collected. **Frequency** data are a count of behavior per amount of time. This is typically used for short, quick behaviors that are easily counted as one discrete unit (for example, shoutouts). **Duration** is the total amount of time a behavior takes, typically used for longer behaviors that may repeat rapidly or without much time in between (for example, crying). **Latency** is the amount of time between when a direction is given and when compliance begins and is typically used to measure attentive-type student behaviors (for example, the amount of time between the direction to start the test and when the student picks up the pencil and begins to write). **Intensity** is the rating given to the behavior, which can be somewhat subjective, but when consistently measured as defined by the staff can be helpful (for example, a tantrum could be a 5 if it involves screaming, lying on the floor, and crying, and a 1 if it just involves lying on the floor in silence). Data can also be collected continuously (meaning every single instance of the behavior is collected), discontinuously (meaning only samples of the behavior are recorded and extrapolated), or partially continuous (meaning the behavior is collected continuously but only for a portion of the opportunities in which it occurs). Continuous data collection obviously gives the most accurate information but is not always feasible or even advisable given the other responsibilities held by staff. For some problem behaviors that do not occur at high rates, a classroom teacher can monitor and report every single instance or total duration of that behavior. Discontinuous measurement is not ideal, though, as it tends to either over- or underestimate behavior. Partially continuous is the best solution, and behavior can be reported as an average across observations or across the same amount of time for multiple days. See sample data collection forms for all methods in the appendices (Appendices 11–4 through 11–8). At this point, baseline data only are being collected, that is, data about the behavior before the official intervention has begun. The student may need to be observed multiple times in multiple settings across multiple days. And it might take multiple people making the observations due to observer effects.

## Writing the FBA

Now that all of the data have been collected, it is time to begin documenting what was learned. Most state boards of education have their own paperwork to be used in conjunction with the IEP paperwork, but in general, the components are the same. (See FBA Template in Appendix 11–9.)

### Student Strengths

Student strengths should be the starting point of any assessment documentation. What are the social and emotional skills the student demonstrates? Does he have any behavioral strengths? What type of effective communication does the student use? What are her interests? What does she like to do during free time or at recess? Who does he choose to spend time with or play with?

### Operational Definition

First, the behavior needs to be defined. This includes baseline rates that were gathered and all of the ABC data, both summarized in narrative and graphic form. Graphs make data easy to examine and establish trends. **Operational definition** just means that the behavior is defined in a way that anyone going in to observe could easily identify and take data on the behavior in question. It should be observable, measurable, objective, clear, and complete.

### Observable and Measurable

Both examples and nonexamples of the problem behavior should be defined in detail. Any contextually specific behaviors and patterns should be identified and comparisons to typical peer behavior should be made. Specifics about the topography (meaning what does the behavior look like with very specific details) of the behavior should be described. For example, instead of saying, "The student engages in physical aggression," a better description would be, "The student engages in hitting behavior, which includes placing an open hand on another student with enough force to leave a mark."

Another example could be, instead of saying, "The student throws tantrums," the description, "The student engages in tantrum behavior, which involves lying on the floor, yelling, 'No,' and kicking legs repeatedly," is more accurate. This allows for more accurate measurement of the behavior in the future. Another portion of the operational definition is how long or how often the behavior occurs. This is typically gathered through duration recording and frequency recording. The duration a behavior occurs will give the "how long" and frequency will give the "how often." A nonexample of this is, "The student regularly throws tantrums." A better example is, "The student engages in tantrum behavior on average two times per day and each instance lasts an average of 3 minutes as measured across 1 week." An important inclusion into the definition is also who is being affected. As noted in the example about physical aggression, the statement "an open hand on another student" made the definition more precise, as opposed to hitting an adult or even themselves.

Those three behaviors are very different. To add another layer, including the setting in which the behavior occurs is helpful. For example, the location "in the general education classroom" could be added to the definition of the tantum behavior, or the physical aggression definition could include "during unstructured activities." The behavior should also have a specific beginning and end to make measurement more straightforward if relevant.

## Objective

Objectivity in defining behavior means not ascribing intent or emotion to the situation. Adjectives do not have a place here, nor do motives. As was mentioned previously, students are not engaging in behavior to be mean or create havoc in the environment. There is an underlying cause (aka the function!).

## Clear

As has been mentioned, being specific about the contents of the definition is important so that everyone involves knows the exact behavior being measured and ultimately intervened upon. Vagueness at this point leads to frustration and difficulty determining functions and whether interventions actually work or not.

## Concise

Other pieces that can be included, if it is deemed helpful, could be triggering events (i.e., in the presence of a specific student) or setting events (i.e., when a demand is being presented). However, the definition could get too long and cumbersome to be meaningful at a certain point, so be mindful of keeping the definition thorough but concise. Common problems with defining target behaviors include behaviors that are (1) defined too generally, (2) don't pass the "dead man's test," and (3) are missing measurable baseline data.

When choosing behaviors to define, prioritize two to three behaviors. In the case of behavioral intervention, too much really is too much. Focus on behaviors that are dangerous or severe, are high frequency or present regular opportunities to learn new skills, are acting in place of foundational behaviors, or are enduring, chronic behaviors. When thinking about the behaviors to target, ask yourself the following questions. How severe or problematic is the behavior? Is it a long-standing problem? How difficult might the behavior be to change? Is the behavior occurring in multiple settings? How easy is it going to be to change those settings? Are there other behaviors that need to be addressed first? Is the student missing any prerequisite skills necessary to complete the task?

## Setting/Environmental Variables

Environmental variables to consider include relationships with peers, family events or relationships, activities being conducted, medications, biological events, or other overarching occurrences. Setting events are situationally specific, like room temperature, staff present, physical layout of the classroom, the instructional activity, the time of day, a disruption in the routine, and a problematic interaction with a peer, among others.

### CASE STUDY—SECONDARY— ENVIRONMENTAL VARIABLES AND SETTING EVENTS

*In Lily's case, the environmental variable of family relationships is heavily impacting the challenging behavior she is demonstrating at school. Her parents' recent divorce seems to be affecting her by increasing the symptoms of anxiety she is experiencing at school. The setting events that appear to be situationally specific in eliciting the target behavior are during English class and writing class, as well as during PE.*

## Setting

Providing a detailed description of the environment in which the behavior occurs is the next step in FBA documentation. Aspects of the environment can explain why an antecedent results in a problem behavior one day and not the next, and why some days a consequence is more effective as a reinforcer or punisher than others. Appendix 11–10 contains a classroom climate survey.

## Antecedents

The difference between antecedent events and setting or environmental context is the difference in proximity to the behavior. Setting or environmental events are distant from the student and can be more difficult to identify and in general make the antecedent events more or less powerful. Antecedent events are immediate and easier to identify. They are observable where the others typically are not. Also often referred to as "triggers," antecedents seem to act as a catalyst for the behavior to occur while setting events are slow acting and take a lot more investigative work to determine their presence. It is important not to neglect those distant future events, however, in the consideration of factors impacting the behavior. The antecedent portion of the FBA should include a description of the relevant events that precede the target behavior (Iovannone, Anderson, & Scott, 2017).

## Consequences

What is the result of the target behavior? What did the student gain? What was the response of others to the student? In this section, maintaining consequences for the challenging behavior should be summarized with an eye toward ultimately defining the function of the behavior. Appendix 11–4 also contains information on collecting ABC data.

## Hypothesis of Behavioral Function

At this point, there is a full summary of the record reviews, interviews, observations, and data collection to inform potential hypotheses about why the challenging behavior is occurring. This hypothesis will describe the relationship between the behavior, the antecedent events (events, times, situations, etc.) that predict when the problem behavior will or will not occur, and the maintaining consequences of that behavior. Testing your hypothesis can be tricky in the case of very complex behaviors, as actual experimental manipulation of environmental events to systematically identify the antecedent events that trigger problem behaviors and the consequences that reinforce problem behaviors (i.e., a functional analysis) should only be conducted by a trained behavior analyst. Once a behavior intervention plan is developed based on the contents of the functional assessment, however, the team will typically be able to identify whether the hypothesis was correct. This will be discussed further in the next chapter.

Review the information that has been gathered up to this point. If the team feels that they have enough information, a hypothesis (realistically, a well-educated guess) about the function of the behavior can be determined. Remember, there are four functions of behavior in which all behaviors fall. In the education realm, sometimes other functions are discussed (like control or manipulation), but empirically speaking, all behaviors exist as a function of the following:

Based on the accumulation of the record review, the interviews with relevant parties, observations of the student in various settings, and any additional assessment that was done, patterns in the data should emerge that indicate which function the target behavior is meeting for the student. Taylor and Abernathy (2016) developed a Behavior Intervention Flowchart, which could be very helpful in this hypothesis decision-making process and was developed to help teachers who are unfamiliar with this process make better informed decisions. If no clear pattern has emerged, determine where the question marks exist in the information and go collect whatever is needed for clarification. Something else to consider is that a behavior may be (and in schools where there are variables galore) multiply maintained. That is, the behavior serves more than one function. If the team believes this to be the case, try to isolate the variables in the data and look again for patterns to support placing both functions in the hypothesis.

# CASE STUDY—ELEMENTARY—FUNCTION

*The function of Xavier's property destruction behavior is determined to be a combination of escape from a nonpreferred task (perceived as difficult or not enjoyable) and attention (gained adult attention as a result of the problem behavior).*

# CASE STUDY—SECONDARY—FUNCTION

*The function of Lily's "shutting-down" behavior is determined to be a combination of escape from a task (perceived as stressful due to anxiety responses) and automatic/sensory (anxiety symptom reduction).*

## Evaluate the FBA

As a last step before developing a behavior plan, the FBA should be evaluated for integrity. When it comes to an assessment, integrity refers to the degree to which the information gathered or the tools used are answering the relevant questions and are actually measuring what they say they are measuring. For the FBA, the self-assessment tool in Appendix 11–11 helps do just that. The team will answer questions about each step in the process and what was recorded in the document to ensure all the relevant people were involved, the information gathered was thorough, the data collected were complete across settings and people, the data collected were accurate, and any other relevant variables are considered. Just like asking students to review their work before turning in the finished product, the team should review the FBA to ensure it is precise and comprehensive. Do not skip this step, as without a very high-quality FBA, the BIP will suffer.

## How to Read an FBA

As is often the case in these transient days, a student will move into a district with an FBA already in place. The formatting will likely be different, but all the major components should be there. Look for the major components that were discussed here and ask the following questions:

1. Is the target behavior described so that, even without knowing the student, anyone can point it out?
2. Is there a section that describes the student's history and background? Does it give a summary of diagnosed conditions? Does it rule out medical conditions as a reason for the behavior?
3. Was it written by a team or just one person?
4. How much time was taken in the data collection process? Are baseline data reported for just one instance or were multiple days considered?
5. Is the function (or functions) of behavior reported one of the four functions? Or is it something else entirely?
6. Is the hypothesis of function grounded in the data?
7. Is there a clear flow from start to finish linking the information gathered to the hypothesis?
8. Does the team consider the student's strengths and does the FBA give a clear picture of the student?

The FBA self-assessment tool can also act as a good guide to interpret another team's work and ensure all the necessary components are present.

## CHAPTER SUMMARY

Functional Behavior Assessment (FBA) is a group of tools vital to a special educator's practice. Students with emotional and behavior disorders demonstrate challenging behaviors that can be tricky to decipher. The FBA helps to answer the "why are they doing that?" question and gives the team the tools to craft an effective plan to reduce that behavior. This chapter will help a team develop an FBA through strategic but straightforward methods that can stand up to scrutiny and make the BIP process easier.

## DISCUSSION QUESTIONS

1. Do you have a student for whom an FBA would be appropriate? Why and for what target behavior?

2. How closely is your school team following this procedure? What changes could be made?

3. How might the IEP of an EBD student improve with an FBA included?

4. Why do you think the FBA process is often overlooked for EBD students?

## REFERENCES

Baer, D. M., Wolf, M. M., & Risley, T. R. (1968). Some current dimensions of applied behavior analysis. *Journal of Applied Behavior Analysis, 1*(1), 91–97. doi:10.1901/jaba.1968.1-91

Duker, P. C., & Sigafoos, J. (1998). The Motivation Assessment Scale: Reliability and construct validity across three topographies of behavior. *Research in Developmental Disabilities, 19*(2), 131–141. doi:10.1016/S0891-4222(97)00047-4

Gable, R. A., Quinn, M. M., Rutherford, R. B., Jr., & Howell, K. (1998). Addressing problem behaviors in schools: Use of functional assessments and behavior intervention plans. *Preventing School Failure: Alternative Education for Children and Youth, 42*(3), 106–119.

Gresham, F. M., Watson, T. S., & Skinner, C. H. (2001). Functional behavioral assessment: Principles, procedures, and future directions. *School Psychology Review, 30*(2), 156–172.

Iovannone, R., Anderson, C., & Scott, T. (2017). Understanding setting events: What they are and how to identify them. *Beyond Behavior, 26*(3), 105–112. doi:10.1177/1074295617729795

Iwata, B. A., & DeLeon, I. G. (1995). *The Functional Analysis Screening Tool (FAST)*. Unpublished manuscript, University of Florida.

Lewis, T. J., Scott, T. M., & Sugai, G. (1994). The Problem Behavior Questionnaire: A teacher based instrument to develop functional hypotheses of problem behavior in general education classrooms. *Diagnostique, 19*(2–3), 103–115.

Matson, J. L., Tureck, K., & Rieske, R. (2012). The Questions About Behavioral Function (QABF): Current status as a method of functional assessment. *Research in Developmental Disabilities, 33*(2), 630–634. doi:10.1016/j.ridd.2011.11.006

O'Neill, R. E., Horner, R. H., Albin, R. W., Sprague, J. R., Storey, K., & Newton, J. S. (1997). *Functional assessment and program development: A practical handbook.* Brookes/Cole.

Steege, M., Pratt, J., Wickerd, G., Guare, R., & Watson, S. (2019). *Conducting school-based functional behavioral assessments: A behavior analytic problem solving model* (3rd ed.). Guilford.

Sugai, G., Lewis-Palmer, T., & Hagan-Burke, S. (2010). Overview of the functional behavioral assessment process. *Exceptionality, 8*(3), 149–160. doi:10.1207/S15327035EX0803_2

Taylor, S. S., & Abernathy, T. V. (2016). Behavior Intervention Flow Chart: A strategic tool for managing challenging behaviors. *Creative Education, 7*, 2423–2432. doi:10.4236/ce.2016.716232

Van Acker, R., Borenson, L., Gable, R. A., & Potterton, T. (2005). Are we on the right course? Lessons learned about current FBA/BIP practices in schools. *Journal of Behavioral Education, 14*(1), 35–56. doi:10.1007/s10864-005-0960-5

Walker, J. D., & Hott, B. L. (2015). Navigating the manifestation determination process: A teacher's perspective. *Beyond Behavior, 24*(3), 38–48. doi:10.1177/107429561502400306

## APPENDIX 11–1
## ICEL/RIOT Matrix

| Domain | Review | Interview | Observe | Test |
|---|---|---|---|---|
| **Instruction** How the curriculum is taught. Question to ask: Is the curriculum being differentiated to meet the needs of the student? Considerations: • Classroom management techniques • Presentation style • Cooperative learning • Opportunities to respond • Student interactions with peers and teacher | Lesson plans Permanent products Academic and SEL benchmark data Report cards Length of time to complete assignments | Talk to relevant individuals about the following: Instructional decision making Permanent product output methods Grouping structures Any accommodations and modifications used for all students Behavioral management practices Procedure for determining mastery of content Schedule of instruction across a typical week | Ensure multiple observations are made to examine the following: Classroom teacher's instructional style/preferred style of presenting academic information Use of empirically based teaching practices Communication patterns with target student during instruction Opportunities to respond for all students compared with target student Large-group instruction duration vs. small group vs. independent seat work | Classroom Climate Survey (Appendix 11–10) Checklist for Effective Instruction (Appendix 11–4) |

*continues*

| Domain | Review | Interview | Observe | Test |
|--------|--------|-----------|---------|------|
| **Instruction** *continued* | | Pattern of student performance<br><br>Expectation for pacing of curriculum<br><br>Technology used in the classroom<br><br>Student response to instructional practices and any modifications made for the target student | Use of positive reinforcement during instruction<br><br>Quality of teacher-student interaction<br><br>Student time on task compared with peers<br><br>External supports<br><br>Teacher report in interview vs. actual classroom events | |
| **Curriculum**<br>Content of what is taught, including scope and sequence and pacing<br><br>Question to ask: Is the curriculum appropriate for the target student? | Examine the curriculum that was chosen by the district or the teacher for the following:<br><br>Evidence base<br><br>Implementation integrity<br><br>Any modifications or accommodations made to curriculum | Talk to relevant individuals about the following:<br><br>Core curriculum<br><br>Supporting curriculum<br><br>Supplemental teaching materials<br><br>Flexibility to modify curriculum<br><br>Use of data-based decision making | Ensure multiple observations are made to examine the following:<br><br>Student and peer response to the curriculum<br><br>Variety of opportunities to engage with content<br><br>Opportunities for student engagement and active responding | Reading level of textbooks and other resources<br><br>Readability and difficulty of tests |

| Domain | Review | Interview | Observe | Test |
|---|---|---|---|---|
| **Curriculum** *continued*<br><br>Considerations:<br>• Difficulty<br>• Materials used<br>• Sequencing<br>• Format<br>• Relevance | Published scope and sequence and alignment to that<br><br>Permanent products<br><br>Benchmarks and standards | Pacing expectations<br><br>Philosophical orientation of the curriculum<br><br>Level of texts<br><br>Prerequisite skills needed to engage with content<br><br>Expectations for mastery of content<br><br>Technology integration<br><br>Social validity of content | Performance options | |
| **Environment**<br><br>*School*<br>The environment where instruction takes place<br><br>Question to ask: How is the environment impacting learning?<br><br>Considerations:<br>• Distractors<br>• Peers | *School*<br>Published, posted, and communicated school rules and expectations<br><br>Physical layout of school, classrooms, property, and transportation<br><br>Daily schedules required by school and district<br><br>Time out of classroom | *School*<br>Talk to relevant school individuals about the following:<br><br>Situational expectations and rules<br><br>Peer group<br><br>Organization of the classroom<br><br>Schoolwide and classroom behavior systems | Ensure multiple observations are made to examine the following:<br><br>Physical arrangement of learning spaces<br><br>Levels of lighting, noise, temperature<br><br>Distractions in the environment<br><br>Signals for transitions | Systematic observation<br><br>School climate survey results |

*continues*

**APPENDIX 11–1.** *continued*

| Domain | Review | Interview | Observe | Test |
|---|---|---|---|---|
| **Environment** *continued* | *Home* | Mentoring available | Level of activity in the classroom | |
| • Expectations for behavior and academics | Attendance records | Talk to parents or guardians about: | Reported vs. actual environment | |
| • School culture | Parent participation in school activities | Sleep habits | Patterns of interactions with peers and school staff | |
| • Attitudes | Mobility | Nutrition habits | | |
| • Class size | Disciplinary records | Homework routines | Patterns of interaction outside of the regular school day | |
| *Home/community* Where the student spends time outside of school | Supports being provided to the student beyond general education | Extracurricular activities | | |
| | | How time is spent outside of school | | |
| Question to ask: How does the environment outside of school support performance at school? | Parent communication and availability | Expectations at home | | |
| | Extracurricular activities and supports | Attitudes about school | | |
| | | Consistency of routines and discipline between home and school | | |
| Considerations: | Siblings | School/family engagement | | |
| • Distractions | | | | |
| • Supports | | | | |
| • Expectations | | | | |
| • Beliefs/attitudes | | | | |
| • Attendances/tardies | | | | |
| • Patterns of involvement | | | | |

| Domain | Review | Interview | Observe | Test |
|---|---|---|---|---|
| **Learner**<br><br>The target student<br><br>Question to ask: Have all difficulties with curriculum, instruction, and environment been ruled out before the problem is considered central to the learner?<br><br>Considerations:<br>• Motivation<br>• Prerequisite skills<br>• Executive function skills<br>• Habits<br>• Abilities<br>• Impairments<br>• History of instruction | Permanent products created by the student versus those created by peers<br><br>Cumulative file (permanent and temporary)<br><br>Health records<br><br>Assignment notebook<br><br>Attendance and disciplinary records<br><br>Response to intervention and special education records | Talk to the student themselves about the following:<br><br>Self-perception<br><br>Needs<br><br>Learning style<br><br>Beliefs<br><br>Self-determination<br><br>Friends<br><br>Perception of home environment and responsibilities<br><br>Goals and aspirations<br><br>Talk to the parents or guardians about the following:<br><br>Health impact on learning<br><br>Neurological impairments<br><br>Perceptions or expectations on learning, behavior, speech, or motor needs<br><br>Family engagement | Ensure multiple observations are made to examine the following:<br><br>The student's learning style compared with instructional style<br><br>Use of technology<br><br>Target behavior, antecedents, conditions, consequences<br><br>Transitions<br><br>Time on task<br><br>External supports necessary to sustain engagement<br><br>Processing speed<br><br>Barriers to access instruction<br><br>Behavioral interventions already occurring in the classroom or other settings specifically targeting the student | Standardized academic assessment<br><br>Cognitive assessment<br><br>Preference assessment<br><br>Motivation rating scales<br><br>Behavior rating scales<br><br>Progress monitoring<br><br>Social emotional health<br><br>Setting events checklist |

# Record Review Template

| Demographic Information | | |
|---|---|---|
| Student Name: | | DOB: |
| Current Grade: | Current School: | Current Teacher: |

| Educational History | | | | | |
|---|---|---|---|---|---|
| Preschool: *Circle response for each* | Attended? Y/N | Public or private | 3 years old 4 years old | IFSP/504 | Notes: |

| Grade | School/ District | Teacher | IEP/504 | Typical Pattern of Performance | Notable Events |
|---|---|---|---|---|---|
| K | | | | | |
| 1 | | | | | |
| 2 | | | | | |
| 3 | | | | | |
| 4 | | | | | |
| 5 | | | | | |
| 6 | | | | | |
| 7 | | | | | |
| 8 | | | | | |
| 9 | | | | | |
| 10 | | | | | |
| 11 | | | | | |
| 12 | | | | | |

## Standardized Assessment Scores

### Academic Curriculum-Based Assessment Benchmarking

| Tool used: | Reading: | Percentile: | Math: | Percentile: | Notes |
|---|---|---|---|---|---|
| | | | | | |

### Districtwide Assessment

| Tool used: | Reading: | Percentile: | Math: | Percentile: | Notes |
|---|---|---|---|---|---|
| | | | | | |

### Statewide Assessment

| Tool used: | Reading: | Percentile: | Math: | Percentile: | Notes |
|---|---|---|---|---|---|
| | | | | | |

### Other

| Tool used: | Reading: | Percentile: | Math: | Percentile: | Notes |
|---|---|---|---|---|---|
| | | | | | |

## Review of Special Education Participation

| | | |
|---|---|---|
| Grade initially made eligible for sped: | | Date: |
| Initial category(ies) of eligibility: | | |
| Current eligibility: | | |
| Summary of current goals: | | |
| Summary of current services: | | |
| Summary of past goals: | | |
| Summary of past services: | | |
| Any additional notes: | | |
| If 504 plan, describe needs and accommodations: | | |

*continues*

| Review of Medical Records | | |
| --- | --- | --- |
| *Medical and Psychological Diagnoses* | | |
| Diagnosis | Date | Diagnosing Physician/Psych |
| | | |
| | | |
| | | |
| | | |
| | | |
| | | |
| Notes or relevant recommendations for school environment: | | |

# APPENDIX 11–3

## Structured Interview

**Functional Assessment Interview**

Student: _____    Date of Interview: _____

Interviewer: _____    Respondent(s): _____

What are the student's strengths? What is he or she good at? What does he or she enjoy doing?

Describe the behavior that causes the most difficulty for you:

Is the behavior a safety concern for this student/other students/adults?

When does the behavior typically happen? Where is it most likely to happen?

*continues*

**APPENDIX II–3.** *continued*

Where is the behavior least likely to happen? When is it least likely
to happen?

With whom is the behavior most and least likely to happen?

What activities are most likely to produce the behavior? Least likely?

Is there anything that I did not ask about that often seems to set off the
behavior? Does the student appear to have any sensory-seeking or avoiding
behaviors? Any areas of deficit that weren't discussed yet? Any particular
preferences or peculiarities compared to peers that cause difficulties?

Does the student ask for help? If so, how? How often?

Does the student respond appropriately to requests or directions? How many steps can he or she follow (and how does that compare with peers)?

Is the student aware of the implications of his or her actions? Does he or she understand how others see him or her?

What are the student's preferences? (food, drink, objects, toys, activities, people, places, etc.)

Adapted from the Functional Assessment for Teachers from the Student Services Department of Newfoundland Labrador, Canada. Retrieved from https://www.gov .nl.ca/eecd/rewrite.php?rewrite_uri=/forms/studentsupport/FAI-Teachers.pdf

# Antecedent-Behavior-Consequence
## Data Collection Form

Target behavior(s): _____

Student: _____

| Date and Time: Environment: | Antecedent | Behavior | Consequence |
|---|---|---|---|
|  |  |  |  |
|  |  |  |  |
|  |  |  |  |
|  |  |  |  |
|  |  |  |  |
|  |  |  |  |

# Frequency Data Collection Form

Target behavior(s): _____

Student: _____

| Date and Environment: | Start Time: | End Time: | Tally Behaviors: | Total: |
|---|---|---|---|---|
| | | | | |
| | | | | |
| | | | | |
| | | | | |
| | | | | |
| | | | | |

# Duration Data Collection Form

Target behavior(s): _____

Student: _____ Date: _____

| Environment: | Start Time: | End Time: | Notes: | Total Duration: |
|---|---|---|---|---|
| | | | | |
| | | | | |
| | | | | |
| | | | | |
| | | | | |
| | | | | |
| | | | | |
| | | | | |
| | | | | |
| | | | | |
| | | | | |
| | | | | |
| | | | | |
| | | | | |
| | | | **Total day's duration** | |

# Latency Data Collection Form

Target behavior(s): _____

Student: _____ Date: _____

| Environment: | Stimulus: | Amount of Time Before Behavior Begins: |
|---|---|---|
|  |  |  |
|  |  |  |
|  |  |  |
|  |  |  |
|  |  |  |
|  |  |  |
|  |  |  |
|  |  |  |
|  |  |  |
|  |  |  |
|  |  |  |
|  |  |  |
|  |  |  |
|  |  |  |
|  |  |  |
|  |  |  |

# Intensity Data Collection Form

Target behavior(s): _____

Student: _____  Date: _____

1 = _____  2 = _____  3 = _____

| Environment: | Setting Events: | Behavior Intensity Rating: | | |
|---|---|---|---|---|
| | | 1 | 2 | 3 |
| | | 1 | 2 | 3 |
| | | 1 | 2 | 3 |
| | | 1 | 2 | 3 |
| | | 1 | 2 | 3 |
| | | 1 | 2 | 3 |
| | | 1 | 2 | 3 |
| | | 1 | 2 | 3 |
| | | 1 | 2 | 3 |
| | | 1 | 2 | 3 |
| | | 1 | 2 | 3 |
| | | 1 | 2 | 3 |

# Functional Behavior Assessment Template

### Functional Behavior Assessment Documentation

Complete an FBA form for each target challenging behavior in question. Select no more than two to three challenging behaviors to intervene upon at any given time.

Target Behavior: _____

---

**Student Strengths and Preferences:** Describe the student's strengths, including academic, social, emotional, functional, cognitive, communication, and behavioral strengths. Also report on results of preference assessment for potential reinforcers.

<br><br><br><br><br>

**Operational Definition:** Include a description of the topography of the behavior and include baseline data (frequency, duration, intensity, latency) as relevant.

<br><br><br><br><br><br><br>

**Environmental Variables and Setting Events:** Describe any environmental variables or events happening in close proximity that may be affecting the student and contributing to the challenging behavior. Also include any other relevant background information here.

<br><br><br><br><br><br>

---

*continues*

**Setting:** Describe the setting in which the behavior occurs, including information about the physical location, time of day, and persons present.

**Antecedents:** Describe the relevant events that typically occur directly preceding the target behavior.

**Consequences:** Describe the response to the target behavior that appears to be acting to maintain the behavior.

**Hypothesis of Behavior Function:** What is the relationship between the behavior and the environment in which it occurs?

# Classroom Climate Survey

Answer the following questions as honestly as possible. Check the box that best describes your feelings. It is completely anonymous and just intended to help the teacher improve the classroom setting.

|  | Strongly Agree | Agree | Disagree | Strongly Disagree |
|---|---|---|---|---|
| My teacher makes me feel as though he or she really cares about me. | | | | |
| My teacher tries to understand how students feel. | | | | |
| Students in this class treat the teacher respectfully. | | | | |
| This class stays busy and does not waste time. | | | | |
| My teacher explains topics in a variety of ways to help me understand the content. | | | | |
| My teacher explains things clearly. | | | | |
| We learn a lot almost every day in this class. | | | | |
| The students learn to correct mistakes and learn from them in this class. | | | | |
| My teacher makes the lessons interesting. | | | | |
| I learn a lot in this class. | | | | |
| All students speak about and share in this class. | | | | |
| My teacher respects my ideas and suggestions. | | | | |
| My teacher checks that all students understand what is being taught. | | | | |

# APPENDIX 11–11

# FBA Self-Assessment

| Criterion | | Rating<br>0 = not complete<br>1 = partially complete<br>2 = thoroughly complete | Score |
|---|---|---|---|
| 1. Gather information | Include key individuals in the initial assessment meetings. | 0  1  2 | __ / 8 |
| | Review all relevant records. | 0  1  2 | |
| | Collect informal direct observation data. | 0  1  2 | |
| | Interview all relevant parties who have direct experience with the student. | 0  1  2 | |
| 2. Student strengths and preferences | Describe at least five student strengths across domains. | 0  1  2 | __ / 6 |
| | Describe desirable actions the student is capable of doing instead of the problem behavior. | 0  1  2 | |
| | Student preferences were assessed and reported. | 0  1  2 | |
| 3. Environmental variables and setting events | All environments considered. | 0  1  2 | __ / 4 |
| | Considers situationally specific events. | 0  1  2 | |
| 4. Operational definition | Definition is objective. | 0  1  2 | __ / 10 |
| | Definition is clear. | 0  1  2 | |
| | Definition is concise but complete. | 0  1  2 | |

| | Criterion | Rating<br>0 = not complete<br>1 = partially complete<br>2 = thoroughly complete | | | Score |
|---|---|---|---|---|---|
| 4. Operational definition<br>*continued* | Baseline data are provided on the frequency, duration, and intensity of behavior. | 0 | 1 | 2 | |
| | Target behaviors are broken up if more than one is reported and described separately. | 0 | 1 | 2 | |
| 5. Setting | Identify the time(s) of day when the behavior is most and least likely to occur. | 0 | 1 | 2 | __ / 8 |
| | Identify settings in which behavior is most and least likely to occur. | 0 | 1 | 2 | |
| | Identify persons most likely to be present when challenging behavior occurs. | 0 | 1 | 2 | |
| | Describe setting for each target challenging behavior identified. | 0 | 1 | 2 | |
| 6. Antecedents | Based on record review and interview and confirmed in observation. | 0 | 1 | 2 | __ / 8 |
| | Objective and observable description. | 0 | 1 | 2 | |
| | Description focuses on environmental occurrences. | 0 | 1 | 2 | |
| | Events are described in terms of the proximity to target behavior. | 0 | 1 | 2 | |

*continues*

| | Criterion | Rating<br>0 = not complete<br>1 = partially complete<br>2 = thoroughly complete | Score |
|---|---|---|---|
| 7. Consequences | Events are described in terms of proximity to target behavior. | 0   1   2 | __ / 6 |
| | Variables are identified that can be easily modifiable. | 0   1   2 | |
| | All environmental variables are considered (people present, activities or objects removed or accessed). | 0   1   2 | |
| 8. Hypothesis of function(s) | One or more of the four functions of behavior are identified and based on data. | 0   1   2 | __ / 4 |
| | Written in observable and measurable terms. | 0   1   2 | |

Adapted from Sugai, Lewis-Palmer, and Hagan-Burke (2010) and O'Neill et al. (1997).

# Behavior Intervention Planning

*With Contributions from Sarah Heiniger*

---

## KEY VOCABULARY

Behavior Intervention Plan (BIP)
Negative Reinforcement
Positive Reinforcement
SMART Goals
Social Validity

## LEARNING OBJECTIVES

By the end of this chapter, you should be able to . . .

- Determine acceptable and socially valid alternatives to challenging behaviors.
- Accurately determine if hypothesized function of behavior is correct.
- Develop effective interventions.
- Determine whether an intervention is effective using data-based decisions.
- Collect accurate data and use that data to make decisions.

# INTRODUCTION

Now that a fully developed hypothesis of behavior function has been developed (see Chapter 11 on Functional Behavior Assessment), that information can be used to craft a **Behavior Intervention Plan (BIP)**. Students with EBD often require a formal BIP to support access to a quality education and meaningful social progress. A BIP should be designed to create environments and patterns of support around the student that nullifies the current maintaining consequences. The challenging behaviors they were engaging in should no longer be effective, should no longer be the most efficient means, and/or should be contextually irrelevant in terms of getting their wants and needs met (Sugai et al., 2010).

In addition, a formal BIP might be required by your school district's policy or even by law. There is a provision in the Individuals with Disabilities Education Act (2004, 34 CFR §300.324(a)(2)(i)) that the school team must consider use of positive behavior interventions and supports when a student's behavior is impeding their learning or that of other students. Interpretations of the law go further, though; the IEP team can use an FBA and BIP proactively if everyone deems it appropriate for the student. In Section 34 CFR §300.530(e) of the IDEA, if a student's misconduct is found to be a manifestation of their disability, an FBA and BIP are required. From a best practice perspective, if a student has difficulty managing their own behavior (whether externalizing or internalizing), a formal examination of that behavior and a formal plan for intervening are probably warranted. If the IEP team has determined that an FBA is warranted, then it is likely the behavior is impacting the student's ability to access the educational environment. And if a high-quality FBA was conducted, then the team is in a good position to craft a highly effective BIP.

## Plan Development

As noted in Chapter 11, the Functional Behavior Assessment and BIP process follow the steps of the problem-solving process. The FBA encompasses the first two steps (problem identification and problem analysis) and the BIP encompasses the final three steps (plan development, plan implementation, and plan evaluation). We will begin with a discussion on developing the plan.

## Social Validity

The concept of creating a socially valid behavior plan is really important. A team needs to think about how the behaviors that a student is learning will fit into the broader school community by asking the following questions: Will this behavior help the student be a better member of the community? Will other people around the student respond better or worse with this alternate behavior in place? Is the student going to be able to access the environment more easily? Will this behavior make the student fit in better or stand out more? Does this behavior plan promote the concept of the least restrictive environment?

An individualized, high-quality BIP ought to be based on the hypotheses developed from the FBA, include plans for both reducing challenging behaviors and increasing replacement skills, focus on measurable outcomes, identify the roles and responsibilities of all involved people, clearly define the necessary supports for success, and be socially valid. This is accomplished by thoroughly examining all of the information collected through the functional assessment process as a team, choosing replacement behaviors that meet the identified function of the target behavior in a more socially appropriate manner, identifying how the environment will be modified to support behavior change, planning for instruction to teach replacement skills, considering all accommodations and modifications to the environment that could be necessary to support behavior change, structuring a plan of reinforcement, considering how continued challenging behaviors will be addressed, and planing for ongoing data collection to determine if the plan is effective. For components of a BIP, see Table 12–1.

**Table 12–1.** BIP Components

| Step | Description |
| --- | --- |
| Summarize FBA and Previous Interventions Attempted | In a brief paragraph or two, summarize the information gleaned from the FBA process and any previous interventions attempted to modify the challenging behavior |
| Identify Replacement Behavior | Describe the chosen replacement behavior or behaviors, if multiple are needed or if there are several approximations toward the ultimate replacement behavior |
| Accommodations and Modifications | How is the environment going to be modified to support behavior change? What pieces will be removed, what pieces will be added, what pieces will be changed? What accommodations does the student need made either to the instruction or learning situations to be successful? |
| Instruction, Curriculum | Is the current curriculum and instruction appropriate for the student? Do any modifications need to be made to the classroom instruction and/or intervention instruction? What additional instruction needs to take place in order to teach the replacement behaviors? Is an additional curriculum required? Who will do the teaching and when? |

*continues*

**Table 12–1.** *continued*

| Step | Description |
|---|---|
| Reinforcement Procedures | How will the replacement behavior be reinforced? How often? By whom? When? And where? |
| Restrictive Disciplinary Measures and Crisis Plan | If a challenging behavior occurs, how will it be handled? If there a crisis situation, what is the plan in place to address it? |
| Data Collection Procedures | How will ongoing data be collected about the challenging behavior? How will ongoing data about the replacement behaviors be collected? |

## SUMMARIZE THE FBA

### CASE STUDY—ELEMENTARY— FBA SUMMARY

*Xavier has many strengths, including above grade-level mathematics skills and enjoying peer relationships. Xavier has good functional student skills and is able to follow directions and complete classroom routines when motivated. When a preference assessment was conducted, Xavier showed interest in playing on the iPad, having stories read to him, and anything involving superheroes. The target behavior decided upon by the team was property destruction, which is defined as swiping classroom materials off tables, knocking over chairs or stools, ripping up papers (either his work or others), or otherwise throwing objects on the floor. This behavior happens in baseline on average three times per day and lasts anywhere from 5 minutes to 90 minutes. Environmental variables that appear to have an impact on Xavier is when something is changed in the classroom, whether that change is physical (desks moved around) or staff (substitute teacher). Setting events that impact him include the diagnosis of attention-deficit/hyperactivity disorder and mood disorder not otherwise specified (NOS), when it appears he did not sleep well the night before (observed through physical indicators), and if he has not eaten yet that day.*

The setting in which the problem behavior occurs is only in the general education kindergarten classroom, not in any of the special (music, art, physical education) classrooms. There is no clear pattern as to time of day or persons present, as behaviors happen across the entire afternoon (Xavier attends only afternoon kindergarten). Antecedents have been identified as when Xavier is presented with a creative craft-type activity, when asked to transition before fully completing his task, or when he is presented with a handwriting task. Current consequences that are maintaining the behavior include being allowed to escape the task because of the intensity of the behavior he demonstrates or getting attention one-on-one from adults in the environment when he is removed from the group or even from the classroom. The current hypothesis of the behavior function is that the property destruction behavior is dually maintained by attention and escape functions.

## CASE STUDY—SECONDARY— FBA SUMMARY

*Lily is a very hardworking student who has developed numerous friendships. She was an active participant on the soccer team and in the photography club. The target behavior for Lily is what the team is calling "shutting down," that is, a lack of participation in class (appearing withdrawn in class, sitting at her desk without participating in the discussion while keeping her head down, and when assignments or tests are presented at school, she will either only complete them partially or not begin work at all). Environmental variables that are impacting Lily's behavior include specific subject areas (writing and English), whole-group tasks, or independent seatwork. Setting events appear to be the impact of her parents' divorce, recently ceased highly preferred events (end of soccer season), and her best friend moving away. The setting in which the behavior occurs is in the ELA classroom and the creative writing classroom. Antecedents for the behavior are being presented with a task or a whole-group discussion. Maintaining consequences include escaping the task (by refusing to participate, she does not actually complete the task). The function of Lily's "shutting-down" behavior is determined to be a combination of escape from a task (perceived as stressful due to anxiety responses) and automatic/sensory (anxiety symptom reduction).*

## Starting the BIP Process

In beginning the BIP, it can be a good idea to take a step back and examine the FBA summary. Read through the document and summarize it in a paragraph or two. Ensure that the information it contains can be easily understood by a third party unfamiliar with the student, is cohesive, and does not leave any questions unanswered. A useful tool to help get the facts from the FBA into a practically applicable BIP is the competing behavior pathways chart.

The competing behavior pathways chart is a clear visual to help the team see where the behavior is at currently, where it should ultimately be (desired replacement behavior), and an alternative behavior that is acceptable in the meantime. The chart represents what is known in behavior analysis as the three-term contingency. This can be thought of as Antecedent-Behavior-Consequence (ABC) or also as stimulus-behavior-reinforcement when the focus is on teaching the replacement behavior. The student is reacting to something (the antecedent) whether it is an instruction or something in the environment, then behaving (either in a problematic way or in a more acceptable way), and then that behavior is being reinforced (the maintaining consequence for the problem behavior or with something else that acts as a reinforcer to increase the more acceptable or desired replacement behavior). The setting event acts as a motivator or abolisher to make the consequences more powerful. For example, if the student has not eaten since dinner the night before and it is the middle of the morning, the student might engage in problem behavior to escape the classroom and get a snack (because the student has learned the team gives him a snack whenever he begins to "act cranky"). Another example might be that the student has math class right before English class, and math is particularly difficult and results in increased levels of anxiety, so when difficult content is presented in English class, the motivation is already high to "escape" the context by putting her head down on her desk and ignoring instruction.

## Example of Competing Behavior Pathway Completed for Xavier

Only put one target behavior at a time into the competing behavior pathway chart, but make as many separate charts as needed to include all of the relevant target behaviors. Refer to Chapter 11 for a more detailed explanation of functions of behavior. Include setting events (what happens going into the actual immediate event itself—does the student have a medical condition? Was there a recent holiday from school? Does the student have a learning disability? Was there deprivation from something? Did the student have a fight with friends?). Then the antecedent events (what happens exactly right before the challenging behavior occurs) are recorded. This can include any student triggers that make it evident that a challenging behavior is about to erupt. Then the behavior itself is defined.

In the FBA, there was not a discussion about alternatives to the challenging behavior. In the competing behavior pathway chart, this is the start of identifying some other behaviors that the student could use to get the same need or want met. In every case, there will be the most ultimate desired behavior. Also, in most cases, that desired behavior is at least one step further than a student is able to accomplish just through prompting and reinforcement alone. It helps to choose at least one acceptable alternative behavior that the student already has in their repertoire (and maybe more than one) so that everyone on the team understands the current approximation. This process can sometimes be frustrating as an educator, as the student is "capable of more" or that instructional time is being wasted. These are valid concerns, but adding frustration to the student is not going to result in growth, and in the beginning stages, small growth should be celebrated. Appendix 12–1 contains a competing behavior chart.

In the example above is the target problem behavior in which Xavier engages. He reports getting so agitated that the "only thing" that relieves those feelings is to destroy something in the classroom. Leaving the table and choosing an alternate activity is not the teacher's first preference (because then he is losing instruction), but when it takes the place of destroying another student's hard work, that is a success (in the short term). It meets the need of escaping the aversive work and allows him to remain a positive member of the community. The student can be easily prompted to engage in that behavior alone, because he is presently getting out of his seat and roaming the room in a destructive way. Teaching can occur to use other strategies to keep the behavior there while also teaching a calming progression with a visual simultaneously that can replace the ripping or swiping. And then finally, Xavier can be taught to maintain an outwardly calm exterior while silently using the calm-down progression and removing himself from the situation. All meet the function of escape from the tension associated with the task (whether by physically getting away from it or reducing the difficulty by taking away the emotional tension). Obviously, there are other alternatives that could be plugged into that scenario, but this is just one example.

## Acceptable Alternatives to the Problem Behavior

When selecting acceptable replacement behaviors, whether the penultimate behavior or otherwise, there are several considerations. This will be the ultimate desired alternative. First, consider the context and how the typical student is expected to behave. Do not set the goal higher than what a typical peer is able to achieve. Plans can run awry when this happens. The observation portion of the FBA can be helpful here in defining what other students do during the target context. There is obviously an ideal student performance in every teacher's mind, but in reality, the average student does not attend all of the time, misbehaves some of the time, treats others poorly every once in a while, and is allowed to have bad days. Just because the target student has a plan does not mean these variables do not apply. When crafting the approximations of behavior that will be acceptable, consider the student's current skill repertoires. How much additional instruction will be required to get the student to demonstrate the replacement behavior without prompting? Repertoires can be built upon, and if the student can be successful and independent at a slightly less ideal behavior, then start there and instruct further to the ultimate behavior along the way. Building too much prompting into the plan (whether it comes from a person or in the environment) decreases the level of independence with the skill and places too much importance on something that, if absent, could derail the plan.

Another very important factor to consider when choosing replacement behaviors is the function. Does the alternate behavior meet the same function as the target challenging behavior? If not, it is not actually going to work as a replacement behavior.

Make sure that the replacement behavior(s) are just as or even more efficient than the problem behavior at getting the student what they need and are easily reinforced. This is where environmental modifications and/or accommodations to the student's programming and staff training come in. When a new behavior is taught, the behavior must contact reinforcement immediately and meaningfully to strengthen that behavior (either increase the likelihood that it will happen again in the future and/or increase the degree of independence with that behavior). If quick, salient reinforcement of the behavior cannot be provided, then that new behavior probably will not stick. The team should also consider all of the consequences from the target and replacement behavior. There are sometimes unintended consequences that, if the plan is thoroughly discussed and reviewed as a team, can be avoided so as not to create another problem behavior monster.

Finally, ensure that the behavior is socially valid. **Social validity** means that a behavior is important to the context, is meaningful for being able to participate in that setting, and is a behavior most other individuals see as appropriate or valued. Is it an important behavior that all students should demonstrate? Is it going to help the student be a better member of the community? Is the behavior going to allow the student to get along better with peers?

Before progressing further, a discussion of reinforcement and punishment is important (Table 12–2). These two concepts are two sides of the same coin, and even though punishment has some pretty intense connotations, in reality, it is used every day and can be very effective when it is deemed necessary. Reinforcement means increasing the likelihood that the behavior will happen again in the future or increasing the strength of that behavior. Punishment means anything that is decreasing the likelihood that the behavior will occur again in the future or decreasing the strength of that behavior. In behavior analysis, the term "positive" just means an addition to the environment. When **positive reinforcement** is discussed, it means adding something preferred by the student to the environment that results in that increase in behavior. **Negative reinforcement** means taking something aversive away from the environment to increase the behavior. Again, punishment is just the inverse of that. Positive punishment is adding an aversive to decrease the behavior, and negative punishment is removing a preferred to decrease the behavior.

**Table 12–2.** Reinforcement and Punishment

| | **+**<br>*(add to the environment)* | **–**<br>*(remove from the environment)* |
|---|---|---|
| **Reinforcement**<br>INCREASES the likelihood of behavior in the future | Positive Reinforcement | Negative Reinforcement |
| **Punishment**<br>DECREASES the likelihood of behavior in the future | Positive Punishment | Negative Punishment |

It is important to have a firm grasp on this concept, because when designing a behavior plan, both additions to and subtractions from the environment can act effectively. Look at Xavier's behavior. He is actively trying to avoid work that is too difficult for him. In considering the function, the team could design interventions that allow him to escape the work in a more functional way. This is not the typical sticker chart for buckling down and getting the work done, but because it meets the function, it will likely be more effective in the short term while the other skills are addressed.

Reinforcement can be provided at different rates and using different methodologies but should always be based on the student's preference. Not all students like verbal praise, nor do all students like sticker charts. Primary reinforcers (i.e., those based on basic physical needs of food, water, rest, shelter, health, and physical touch) are always effective, but that does not mean they are appropriate in all settings. This will be discussed in the following sections on plan development and skill acquisition, but rate and type of reinforcement need to match the student's level of learning, ability, and preferences. Remember, no matter what you are offering, if the addition of an object or attention does not change the student's behavior, then that object or attention is not a reinforcer.

## Hypothesis Testing

Implementation of the BIP is an essential test of the hypothesis about the function the target behavior is serving. To ensure the strongest hypothesis, the functional behavior assessment should have triangulated the data (at least three pieces of objective data supporting that conclusion) to create a validated hypothesis statement. That hypothesis should also be alterable, in that it acts as a variable in the environment that can be manipulated and fits within the resources available. The hypothesis statement should not be so rigid as to have to be discarded as soon as one small part is disproved. In addition, and this should go without saying, but the team should agree on the hypothesis. If the team is undecided, then perhaps the functional behavior assessment is not as complete as it could be. If this process is newer to a school building or district, there may be the odd team member out who disagrees with the concept as a whole or does not necessarily buy in, but as long as that person is willing to test it out and will follow the plan, then the process can move forward.

## INTERVENTION

### Planning

Once all of those pieces are in place, socially valid interventions that are strongly rooted in behavior analytic science and good teaching practice should be developed. Likely, the members of the team sitting around the table have many combined years of experience working with students and have wonderful ideas about things to try. A two-pronged approach to planning should occur in the BIP: problem behavior reduction and replacement skill building. A good plan incorporates considerations for both, as taking away behavior leaves a vacuum into which another behavior will occur. And in all likelihood, that behavior will be another problem causer rather than a prosocial alternative. In addition, intervention should be considered at all layers of instruction: whole group, small group, and individual. If the whole classroom setting is not conducive to promoting appropriate behavior, no amount of individual intervention is going to change the student's behavior in that setting in the long term without significant intrusive and costly procedures.

Secondary level intervention—namely, behavior interventions that are easy to administer by the classroom teacher without a lot of additional instruction or time—should be in place or have been tried before a formal BIP is developed (which should have been documented in the FBA). These might continue as a layered approach or be completely replaced by the more intensive BIP. This level of intervention can act as a good link to the general education teacher if more support is provided to the target student to maintain that relationship. If a paraprofessional is added or the student is receiving more instruction from a special education teacher or a social worker and the classroom teacher loses interaction, it will be difficult to build that back up as the student's skills are generalized and support is faded.

Finally, the team should consider the individualized and intensive-level interventions to apply to meet the function and provide the student with appropriate, socially valid, and useful replacement behaviors. Once the replacement behavior has been identified, the intervention to teach and maintain that behavior is individually crafted. This intervention is not just adding a curriculum to the student's day or a token economy. The various needs of the student and various settings in which the target behavior occurs should be considered.

## Problem Behavior Reduction Strategies

This is likely the first place a team will start, as the challenging behavior itself has been disruptive to the student's learning and that of others. These strategies act as barriers between the behavior and the maintaining consequences to quickly reduce the problem. These cannot be left as the only strategies in the plan, as another problem behavior will pop up in place of the first target behavior when no other replacement behavior is taught. There is no vacuum in behavior; when one behavior exits, another will take its place. In addition, when these strategies are used without additional positive and proactive strategies, relationships can be damaged and behavior can worsen.

Response blocking is a technique to interrupt the behavior-consequence pattern. It can involve literal blocking of a student hitting themselves or someone else, or reaching to grab someone else's belongings. It can also be a figurative blocking of attention if that is the function. Extinction has traditionally been used to completely remove all contact to reinforcing consequences from challenging behavior. The difficult part about extinction is that it needs to be implemented 100% of the time, which is nearly impossible to do in the school setting. As much as it possible, though, staff can participate in planned ignoring and not allow for much escape to facilitate the removal of reinforcement from those behavioral functions. It is also much more preferable to approach problem behavior with a package of challenging behavior response plus plan for differential reinforcement and to avoid the traditional procedures that involved putting hands on students and forcing them to stay in aversive settings without teaching alternatives.

When challenging behavior does rear its ugly head, using strategies like prompting more appropriate behaviors, asking if the student needs help, and waiting nearby until the behavior seems to be de-escalating are all more respectful and more manageable response strategies. Offering help can take the form of just saying, "Do you need help with something?" It could also be just stepping in to help or something like, "You can do it yourself or I can help you with that." Prompting includes giving choices: "Do you want this or that?" "How about we go for a walk or get a snack?" It could also include basic statements like, "Use your calm-down chart," or "Remember to do whole-body relaxation." High-probability behaviors (that is, those a student is really likely to do no matter what the situation) can also be prompted, as long as they are not considered reinforcing to the problem behavior. When all else fails, wait for the behavior to de-escalate somewhat and then try to intervene again while keeping everyone around safe from harm. However, if the challenging behavior continues to escalate, the crisis prevention measures that the school has in place should be put into motion. At that point, the team can determine whether a student is posing a threat to himself or others and will act accordingly. But it is very important to follow the procedures of the school district and building in cases like this.

In essence, problem behavior reduction just involves removing the reinforcement from the situation. In the ABC terminology, the behavior is not coming into contact with the consequence that it was before, which was acting to reinforce that behavior over time. The function that used to be met with that behavior is not any longer. The BIP team needs to carefully examine the information that was gathered and craft a specific plan around how staff will remove that C from the A-B-C chain and transfer it to something else.

## Differential Reinforcement

Differential reinforcement methodologies act to shift reinforcement away from a target challenging behavior and onto an identified replacement behavior. Defining this in the BIP is helpful, especially for team members who may not have as much practice applying these types of practices. There are four different types of differential reinforcement: (1) alternative, (2) incompatible, (3) other, and (4) low rates. Also important to consider is a plan for noncontingent reinforcement, which provides the student to access whatever is going to meet that functional need met without having to demonstrate a behavior to get it, which is where practices like a "sensory diet" come into play to satiate a student without making them "jump through hoops" to get there. The schedules of differential reinforcement are referred to as DRA, DRI, DRO, and DRL. See Table 12–3 for details of each and when to use which strategy over another.

## DRO

DRO is often used in instances of self-injurious behavior, which can be common in students with EBD. Typically, for this schedule, the team will base the interval length on the baseline data that were collected in the FBA process to determine. If that information was not recorded during the FBA, an inter-response time (IRT) can be calculated. Once the behavior starts occurring, start the timer. Keep the timer going even after the behavior stops, and stop it when the behavior starts again. This is known as the IRT, or the time between behaviors. Keep going until there are enough data gathered to determine an average IRT (preferably across several different days and different types of activities). It is best to start with a fixed schedule for ease of use and then fade to a variable schedule, which might result in more long-lasting elimination of the target challenging behavior. Another option is to include an escalating schedule of reinforcement, in which a successful interval without the target behavior results in a reinforcer being delivered as well as a

**Table 12–3.** Types of Differential Reinforcement

| Differential Reinforcement of . . . | Definition | Example | When to Use |
|---|---|---|---|
| Alternative Behavior (DRA) | Reinforcing any behavior that could act as an alternate replacement to the target challenging behavior, but meets the same need | Reinforce instances of hand raising instead of shouting out behavior | When there is an acceptable substitute behavior that is not necessarily incompatible but meets the same function, when no good incompatible substitute exists |
| Incompatible Behavior (DRI) | Reinforcing any behavior that could not occur at the same time as the target challenging behavior, but meets the same need | Reinforce chewing gum instead of chewing on a shirt | When the behavior needs to be removed, but a replacement is necessary due to function |
| Other Behavior (DRO) | Reinforcement provided after a pre-determined period of time during which target challenging behavior does NOT occur | Reinforcement provided after a period of 5 minutes during which the student does not shout out | When the goal is for the behavior to be removed completely, when the entire period can be observed; when student has a good repertoire of other independent behaviors; in conjunction with other reinforcement |
| Low Rates of Behavior (DRL) | Reinforce a behavior less often that is good in essence but occurs too often | Reinforce the behavior of small group discussion participation by acknowledging student response only 3 times instead of high rate of 15 times in 15 minutes. | When the behavior itself is appropriate, but occurs too often |

slightly increased subsequent interval length. This allows for a reinforcement schedule that might fit better with the environment (more naturally occurring) and does also serve the same purpose as an intermittent schedule to solidify the absence of behavior over time. Regardless of the schedule initially chosen, the goal should be to increase the interval over time as the student is successful, which should be written into the BIP (Vollmer & Iwata, 1992). The team should write into the BIP when the goal will be increased. The goal duration length should only be adjusted according to the data and on the schedule the team has agreed to. If the goal is adjusted too quickly, there may be a backslide in behavior. If it is not adjusted quickly enough, the student may become dependent on a specific schedule of reinforcement.

When implementing, the team should decide whether or not to include the student in the full procedure. Some students really benefit from the visual of a timer to help remind themselves of the behavior they should (or should not, in this case) be performing. For other students, the idea that they are being timed and monitored might result in increased levels of anxiety, so the timing may need to be more covert and reinforcement is not presented to them as obviously (Vollmer & Iwata, 1992). See Table 12-4 for steps to implement DRO.

**Table 12–4.** Steps to Implement DRO

1. Check baseline data in FBA for how often the behavior occurs and the amount of time between behaviors.

2. Decide upon a good interval length, at or slightly below the average IRT that was measured.

3. Set a timer for the pre-determined interval length. Make the student aware, if that is part of the BIP.

4. When timer goes off, provide reinforcement if the target behavior did not occur. If it did occur, let the student know they did not earn the reward and can have another try (or see troubleshooting tip below). Use an appropriate option for reinforcement based on student preference. Also develop a fading schedule from artificial to more naturalist methods of reinforcement, but be flexible to the timing.

5. Repeat Steps 1 to 4. Increase goal when appropriate.

Troubleshooting: If the student does engage in the problem behavior during the interval, the timer can be "reset" and the interval starts over. If this happens too often, the team should consider shortening the interval or layering on an additional type of differential reinforcement.

## DRA and DRI

The DRA schedule is used to systematically reinforce acceptable behaviors that look different from but are not necessarily physically incompatible with the target behavior. DRI is when the behaviors are indeed physically incompatible (meaning the two behaviors cannot be performed at the same time). They can both be discussed as variations on each other as DRI is essentially an example of a DRA, just with more specificity. It is like the rectangle versus the square; a square is always a rectangle, but a rectangle is not always a square. By way of example to further illustrate, consider the target challenging behavior of reading very loudly during silent reading. An incompatible behavior might be whispering to self, as a student cannot whisper and yell at the same time. A more preferred but not necessarily incompatible behavior is silent reading, as the student could indeed be reading in his head and out loud at the same time. Another example: Consider the target challenging behavior of "shutting down" (defined as not performing the work of the test) when faced with a test that is perceived as difficult by a student with anxiety. An incompatible behavior might be seen as picking up the pencil and reading the instructions. An alternative behavior might be engaging in internal calming behaviors that do not look dissimilar to the shutting-down behavior and are not actually incompatible but are different and getting the student one step closer to beginning the test.

A schedule for reinforcing the alternative or incompatible behavior should also be included in the BIP, as well as a plan for fading. Again, after ensuring the behavior is within the student's repertoire, the behavior should be reinforced in the relevant context quite often at first (typically fixed ratio on a very frequent schedule), then faded to a less frequent fixed and finally to a variable ratio over time. Finally, artificial reinforcement should be faded to more natural reinforcement if possible. For the examples above, an artificial reinforcer for the whispering-to-self behavior could be a tally mark on a "behavior rewards chart" that is covertly shown to the student during reading time. A more natural reinforcer is having peers sit close by during silent reading because their reading is not constantly interrupted any longer. For the test anxiety example, an artificial reinforcer could be teacher praise and soothing statements whispered to the learner; a more natural reinforcer is the lack of anxious feelings when encountering a test or finishing a test with the rest of the class and getting a good grade. Beginning with artificial reinforcement does sometimes appear to be a step backward. Is it really helpful to provide students with tokens or toys or edibles or extra attention when they are just doing what is expected of every other student? The truth is, students with EBD often have a lack of intrinsic motivation to perform or achieve, and that needs to be built over time. The only way to do so is by beginning with external forms of reinforcement and fading those back over time, pairing those with more naturally occurring forms of reinforcement, until the artificial/external reinforcement can be faded back completely (Vollmer & Iwata, 1992). See Table 12–5 for steps to implement a DRI or DRA.

**Table 12–5.** Steps to Implement DRI/DRA

1. Check baseline data in FBA for either the duration, the frequency, or the intensity of the target challenging behavior.

2. Determine an acceptable alternative (or incompatible) that makes sense for the setting, meets the functional need of the challenging behavior, and keeps the student from engaging in the challenging behavior.

3. Determine a schedule for reinforcement for the behavior and an appropriate option for reinforcement based on student preference. Also develop a fading schedule from artificial to more naturalist methods of reinforcement, but be flexible to the timing.

4. When timer goes off, provide reinforcement if the target behavior did not occur. If it did occur, let the student know they did not earn the reward and can have another try (or see troubleshooting tip below).

5. Repeat Steps 1 to 4. Increase goal when appropriate.

Troubleshooting: If the student tends to default to the challenging behavior more often than the replacement behavior, consider the need to change the replacement behavior or to spend more time teaching that behavior outside of the actual context.

## DRL

DRL should be used when the target challenging behavior is an appropriate behavior in and of itself, but the rate at which the student engages in the behavior makes it problematic. Hand raising is a classic example, and every teacher has that overeager student whose hand shoots up for every possible opportunity to answer a question. Raising a hand is not a behavior to extinguish, but doing so too often can lead to negative feelings toward that student by others and disruptions in instruction. Speed eating is another good example. It would never be a good idea to do away with the behavior of eating, but eating too fast can result in choking, difficulties with digestion, and socially awkward experiences (Vollmer & Iwata, 1992). A DRL can be based on frequency, latency, or interresponse time and, much like with the DRO schedule, can and should be varied over time. The team could start with a very low (ambitious) goal to a rate that is acceptable and typical of a peer or could start with a higher goal and systematically decrease the goal over time. That decision will depend upon the student and whether jumping right to a very ambitious goal will actually reduce the behavior completely rather than just reduce the rate. It is important, however, not to set the goal to a rate lower than what a typical student performs. When designing the reinforcement schedule, be specific. For the hand-raising behavior, say the goal is for the student to only raise her hand three times during 15 minutes of instruction. Does the teacher reinforce the first three instances and then nothing else for the remainder of the 15 minutes? Does the teacher wait and only reinforce during the last 3 minutes of those 15 minutes? Does the teacher reinforce the first instance, then reinforce on a variable schedule after that time until all three have been met? These are the types of questions that must be considered when designing a DRL intervention.

Involving the student in the intervention planning can be helpful. For the student that is capable of monitoring their own behavior, just knowing that the behavior is happening too often and knowing the goal might be enough to reduce the rate of behavior. Another student might need some visual support to serve as a reminder during the specified time period. Tally marks on the board that are erased each time a behavior occurs, a specified number of tickets that must be turned in when behavior occurs, or something similar can be a visual trigger that the student is running out of opportunities. See Table 12–6 for steps to implement a DRL.

**Table 12–6.** Steps to Implement DRL

| |
|---|
| 1. Check baseline data in FBA for either the frequency of the challenging behavior. |
| 2. Determine a goal for the low rate of behavior. This is typically based on what peers are doing in the same context. Decide to start with either a graduated goal or a highly ambitious goal. |
| 3. Determine an appropriate option for reinforcement based on student preference. Also develop a fading schedule from artificial to more naturalist methods of reinforcement, but be flexible to the timing. |
| 4. As you are tracking rate, the responses per a period of time is going to be counted. Start the timer, and only provide reinforcement for the rate of behavior identified. |
| 5. Repeat Steps 1 to 4. Increase goal when appropriate. |
| Troubleshooting: If the student begins to cease the behavior entirely when the intervention is begun, consider increasing the rate allowable for reinforcement and set up changing criteria over time. |

When the replacement behavior has been identified, a schedule for reinforcing that behavior should be established using one of these differential reinforcement methods. Once that replacement behavior has been taught in isolation (if it is not already in the student's repertoire) as detailed below, the behavior can be reinforced in the setting in which the target challenging behavior occurs.

## CASE STUDY—ELEMENTARY— DIFFERENTIAL REINFORCEMENT

*Xavier will receive noncontingent attention from staff members other than the classroom teacher on a variable interval schedule to help satiate the need for attention from adults. The team is working under the assumption that all students deserve attention from the staff in the building, and this is not something he should always have to work for. Because Xavier is specifically trying to obtain attention from the classroom teacher, the team is also implementing a DRL intervention with tickets that Xavier can trade in for attention from the teacher. The classroom teacher will also implement a DRO schedule during which she will have a timer and provide reinforcement to Xavier in the form of attention for every 5 minutes he does not engage in a problem behavior for two weeks and then increase the interval from there.*

## CASE STUDY—SECONDARY— DIFFERENTIAL REINFORCEMENT

*Lily is attempting to escape from tasks, so the team determined that would be allowable on a low-rate schedule. They implemented a DRL so that she could "opt out" of an assignment or test to be completed at a later time or date in a small-group setting once per day if she gives the teacher a nonverbal signal. They also want her practicing the behavioral relaxation strategies she is learning in private therapy to manage her anxiety symptoms, so will provide reinforcement according to a DRI when they notice her using those strategies by giving her bonus points to use toward an upcoming assignment.*

## INTRODUCTION TO REPLACEMENT BEHAVIOR

When developing a plan for teaching the replacement behavior, the stages of learning and reinforcement at each level need to be considered. The team should plan for resource use, types of reinforcement necessary at each stage, data collection at each stage, and the amount of time each stage may take. New behavior learning moves through the following stages: (1) acquisition, (2) fluency, (3) maintenance, and (4) generalization.

New skill acquisition typically requires more intensive instruction and high rates of reinforcement. The students who require a BIP typically are not learning the skills necessary from the core instruction or from small-group scenarios, so 1:1 or 1:2 level instruction should be considered. There are curriculums that may teach some of the replacement skills that the team is looking for, which are important but often take multiple sessions over the course of weeks or months to develop skills. More immediate replacement skill instruction will likely need to be taught. Skills may need to be broken down into small components and regular repetition of teaching should occur. Modeling, self-monitoring, role-play, behavioral rehearsal, and behavior contracting could all be a part of a BIP. Given the intensity of the teaching situation, the student may need to be removed from their current setting for a time at the beginning stages, or intervention may be possible within the general education classroom. At this stage, a high rate of reinforcement also needs to be present. Fixed ratio reinforcement is the schedule of choice when introducing a new skill. As it is practiced, the schedule can be shifted to variable ratio. For example, if the student really enjoys verbal praise, when teaching a new skill, a statement of "That was awesome!" or "Well done" could be made after every demonstration of the replacement behavior. Then, over time, that could be faded to after every third time and then again to a variable schedule of verbal praise around an average of five demonstrations. The acquisition phase focuses on accuracy of the response across opportunities, not speed. A goal at this stage might look like this: "Xavier will demonstrate the stages in his visual calming schedule with 100% accuracy across five opportunities in a 1:2 group with the social worker by March 3."

## Schedules of Reinforcement

Reinforcement is a vital part of learning a new skill that it must be detailed into the BIP for consistency, which is provided in Table 12–7. One of the biggest problems that arise with BIP implementation is the inconsistency or lack of reinforcement for replacement behaviors, so the student either reverts to the old challenging behavior or comes up with a new one to get that functional need met.

### CASE STUDY—ELEMENTARY— REPLACEMENT BEHAVIOR PLAN

*The team identified that Xavier has a few missing skills that need to be taught. He needs instruction on recognizing his body's signs of emotion, responding to those, and regulating his emotions. He will meet with a social worker 1:1 to develop that skill through instruction using a social skills curriculum and behavior relaxation training. The social worker will also develop a calming visual with Xavier's support and teach him to utilize that in the 1:1 setting and then generalize that to the classroom. He also needs instruction on different options he can choose in the classroom to still show good student behaviors without disrupting the group or destroying other people's belongings. The special education teacher and classroom teacher will model for Xavier different activities he can choose in the classroom and how to indicate he wants to do that.*

**Table 12–7.** Schedules of Reinforcement

| | | Fixed | Variable |
|---|---|---|---|
| Response-based reinforcement—reinforce instances of a replacement behavior on a schedule according to the number of responses | Definition | Fixed Ratio—reinforce according to a fixed number of responses<br><br>Schedule is defined by a number<br><br>EX: FR1 = reinforce every instance of the behavior<br><br>FR3 = reinforce every third instance of the behavior | Variable Ratio—reinforce according to an average number of responses, varying the ratio<br><br>EX: VR5 = reinforce an average of every fifth instance of the behavior (3rd time, 7th time, 5th time = average 5) |
| | Example | A student is called on every 3rd time he raises his hand in class. | A student is called on after he raises his hand 1 time, then 3 times, for an average of 2. |
| | Uses | Use to reinforce new replacement behaviors being taught (low rate FR schedules) or replacement behaviors being taught to fluency (higher rate FR) | Use to reinforce replacement behaviors being taught to fluency (low rate VR schedules) or those being maintained or generalized into the classroom setting (high rate VR schedules) |
| | Advantages | Builds a high response rate | Maintains a consistent response rate over time |
| | Disadvantages | May result in inconsistent learning if not applied consistently, learner can satiate, resource intensive | Not effective for teaching new behavior |

**Table 12–7.** *continued*

| | | Fixed | Variable |
|---|---|---|---|
| Time-based reinforcement—reinforcement based on periods of time (either during which the challenging behavior did not occur or the replacement behavior did occur) | Definition | Fixed Interval: Reinforcement is provided after a specific amount of time as long as the target behavior is occurring (or not occurring)<br><br>EX: FI3 = reinforcement provided after 3 minutes | Variable Interval: Reinforcement is provided after a specific amount of time across an average amount of time as long as the target behavior is occurring (or not occurring)<br><br>EX: VI3 = reinforcement provided after varying intervals of time as long as the average is 3 min (5 min, then 1 minute, then 3 minutes) |
| | Example | The student is provided with reinforcement after 5 minutes of independent seat work.<br><br>The student is provided with reinforcement after 5 minutes of no blurting out | The student is provided with reinforcement after 5 minutes of independent seatwork, then again after 1 minute of independent seatwork, then again after 3 minutes. |
| | Uses | Use to reinforce skills in the fluency building stage or to reinforce consistent periods without problem behavior | Use to maintain or generalize skills across settings |
| | Advantages | Easy to implement | Maintains behaviors well over time |
| | Disadvantages | If monitoring is not continuous, a drop in responding could occur following reinforcement | Not effective for teaching new behaviors |

Fluency is a stage of learning that is often missed in this era of education. A skill is not truly mastered unless it is readily and quickly available to the learner, that is, it can be retrieved quickly from long-term memory and is able to be performed with independence and to the set criteria at a high rate. This is especially important when thinking about replacement skills for challenging behaviors. If the replacement behavior is not easily retrievable and built into the muscle memory, the behavior (i.e., the original challenging behavior) will jump to the forefront once again. A skill needs to be demonstrated within the context of skill acquisition first before assessment of fluency is attempted. Fluency practice could look like practicing a skill multiple times back to back across a specific amount of time (i.e., doing full-body relaxation over and over for a minute) or responding quickly across multiple presentations (i.e., giving a possible strategy to use in response to a multiple fictional scenario quickly across 1 minute). A goal at this stage might look like this: "Lily will fluently and accurately describe how her body responds (physical manifestations) when feeling specific emotions for at least 20 emotions in 1 minute by November 17." The natural reinforcement schedule at this phase is interval, or time, based. It interrupts fluency to be interjecting reinforcers after demonstration of a skill; much more organic is to provide reinforcement after the time has expired. Perhaps for Lily, she enjoys periods of quiet after engaging in a lot of talking during a social work session, so after doing the timed minute of fluency demonstration, she gets to spend 2 minutes in a quiet activity of her choosing. Again, this stage is built upon the previous skill acquisition phase and in preparation for the next phase of maintenance.

After a skill is practiced fluently, it should be stable over time. The skill should be "maintained" when checked a few days, a few weeks, or even a few months later under the same conditions but without that intensive practice in between. Typically, when working on replacement behavioral skills, after a few days, the skill might be checked for maintenance and then transferred to the generalization stage, which is the most important stage of the process. Generalization is when the skill is taken from the practice setting to real life, where the original challenging behavior was occurring. At this stage, the student should be able to, with some support, take the skill they have been working on back to the classroom setting and use it with success. There may be some backsliding, but on the whole, success should be had. If this is not true, circle back and determine if something was missed in teaching the replacement skill, if some challenging behavior is still being reinforced, or if some environmental modification that is necessary is not present. If generalization is occurring, fading of all external supports and accommodations can be attempted until the student is functioning under the least restrictive set of conditions. Reinforcement schedules during the generalization phase are ideally within the variable column, either variable ratio or (preferred) variable interval. It is much easier to keep track of intervals in a classroom setting than instances of a behavior, especially for the longer term. The only downside to this is, if a behavior is not being monitored continuously throughout the interval, responding can dip according to the schedule. However, utilizing a variable schedule typically course corrects for this problem, as the student does not know when their behavior is potentially being reinforced, thus setting the stage for continuous performance with the hope of recognition. At this stage, reinforcement can and should be much more natural. Any artificial methods have hopefully been faded to easier to implement and natural methods that align with the the setting. Verbal praise, whole-class or group contingencies, nonverbal recognition, being called on, being included in conversations, scores or points on assignments, and even more distant methods of reinforcement like a token system at home or praise from an administrator should be considered.

Something to remember as an overarching principle across the process of behavior plan development: You cannot force someone to change their behavior, but you can modify the environment and change your behavior to increase the likelihood of student behavior change. The plan itself describes not only the student's replacement behaviors but also those of the adults around the student.

## WRITING GOALS

Now that all the components of the plan have been identified, an actual goal to work toward is needed. A SMART goal should be written and, as has been noted, can be modified if necessary but should be based upon the baseline data and information gathered in the FBA process. **SMART** stands for *Specific, Measurable, Attainable, Relevant, and Time-bound.*

Specific goals include the criteria that have been discussed up to this point. The behavior should be objectively described so that anyone could step into the monitoring of this goal and have no problem whatsoever determining which behavior to track. It should also include the contexts and people involved around the behavior so the behavior being tracked can be compared to itself. If the behavior in question only occurs in PE and around a small group of specific peers, counting that behavior in the classroom and then trying to compare the two will give some consternation.

Measurable goals have something to count, whether it be frequency, duration, intensity, or latency. The same type of data should be counted each time. Multiple dimensions could be counted for one behavior, but those cannot be compared to each other.

The goal set should be attainable. Ambitious goals are important, but if the goal is too ambitious, everyone will become frustrated as it will seem that no progress is occurring. The goal should be set based on the baseline data and, in comparison, with the typical expectations for behavior in that setting.

Relevant goals are socially valid goals. This means that the behavior for reduction and the replacement behaviors are important for the individual to grow as a student and to work better within the school setting. Relevant goals are not arbitrary and have buy-in from the student and the team. Relevant goals are also not overly ambitious and may be approximations of the ultimate desired behavior.

Time-bound means that there is an end date in sight but also an end date with meaning. A goal should not be set for 6 months in the future that will in all likelihood only take 6 weeks to complete. Likewise, if the behavior if dramatically impacting the student performance, some sort of measurable change needs to happen relatively quickly. At least six to eight data points need to be taken in order for any decision making to occur, so consider that in the goal deadline. If the goal set needs to include multiple changes over time before reaching the ultimate replacement behavior, that can be written into the goal as well. Both short-term and long-term goals can be written (see BIP plan template in Appendix 12–2).

---

 **CASE STUDY—ELEMENTARY—GOALS**

*Long-term goal: By April 1, Xavier will have reduced and maintained instances of property destruction to zero per day across 3 months.*

*Short-term goal: By February 1, Xavier will respond to visual cues and brief teacher prompts when problem behavior triggers are observed or when behavior is just beginning to escalate to reduce intensity of behavior from an average of 3 to an average of 1 across 2 weeks.*

*Short-term goal: By March 1, Xavier will choose an alternative activity instead of the one presented to the whole class when prompted by staff observing behavior triggers.*

---

## PLAN IMPLEMENTATION

Likely, you as the reader are going to be serving in a leadership role on the BIP team. Leave the room with a plan of action for implementation integrity or you will likely be met with unhappy team members over the next few days who either don't understand their role or are claiming the plan you developed is garbage.

Now that an evidence-based BIP is written, it needs to be implemented. No matter how sound the plan, if it cannot be easily implemented with integrity by the key players in the situation, it is not worth the paper it is printed upon. A core consideration when crafting the plan is whether the staff actually implementing the plan have a say in the plan's creation. Typically, a BIP team includes the staff working with a student, including bus drivers, cafeteria monitors, teachers, counselors, behavior specialists, and/or school psychologists. If that team member is not included, they may not be able to tell the team about a very specific variable in the environment that was overlooked, that they maybe do not have the background knowledge to conduct the intervention, or that they do not know how they will manage the expectation for data collection. The team should also consider how to determine if the plan was implemented with integrity.

Fidelity of implementation is important. Possibly worse than not implementing the plan at all is a plan that is implemented poorly. This typically results in frustration on the part of the staff and the student and a claim of "This plan isn't working!" when in reality, the plan was not really implemented correctly. And if the team has no idea of why the plan is not working, trying to modify it is next to impossible. Use the implementation fidelity checklist found in Appendix 12–3 as a neutral prompt to ensure all pieces of the BIP have been implemented accurately. Having a tool like this allows for feedback on implementation to come from an external source, rather than coming across as finger pointing and resulting in hurt feelings.

Take the formal plan and assign action steps with clear behaviors and deadlines. Check that each team member can verbally describe their participation in the plan and the rationale for their participation. If a team member does not understand the "why" behind what they are assigned, chances are they may not proceed in the face of difficulty. It also helps to include the team members who will be plan implementers because they are in the target context day in and day out and will be able to speak to making the plan appropriate for that environment. Also ensure that each team member understands what to do in the case of bumps in the road. Sometimes bumps are little, such as the data collection form is too cumbersome or the chosen reinforcer does not appear to be effective. Sometimes the bumps are rather massive, such as the intervention resulted in a CPI hold. If the team has thoroughly planned for anything that might go wrong and discussed it before implementation began, each member will be better prepared when the rains come down and can adjust accordingly without panic.

The action plan should also include start dates and roll-out plans. Perhaps the first part of the plan needs to be completed before any other subsequent pieces are implemented. Include a communication plan between team members to solidify those pieces. Monitor implementation as the plan roll-out progresses and do not proceed to the next step until the preceding steps have been done effectively. Do not focus on too many behaviors at once. The team may have targeted multiple behaviors as challenging, but it can be too much (both for the student and the interventionists) to work on and keep track of that many procedures at once. Do plan for regular reviews of the plan, especially upfront, and make sure the roll-out plan is scaffolded over time. Also plan for regular observation of the interventionists and provide for built-in coaching along the way. No person is perfect, and having an extra set of eyes to watch out for any unconsidered variables is an important part of any behavioral plan implementation. One of the reasons for poor implementation of BIPs is the team members' lack of familiarity with the plan (Walker & Barry, 2017). This can result from lack of collaborative discussions and a lack of a clear plan for implementation. See Appendix 12–4 for an implementation action plan template. Use this template to support self-examination and as a guide for notetaking during team discussions. Being able to ask questions and gain clarification, as well as work through any concerns or barriers, is an important benefit of using this tool to facilitate implementation conversations.

## MONITORING PROGRESS

Part of the written BIP should include a plan for progress monitoring. The who, what, where, when, why, and how of the monitoring should be addressed, with examples in Table 12–8. The actual examination of that progress monitoring data will be discussed in more depth in the plan evaluation section, but for the purposes of plan implementation, the following need to be addressed.

**Table 12–8.** The Wh's of Progress Monitoring

| | |
|---|---|
| Who | Who will be observing and recording the data? Who will be graphing the data? Who will take inter-observer agreement data? |
| What | The type of data being collected The target behavior being observed |
| When | During what times of day or days of the week? During what activities, classes, or subjects? During unstructured or structured times? When which people are present? Under what set of conditions? Are there any times that data should NOT be collected? Should the different times be defined on the chart? Is data being taken continuously and all the time? Is data collection only required during specific times? Is just a sampling of data going to be taken? |
| Where | In what environments should data be collected or not collected? Should the locations be differentiated on the data collection tool? |
| Why | What is the purpose of collecting the data? |
| How | What is the tool used for recording data? Are any other additional materials needed to take the data? Does the staff taking data need additional training in order to take accurate data? |

Consider this as well: Too much data can just be too much data. This data can be cumbersome to collect and even more cumbersome to sift through and report on. Narrow the focus. Make the data collected not overly burdensome for the collector while at the same time being meaningful to use for decision making. The collection process should be straightforward and purposeful. The data should also be graphed for ease of visual inspection (see Vanselow & Bourret, 2012, for tutorials on graphing using Excel, which is specific to graphing behavior data, but more up-to-date tutorials can likely be found via a quick Google search). A graphic display of data clearly shows the relationship between the dependent and independent variables in the situation, serves to summarize the data collected, and facilitates more accurate analysis (Cooper et al., 2019). Graphs serve as an effective source of feedback to those involved in the intervention and a more immediate access to the record of the behavior than sifting back through the numbers. The essential components of the graph are detailed on Table 12–9. Behavior data can be graphed using line graphs, bar graphs, cumulative data, semilogarithmic charts, or scatterplots. The graphs typically used for recording reduction of problem behavior are the line graphs using an equal interval scale and a semilogarithmic chart (also known as the Standard Celeration Chart [SCC] used in precision teaching), which charts the frequency of behavior over time on a proportionally scaled axis. See Pennypacker and Lindsley (2003) for a primer on using the SCC.

**Table 12–9.**  Essential Components of a Graph

1. Goal statement (including operational definition of the target behavior)
2. Graph titles and labels
3. Baseline data
4. Phase or condition lines
5. Goal line
6. Trend line

## PLAN EVALUATION

At the start of implementation, the plan should be reviewed at least every other week. The team leader should check in with the team members within that time to ensure that implementation is occurring correctly. Observation for interobserver agreement on data collection should be done, as well as observation of actual implementation of the intervention (see the implementation integrity checklist in the appendices). Visual inspection of the data on a graph should take place during this time as well, and if any major irregularities are occurring, all involved staff should be interviewed to determine what is going wrong. For help in decision-making with graphs, see Table 12–10. Ask the staff involved if the plan continues to seem reasonable and maintainable. If they are feeling burnt out already after just a few weeks, the likelihood of long-term fidelity is low.

**Table 12–10.** How to Make Good Decisions Based on Visual Analysis of a Graph

1. Are there are least 6 to 8 data points?
2. Increase goal if:
   a. Trend line is steeper than the goal line
   b. There are at least 3 data points above the goal line
3. Change intervention if:
   a. Goal line is steeper than the trend
   b. There are at least 3 data points below the goal line
4. Maintain the intervention if:
   a. Goal line is consistent with trend line
   b. At least 3 of the data points are consistent with the goal line

After the initial few weeks, check in every 3 to 5 weeks. The team should examine the data more often than that, and conditions should be added to the chart to communicate effectively the changes to the plan according to the rollout. Meeting together as a team, verbally reviewing the data, documenting any progress and changes made to the plan, and getting any anecdotal input are a vital part of behavior intervention. Even though meetings can be difficult to squeeze into already busy school staff schedules, they make a difference. Getting all of the stakeholders together (especially the paraeducators or other frontline staff who are doing the implementing and data collection) to discuss progress will ultimately save time and energy.

In general, the more data present on the graph and the greater the stability of those data (i.e., the data points are tightly grouped around the trend line), the more confidence the team can have that the decisions they make are valid. The more variable the data (i.e., the data points are spread widely around the trend line), the less accurate decisions will be. If this is the case, either more data should be collected or the team should look at the accuracy of the data being collected.

After several rounds of checking every 3 to 5 weeks, the team can shift monitoring to less frequent intervals. It may be decided that actual progress monitoring can be spaced out as well. Depending upon how the student is responding to the plan, changes to the plan can be made as well. The intervention might be changed, the goal might be increased, another setting might be added, and the replacement behavior might be modified to more closely meet peer standards. Continued checks for implementation integrity should be made and trends in student progress should be analyzed. For questions to ask to ensure a quality BIP (Table 12–11). Just remember that this is a team process, and including all of the members is important for success.

**Table 12–11.** BIP Self-Check

| Self-Check: Does your BIP? |
| --- |
| Describe how others around the student will change? |
| Describe how the environment will change? |
| Use technically sound principles of applied behavior analysis? |
| Use interventions grounded in research? |
| Fit the setting in which the behavior occurs? |
| Allow for easy implementation by staff? |
| Account for barriers to implementation? |

## CHAPTER SUMMARY

School teams have to plan for problem behavior reduction more and more in the current day and age. The skill of developing a BIP based on an FBA is one that every special education teacher needs to have in his or her arsenal. The procedures in this chapter make the process straightforward and, when based on the science described, will produce a plan that will help students with emotional and behavioral disorders fit more successfully into their school environments and become better integrated and supportive members of their communities.

## DISCUSSION QUESTIONS

1. How does writing a BIP for a student with externalizing behaviors differ from that of a student with internalizing behaviors?

2. Is the concept of differential reinforcement new to you? How might you implement that with a student tomorrow?

3. What are the common behavioral interventions you are familiar with? How might those fit into a BIP?

4. Why is it important to have strong Tier 1 (for all students) behavior systems and curricula?

5. How can you incorporate implementation integrity checks into BIPs that are already in effect?

## REFERENCES

Pennypacker, H. S., & Lindsley, O. R. (2003). *Handbook of the standard celeration chart.* Cambridge Center for Behavioral Studies.

Sugai, G., Lewis-Palmer, T., & Hagan-Burke, S. (2010). Overview of the functional behavioral assessment process. *Exceptionality, 8*(3), 149–160. doi:10.1207/S15327035EX0803_2

Vanselow, N. R., & Bourret, J. C. (2012). Online interactive tutorials for creating graphs with excel 2007 or 2010. *Behavior Analysis in Practice, 5*(1), 40–46. doi:10.1007/BF03391816

Vollmer, T. R., & Iwata, B. A. (1992). Differential reinforcement as treatment for behavior disorders: Procedural and functional variations. *Research in Developmental Disabilities, 13*(4), 393–417. doi:10.1016/0891-4222(92)90013-V

Walker, J. D., & Barry, C. (2017). Improving outcomes of behavioral intervention plans. *Intervention in School and Clinic, 53*(1), 12–18.

## APPENDIX 12–1

# Competing Behavior Pathway with Successive Approximation

Student: _____ Grade: _____ Date: _____

Ultimate goal replacement behavior: _____

How does it meet the same function? _____

Define successive approximations to the ultimate goal behavior, starting with 1 being the first replacement behavior to introduce that is easy for the student to demonstrate, is easily reinforced, is likely to occur in that setting, and meets the same function as the problem behavior. Add as many as you need to get the student to the ultimate replacement behavior.

| Acceptable Alternative | Define Behavior | How Does It Meet the Same Function? |
|---|---|---|
| 1 | | |
| 2 | | |
| 3 | | |
| 4 | | |

*continues*

**APPENDIX 12–1.** *continued*

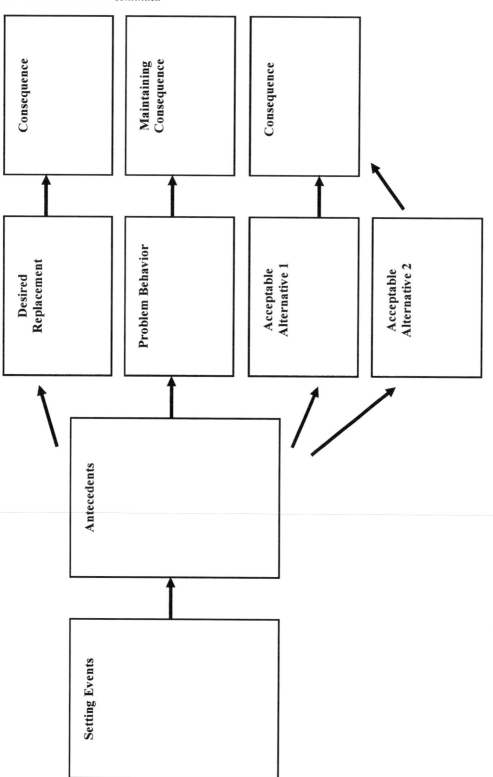

# BIP Template

| | |
|---|---|
| **Student information** | Name:                    Grade:<br><br>DOB:                     Date: |
| **Team members** | |
| **Target challenging behavior**<br><br>Operational definition | |
| **Summary of FBA and previous interventions attempted** | |
| **Replacement behavior**<br><br>Define the chosen replacement behavior or behaviors; describe successive approximation if needed. | |
| **Universal modifications**<br><br>How does the core curriculum and supports provided to all students help this student? What changes need to be made to better support all learners at this level? | |

*continues*

| | |
|---|---|
| **Accommodations and modifications**<br><br>How is the environment going to be modified to support behavior change? What pieces will be removed, added, or changed? What accommodations does the student need made to the instruction or learning situations to be successful? | |
| **Method of teaching the replacement behavior**<br><br>Is the current curriculum and instruction appropriate for the student? Do any modifications need to be made to the classroom instruction and/or intervention instruction? What additional instruction needs to take place in order to teach the replacement behaviors? Is an additional curriculum or staff training required? Who will do the teaching and when? | |
| **Reinforcement procedures**<br><br>How will the replacement behavior be reinforced? How often? By whom? When? And where? | |

| | |
|---|---|
| **Consequences for challenging behavior**<br><br>What response will be made if challenging behavior occurs? | |
| **Restrictive disciplinary measures and crisis plan**<br><br>If an out of the ordinary challenging behavior occurs, how will it be handled? If there is a crisis situation, what is the plan in place to address it? | |
| **Data collection procedures**<br><br>How will ongoing data be collected about the challenging behavior? How will ongoing data about the replacement behaviors be collected? | |
| **Timeline**<br><br>When will the intervention commence? When will the plan be evaluated? How often will the plan be evaluated? When is the next team meeting? | |

*Create a new BIP for each target behavior being addressed.

# BIP Implementation Fidelity Checklist

**Student:**                           **Today's date:**

**Fidelity check completed by:**        **BIP date:**

**Meeting Participants and Roles:**

|  |  |  |
|---|---|---|
|  |  |  |
|  |  |  |
|  |  |  |

## BIP Document Review:

| | | |
|---|---|---|
| Do interventions match function of behavior? | Yes | No |
| *If no, reconvene team to examine the FBA and take further data.* | | |
| Is there a plan for instruction of replacement behaviors? | Yes | No |
| *If no, reconvene team to develop an instruction plan to do so.* | | |
| Are replacement behaviors aligned with function of behavior? | Yes | No |
| *If no, reconvene team to examine the FBA and develop new replacement behaviors.* | | |
| Is there a plan for reinforcement of replacement behaviors? | Yes | No |
| *If no, reconvene team to develop a systematic plan for reinforcement.* | | |
| Is the BIP clearly written and easily understood by each team member? Can each team member state his or her role in the implementation process? | Yes | No |
| *If no, reconvene team to clarify implementation of the plan.* | | |

## BIP Document and Observation Review:

| BIP Component | Brief Overview | Observation Review<br>0 = no opportunity<br>1 = observation did not reflect written plan<br>2 = observation reflected some components<br>3 = observation reflected all components | Next Steps<br>1 = review for fidelity<br>2 = review plan<br>3 = no review necessary | Anecdotal Notes |
|---|---|---|---|---|
| Challenging behavior clearly being targeted | | 0 1 2 3 | 1 2 3 | |
| Instruction of replacement behavior | | 0 1 2 3 | 1 2 3 | |
| Procedural prevention of challenging behavior | | 0 1 2 3 | 1 2 3 | |
| Opportunities created to reduce challenging behavior | | 0 1 2 3 | 1 2 3 | |
| Environmental modifications in place | | 0 1 2 3 | 1 2 3 | |
| Reinforcement of replacement behavior | | 0 1 2 3 | 1 2 3 | |

*continues*

| BIP Component | Brief Overview | Observation Review 0 = no opportunity 1 = observation did not reflect written plan 2 = observation reflected some components 3 = observation reflected all components | Next Steps 1 = review for fidelity 2 = review plan 3 = no review necessary | Anecdotal Notes |
|---|---|---|---|---|
| Feedback given on replacement behavior | | 0 1 2 3 | 1 2 3 | |
| Consequences for challenging behavior | | 0 1 2 3 | 1 2 3 | |
| Data collected on challenging and replacement behavior | | 0 1 2 3 | 1 2 3 | |

Modified from Walker and Barry (2017).

# BIP Implementation Action Plan Template

Meeting Date: _____

**Meeting Participants and Roles:**

| | | |
|---|---|---|
| | | |
| | | |
| | | |

| BIP Component | Person Responsible | Action Plan with Measurable Outcome | Target Date of Completion |
|---|---|---|---|
| | | | |
| | | | |
| | | | |

Barriers/questions/concerns that need to be addressed prior to implementation (give details along with solutions for those barriers, who is responsible for changes, and deadlines for reporting back to the team):

| |
|---|
| |

# 13

# Progress Monitoring: Assessment and Measurement

*With Contributions from Wilhelmina Van Dijk
and Nicolette M. Grasley-Boy*

## KEY VOCABULARY

Computer-Adaptive Testing

Continuous Recording

Curriculum-Based Measures

Curriculum Sampling Approach

Direct Observation

Discrete Behaviors

Dosage

Event Recording

Implementation/Treatment
Fidelity

Indirect Assessment

Interval Recording

Latency

Momentary Time Sampling

Norm-Referenced Assessment

Quality

Reliability

Responsiveness

Treatment Delivery

Treatment Receipt

Validity

## LEARNING OBJECTIVES

By the end of this chapter, you should be able to . . .

- Explain the difference between event recording, daily behavior report cards, norm-referenced rating scales, and permanent products as they relate to progress monitoring.

- Choose a behavioral progress monitoring tool appropriate for the behavioral goal.

- Create a tool for collecting behavioral progress monitoring data.

- Differentiate between direct and indirect assessment of behavior and list examples of each.
- Explain the benefits of curriculum-based measures for academic progress monitoring.
- Choose a curriculum-based measure appropriate for an academic intervention.
- Describe the five elements of implementation fidelity.
- Construct a plan to monitor implementation fidelity based on the focus of an intervention.
- Explain the differences between treatment delivery and treatment receipt.
- Apply the steps to graphing when tracking student progress.

## INTRODUCTION

In addition to behavioral issues, many students with EBD have trouble keeping up with the academic demands of their education. Research indicates that students with EBD often are behind in mathematics and spelling, and often have unidentified language impairment. It is unsurprising that many students with EBD receive interventions to help them increase their academic skills and decrease problematic behavior. Despite this fact, these students often do not make as much progress as peers with different disabilities, such as LD, because the specifics of their disability negatively interact with the academic interventions. It is important to signal potential issues as they arise and adapt both academic and behavioral interventions to meet the needs of these students. To be able to adapt interventions early, teachers need detailed information on their students' skills through frequent progress monitoring of behavioral and academic goals. Additionally, teachers will need to know if the lack of potential progress is a result of nonresponse of the students or the result of an intervention that was not delivered optimally. In this chapter, the most common ways to monitor students' progress toward behavioral and academic goals will be shared, as well as ways to check if interventions were delivered as intended.

## CASE STUDY

*For Erica to be ready to take prealgebra in sixth grade, Ms. Wright conducted a thorough assessment of her mathematics skills. Ms. Wright discovered that Erica has the necessary computational skills to solve number problems but has trouble integrating these skills in word problems. To help Erica and some other struggling students with their mathematics skills, Ms. Wright has started to use schema-based instruction with a small group of students three times a week. Additionally, Erica is using a self-monitoring strategy to keep her from calling out during the small-group instruction.*

*After settling into the routine of the small groups, Ms. Wright has the impression all students in the group are improving their mathematics skills and Erica seems to have decreased her externalizing behavior. To prepare for a meeting with Erica's IEP team, Ms. Wright wants to have evidence beyond her impressions that the two interventions are helping Erica. She decides it will be necessary to keep detailed data on Erica's progress. She remembers reading about the importance of progress monitoring, but she's unsure exactly what type of data will show that her approach is working.*

Ms. Wright is facing a daunting task. She will have to decide if she needs to collect data on Erica's behavior during the schema-based small group intervention, on Erica's word problem-solving skills, or both. She also needs to provide evidence that the way she implemented the schema-based instruction is consistent with the intention of the developers. Many teachers will face similar tasks due to the interplay between students' behavioral and academic goals.

## COLLECTING BEHAVIORAL DATA

There are many options for collecting progress monitoring data, including systematic direct observations, daily behavior report cards, norm-referenced behavior rating scales, and permanent products (Gage & McDaniel, 2012; Riley-Tillman et al., 2005). When choosing a data collection system, teachers must consider the type of behavioral data they need to collect (e.g., specific behaviors, behavior ratings) along with the feasibility of collecting that data in the classroom or across other educational settings. Conley and colleagues (2019) suggest behavioral support teams prioritize a small number of behaviors for data collection using measures that are easy to implement for all staff involved. The support team should also ensure the chosen measures are sensitive to small changes in behaviors during the time allotted for data collection prior to the next team meeting to assess progress. Finally, it is imperative to consider when and how often data collection will occur, and this should ideally coincide, at least in part, with when the behavior problems were occurring in the first place.

## Direct Observation of Specific Behaviors

Students often have goals that rely on measuring specific or discrete behaviors, either appropriate or inappropriate, and monitoring them for change following intervention implementation. For example, one student's goal may be to increase time on task during independent seatwork in reading class. Another student's goal may be to decrease callouts during math class to two or fewer per period. To monitor these goals, teachers must directly observe the goal behaviors during the specified times. During direct observations, some aspects of a behavior are recorded as they occur in real time. Depending on the behavior and goal, teachers may need to observe specific dimensions of the behavior, including frequency/rate, duration/percentage of time, latency, or percentage of correct demonstrations. All direct observations require that the behavior is operationally defined for the observer, including examples and nonexamples, and that this definition is easily accessible and included on the observation form. Direct observations can be conducted by the classroom teacher while they are instructing or managing the classroom, but it is highly recommended that another staff member serves as the observer, when possible, to increase the accuracy of the behavior measurement.

### Event Recording

Direct observations often use event recording, or continuous recording, which can be broken into two main types: (a) frequency recording and (b) duration recording. Frequency recording is simply tallying the number of times a behavior occurs and is used for observing discrete behaviors that are brief in duration (e.g., calling out, raising hand, leaving seat without permission). Frequency recording is typically done over a specified period that allows the observer to calculate a rate of behavior. For example, a teacher may observe the number of times a student leaves her seat without permission during a 20-minute small-group math lesson. The teacher can take the final tally of behaviors and divide it by the number of minutes in the observation to find the rate of seat leaving per minute. If she observes the student getting out of their seat without permission five times during the 20-minute lesson, she would divide 5 by 20 to get a rate of 0.25 instances per minute. Including a time component when conducting frequency recording is highly advisable for progress monitoring as it puts the behaviors on a common scale for comparison. It also enables teachers to use data from different amounts of time, which may be helpful when there are schedule disruptions during the observation such as fire drills.

## Duration Recording

Duration recording is observing the length of time a behavior occurs and is best suited for behaviors that are not brief, for example, academic engagement and time in or out of seat. Duration recording is also used when measuring the latency of a behavior, that is, the length of time between a prompt and the start of the behavior. For instance, a teacher may observe how long it takes a student to begin an academic task after being prompted. In some cases, it may be useful to use duration to calculate the percentage of time engaged in a particular behavior. For a student whose goal involves monitoring on-task behavior during a 30-minute science lesson, the observer would track the duration of on-task behavior along with the total time of the observation and divide on-task by total time to get a percentage of time on task. If the teacher observes the student on task for 15 minutes of the 30-minute lesson, they would divide 15 by 30 and multiply by 100 to find the student was on task 50% of the period. Similar to rate, this can help when there are inconsistencies or disruptions to the total observation time.

## Interval Recording

Another type of direct observation procedure is called interval recording. There are several types of **interval recording**, but in general, they all involve getting a sample of a behavior across intervals in a given time period based on whether or not it occurred during each interval, rather than counting each occurrence or the exact length of time. Though it may over- or under-estimate the behavior compared to event recording (Ledford et al., 2015), interval recording is a useful direct observation tool. When observing using interval recording, the observation must first be broken into equal intervals (e.g., 10 seconds, 1 minute), and the observer must use some form of timer, preferably one that will not disrupt students, to signal the beginning of each interval. Both the specific behavior to be observed and the observer's role will help determine an appropriate interval length. The current frequency or duration of the behavior can be used to inform interval length. For low-frequency behaviors, a longer interval may be adequate, but higher-frequency behaviors may need a shorter interval to capture times they are *not* occurring as well. Short-duration behaviors are better captured using smaller intervals, while longer behaviors can be measured with longer intervals. When the teacher is responsible for both observing and instructing, it is helpful to use a longer interval both to allow time to catch the behavior as well as reduce the number of times she may need to disrupt instruction to record for each interval.

There are three types of interval recording: (a) whole interval, (b) partial interval, and (c) momentary time sampling (Alberto & Troutman, 2013; Cooper et al., 2007). In whole-interval recording, the interval is only marked if the behavior occurs for the *entire* interval. Whole-interval recording lends itself well to duration-based behaviors, such as on/off task. For partial-interval recording, the interval is coded if the behavior occurs at *any* point in the interval for *any* amount of time. This type works well with frequency-based behaviors, such as hand raising. Finally, **momentary time sampling** involves only observing the presence or absence of the behavior briefly (e.g., 1 to 3 seconds) at the end of the interval. This type also works well with duration-based and high-frequency behaviors (Lee et al., 2011).

When using interval recording, it is important to refer to the behavioral occurrence as the *percentage of intervals observed/not observed* rather than the frequency/rate or duration/percentage of time. Following an observation, teachers count the number of intervals in which the behavior occurred and did not occur. The choice to report and monitor occurrence or nonoccurrence will depend on the target behavior for each student. Once teachers have these sums, they will divide the number of intervals with an occurrence (or nonoccurrence) by the total number of intervals observed, then multiply by 100 to obtain the percentage of intervals observed (or not observed).

## Benefits

Although they are the most time- and resource-intensive, direct observations can provide some of the most accurate measurements of a behavior during the specified time period. They are sensitive to small changes in behaviors, which is a key for progress monitoring behavior goals. Behavior increases or decreases are likely to be noticeable sooner with direct observation tools than with other measures, such as norm-referenced rating scales or office discipline referrals. This also improves the data-based decision-making process in that the team is able to make decisions sooner and based on robust data. Direct observations may also lead to more accurate samples of the behavior during the specified time period as they are real-time measurements of the behavior as it occurs.

## Barriers

Direct observations can be difficult to conduct if the observer is responsible for teaching and managing the classroom at the same time. They require a great deal of attention directed toward the target student, which can be difficult depending on the lesson content or other students' behaviors. The skill of direct observation can also be difficult to learn or teach another observer, and interval recording systems require an extra element of attention to accurately record each interval on the form at the correct time throughout the observation. Additionally, direct observation data may not generalize to other times or contexts that are not observed (Cook et al., 2014). For instance, it is possible that a student who has difficulty staying on task during whole-group reading instruction does not have the same trouble during small-group math instruction. As such, it is imperative that data collection (and intervention implementation) be coordinated to target specific contexts for which the BIP was developed.

## DAILY BEHAVIOR REPORT CARDS

Daily behavior report cards (DBRCs) are adaptable progress monitoring systems for collecting behavioral data that also lend themselves to data sharing across stakeholders (e.g., teachers, students, parents). When using DBRCs for progress monitoring, they should specifically note the behavior(s) being rated *at least* once per day, and this rating should be shared among stakeholders daily (Riley-Tillman et al., 2005). The opportunity to give students behavioral feedback and communicate daily behaviors to guardians is one of the key elements of the DBRC. Ratings may also take several forms, including numeric performance scales, visual performance scales, and percentage estimates. Depending on the student's needs, DBRCs can also be used as an effective intervention technique, particularly when used across the school day and when home involvement is high (Vannest et al., 2010).

### Benefits

DBRCs are highly adaptable to various behavioral and data collection needs. Ideally, they should target one or a small number of behaviors. They are particularly useful for addressing behaviors that occur throughout the school day in various contexts and prompt teachers to provide ongoing feedback at several points during the day. This can facilitate communication between teachers and help identify contexts during which the student is successful or requires more support. DBRCs were also developed as a home communication tool that can enable parent/guardian involvement.

### Barriers

DBRCs rely on perceptions of target behaviors rather than direct observations; thus, DBRCs may be less accurate when measuring behavioral occurrences as they are typically estimates or ratings across a full day. DBRCs also require training for all staff who will rate the student each day. Depending on the number of teachers and their familiarity with DBRCs, this may require a great deal of additional training on rating and providing feedback to the student. Given this, it is important to ensure other staff are using the rating system correctly and appropriately. It is also critical to communicate to caregivers how to appropriately use and respond to DBRC ratings at home. Parents/guardians should be provided information on the DBRC, including how the student is rated, what the rating means, and how to celebrate meeting goals or use unmet goals as learning opportunities rather than punishment opportunities. Finally, the support team must plan how to respond if the DBRC is lost or destroyed during the day.

## NORM-REFERENCED RATING SCALES AND PERMANENT PRODUCTS

Behavioral data may also be collected using norm-referenced rating scales, permanent products, or otherwise existing behavioral data. These may include norm-referenced behavioral ratings (e.g., Behavior Assessment System for Children [BASC-3; Reynolds & Kamphaus, 2015]; Child Behavior Checklist [CBCL] and Teacher Report Form [TRF; Achenbach & Roscorla, 2001]; Behavioral and Emotional Rating Scale [BERS-2; Epstein, 2004]), office discipline referrals, suspension counts, attendance data, self-management forms, or task completion checklists (Gage, & McDaniel, 2012; Riley-Tillman et al., 2005). Some of these data sources are particularly useful early in the FBA process as they do not require additional time or resources to collect information that can help identify issues.

### Benefits

Permanent products such as office discipline referral, suspension, and attendance data require little to no additional time or resources as they are typically collected across school systems. Similarly, forms that rely on student self-monitoring or self-management (e.g., task completion checklists) may take up less staff time after an initial period of teaching the student to use the form. While they do require staff, student, or parent time, many norm-referenced behavioral rating tools are designed to be completed outside of instructional time and do not require direct observation of the behaviors. Additionally, many of these rating scales are simple to complete and do not require additional training for the rater to use them (Riley-Tillman et al., 2005).

## Barriers

Permanent products tend to be less time- and resource-intensive, but there is a trade-off with accuracy and sensitivity to change. **Norm-referenced assessment** tools rely on retrospective ratings and individual perceptions of behaviors (Cook et al., 2014). Relying on adult perceptions may be potentially prone to bias or inaccuracies given time passage between ratings. These tests, in particular, may not be able to measure behavioral improvements, especially when assessments are repeated within a short period of time (Riley-Tillman et al., 2005). Depending on initial rates of behaviors, office discipline referrals or suspensions also may not change enough during progress monitoring periods to make effective decisions about the intervention(s). Although some permanent products require little to no additional staff time or resources, those that rely on students to collect their own data (e.g., self-management forms, checklists) will need to be taught after they are introduced to the student and should include a period of ongoing feedback on their use before the student can complete them independently. Finally, in many cases, it is unlikely that progress monitoring can rely solely on permanent product data, particularly administrative data such as referrals or suspensions, given these may not be closely linked to behaviors targeted in the BIP.

## EXAMPLES OF BEHAVIORAL DATA COLLECTION SYSTEMS

### Paper and Pencil

There are many existing options for low-tech paper-and-pencil behavioral data collection systems. This format also lends itself well to easy customization for many contexts and behavioral goals.

### *Event Recording*

When developing a paper-and-pencil event recording system, you should begin by identifying the specific behavior(s) that will be recorded. Next, determine if you will use event or interval recording and, if using interval, what type of interval recording and the interval length. Finally, develop or adapt a data recording form to meet your needs. Make sure the form includes space for the necessary student identifying information, date, observation start and end time, instructional context, specific behavior(s) and operational definition(s), and data recording space. Depending on the measurement method, this may be a blank space for tallying behavior counts or writing the total recorded elsewhere like on Post-It notes or by using a stopwatch, or interval recording spaces. Tips for event recording are in Table 13–1.

**Table 13–1.** Event Recording Tips

**Tools for frequency recording:** Event recording can be especially difficult if you are teaching or managing the rest of the classroom at the same time. Try carrying a Post-It note or piece of masking tape to tally behaviors as you see them, or use a golf counter or other device that advances a tally when you click. Another method is to place some pennies in your pocket or rubber bands on your wrist and move one to the other side each time you observe the behavior, then count the total number moved at the end of the observation period.

**Tools for duration recording:** Invest in a stopwatch or use a stopwatch smartphone application when collecting duration data. Use a tool that you can carry around the classroom with you that will not get in your way or be a distraction to yourself or students. If these options do not work, make sure you have a clock in view to note start and end times of the behavior, but remember that this may not lend itself well to brief (<1 minute) behaviors.

**Enlist help:** If possible, have another staff member help with data collection. Make sure you are able to train them to use the system and that they are able to conduct enough observations during the progress monitoring period.

**Keep it simple:** Work to find an event recording system that is feasible for you. Consider what will work for you in the context of where you need to collect direct observation data along with what behaviors you will need to observe. Once you select a method, try it out a few times before altering it. Seek input from other behavioral support team members or staff with behavioral training when available.

**Keep it consistent:** Make sure you conduct observations at the same time(s) throughout the progress monitoring period. Remember—behaviors often vary across contexts! Behaviors observed during reading are not necessarily going to be the same during science. It is critical to collect and compare during the same context for the best progress monitoring.

## Daily Behavior Report Cards

For Daily Behavior Report Cards (DBRCs), the support team will first need to determine which behavior(s) will be tracked and how many times per day it will be rated. The team will also need to determine the rating system, which should be at an appropriate level for the student to understand. For example, older students may do well with a rating scale where 2 shows they engaged in the appropriate target behavior(s) with one or no reminders during the rating period, 1 shows they needed two to four reminders, and 0 shows they did not engage in the appropriate target behavior(s) with five or more reminders. Younger students may need a simpler system, such as one using a smile and frown face, or just "yes" and "no." Students can also be taught to use their DBRCs for self-monitoring behaviors.

## Electronic

Among electronic direct behavioral observation data collection systems, the School-Wide Classroom Observation and Analysis (SCOA; Anderson, 2012) iOS application stands out for its low cost and ease of use. SCOA can be used to collect student and teacher behavior data during a set observation period and is preprogrammed with a number of specific behaviors for both, including student engagement and teacher praise (see https://louisville.edu/education/abri/assessment/scoa-application.pdf for full list of behaviors). Additionally, SCOA makes it easy for users to program additional behaviors of interest. It is important to note, however, that SCOA can only be used for frequency and duration recording at this time, but data are provided that allow the user to later convert these to rate and percentage of time observed, respectively. At the conclusion of an observation, the user has the option to email the summary table, which can be used to graph results later using Excel or by hand. Saved observations are also accessible in the application for later reference.

## Academic Progress

As with behavioral data, it is important to monitor students' progress on academic skills. Progress monitoring is a form of formative assessment that is conducted frequently during a prolonged period of time. Assuming the intervention is appropriate for the students' deficits, students should show growth in the target skills, indicating the intervention can continue. If students are not progressing as expected, instruction for these particular students may need to be changed (Clemens et al., 2018). For several decades, research has shown that adjusting instruction based on data leads to better student outcomes (Filderman et al., 2015; Fuchs & Fuchs, 1986; Stecker et al., 2005).

Because progress monitoring happens frequently during a longer period of time, it is essential to use assessments that have the ability to detect small changes in student ability. Standardized, norm-referenced, and computer-adaptive tests generally lack the sensitivity to detect such changes in students' abilities. These tests may be able to show growth over longer periods of time, such as at the end of 9-week teaching cycles, or the traditional fall-winter-spring assessment periods. Conversely, curriculum-based measures (CBMs) do have this sensitivity and can be used for specific skills and more general outcomes (Clemens et al., 2018; Hosp, Hosp, & Howell, 2016).

# STANDARDIZED TESTS: NORM-REFERENCED TESTS AND COMPUTER-ADAPTIVE TESTING

## Norm-Referenced Tests

Using norm-referenced tests, teachers can estimate how a student is doing compared to a norming group of students of the same age. Many norm-referenced tests cover a wide range of tasks or skills with items increasing in difficulty. Others have a more specific focus, such as decoding skills or picture vocabulary. The main reason norm-referenced tests are not particularly useful as progress monitoring tools is because they rank students according to their relative standing. A commonly used metric to rank students is the percentile score. This metric does not capture absolute growth well, especially when students are low performing. First, a student's raw score is converted into a standard score according to their age. Then, this standard score is used to rank students. A student with a standard score of 40 on a test with a mean of 100 and a standard deviation of 15 will be ranked lower than the first percentile. If this student increases their performance with 20 standard score points to 60, they will still be ranked lower than the first percentile. The absolute growth does not result in a relative growth. This is different from a student scoring at the mean. A standard score of 100 has a relative standing at the 50th percentile. A 20 standard score point improvement to 120 increases the relative standing to the 91st percentile.

## Computer-Adapted Tests

A method of testing used increasingly in schools is through computer-adapted tests (CATs). CATs can provide more precise estimates of abilities than traditional standardized tests. CATs do this by changing the difficulty of items presented to a student taking the test based on their performance on previous items. If a student consistently answers items correctly, CATs will increase the difficulty of the items. Conversely, if a student answers incorrectly, CATs will decrease the difficulty of the items. Each student, therefore, will respond to a different set of items. In cases where students are consistent in their abilities, CATs are able to estimate this ability faster than traditional standardized tests. While some developers of CATs have promoted them as progress monitoring systems (e.g., STAR 360 by Renaissance Learning), most developers caution against using the measures more than once a month or even more than four times a year.

## Curriculum-Based Measures

Curriculum-based measures (CBMs) are generally brief samples of student performance (Deno, 1985; Fuchs, 2004; Hosp et al., 2016). CBMs can reflect general skills in a specific academic area, such as decoding or written expression, or the current content of a specific curriculum used in the classroom. Some well-known curriculum-independent CBM tools are AIMSweb, DIBELS, and Fastbridge.

Research has consistently shown that CBMs created independent of a specific curriculum have advantages over teachers creating their own CBM. For example, in independent CBMs, the difficulty level of probes is easier to control ensuring probes stay consistent. Additionally, the same measures can be used across curricula giving teachers the opportunity to compare the current skill level of their students not only to their previous performance but also to other students. Finally, the content in the probes is likely unfamiliar to students, limiting the inflation of scores (Fuchs & Deno, 1994). Through the use of CBMs with specific and systematic decision rules on adaptation of instruction, teachers increase their understanding of the skills and academic progress of their students.

Choosing the specific CBM for progress monitoring will depend on at least two things: the age of the students and the specific focus of the intervention. If a curriculum-independent CBM does not reflect the focus or content of an intervention, teachers may have to construct their own CBM.

Most CBM measures in elementary grades last between 1 and 5 minutes and are administered one-on-one. In upper elementary and beyond, CBM measures often take longer than 5 minutes and several measures can be administered to a group of students, for example, Maze tasks, written expression tasks, spelling measures, and vocabulary tasks. All curriculum-independent CBMs have specific instructions on how to conduct them. Typically, CBMs will start with one or two practice items to make sure students understand the task. In order to be able to compare scores, it is important to follow the instructions for administration carefully. Imagine the different reactions of students when asked "to read as much as you can" or "to do your best reading." The first group of students may resort to speed-reading, resulting in higher rates of words per minute with little understanding, while the second group may have lower total of words read correctly but showed understanding by including proper intonation.

To make sure results are consistent across measurements and that they are not influenced by factors unrelated to the students, it is important to keep the same routine when conducting progress monitoring probes. For example, probes should be conducted on the same day of the week, since growth from Monday on Week 1 to Wednesday on Week 2 (7 instructional days) is likely higher than growth from Wednesday on Week 2 to Monday on Week 3 (3 instructional days). It also matters if probes are conducted before or after instruction. There is no research to show that either of the two is better. Finally, there is a need for consistency in setting. It is preferable to conduct progress monitoring in an environment free from distraction, such as an empty classroom, or the hallway. However, this is often not feasible for teachers. Conducting probes in the regular classroom is also possible, provided the other students are working independently and quietly. In this case, make sure the student being probed is facing away from the other students and can hear the instructions well.

Just as many commercially available CBMs provide instructions on how to conduct them, they also have scoring instructions. Many of the early literacy and reading measures, for example, include hesitations (i.e., thinking time over 3 seconds for an item) as errors, besides skipped items and items gotten wrong. The total number of correct items within the time frame of the probe is then counted as the score. As with administration of CBMs, it is important to be consistent in scoring. If teachers deviate from the scoring instructions, the scores of their students are not comparable with other students. It is possible, however, that the recommended scores are not sensitive enough to change. Consider a student having trouble with addition and subtraction. Their score on a math fact CBM scored as total problem correct per minute will not increase much if they can correctly add or subtract numbers lower than 10 but are not yet able to carry digits. Measuring these students' skills through the number of digits correct may reflect their growth more accurately.

In some cases, the content or focus of an intervention is not compatible to any CBM. In this case, teachers can construct their own CBM. This is sometimes referred to as a *curriculum sampling* approach (Fuchs, 2004). In a **curriculum sampling approach**, teachers gather a large set of items reflecting the content of the intervention. In content area instruction, for example, this could involve a large set of vocabulary items or Maze probes. In mathematics, a set of algebra problems could be identified. Next, from this larger set, smaller sets with an equal number of randomly selected problems are created. If multiple skills are targeted, each probe should have an equal number of items within each skill area. Finally, the probes are created and randomly selected for administration. Some tools exist to help with constructing curriculum-dependent CBMs. On the intervention central website (www.interventioncentral.org), teachers can construct their own letter-naming fluency probes, reading fluency probes, maze probes, writing probes, and math fact fluency probes, as well as keep charts and make reports. (Additional information about CBMs is located in Appendix 13–1.)

## Implementation Fidelity

Assessing students' academic progress and behavioral improvement is only one part of progress monitoring. It is also important to know if the changes in progress are indeed due to the intervention and, conversely, when students are not making adequate progress, if this is the result of an intervention not implemented as the designers had intended. In other words, the way a teacher currently presents the intervention is not identical to the presentation idealized by its developers. For example, students may not make the expected growth in phonemic awareness if an intervention that is designed to be offered every weekday for 20 minutes is offered 3 days a week for

15 minutes. Or, students may not be able to internalize a paraphrasing strategy and therefore not do well on a writing assessment if an interventionist only provides modeling and guided practice but leaves out the originally included independent practice of the strategy. Similarly, teachers that praise students for staying in their seats inconsistently may see less reduction in out-of-seat behavior than teachers praising students according to the prescribed ratio.

Both behavioral and academic interventions consist of one or more essential steps or expected teacher behaviors (Century & Cassata, 2014). In other words, those steps that are crucial to the success of an intervention can be used to define the intervention. Executing an intervention as intended by following all essential steps is often referred to as **implementation fidelity** or **treatment fidelity** (e.g., Moncher & Prinz, 1991; O'Donnell, 2008; Yeaton & Sechrest, 1981). Currently, implementation fidelity is considered a multidimensional construct (Gresham, 2014) with five elements under its umbrella: Adherence, Differentiation, Dosage, Quality, and Responsiveness (Dane & Schneider, 1998). The first element, *adherence*, is used to indicate if all of the individual steps of an intervention were followed. Second, checking for *differentiation* means to make sure the intervention is different from regular instruction or a second intervention (Moncher & Prinz, 1991). This is not to be confused with differentiating instruction, which refers to adapting instruction to better suit a student's strengths and needs. Third, the amount of exposure students have had to an intervention is captured by **dosage**. Fourth, even if all elements of an intervention were implemented, there may be a difference in the *quality* of this delivery. Elements of **quality** could be related to how well each of the steps were implemented or to enthusiasm, organization, and preparation of the teacher. The fifth and last element of implementation fidelity is **responsiveness**. This refers to how students respond to the intervention and can be indicated by their enthusiasm, their level of engagement, or their independent use of strategies outside of the intervention. It is important for teachers to observe more than one type of fidelity when checking implementation fidelity, since each type measures a different aspect of implementation fidelity that are not necessarily interchangeable. This is why teachers should understand the relations between the elements as well. To illustrate, a teacher may perform all the steps of an intervention by following a provided script to the letter, but they may do so mechanically, without feeling. Or, a teacher may implement an intervention with perfect adherence and good quality by performing all steps with enthusiasm, but since the intervention is too similar to regular instruction, a student does not respond well and their gains are small.

## Observation of Implementation Fidelity

Just as in observation of student behavior, there are two main ways to observe for implementation fidelity: through direct assessment by observing discreet behaviors (either live or through recordings) or through indirect assessment using global ratings of behaviors.

## Direct Assessment

The direct assessment method for implementation fidelity is identical to direct assessment of student behaviors described above, and the same type of considerations apply (Gresham, 2014). In terms of representativeness, that is, to what extent does this observation relate to a regular session, direct observations should occur a number of times. Usually, 20% is recommended for a daily intervention; this means observations should occur once a week. Choosing the days randomly is best, since it will reduce the observer effect. Often, having an observer in the classroom increases the fidelity of an interventionist, and this results in an observation less representative of the big picture fidelity (Gresham, 2014). Understandably, having multiple observations to ensure representativeness is a big burden on teachers, even when buddy systems are in place, and using audio or video-recordings of their own teaching may be preferable over having a separate observer in the classroom. Besides the frequency of the observation schedule, it's important that the length of an observation is relatively consistent across observations. Ideally, the complete intervention is observed, especially when adherence is the focus of observation.

## Indirect Assessment

In addition to direct observation of implementation fidelity, there are several ways teachers can assess implementation fidelity indirectly. These indirect assessments include self-report measures, conducting behavioral interviews after a session, and permanent products, such as session notes (Gresham, 2014). The benefit of using indirect assessments is that they take a lot less time to complete and often do not necessitate involving a second person. For example, teachers who plan reading intervention sessions according to a prescribed outline can turn in their plans with checks for things that were actually executed. Self-checklists are a different way to indirectly assess implementation fidelity. For example, a teacher may be asked to fill out a daily behavior chart, indicating on a scale from 1 to 10 how well they implemented an intervention.

A disadvantage of using indirect assessments is their lower rates of specificity, since they cannot capture the same amount of individual behavior. Imagine the difference in measuring student engagement either directly or indirectly. Using a frequency count, an observer can easily tally the number of times a student responds to a teacher initiated OTR. This data can then provide a specific rate of engagement in a lesson. Conversely, a 5-point Likert scale asking a teacher how engaged a student was may not give the same level of specificity. A second disadvantage of indirect assessments is that self-reports of behavior are typically higher than reality. In other words, people tend to overestimate their own performance (Noell & Gansle, 2014). Using both direct and indirect measures may strengthen the evidence for implementation fidelity.

A simple trick for self-observation is to laminate an intervention checklist and use nonpermanent marker to check off the steps as they are implemented. At the end of the intervention, these checks can be transferred to a more permanent data file, such as a spreadsheet. It is not only important to calculate the percentage of steps completed (dividing the number of steps implemented by the total number of steps in an intervention and multiplying by 100), but also to check for patterns in implementation. For example, it's possible a specific step gets systematically skipped. This represents the difference between adherence to the protocol during a session (*accuracy*) and adherence to the protocol elements (*consistency*) (Gresham, 2014).

## WHAT TYPE OF DATA TO COLLECT?

For most interventions, adherence will be a major focus for measuring implementation fidelity. However, the type of additional fidelity data that are of importance is dependent on the focus of the intervention. For example, if a student is working on increasing math fact fluency, the number of practice opportunities is important. This means teachers should collect data on the dosage of the intervention. In this case, dosage can be described as the number of math facts in the session. Just as in observation of behavioral frequencies, dosage can be measured as a total number, or a rate per minute. If a major part of an intervention includes generalization of skills, such as not speaking out of turn, into the general classroom, measuring responsiveness is important.

The type of fidelity data to observe is not the only decision to make when checking for implementation fidelity. It is also important to make a distinction between measurement at the teacher level and the student level. This is a distinction between **treatment delivery** (teacher level) and **treatment receipt** (student level) (Noell & Gansle, 2014). To illustrate, dosage can be measured from the teacher's standpoint as the number of math facts presented or, from the student's perspective, the number of problems attempted. The decision between collecting data on the teacher or the student provides data that answer different questions. Collecting data on the teacher helps answer whether the intervention in general is implemented as intended. If this is true, all students are supposed to make progress toward their goal. Collecting data on individual student behavior can help a teacher figure out why a certain student is making less progress than anticipated, while most other students receiving the same intervention are doing all right.

## CHOOSING IMPLEMENTATION FIDELITY MEASURES

### Existing Measures

In some cases, developers have established the essential parts of interventions and will provide checklists or other resources that can help interventionists implement the intervention with fidelity. In most cases, however, detailed research on what enhances or impedes student learning has not been done, or fidelity measures of this specificity are not available (Century & Cassata, 2014). The complexity and wide variety of many academic interventions make implementing with fidelity difficult (Gresham, 2014; Johnston & Pennypacker, 1993) and have hindered the development of standardized measures of implementation fidelity.

### Making Your Own Measures

When the right tool for assessing implementation fidelity does not exist, teachers need to make their own. The most important aspects of a tool are validity and reliability. A tool has **validity** if the interpretation of the test is appropriate for the context. In the case of implementation validity, we want to first make sure that the tool captures the essential steps or elements of the intervention in a coherent way. An intervention is complex if it consists of four different elements with five activities within each element. An adherence tool might consist of a checklist of only the four main elements. On the other hand, a checklist with 20 activities is also possible. Other combinations would not make sense. Consider, for example, a checklist with 12 items: 1 item for each of the first two elements and 5 items for each of the last two elements. This combination makes interpretation of adherence problematic and less valid. If the values obtained with a tool are consistent within a context, a tool has **reliability**. This means that two people observing the same intervention session should reach the same score and that different intervention sessions in which behaviors are consistent should receive the same score. In order to make sure an implementation fidelity tool has adequate reliability and validity, the specific implementation fidelity aspects of interest need to be operationally defined. In other words, they need to be stated in specific, behavioral terms that will facilitate accurate measurement (Gresham, 2014).

### Graphing Progress Monitoring Data

Keeping track of students' progress toward behavioral and academic goals over time is essential. For most goals, graphing is a great way to monitor these data that can easily allow teachers to see changes in interventions across that time period. Graphing can be done manually or electronically. Additionally, encouraging students to help graph their own data can be both educational and motivating for students (Förster & Souvignier, 2014; Hudson et al., 2005).

## Manual Graphing

Graphing behavioral or academic data by hand is easy and requires little to no technology. Graph paper (i.e., gridded) and a pencil or pen are the only necessary tools, though a ruler/straightedge may also be helpful. Setting up the correct spacing and units on a graph may take some trial and error at first but is helpful to better think about the behavior to be tracked and how often to graph the data. (See Appendix 13–2 for support in making graphs by hand.)

## Electronic Graphing

While graphing by hand is a low-tech option that can easily be taken anywhere, graphs can also be created electronically using spreadsheet software such as Microsoft Excel. Electronic graphs are easier to use when data collection takes place over a long period of time but take slightly more time to set up. (Step-by-step directions for making graphs in Excel are located in Appendix 13–3.)

## CHAPTER SUMMARY

Many students with EBD struggle with academics in addition to behaviors. It is important to gather data frequently both on student performance and teacher behaviors in order to adapt interventions and to optimize outcomes for students. The focus of this chapter was to provide an overview of progress monitoring of interventions for students with EBD. We discussed several options for systematically collecting behavioral data, the types of questions each collection method is appropriate to measure, and advantages and disadvantages of methods. There are many assessment options for academic progress monitoring (e.g., norm-referenced tests, computer-adaptive tests, and CBMs). We also discussed characteristics, advantages, and limitations, as well as implementation fidelity and its importance for interventions. Assessment and measurement were explained for both behavioral and academic goals. After an overview of the different components of implementation fidelity, we provided details on options for observation systems, elements, and measures. Finally, we described low- and high-tech procedures for graphing data.

**DISCUSSION QUESTIONS**

1. Discuss how to use (a) event recording, (b) daily behavior report cards, (c) norm-referenced rating scales, and (d) permanent products when progress monitoring behavioral goals, along with the advantages and disadvantages of each method.

2. Jade's teacher noticed that she calls out frequently during her whole-group science class.
   a. Discuss which behavioral progress monitoring tool would be best for assessing this behavior before and after intervening.
   b. How would you track Jade's behavior, based on the progress monitoring tool you chose, before and after intervention? Remember to include key details such as the date or session and when the intervention began.

3. What are the benefits of CBMs for academic progress monitoring?

4. Describe the five elements of implementation fidelity.

5. What is the difference between treatment delivery and treatment receipt?

 **RESOURCES**

https://www.earlywood.org/Page/556

https://intensiveintervention.org/about-charts-resources

https://www.interventioncentral.org/teacher-resources/graph-maker-free-online

## REFERENCES

Achenbach, T. M., & Rescorla, L. A. (2001). *Manual for the ASEBA school-age forms and profiles*. University of Vermont Research Center for Children, Youth, & Families.

Alberto, P. A., & Troutman, A. C. (2013). *Applied behavior analysis for teachers* (9th ed.). Prentice Hall.

Anderson, J. (2012). *School-wide Classroom Observation and Analysis (SCOA) (Version 1.8)* [Mobile application software]. Retrieved from http://itunes.apple.com

Century, J., & Cassata, A. (2014). Conceptual foundations for measuring the implementation of educational innovations. In L. M. Hagermoser Sanetti & T. R. Kratochwill (Eds.), *Treatment integrity: A foundation for evidence-based practice in applied psychology* (pp. 81–108). American Psychological Association.

Clemens, N. H., Widales-Benitez, O., Kestian, J. Peltier, C., D'Abreu, A., Myint, A., & Marbach, J. (2018). Progress monitoring in the elementary grades. In *Handbook of response to intervention and multi-tiered systems of support* (pp. 175–197). Routledge.

Conley, K. M., Everett, S. R., & Pinkelman, S. E. (2019). Strengthening progress monitoring procedures for individual student behavior support. *Beyond Behavior, 28*(3), 124–133. doi:10.1177/1074295619852333

Cook, C. R., Volpe, R. J., & Delport, J. (2014). Systematic progress monitoring of students with emotional and behavioral disorders: The promise of change-sensitive brief behavior rating scales. In H. M. Walker & F. M. Gresham (Eds.), *Handbook of evidence-based practices for emotional and behavioral disorders* (pp. 211–228). Guilford.

Cooper, J. O., Heron, T. E., & Heward, W. L. (2007) *Applied behavior analysis* (2nd ed.). Pearson.

Dane, A. V., & Schneider, B. H. (1998). Program integrity in primary and early secondary prevention: Are implementation effects out of control? *Clinical Psychology Review, 18*(1), 23–45. doi:10.1016/S0272-7358(97)00043-3

Deno, S. L. (1985). Curriculum-based measurement: The emerging alternative. *Exceptional Children, 52*(3), 219–232. doi:10.1177/001440298505200303

Epstein, M. H. (2004). *Behavioral and emotional rating scale* (2nd ed.). Pro-Ed.

Filderman, M. J., Toste, J. R., Didion, L. A., Peng, P., & Clemens, N. H. (2018). Data-based decision making in reading interventions: A synthesis and meta-analysis of the effects for struggling readers. *Journal of Special Education, 52*(3), 174–187. doi:10.1177/0022466918790001

Förster, N., & Souvignier, E. (2014). Learning progress assessment and goal setting: Effects on reading achievement, reading motivation and reading self-concept. *Learning and Instruction, 32*, 91–100. doi:10.1016/j.learninstruc.2014.02.002

Fuchs, L. S. (2004). The past, present, and future of curriculum-based measurement research. *School Psychology Review, 33*(2), 188–193.

Fuchs, L. S., & Deno, S. L. (1994). Must instructionally useful performance assessment be based in the curriculum? *Exceptional Children, 61*(1), 15–24. doi:10.1177/001440299406100103

Fuchs, L. S., & Fuchs, D. (1986). Effects of systematic formative evaluation: A meta-analysis. *Exceptional Children, 53*(3), 199–208. doi:10.1177/001440298605300301

Gage, N. A., & McDaniel, S. (2012). Creating smarter classrooms: Data-based decision making for effective classroom management. *Beyond Behavior, 22*(1), 48–55. doi:10.1177/107429561202200108

Gresham, F. M. (2014). Measuring and analyzing treatment integrity in psychotherapy research. In L. M. Hagermoser Sanetti & T. R. Kratochwill (Eds.), *Treatment integrity: A foundation for evidence-based practice in applied psychology* (pp. 109–130). American Psychological Association.

Hosp, M. K., Hosp, J. L., & Howell, K. W. (2016). *The ABCs of CBM: A practical guide to curriculum-based measurement.* Guilford.

Hudson, R. F., Lane, H. B., & Pullen, P. C. (2005). Reading fluency assessment and instruction: What, why, and how? *The Reading Teacher, 58*(8), 702–714. doi:10.1598/RT.58.8.1

Johnston, J. M., & Pennypacker, H. S. (1993). *Readings for strategies and tactics of behavioral research.* Lawrence Erlbaum.

Ledford, J. R., Ayers, K. M., Lane, J. D., & Lam, M. F. (2015). Identifying issues and concerns with the use of interval-based systems in single case research using a pilot simulation study. *Journal of Special Education, 49*(2), 104–117. doi:10.1177/0022466915568975

Lee, D. L., Vostal, B., Lylo, B., & Hua, Y. (2011). Collecting behavioral data in general education settings: A primer for behavioral data collection. *Beyond Behavior, 20*(2), 22–30.

Moncher, F. J., & Prinz, R. J. (1991). Treatment fidelity in outcome studies. *Clinical Psychology Review, 11*(3), 247–266. doi:10.1016/0272-7358(91)90103-2

Noell, G. H., & Gansle, K. A. (2014). The use of performance feedback to improve intervention implementation in schools. In L. M. Hagermoser Sanetti & T. R. Kratochwill (Eds.), *Treatment integrity: A foundation for evidence-based practice in applied psychology* (pp. 161–184). American Psychological Association.

O'Donnell, C. L. (2008). Defining, conceptualizing, and measuring fidelity of implementation and its relationship to outcomes in K–12 curriculum intervention research. *Review of Educational Research, 78*(1), 33–84. doi:10.3102/0034654307313793

Reynolds, C. R., & Kamphaus, R. W. (2015). *Behavior assessment system for children* (3rd ed.). NCS Pearson, Inc. (BASC–3).

Riley-Tillman, T. C., Kalberer, S. M., & Chafouleas, S. M. (2005). Selecting the right tool for the job: A review of behavior monitoring tools used to assess student response-to-intervention. *California School Psychologist, 10*, 81–91. doi:10.1007/BF03340923

Stecker, P. M., Fuchs, L. S., & Fuchs, D. (2005). Using curriculum-based measurement to improve student achievement: Review of research. *Psychology in the Schools, 42*(8), 795–819.

Vannest, K. J., Davis, J. L., Davis, C. R., Mason, B. A., & Burke, M. D. (2010). Effective intervention for behavior with a daily behavior report card: A meta-analysis. *School Psychology Review, 39*(4), 654-672.

Yeaton, W. H., & Sechrest, L. (1981). Critical dimensions in the choice and maintenance of successful treatments: Strength, integrity, and effectiveness. *Journal of Consulting and Clinical Psychology, 49*(2), 156–167. doi:10.1037/0022-006X.49.2

# Descriptions of Main CBM Tasks

| Area | Specific Skill | Description of Task |
|------|----------------|---------------------|
| Early Literacy | Letter Naming Fluency | • Students are given a page with random letters, both lower- and uppercase, and are asked to name as many letters as they can. Most CBMs arrange letters page-like and students should name the letters left to right, top to bottom.<br>• Giving the wrong name, hesitating more than 3 seconds, and skipped letters are marked as errors.<br>• The total number of correct letters named in the minute is the final score. |
| | Letter Sound Fluency | • Students are given a page with random letters, both lower- and uppercase, and are asked to give the sound of as many letters as they can. Most CBMs arrange letters page-like and students should give the sounds of the letters left to right, top to bottom.<br>• Giving the wrong sound, hesitating more than 3 seconds, and skipped letters are marked as errors.<br>• The total number of correct letter sounds named in the minute is the final score. |
| | Word Identification Fluency | • Students are given a list with real words and are asked to read as many words as they can. Most tests start easy, with isolated letters or CV/VC words, and increase in difficulty as the list progresses.<br>• Pronouncing the word incorrectly, hesitating for more than 3 seconds, and skipped words are marked as errors.<br>• The total number of correct words is the final score. |
| | Nonsense Word Fluency | • Students are given a page or list with pseudo-words and are asked to read as many words as they can. Most standardized assessments start easy and grow increasingly harder. CBMs typically only use CVC words and students are encouraged to pronounce as many letter sounds as they can if they do not know the whole word. |

*continues*

| Area | Specific Skill | Description of Task |
|---|---|---|
| Early Literacy *continued* | Nonsense Word Fluency *continued* | • Pronouncing the word incorrectly, hesitating for more than 3 seconds, and skipped words are marked as errors.<br>• The total number of correct words is the final score. For CBMs, the total number of correct letter sounds can be counted as an alternative to correct words. |
| | Phonemic Segmentation Fluency | • Students are asked to say each sound in an orally presented word individually.<br>• All segments of words separated by the students are counted as correct. A higher score indicates students are able to distinguish individual sounds better. For example, black: /bl/ /ak/ is 2 points, but /b/ /l/ /a/ /k/ is 4 points. |
| | Spelling | • Students are orally presented with a list of words, ranging between 12 and 17 words. The pace of presentation is usually standardized to 7 to 10 seconds per word.<br>• Students' skills can be determined in two ways: (a) as the total number of words spelled correctly (WSC) or (b) as the number of correct letter sequences (CLS).<br>• Using CLS, each correct initial and final letter is awarded 1 point, and each correct sequence of two letters is awarded an additional point. The number of points for each word is one more than the number of letters in a word. The total number of CLS is a student's score. |
| Reading | Oral Reading Fluency | • Students are presented with a story and asked to read the story with their best reading (not speed reading). If a student hesitates for more than 3 seconds, the unknown word is provided to the student.<br>• Pronouncing words incorrectly, hesitations, skipped words, and changing the order of words are marked as errors.<br>• Typically, three probes are administered. The total number of correct words read per minute is counted as the score for each probe, and the median score is taken to represent the students' final score. |

| Area | Specific Skill | Description of Task |
|------|----------------|---------------------|
| Reading *continued* | Maze | • Students are presented with a story of which some words are replaced with blanks. Typically, blanks appear at fixed intervals (e.g., each seventh word). Students are asked to read the story silently and circle the choice that would complete the sentence best. Choices often differ phonetically, syntactically, or semantically but are alike in length.<br>• The total of correct answer choices is a student's score. |
| | Multiple-Choice Reading Comprehension | • Students are presented with a story. After reading the story, students answer questions about the story that assess their literal and inferential understanding.<br>• The total of correctly answered questions is a student's score. |
| Vocabulary | Picture Naming Fluency | • Students are presented with a series of picture tiles representing nouns commonly used in basal readers and children's books. Students are asked to name as many of the picture they can.<br>• The total number of pictures named correctly is a student's score. |
| | Reverse Definition Fluency | • Students are presented with formal definitions of nouns commonly used in basal readers and children's books. Students are asked to provide the noun being defined.<br>• The total number of nouns named correctly is a student's score. Timing is paused when definitions are presented. |
| | Vocabulary Matching | • Students are presented with a list of vocabulary words on one side of a paper and definitions (with a small number of distractors) on the other side of the paper. Students are asked to match words with their definitions.<br>• Often Vocabulary Matching tasks are applied to content areas as a specific set of words representing an area can more easily be identified.<br>• The total number of words matched correctly is a student's score. |

*continues*

| Area | Specific Skill | Description of Task |
|------|---------------|---------------------|
| Vocabulary *continued* | Multiple-Choice Vocabulary Measures | • Students are presented with words and a choice set of words or phrases. Students are asked to choose the word or phrase matching the target word.<br>• The total number of correct choices is a student's final score. |
| Written Expression | Story Starter | • Students are provided with either a picture or an introductory sentence or two. After a minute of thinking time, students are asked to write a story.<br>• Stories can be scored in a number of different ways: (a) the total words written, regardless of spelling or grammatical accuracy; (b) the number of words spelled correctly (WSC); and (c) the number of correct writing sequences (CWS) where each adjacent pair of words correct in spelling, punctuation, and grammar is given a point. |
| Early Numeracy | Oral Counting | • Students are asked to count starting at 1 as high as they can.<br>• The last correct number before making a mistake is the student's score. |
| | Number Identification | • Students are given a list of randomly ordered numbers and asked to identify as many as they can. |
| Mathematics | Computation | • Students are given a list of math computation problems and asked to solve as many as they can.<br>• Using math facts gives an indication of general math computation skills. Using a sample of problems from the current curriculum will provide information on growth in a particular skill.<br>• Students' skills can be determined in two ways: (a) as the total number of problems solved correctly or (b) as the number of correct digits (NCD). Using NCD, each digit in an answer is given a point. The total number of correct digits is a student's score. On some measures, problems are awarded different numbers of points depending on their difficulty. |

| Area | Specific Skill | Description of Task |
|---|---|---|
| Mathematics *continued* | Concepts and Applications | • Students are presented with a test booklet containing approximately 30 items. They are asked to solve the problems in order and mark those they do not know. Students may need to provide the answer to a problem or select the correct answer in a multiple-choice format.<br>• The content reflects the five strands of mathematical proficiency and focus on problem solving, logical reasoning, and analytical skill application.<br>• Correct answers are awarded differing number of points depending on their difficulty. The total number of points a student received is their final score. |
| | Estimation | • Student are presented with a 40-item multiple-choice measure including computation estimation and word problem estimation tasks. |
| | Quantity Discrimination | • Students are presented with a list of paired numbers and asked to identify the larger number in a pair or to provide the appropriate proportion symbol ($<$ = $>$).<br>• The correct number of pairs identified is the student's score |
| | Missing Number | • Students are presented with sets of number sequences. One number in the sequence is missing. The position of the missing number varies across sequences. Students are asked to fill in the missing number.<br>• The total number correct is the student's score. |

# APPENDIX 13–2

# Steps for Making Graphs by Hand

1. With your graph paper situated horizontally, draw a horizontal line on a gridline near the bottom of the page (leave some room below to record dates, etc.). This will be referred to as your x-axis and will always be used to represent time on your graph.

2. Draw a vertical line on a gridline near the left edge of the paper, also leaving room to write. This will be referred to as your y-axis and will be used to plot the behavior or academic data.

3. Determine the spacing and units (e.g., weeks, sessions) that you will mark on your x-axis. It is important to use a unit that will remain constant across the progress monitoring period. When making this decision, consider how often you will be collecting progress monitoring data along with how long the intervention period may last. Though not ideal, it will be okay to extend the graph to another page if data collection continues for a longer period of time than a single page can accommodate.

4. Determine the spacing and units (e.g., rate of behaviors, percentage correct, words correct per minute) that you will mark on your y-axis. These units should also be equally spaced, and it is important to consider the current and expected level of the behavior when establishing this spacing.

5. If you have baseline (i.e., preintervention) data, record that on the graph first. Always start at the left side of the graph and work right as you plot data to represent the passage of time, connecting each point with a straight line. Also make sure to indicate the date or session the data were collected on your x-axis, using the unit spacing you determined earlier. It is best to include breaks if there are gaps in the data to give the behavior support team the most information, along with the reason for the gap (e.g., absence, schedule disruption, refusal) if possible.

6. At the end of the baseline data, make some mark (e.g., dotted vertical line) to indicate the beginning of the intervention data. This will make it easier to compare the changes later.

7. Record data collected during the intervention period to the right of the line made in Step 6, continuing to note the date or session on the x-axis. Also continue to make notes of any disruptions to data collection, changes to the intervention, or additional interventions to monitor their impact on behavior. Continue recording data, adding new pages as needed, until progress monitoring for that behavior is discontinued.

# Steps for Making Graphs in Excel

| | |
|---|---|
| 1. In a new spreadsheet, label your first column as Date/Session, your second as the behavior, and the third as Notes. | |
| 2. Fill in baseline data (if applicable). Note any data collection issues in the Notes column. | |
| 3. Continue filling in progress monitoring data as they are acquired, noting when the intervention began and any data collection issues as they come up. Leave data column blank when the student is absent or data collection is missed for another reason. | |
| 4. When ready to create a graph, select the date and behavior cells you want to include. | |
| 5. Under the Insert tab, select the line charts and choose your preferred style. It will automatically create your graph and place it on the spreadsheet. | |

*continues*

| | |
|---|---|
| 6. To place a break between the baseline and intervention data, select the first point in intervention, double click, and change the formatting to "No line." Repeat for any other large changes (e.g., intervention change, removal of intervention). | 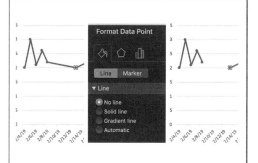 |
| 7. The Insert tab also has options to add a text box or vertical line to add notes or intervention changes. Alternatively, these can be added by hand if the graph is printed for support team review, but it is important to keep records of when they happen along with the data. | 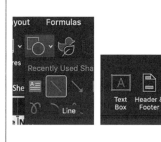 |

# INDEX

Note: Page numbers in **Bold** reference non-text information.